What Zoos Can Do

The Leading Zoological Gardens
of Europe 2010 - 2020

Anthony Sheridan

Special Thanks

I have very many people to thank for helping me to produce this book. Most are listed on page 143.

Above all, I thank Jane, my wife, who has devoted much of her time, particularly during late autumn and winter 2010-11, to help me with computer work, improving my texts and supporting my full time involvement in this project.

I also thank my younger daughter, Rachel, a wildlife photographic enthusiast, and my long suffering publisher, Klaus Schüling, for his unfailing support of this project.

Anthony D. Sheridan,
Radlett, England
March 2011

ISBN 978-3-86523-183-3

SCHÜLING VERLAG

Münster 2011

Contents

Foreword

It's just half a century ago that our knowledge about wild animals was rather limited and the zoo and wild animal medicine was in its infancy. The way zoos animals were kept at that time rarely met their needs; rather the animals were considered show-pieces and kept in basic cages. Accordingly, sustainable keeping and breeding was rare in many species and, where necessary, replacement could easily be obtained from the wild. Zoo education hardly existed, and the legal framework in which the zoos operated was simple – there was no endangered species convention, no animal welfare laws and only limited animal health regulations.

This has all changed. The zoos are rapidly developing from simple animal collections to con-servation centres, as suggested by the World Zoo Conservation Strategy of 1993. It has become a trend to immerse both animals and guests in the same re-created naturally looking surroun-dings, and instead of organising tea-parties for chimps, the zoos have developed behavioural enrichments programmes for many species. The longevity of zoo animals now exceeds that of their wild cousins, and many coordinated breeding programmes have become so successful that measures have to be taken to limit the numbers of offspring. Zoo education, now an essential part of the zoos' activities, no longer aims just at providing information, but also at developing in visitors an awareness of environmental issues.

Zoos assume a task which the Biodiversity Convention has attributed to its Party States and which becomes increasingly important the more natural habitats are being destroyed and the more climate change is progressing. Accordingly millions of Euros from tax revenues are inves-ted into making the zoos fit for the 21st century, but at the same time an ever growing flood of regulations issued by the European Union and the individual countries makes life for zoos more difficult. An analysis of the conditions under which zoos operate today and of possible scenarios for the future, as provided by the present book, is extremely useful and certainly will contribute to the discussions about the future of zoos. I therefore hope that Anthony Sheridan's book will find a wide readership within and outside the zoo world.

Liebefeld-Bern, 30 March 2011

Dr. Peter Dollinger
Executive Director of the German Association of zoo directors
and the Swiss Association of Scientific Zoos

CHAPTER 1

Introduction

WHAT ZOOS CAN DO is designed to be a non-technical comprehensive survey of Europe's leading zoological gardens in 2010 and to forecast how they will develop over the next ten years. The information has been gathered on extensive visits made to 80 selected leading zoological gardens in 21 European countries during 2008 to 2010, including many return visits to the largest collections, interviews with Zoo Directors and Managers and analysis of collected data.

In this book, I have attempted to look at, analyse and understand each of these selected zoos- their strengths, weaknesses and opportunities. Within Europe, they are the shop window for the diversity of the world's animal species. Zoos have not only to be the most popular, widely visited, delightful and pleasurable visitor attractions in their area, but they also to be a source of inspiration, enlightenment and motivation. They have to be a clarion call to Europe's citizens to act individually and collectively – through their politicians, sponsors, donors and other supporters – to bring conservation issues to the top of the political agenda. Zoos need to persuade their visitors to help conservation by being conscious of these issues and react accordingly in their personal purchasing decisions and in discussions with their families and friends.

Europe's leading zoological gardens contain the majority of the oldest and arguably of the best zoos in the world. They work together closely to ensure maximum welfare and local breeding of rare species within Europe (ex-situ conservation), to assist with conservation projects in the species' original habitats (in-situ conservation) and carry our research available to the zoo world and further afield through their active and well supported regional organisation EAZA (European Association of Zoos and Aquariums). Europe's 3000 or so zoos and aquaria are estimated to attract 160 million visitors annually, a figure that is growing and is higher than for any other paid visitor attraction in Europe. The majority of school children will visit a zoo at least once on an organised educational visit during their school life, and most adults will have visited a European zoo within recent years.

Zoological gardens matter greatly. They consume large sums of public and private finance. They feature very frequently in the media. They are often the No. 1 city attraction but still need to meet the increasingly high standards required by European and national legislation as well as expected by their actual and potential visitors.

This book endeavours to discuss these subjects as well as to give detailed information on each of the 80 selected zoological gardens. It is designed to be of real value to all those interested in visiting zoos, in financially supporting zoos, as well as those working in or for zoos. It contains a wealth of comparative information and material, some of which has not been published elsewhere, on Europe's leading zoological gardens. The investments currently being realised in these zoos, amounting to over EUR 750 million during 2010-15, are very significant and should contribute substantially to the further improvements urgently required to meet current standards and expectations.

INTRODUCTION

I have enjoyed meeting and getting to know so many leading Zoo Directors, and visiting their delightful zoos. I have learned much and continue to do so. I am excited with the progress made in recent years and the determination of these zoos to continue to invest in new and better facilities. Only by so doing, can our great zoos in Europe continue to attract more visitors and respond positively to the demands of animal welfare enthusiasts. I hope that this book will encourage more people to visit these zoos, more public and private institutions to support financially these zoos, and that it will foster an even greater understanding of the ever increasing importance of good zoos in a world where wildlife habitats are disappearing at an alarming rate.

Carl Hagenbeck, Father of the 21st Century Zoo

CHAPTER 2

Selection of Zoological Gardens

Introduction

There are estimated to be about 3000 zoos, aquariums, safari parks, and other animal collections in Europe; of these, about 300 are members of EAZA. This survey includes only zoological gardens or animal parks containing substantial zoological gardens. It is difficult to draw a line and each marginal case has been considered on its merits.

Zoological Gardens

The great majority of visitors go to zoological gardens rather than to safari parks, bird parks, aquariums or seaworlds or other wildlife attractions. Most organised school visits and university projects are similarly focussed on the same zoological gardens.

The true zoological garden contains an extensive animal collection, concentrated on mammals, birds and reptiles, set in attractive and varied botanical landscapes, preferably including good water features and undulating topography. They will include a good and varied tree cover, as well as an attractive botanical offering. The buildings should be pleasing, its grounds clean, attractive and well organised, and its location providing a real oasis if within or adjacent to a city.

Selection

My listed zoological gardens comprise the most visited, comprehensive and important collections of mammals, birds and reptiles in Europe. 80 zoos from 21 European countries are included. All of them have been personally visited, many on several occasions, and usually the Zoo Director has been met and interviewed in connection with my detailed questionnaire, which has been completed for each listed zoo. All of these zoos are "good" zoos; each has its own strengths and weaknesses. Each zoo is different, but all are delightful to visit. I have been privileged in meeting and, in many cases, getting to know the Zoo Director; this has helped greatly in understanding each zoo and how it may look in 2020.

National Locations

I have defined Europe in its original geographical sense and then decided to draw a boundary including all EU and EEA countries; this, of course, then excludes Russia, Ukraine, Belarus and nearly all Balkan countries. Taking account of other criteria mentioned below (comprehensive range of species, visitor numbers, EAZA membership and overall standards), it appeared that there are no appropriate zoos in the following countries within the defined geographical area – Bulgaria, Cyprus, Greece, Iceland, Lithuania, Luxembourg, Malta, Norway and Romania. The remaining 21 countries are represented.

Accreditation

All selected zoos must be full members of EAZA as at 31.12.09. This important organisation was established in 1988. Its objectives are the promotion of co-operation for the furtherance of wildlife conservation, particularly through internationally co-ordinated breeding programmes of wild animals, the promotion of education, particularly in terms of biodiversity and environment, the promotion of scientific study and the representation of the interests of its members particularly in supra-national authorities. It has minimum standards for membership, although it should be noted that early members were accepted without the same rigorous testing and evaluation required of applicants today! Therefore, there is a substantial variety of standards of member zoos; re-accreditation is now receiving attention within EAZA and minimum standards are likely to be more uniform within the next few years.

Comprehensive Range of Species

In order to limit and manage my investigations and taking account of the clear priorities of zoo visitors and their most popular species, I decided to limit my analysis and reports to mammals, birds and reptiles. Each selected zoo must have a comprehensive collection of each of these 3 groups. Within each of these 3 groups, I have identified and listed "iconic" species, which are the most popular with visitors and generally expected to be included in a comprehensive collection. These "iconic" species receive special attention and marks, and are analysed separately in this book.

I recognise that amphibians, fish and invertebrates are of major importance and are just as much a part of the animal world and of biodiversity. In the case of fish, specialised aquariums and marine worlds attract many visitors particularly interested in these species.

Visitor Numbers

These are of major importance to every zoo, as they are usually the major source of income, are crucial in establishing the importance of the zoo to the locality and country, and therefore of key importance in relationships with politicians, the media, advertisers, donors and other supporters, and to morale and standards of their own staff and the wider zoo world.

La Palmyre

Dresden

Actual visitor numbers should be straightforward, but this is not the case in practice! Few zoos really know the exact numbers of their visitors, taking account of free entries (primarily very young children) and the actual use of annual entrance tickets (or season tickets). Further reference to this subject is made in this book. I have looked at visitor numbers over the period 2004-2010, and taken account of trends and likely developments.

The major zoological gardens (Group A) will have in excess of 1 million visitors annually or very close to this figure, and the remainder (Group B) will have in excess of 500,000 with certain exceptions, primarily in smaller countries, but where all other criteria for inclusion in the survey are met. Necessarily, there are some marginal decisions or exclusions but great care has been taken to be fair and impartial in my final selection.

Employment

For similar reasons to those mentioned for Visitor Numbers, employment significance is of real importance. In addition, larger employment zoos enable a better career ladder for ambitious staff and enable more senior posts to be established. Vacancies for Zoo Directors and other senior staff are likely to attract larger numbers of applicants in those zoos with larger staffing. More senior posts can be established.

In order to make fair comparisons and to recognise the total impact on local employment, totals of employment include not only staff employed directly by the zoo but also by contracted out facilities, such as catering and/or retail services, and staff provided by other authorities, such as City Council maintenance, cleaning or gardening staff. Account is also taken of part-time and seasonal staff. For Group A zoos, at least 100 staff will be employed, and for Group

B in excess of 50 staff. Many of the largest zoos are responsible directly or indirectly for much larger numbers of staff.

Location of selected Zoological Gardens

The map on the inside of the front cover shows the location of the zoos included in this book. It is noteworthy that only 6 out of 80 are located south of the Alps, namely Bussolengo and Rome in Italy, Lisbon in Portugal, and Barcelona, Madrid and Valencia in Spain. This results from no bias in favour of the more northern European countries but reflects the major division in Europe of interest in and attitudes towards animals and wildlife. Looking at the history of zoos, the pioneering work of zoologists, the visitor numbers and the public and private support for zoos, there is clearly a real north-south dividing line in Europe. There has been and still is a real cultural difference in interest in and attitudes towards all animals and wildlife. Hopefully, younger generations of southern Europeans will gradually change their attitudes in the face of the major global threats to biodiversity in all its forms.

Of the total visitors to Europe's zoos and other wildlife attractions, the 80 listed zoos accounted for nearly 50% of the total. Over 60% of Europe's zoo visitors are from Germany, UK and Netherlands with German visitors alone accounting for nearly 40% of the total.

The exceptional importance of German speaking zoological gardens originates from the 19th century German states, as then constituted, having their own zoos, the long standing zoological interest in those countries, the large sums invested in their zoos in recent years (particularly in the last 15 years) and the enormous media interest and coverage of these zoos in recent years. The 19th century historic dimension also spills over into former German controlled or influenced areas, resulting in early establishment of zoos in cities such as Königsberg/Kaliningrad, Reval/Tallinn, Riga, Breslau/Wroclaw, Pozen/Poznan and Mühlhausen/Mulhouse. The local association of German speaking Zoo Directors – VDZ (Verband Deutsche Zoodirektoren) was the first such

Group A			
Austria	Schönbrunn (Vienna)	Germany	Hellabrunn (Munich)
Belgium	Antwerp	Germany	Münster
Czech Republic	Prague	Germany	Nuremberg
Denmark	Copenhagen	Germany	Wilhelma (Stuttgart)
Eire	Dublin	Hungary	Budapest
Germany	Berlin Tierpark	Netherlands	Artis (Amsterdam)
Germany	Berlin Zoo	Netherlands	Burgers (Arnhem)
Germany	Duisburg	Netherlands	Emmen
Germany	Frankfurt	Netherlands	Rotterdam
Germany	Gelsenkirchen	Spain	Barcelona
Germany	Hagenbeck (Hamburg)	Spain	Madrid
Germany	Hanover	Switzerland	Basel
Germany	Karlsruhe	Switzerland	Zurich
Germany	Cologne	United Kingdom	Chester
Germany	Leipzig	United Kingdom	ZSL London

Group B			
Belgium	Planckendael (Mechelen)	Germany	Rostock
Belgium	Pairi Daiza (Paradisio)	Germany	Wuppertal
Czech Republic	Dvur Králové	Hungary	Sosto
Czech Republic	Plzen	Italy	Bussolengo
Czech Republic	Zlin	Italy	Rome
Denmark	Odense	Latvia	Riga
Estonia	Tallinn	Netherlands	Amersfoort
Finland	Helsinki	Netherlands	Rhenen
France	Amnéville	Poland	Warsaw
France	Beauval	Poland	Wroclaw
France	Doué la Fontaine	Portugal	Lisbon
France	La Fléche	Slovakia	Bojnice
France	Mulhouse	Slovakia	Bratislava
France	La Palmyre	Slovenia	Ljubljana
France	Menagerie (Paris)	Spain	Valencia
Germany	Augsburg	Sweden	Eskilstuna
Germany	Dortmund	Sweden	Kolmården
Germany	Dresden	United Kingdom	Belfast
Germany	Erfurt	United Kingdom	Bristol
Germany	Halle	United Kingdom	Colchester
Germany	Heidelberg	United Kingdom	Edinburgh
Germany	Krefeld	United Kingdom	Marwell
Germany	Opel-Zoo (Kronberg)	United Kingdom	Paignton
Germany	Magdeburg	United Kingdom	Twycross
Germany	Osnabrück	United Kingdom	ZSL Whipsnade

national association, established in 1887, and includes all of the most important zoos in Germany, Austria and Switzerland.

The second most important national group of zoos is in the British Isles, represented by a very active and well organised local association BIAZA (British + Irish Association of Zoos and Aquariums). Historically, several of the oldest 19th century zoos, such as London, Dublin and Bristol, are located in these countries. Today, the leading British zoos are particularly renowned for their conservation and research activities.

The second decade of this century will witness a major expansion in the number of good zoological gardens in Europe. With the gradual implementation of EU Council Directive 1999/22 and its local national consequent legislation throughout the EU and the use of targeted investment funds, such as in Romania, it is anticipated many more zoos will become EAZA members. It is reasonable to expect that a major improvement to zoos in Romania, Bulgaria, Croatia, Serbia, Lithuania and other countries will be a feature of the second half of this decade. This should provide the springboard for a major increase in visitor numbers and interest in biodiversity, conservation and related education.

SELECTION OF ZOOLOGICAL GARDENS

Group B includes 16 Zoos which presently have less than 500,000 visitors annually but which otherwise meet my selection criteria. They are:-		
Denmark	Odense	This zoo has major expansion plans and can be expected to reach 500,000 visitors soon.
Estonia	Tallinn	The national zoo in a small population country.
Finland	Helsinki	The national zoo in a small population country.
France	Doué la Fontaine La Fléche Mulhouse	As free entry zoos have been excluded from my survey, these 3 zoos are widely renowned and add to a fair representation for French zoological gardens.
Germany	Erfurt Halle Krefeld Magdeburg	These 4 zoos were included in the large zoo category in "Der Grosse Zoo-Test" (STERN, Nr. 27, 06-26-2008). Erfurt, with agreed major development programme in progress, can be expected to reach 500,000 visitors soon.
Latvia	Riga	The national zoo in a small population country
Slovakia	Bojnice	The national zoo in a small population country.
Slovakia	Bratislava	The capital city zoo.
Slovenia	Ljubljana	The national zoo in a small population country.
Sweden	Eskilstuna	Officially at least 500,000 visitors are included for the whole entertainments, sports and zoo complex. The zoo has at least 50% of these visitors and is likely to increase in view of its history and development plans.
United Kingdom	Belfast	The national zoo of Northern Ireland in a small population country within the U.K.

Nuremberg

CHAPTER 3

The Role of the Zoo Director

It is hard to exaggerate the importance of the Zoo Director's role in the successful development of a major European zoo in the 21st century. Long gone are the days when this post was filled by a person simply qualified by length of experience in the zoo and appropriate educational background. In today's highly competitive and media influenced world, the Zoo Director can anticipate becoming a nationally known figure, confronted with a wide variety of challenges and opportunities.

This change in the importance of the Zoo Director and the scope of the challenges faced has happened for many reasons, not least the much larger sums required for essential investment in the zoo (typically EUR 100 million over possibly 10 years) to bring the zoo up to modern standards, the need to engage in public debate concerning keeping certain large species in zoos, and the increasing public awareness and concern about biodiversity and environmental issues, reflected in increased media interest. Visitor expectation today is far higher than in the past as a result of increasing competition from the leisure industry.

Therefore, the role of today's Zoo Director is even more demanding and requires the appointment of a highly capable, intelligent, dedicated and multifaceted person. The nature of the Zoo Director's job requires constant availability; the zoo's inhabitants are a full-time, all year round, responsibility and frequently spring unexpected surprises requiring immediate attention. The media are always hungry for newsworthy stories and the more contentious events sometimes require the Zoo Director's diplomatic handling and presentation.

The right appointment is absolutely crucial to the future success of the zoo and the appointing body has a very big responsibility. The importance and significance of the Zoo Director can be compared with that of Chief Executive or CEO in medium sized companies and other organisations; typically he/she may be responsible for at least 200 staff directly or indirectly employed at the zoo. Larger zoos have become more economically important entities in their communities: the modern zoo directors need to be capable of leading a high profile organisation and taking human resources and financial policy decisions. Risk analysis, risk management and ensuring legal compliance are also requirements of the position.

In my meetings with the Zoo Directors of virtually all of the 80 Zoos in my survey, I have been impressed with their commitment, overall calibre and wide ranging qualities they bring to these positions. It is heartening to learn of the keen and increasing interest from well qualified candidates to fill these positions, and this augurs well for the future of these zoos.

In some of the larger zoos, owners have decided to split the role of Zoo Director between two directors, zoological and commercial, as at Köln or München, to take account of the much bigger scope of the role of today's Zoo Director. The success of any such arrangement inevitably depends on the two individuals concerned. The arrangement is usually more successful and more efficient when one of the two individuals clearly has ultimate responsibility and the authority to take a lead and it is likely to be the zoological director who has the knowledge and background to take ultimate authority for the ethical decisions which arise in the zoo.

Other management models may involve a Director-General and a Zoo Director, as at ZSL London and Whipsnade. But the great majority of zoos in my survey are led by a single Zoo Director, supported by many different forms of management organisation.

Background of Zoo Directors

Traditionally, Zoo Directors have been qualified vets, zoologists or biologists. Today, the majority still have one of these qualifications but an increasing proportion is being recruited from other professional backgrounds. This reflects the heavier financial, commercial and media communication components of the job. As at time of writing, the Zoo Directors of my 80 survey zoos are:

Profession	Group A Zoos	Group B Zoos	Total Zoos
Veterinary	8	10	18
Zoology/Biology	15	20	35
Business/Economics	5	11	16
Other	2	9	11

Note: zoos in the EU must, at top management level, have a person qualified in veterinary medicine or zoology.

The near exclusiveness of the Zoo Director being male is also changing, albeit more slowly than in many other high profile professional jobs. At end 2009, the balance was:

Gender	Group A Zoos	Group B Zoos	Total Zoos
Male	27	43	70
Female	3	7	10

Interestingly, by coincidence, Vienna, the top ranked Zoo in my Group A, Beauval, the top ranked zoo in Group B both have female Zoo Directors!

Zoo Directors and Zoo Ownerships

The majority of zoos in this survey are owned or controlled by national, regional or local public authorities; few are owned by companies. The Zoo Director's situation and relationship with his/her Zoo's owners is different, depending mainly on whether they are public or private sector bodies.

For public sector zoos, Zoo Directors may well have a more complex and time-consuming relationship; politicians of various parties may well be involved and frequently the City Mayor may either be on the Board or be personally directly involved, since the City Zoo is frequently the most important paid visitor attraction in the area. The Zoo Director needs to foster good relationships with local politicians associated with the zoo. Contentious issues may well include

Zoo Directors can be grouped, by zoo ownership, as follows:

- Owners of private zoos (e.g. Arnhem, Beauval)
- Appointed by privately owned zoos (e.g. Kronberg)
- Appointed by company owned zoos (e.g. Kolmården, Madrid)
- Appointed by charitable societies (e.g. London, Edinburgh, Dublin)
- Appointed by Government owned or controlled zoos (e.g. Vienna, Bojnice)
- Appointed by municipal or city council owned zoos (e.g. Augsburg, Belfast)
- Appointed by regional council owned zoos (e.g. Stuttgart, Dvur Kralove)
- Appointed by municipally owned or controlled companies (e.g. Berlin, München)

expenditure on conservation from the revenue budget, major investment required to update existing exhibits to conform to new higher standards, visitors' entrance prices, politicians (e.g. Green Party) and public anxiety about keeping certain animals in zoos, acquisition of additional public land for the zoo, and transport and car parking arrangements for the zoo.

For privately owned zoos these issues still pertain although not in a political context. For owner zoo Directors, the situation is much more straightforward as a Committee is rarely involved and decisions can be taken simply and quickly. For the others, whether charitable societies or companies, the relationship between the Zoo Director and the Board of Directors or Trustees – and particularly its chairman – is very important. Main issues are likely to be financial rather than political. The Zoo Director will normally spend much less time in meetings and in writing reports than his colleagues in public sector zoos.

Familie van Hooff, Arnhem

However, the public sector zoo has major advantages in having access to larger sums for investment projects and in receiving subsidies for revenue budgets, often to maintain low visitor entry prices, helping to boost visitor numbers which, in turn, help getting commercial sponsors and more media coverage. Public funding, whether from EU, national, regional or local council sources, is concentrated on public sector zoos. The financial crisis has adversely impacted on some of these zoos.

Nevertheless, individual Zoo Directors can make a big difference in obtaining public funds for major projects, whether the zoo is publicly or privately owned.

Interesting examples over the past 10 years include:

- Dublin Zoo. Major contribution to new capital projects (EUR 40 million) over several years, due to Zoo Director and Prime Minister Bertie Ahern.

- Hagenbeck Hamburg Zoo. Major Government contribution to EUR 20 million "Eismeer" project for polar bears, walruses, penguins and other species.

- Vienna Zoo. Founding of GmbH company and subsequent very large investment in many new facilities, due to Zoo Director and Prime Minister Dr. Wolfgang Schüssel.

These examples and many more result from the Zoo Director's personal efforts and valuable relationship with key politicians.

Management Model

As in other public and private sector organisations, the management model and organisation chart will vary greatly; the Zoo Director will have the main influence on these but has to take account of what he/she inherits before making changes to reflect his/her future policy. The Zoo Director has to attract and retain the most suitable people for key posts, and needs to delegate responsibility where possible. There are many areas of overlap, such as education, conservation and research as well as marketing, media relations and publicity. All of these will concern the Director who will be involved in taking difficult decisions affecting key senior staff. Zoo Directors have to decide which decisions and responsibilities to retain themselves and will be concerned with subjects such as a Master Plan which evinces a clear vision and strategy, attracting major sponsors, relationships with the media, including TV interviews, and direct contact with leading politicians and officials.

Conclusion

The most important decision of the owners of a Zoo today, whether publicly or privately owned, is the appointment of Zoo Director. The evidence of recent years shows that the many success stories of Europe's leading zoological gardens result from outstandingly capable and committed Zoo Directors.

CHAPTER 4

Landscaping and Design

Every zoological garden is different: each unique zoo landscape is one of the great pleasures of zoo visiting. Different sites will have their topographical, geological and climatic peculiarities each with its advantages and disadvantages. The aim of each zoo must be to maximise the natural advantages and compensate for the disadvantages. The ideal site will have substantial deciduous and coniferous mature tree cover, a river flowing through it, lakes and adequate water supplies, a hilly or at least undulating terrain preferably with significant natural rock features and a variety of soils to enable a varied vegetation and botanical features to grow well. Water features will encourage birds, amphibians and other pond dwellers and good vegetation including habitat for rare wild flowers will attract birds, butterflies and insects giving an important added wildlife dimension to the zoo. It is rare to find such a site!

General Landscaping and Design Requirements

General landscaping and design requirements need to be considered in terms of the site as a whole, the individual enclosures from the occupants' viewpoint and those same enclosures from the visitors' perspective.

The topographical and climatic limitations of the site will necessarily form the starting point. What is economically possible to achieve will be the other main consideration.

Amongst the most important improvements, frequently required where these are not naturally present or are not in the required location, is the addition of rocks; artificial rock from specialised suppliers is an increasing feature. Even more expensive for many zoos is increasing water supplies and providing appropriate water features wherever possible.

The most successful zoological gardens give high priority to investment in landscaping and design. Some new zoos (e.g. Gelsenkirchen, Bioparc Valencia) have started with an unpromising flat site and invested heavily in creating the features they would have wished to find on the site at the outset. The great majority of older zoos have gradually improved their sites;

Lisbon

most of them are situated on sites with good mature tree cover. Many city zoos are situated in areas of their cities blessed with woods and parkland.

General Enclosure Requirements

In general, visitors prefer to see animals in as natural an environment as possible, preferably without bars or cages. The concept of moated exhibits and the absence of fences was pioneered by Carl Hagenbeck in Hamburg more than a century ago. Hagenbeck's name remains synonymous with this general design concept which is widely accepted as the desired preferential exhibit form and enables the visitor to become easily absorbed in the world of the animals. Hagenbeck's Hamburg zoo continues to be a leading exponent of this philosophy.

In practice, the concept is not always possible and many species have to be kept in some form of obviously fenced or caged enclosure. Hedging plants and other natural materials can provide a good visitor barrier in many circumstances with the added advantage of attracting birds and insects.

Tree Cover

There should be a variety of deciduous and coniferous trees, providing not only shade for the animals and the visitors, but also nesting places for wildlife, including such charismatic birds as the green parrots that can be seen in Bussolengo, the white storks in Münster or the grey herons in Berlin or Amsterdam. Several zoos make an inventory of their trees, keep careful maintenance records on each of them and provide visitor information on them.

Basel

Well designed enclosures need to consider the following:

- The typical habitat in which the species normally lives.

- The species being able to move normally and to be able to breed where appropriate.

- Visitors being able to see the animals and preferably being able to photograph them. In many cases, visitors may need to linger – and preferably in comfort – to see and appreciate the animals. Visitors cannot reasonably expect instant appearances of shy animals such as Okapi, members of the cat family resting in the afternoon sun or those species living in burrows!

- The welfare of the animals in terms of water supply, shelter and shade, variety of vegetation, trees, bushes, terrain as may be appropriate. For tree climbing species, the availability of suitable trees or substitutes at appropriate heights need to be provided.

- The indoor or shelter requirements appropriate to the species and the prevailing local climate.

- The size of the outdoor enclosure will often be a compromise between the animal occupant's and the visitors' preferences. It is not always necessary to have very large enclosures, even for elephants, if all the other conditions for the welfare of the species are taken into account (including their keepers' relationship with and care for them). On the other hand, there are still far too many enclosures which are now recognised to be unacceptably small.

- The most attractive and interesting outdoor enclosures will contain running water and ideally a waterfall, rocks, mature trees, varied vegetation and ground surfaces; if fenced, they will have (clean!) panoramic windows, preferably designed to avoid sun glare and reflections, and will give the visitors the distinct feeling of seeing the animals in an unforgettable environment preferably from different perspectives and on different levels; they will then be keen to linger and to absorb apt educational/conservation information placed in the area.

Increasingly in Northern Europe there is a need to use both the landscape of the zoo and the expertise available there to help promote healthy tree and shrub species. Recent years have seen disease in horse chestnuts (leaf-mining moth) elms (Dutch elm disease) and in viburnums. The landscape department of the zoo can be alive to this in their planting decisions and when managing vegetation can use pruned tree and shrub material not just for animal feeding but also to build mounds of dead material to support hedgehogs, insects and other wildlife.

Vegetation

Bamboo and other semi-tropical or tropical forms of vegetation are planted in all of the zoos in my survey; this has been a noticeable development in recent years and is a significant cost item. Surprisingly, even in harsher climates in the northern half of Europe, such planting has been successful outdoors. However, the major investment has been in tropical houses, which have been erected over the past two decades, such as Bush at Arnhem and Masaola at Zurich – both around 14,000 sq.m. in floor area. All of these houses accommodate a big variety of tropical vegetation. Whilst much of this vegetation is being imported, there are zoos (e.g. Wilhelma Stuttgart) with substantial botanical houses able to supply other zoos.

LANDSCAPING AND DESIGN

Botanical Gardens

Several zoos in my survey are both zoological and botanical gardens (e.g. Wilhelma Stuttgart, Bristol, Rotterdam); others have a significant botanical element. All of them are conscious of the advantage of investing in a wide range of flora and providing an attractive visitor experience in addition to pleasing those who live and work in the zoo. Most zoos have a gardening department; some belong to their city council owners who co-ordinate these activities over several sites.

As well as having the opportunity to provide visitors with spectacular displays of formal planting with for example the Dahlia exhibitions in Rostock, the zoos have the opportunity and the local expertise and knowledge to use appropriate areas of the zoo for exhibits of indigenous wildflowers vital to a healthy European butterfly population. An excellent example of this concept can be seen at the rear of the new Himalaya exhibit at Twycross.

Ambience

The area of a zoo is not the key factor in determining the best ambience for occupants and visitors. Design and landscaping are the determining factors and will provide the essential ingredient of a key benefit of a visit to a good zoological garden, the feeling of emotional well-being and respite from stress that can come from being in well planned natural green spaces.

This is particularly well illustrated in Zoo Basel, whose renowned landscaper Kurt Brägger (1953 - 88 at Zoo Basel) has created a truly delightful experience in a relatively confined area in the midst of a city.

Kurt Brägger's landscaping design principles[1] define the whole visible world of space from the design of footpaths through to the surrounding nature. The green lungs of the zoo are

---

[1] Zoo Basel 1953 – 88 Kurt Brägger Gartenstaltung by Werner Blaser, Friedrich Reinhart Verlag, ISBN 3-7245-1222-8

Basel

Hamburg

the vital basis of human and animal life. Attention to detail is carried out in every footpath, outdoor enclosure, house, planting, water feature, and choice of material. Animals need to be shown in as natural an environment as possible, preferably safeguarded with almost invisible ditches. Vegetation is subtly planned and true to scale; small shrubs planted nearby and high trees further away, creating an impression of spaciousness. Visitors experience a landscape of small ponds and brooks which encourage them to discover further. The winding footpaths, the landscape pattern and the variety of vegetation put the visitors in a happy frame of mind, able and willing to appreciate the wealth of animal exhibits and the accompanying messages the zoo wishes the visitors to absorb. Wherever possible, complex man-made constructions need to be concealed; some are placed underground whilst others are covered with vegetation; the Vivarium at Zoo Basel (2500 sq m) is two-thirds underground and the remainder nearly covered with vegetation. Enclosure ditches are frequently turned into natural watercourses planted with its natural vegetation. These are just some of the details that can make a big difference to a zoo's attractiveness to visitors, occupants and those working there. Similar design and landscaping ideas are being followed by most of the city zoos in my survey and many of the principles apply to all zoos.

Water Features

The sound of running water is a pleasure for and promotes psychological wellbeing in people and animals alike. It is a big advantage for a zoo to have plentiful natural water supplies and a suitable topography to provide for lakes, rivers, pools and waterfalls on a generous scale. Most zoos suffer from water shortages and this is very evident in too many of the outdoor enclosures. Many zoos are having to invest more in water supplies and infrastructure and in the recycling options for this precious natural resource.

Many "wow" exhibits incorporate running water whilst many of the most disappointing ones are dry.

Animal Houses

Climate dictates the importance and scale of animal houses in Europe's zoos; those located in the warmer part of the continent need to invest much less than those in the more northerly countries.

Nevertheless, visitors expect animals to be well housed and to be able to visit well designed and suitably sized indoor facilities. Apart from the tropical houses, the most significant and expensive houses are for the larger mammals, particularly elephants, giraffes, rhinos, hippos and the apes. Huge investment has taken place in recent years and continues to dominate zoos' capital investment budgets. Today, visitors expect to see far better conditions for the animals, including plenty of roof light, water availability for bathing as well as drinking, a variety of animal enrichment features and an attractively designed and equipped enclosure. Adequate space is really important; in past years, many houses have had too much visitor space at the expense of the animal occupants. These large houses also provide an excellent opportunity to include well presented education/conservation information on the extensive wall space normally available such as in the elephant house in Zoo Köln and in the great apes house in Bratislava Zoo. The outsides of these ever larger houses need to be concealed with as much vegetation as possible and it is good to see increasing use made in zoos of eco rooves like the roof on the new South America house in Vienna Zoo.

Moated Islands

Another relatively recent development is the increasing presence of moated islands, frequently for gibbons, spider and other monkey species. The design and vegetation, as well as tree cover, of such moated islands are of particular importance, and can make the difference between a safe and a risky exhibit, and between a "wow" and a commonplace visitor experience.

For many monkey species living trees are important (many monkeys naturally forage on new green leaves).This is a difficult landscape problem but very successful examples can be seen in Nuremburg where the squirrel monkeys have access via a wire tunnel from their house to an area of deciduous trees and shrubbery. This concept is also successfully managed in many other zoos such as Chester, Whipsnade and Arnhem.

Conclusion

Landscaping and Design are of ever increasing importance in producing a successful zoological garden. The really successful ones will attract many more annual card holders and other repeat visitors, are likely to assist in successful breeding of species within the zoo, and are an incentive for recruitment and retention of zoo staff. Some zoos have in-house expertise but more are realising the importance of outsourcing this work to an increasing number of specialist firms with an enviable track record in successful zoo design.

CHAPTER 5

Education

Education, in its broadest sense, is probably the most important duty of the modern zoo. If real progress is to be made to respond to the challenges of biodiversity loss, habitat degradation, natural resource depletion, climate change and human population growth, people need to be convinced of the seriousness of the present situation and anticipated future trends. Good zoological gardens are in a unique position: they can influence and inspire their visitors to play a key role in reversing present trends and protecting and enhancing biodiversity.

The delightful atmosphere of the good zoological garden is an ideal setting for influencing visitors of all ages. Whilst the majority of visitors wish, in the first instance, to have a day of recreation and enjoyment, there are many ways in which the educational conservation message can be transmitted. In recent years, there has been considerable progress in our leading European zoological gardens, through investment in buildings, staff and equipment, combined with a higher priority being given to education. Most of this has been in Zoo Schools or Education Centres, rather than in the broader context of adult education.

Educational Aims of Zoos as per WAZA/EAZA Strategy:

- To excite, enthuse people about and interest them in the natural world
- To encourage an understanding of conservation issues and visitors' individual roles in them
- To develop public support and action to address conservation concerns
- To develop a sense of place as humans in the natural world and an understanding of the relevance of conservation to everyday life
- To provide a range of experiences, materials and resources to enable visitors to make informed choices in their daily lives which benefit wildlife and the environment

The extent to which the zoos in this survey implement these laudable aims varies very considerably.

Zoo Schools

The formal Zoo School features particularly in city zoos. Frequently supported by the local education authority, the Zoo School will have its own building or rooms and its own staff. and will cater primarily for children of school age in organised classes or groups, accompanied by school teachers. Very large numbers of school children will visit the local zoo either through the Zoo School or in organised school groups, accompanied by teachers, independently of the Zoo School.

Not all schools in the Zoo's catchment area can arrange visits to the Zoo for their pupils; there can be transport and financial problems, personnel difficulties and other reasons. The Zoo School often has to be involved in Outreach programmes, which involve their teaching staff going to the school and substituting, as far as possible, for what would have taken place in the Zoo visit by the pupils. Some of the zoo schools are well organised to carry out such work; more need to be involved in these Outreach programmes to ensure the maximum local exposure to the educational message.

Estimated typical annual numbers of school children on such visits to the 80 zoos	
100,000+	7 Zoos (5 Group A and 2 Group B)
75,000+	5 Zoos (4 Group A and 1 Group B)
50,000+	10 Zoos (7 Group A and 3 Group B)
25,000+	16 Zoos (3 Group A and 13 Group B)
10,000+	17 Zoos (3 Group A and 14 Group B)
5,000+	13 Zoos (5 Group A and 8 Group B)
Total School Children visitors amount to about 2.8 million or an average of 35,000 per zoo (53,000 in Group A and 24,000 in Group B Zoos)	
The Zoos catering for 100,000+ children are Amsterdam, London, Munich, Paradisio now called Pairi Daiza, Prague, Valencia and Zurich.	
These numbers include both children attending the zoo schools and those school class groups visiting the zoo independently with their own school teachers.	

Lisbon

Successful school visits require:

- Good teaching staff, led by the Zoo School's own professional staff. The quality of the teaching staff is of utmost importance. Some zoo schools have their own full-time teaching staff, whilst others may depend on part-time teachers and/or teachers from the local education authority.

- Good facilities. The quality, attractiveness and positioning of the building and, more importantly, the teaching rooms are important both for the teachers and pupils. Preferably, the rooms should not closely resemble typical school classrooms but should be imaginative, exciting and relevant for a Zoo School.

- Equipment and Displays. To be fully effective, the Zoo School needs to have a variety of audiovisual and computer equipment as well as the traditional displays, models, posters and information.

- Animal Presentations. These are important to explain natural behaviour, conservation issues, and care in the zoo and to give children the excitement and interest of real live animals.

- Project Material and Guided Tours. Well constructed projects, including questionnaires, appropriate to given age groups of pupils, supplemented by enthusiastic staff – including volunteers – at various zoo exhibits, are important components of the pupil's day at the zoo. The zoo needs to capitalise on its strengths and ensure that pupils experience the sight, smell, sound and movement of many different species.

Teaching Teachers

Several zoos have expanded their educational programmes by teaching the teachers. Courses are organised and materials provided to instruct the teachers accompanying the pupils on the zoo visit by giving them advance training in the zoo. The advantage of these programmes is that many more classes benefit and that the zoo can assure that the visit of a class, which has not booked a guided visit with a zoo employee, meets the objectives of the zoos' educational goals. If a zoo manages to introduce its own programme into the curriculum of the local schools, this is another reason for teachers to come to the zoo and use it as an education centre.

Adult Education

The most important education role of the zoo is to inform and persuade their visitors of the crucial importance of biodiversity and wildlife conservation in today's world. This requires for each exhibit well designed signage.

The display signage on each exhibit should be supplemented by a Biodiversity/Conservation Centre, preferably housed in a separate building, manned perhaps by well-informed volunteers or students. This could concentrate on the more general biodiversity conservation issues, including the major threats to wildlife, such as bush meat, poaching, Chinese "medical cures", as well as human population growth and its adverse impact on habitats through increased agricultural land and mining and exploration concessions. Issues need to be treated carefully and in a balanced way: for example African bush meat and European over-fishing are similar conservation problems deserving equal attention. Many Zoos, such as Münster, are adding Biodiversity centres and are

Requirements for well designed signage:

- Accurate and attractively presented information in appropriate languages
- Habitat description
- Information on behaviour of the animals
- Breeding information
- Endangerment level in the wild (IUCN list)
- Information on breeding programmes ex-situ (EEPs)
- Conservation work in-situ
- Life expectancy in the wild and in zoos
- What you can do to help conserve the species

illustrating vividly the adverse effect on wildlife conservation through the increasing consumption by the wealthier nations of products such as palm oil; others need to follow.

Visitors are open to receiving information about animals, and are more often receptive to an informal approach. This can take the form of keeper talks, close encounters, hands-on experience, exhibits that allow visitor access (walk-throughs) and conducted tours often led by knowledgeable volunteers or students. Zoos are increasing what they offer in this area, including evening visits and themed talks. Such interpreters all need to be well versed and capable in public presentation skills.

However, much needs to be done to offer a comprehensive adult education menu and this is an area that possibly could qualify for EU funding assistance as a key part of the campaign to increase public awareness of the crucial importance of biodiversity education.

Universities and Colleges

Fortunately, there is clear evidence of increasing interest amongst the student population in biodiversity, wildlife conservation, climate change and related issues; this is likely to continue to increase in the light of the increasing rate of destruction of our planet. The younger generations are more concerned than their parents and grandparents about the possible outcome if present trends continue.

Zoos are increasingly accommodating and assisting students in their relevant degree level work; ideally, there should be a suitably qualified member of zoo staff able to support these students. Many of the projects are helpful to the zoo and some to the wider zoo community.

Many of the leading zoos in my survey go further and have research and conservation departments; well qualified graduates are involved in pure research as well as conservation projects which are both in-situ and ex-situ. This adds to our knowledge of individual species and improves our ability to look after them in captivity as well as helping them in the wild. Two major European zoos, London and Frankfurt, through their zoological societies have very large Research departments and are directly involved each in nearly 100 in-situ conservation projects. The research work carried out, usually in conjunction with leading universities, such as ZSL London with the University of Cambridge, is the equivalent for wildlife as medical research is for the human population.

Bussolengo

Evaluation of Achievement in Education

There is still relatively little known about the real effect of the zoos' educational efforts. More needs to be invested to achieve a better evaluation of the effectiveness of these activities and this would be an ideal university student project.

Cologne

Conclusion

The realisation of the imperative to educate our citizens in Europe about biodiversity conservation is featuring more and more in our leading zoological gardens; however, there is much more that can be done. In these huge numbers of visitors to these zoos is the potential for heightened environmental awareness, improving wildlife conservation and implementing actions for a sustainable future. Financial resources at the zoos are under immense pressure at present; but these areas of activity hopefully will be further supported financially by the EU.
Much progress has been made in buildings and facilities, in staffing, and in improved talks by keepers and volunteers; much remains to be done to bring all the zoos in this survey up to the standards of the best.

Vienna

CHAPTER 6

Ex-Situ Conservation

General Principles - Introduction

Tremendous progress has been made in the last 50 years in the successful breeding of large mammal species from tropical countries within Europe's zoos. 50 years ago it was very rare for elephants and apes to breed successfully in these zoos. Today it is commonplace for the major iconic species to be bred within Europe. In many of our major zoos, the name, date and place of birth of the animal from a major species is publicised. European zoos wish and need to be as self-sufficient as possible, avoiding the importation of animals from the wild and relying on their own breeding programmes within Europe. Import from the wild is undesirable and expensive, not least due to transport costs, and can result in injury or even death for the animal concerned. However, there are instances where there are excess animals in the wild, such as African elephants in southern Africa; wild animals could be destroyed if new homes could not be found for them.

Ex-situ conservation of species refers to conservation in captivity in areas outside the normal homelands of the species. In practice, this refers mainly to breeding programmes and welfare subjects in zoos with a view to maintaining and increasing the captive population.

EAZA (European Association of Zoos and Aquaria)

One of the main reasons for the formation of EAZA was the need to co-ordinate breeding policy within Europe's main zoos so as to become increasingly self-sufficient within Europe.

Beauval

Ex-Situ Conservation

This aim has been developed and translated into EEPs (European Endangered Species Programmes) for threatened species and ESBs (European Studbooks). EAZA member zoos – and those wishing to be members – are obligated to participate in these programmes and register their relevant animals centrally. All the most significant threatened species are now covered by EEPs – more than 150 in total.

EEP (European Endangered Species Programmes)

This is the most intensive type of population management for a species kept in EAZA zoos. Each EEP has a Co-ordinator and frequently a Species Committee to assist the Co-ordinator. The Co-ordinator will have a special interest in and knowledge of the species concerned, and will be employed in an EAZA member zoo.

The EEP Co-ordinator...

- Collects information on the status of all the animals of the species in member zoos
- Produces a studbook
- Carries out demographic and genetic analyses
- Produces a plan for the management of the species, including husbandry manual
- Publishes and communicates research projects
- Recommends, in conjunction with the Species Committee, which individual animals should breed or not breed, and which should be transferred from one zoo to another.

ESB (European Studbooks)

The Studbook Keeper, responsible for a given ESB, collects all the data on births, deaths and transfers of the species from relevant member zoos. The data are entered on special computer programmes, such as ZIMS, which are stored centrally and enable full analyses to be carried out. ESB keepers are also involved in breeding and/or transfer recommendations.

For some species, EEP Co-ordinator and ESB keeper will be the same person.

Problems in Practice

The EAZA policy, logical and sound in principle, inevitably suffers in practice from problems:

- **Voluntary work**. Both the positions of EEP Co-ordinator and of ESB Keeper are voluntary ones. The work concerned is extra to the normal duties of the person concerned. Inevitably, priority in working hours has to be given to the normal function for which the person is employed by the home zoo. This then involves additional hours' work frequently in the individual's own time. For major species, where large numbers of animals are involved in very many zoos, the workload for the EEP co-ordinator is substantial and can average at least 8 hours per week.

- **Communication problems**. Not everyone is fluent or even well versed in English; 30+ countries are involved in EAZA member zoos. Language communication can be a problem and misunderstandings can occur. Also, busy co-ordinators may not be able to respond to urgent matters as rapidly as needed.

- **Breeding policy**. Zoo visitors and the media are particularly fond of baby animals. Zoo Directors have to take this into account and may not always be willing to agree to non-breeding of certain species in their zoo.

- **Transfer policy**. There may be instances where a particular animal is particularly cherished within the zoo – possibly by the Zoo Director's wife or a long-term keeper – and the recommendation to transfer the animal becomes difficult to accept.

- **The Co-ordinator**. This can be a really demanding job, requiring good diplomatic, language and computer skills in addition to the basic requirements of the position. Such persons are in short supply and may be essential to the running of the zoo in which he/she is employed.

I would hope that some special funding, possibly from the EU, could be made available at least for the EEP Co-ordinators of the most demanding species so that extra salary costs to the zoo concerned could be covered, possibly through additional employment and payment for costs of visits to other zoos and Species Committee meetings. This is very important work, essential to successful ex-situ conservation implementation.

EEP Examples

In order to illustrate the important work and significance of EEPs, I have selected two of the most popular species – and amongst my own favourites – the giraffe and the orangutan. These are two of the largest EEPs as both giraffes and orang utans are kept by a very large number of European major zoos. At time of writing, the EEP co-ordinator for the giraffe is at Chester Zoo and for the orang utan at Zoo Karlsruhe.

Ex-Situ Conservation

Giraffe EEP

There are about 800 giraffes kept in 140+ EAZA European member zoos. EEP and ESB functions are carried out by the same person. There is a large species committee of 17 members including 14 members from Zoos in the survey. In the 80 zoos in the survey 29 of the 30 Group A and 37 of the 50 Group B zoos keep giraffes. Zurich, the exception in Group A, plans to add giraffes before 2020. In all surveys, it is one of the 5 most popular animals with visitors to these zoos.

Warsaw

The giraffe, whose native home is in savannah areas in sub-Sahara Africa, has 6 recognised sub-species, namely:

Sub-species	EEP sub-group
Masai	Reticulated
Reticulated	Reticulated
Rothschild's	Baringo
Cape or Southern	Baringo
Kordofan	Baringo
Thornicroft's	-

The EEP effectively includes all but Thornicroft's, which is not present in these zoos, but also includes hybrids which have resulted from breeding in European zoos. The EEP is divided into 2 sub-groups (Reticulated, including Masai; and Baringo, covering the others + hybrids). In the wild, there are estimated to be less than 65,000 giraffes in Africa which is 30% less than 10 years previously. The remaining populations of Rothschild's (less than 650) and of Kordofan (less than 150) are critically endangered.

European zoos try to keep and breed pure sub-species rather than hybrids; most are Reticulated or Rothschild's.

In the wild, 50% - 75% of all giraffes fail to survive their first year. By comparison, in the European Zoos in 2008 only 23% failed to survive their first year. Overall life expectancy is 25 years. Giraffe herds typically consist of 6-12 animals of any combination of sexes and ages at any given moment; all social units are temporary. They live side by side with most of the other herbivores of the African plains. They tend to ignore animals of other species but often feed with zebras, impalas and some other antelopes; oxpeckers frequently live with giraffes. They dwell mainly on dry savannahs and in open woodland, usually associated with scattered acacia growth.

Giraffe Management in Zoos

The main aim of the EEP is to advise and assist their member zoos to provide the best possible conditions for their giraffes, taking account of giraffes' conditions in the wild. Whilst it is not possible to replicate fully the conditions in the wild, much can be done to simulate the most important aspects. Much research has been and continues to be carried out into all aspects concerning welfare of giraffes; the zoos share the results of such research and there is clear evidence that welfare of giraffes in captivity has improved greatly over recent years as a result. Life expectancy in Europe's leading zoos continues to increase; the present target of 20 years+ on average is now within sight (several giraffes have reached 30 years).

Ex-Situ Conservation

The excellent work of the EEP and the recommendations made to member zoos include:

- A core group of at least 3 giraffes should be kept.

- One of 3 models should be followed – small breeding herd of 1 adult male + 2-3 adult females with calves; or large breeding herd of 2+ adult males + 4+ adult females with calves; or single-sex group of either males or females.

- Appropriate indoor house must be provided with attention to details for minimum size, appropriate separation arrangements, materials, flooring (must include resilient surfaces), bedding (at least 50% of surface should have soft bedding material), water supply, food presentation, temperature (20 deg C+), natural daylight (such as transparent roof) and visitor access and viewing arrangements. All of these are advised in detail, taking account of experience and research.

- Outdoor enclosures are specified in terms of minimum size and length, fencing, variety of substrates, variety of feeding stations, adequate fresh water, shelter against sun and wind, and vegetation.

- Nutrition and feeding arrangements. Typically an average giraffe eats 12 kgs daily and the giraffe's nutritional requirements, on which much research is carried out, are challenging! In the wild, their feeding and foraging time varies within 10-12 hours daily, and what they eat there determines the appropriate diet in captivity.

- Social arrangements. The individual characteristics of each giraffe must be taken into account. Any new arrival has to be carefully monitored and observed, both indoors and outdoors.

- Breeding. Recommendations on breeding are made through the EEP and ESB so as to protect the future of the giraffe population throughout the zoos. This involves avoidance of increasing hybrids. However, all zoos with breeding herds value greatly the arrival of baby giraffes. In a few cases, the mother may not take care of her offspring and hand rearing then becomes an option, which is followed on some occasions, requiring the dedication of at least one giraffe keeper!

- Mixed Species exhibits. In principle, both animals and visitors prefer mixed species exhibits including giraffes in savannah type settings. Although not easy in practice and again depending on the individual characteristics of the giraffes and their companion species, they are now commonly in place in many of the zoos in this survey. Much research has been carried out, such as by Dr. Gabriele Hammer (Salzburg University) on such exhibits. Recommendations include compatibility of giraffes with plains zebra, white rhino and impala. At Leipzig Zoo, with one of the best such mixed species savannahs, sable antelopes and gazelles, as well as ostriches, marabous and crowned crested cranes, are also present. Only African savannah species are recommended for mixed species exhibits.

- Transportation. Giraffes are notoriously sensitive and difficult to transport safely and successfully. Recommendations on suitable transport companies are made; in fact, there are only about two who are real specialists in road transport of giraffes within Europe.

- In new inexperienced institutions, mortality rates of giraffes are significantly higher. Keepers and staff less experienced with giraffes and facilities not fully tested for giraffes are key to the higher mortality rate. Consequently zoos new to giraffe keeping have to start with single sex groups.

Orang Utan EEP

In this instance, at the time of writing, the EEP co-ordinator and the ESB keeper functions are carried out by the same person. There is a large Species committee, comprising 15 members of whom 13 are from zoos within the survey and 7 from VDZ member zoos. There are about 320 orang utans kept in 64 EAZA European member zoos. Of the 80 zoos in the survey, orang utans are kept by 20 of the 30 Group A zoos and 22 of the 50 Group B Zoos. It is one of the top 10 most popular animals with the visitors to these zoos.

> **The orang utan ("man of the woods" in local language), whose native home is in the rainforests of Borneo and northern Sumatra in Indonesia and Malaysia, has two recognised sub-species with significantly different physical characteristics, namely:**
>
> • Bornean orang utan (*Pongo pygmaeus*)
> • Sumatran orang utan (*Pongo abelii*)
>
> **In the zoo world, a third type has evolved, namely:**
>
> • Hybrid orang utan (*Pongo HYBRID*)

In the European zoos, 48% are Bornean, 45% are Sumatran and 7% are Hybrids. Of the Borneans, 15% were wildborn and the rest born in captivity, primarily in European zoos; of the Sumatrans, no wildborn have been imported for more than 20 years and over 90% have been born in local captivity. The average annual birth rate in the zoos is 16; in 2009 there were 21 of which 16 survived. Longevity in captivity is up to 52 years.

Position in the Wild

> **The IUCN (International Union for Conservation of Nature) Red List (2007) states that:**
>
> • Sumatran species is "critically endangered"
> • Bornean species is "endangered"

Ex-Situ Conservation

The numbers in the wild are rapidly decreasing. As few as 5,000 or less remain in Sumatra and less than 40,000 (amongst 3 sub-species) in the huge island of Borneo, divided between Sabah and Sarawak in Malaysia and Kalimantan in Indonesia.

Both species are particularly vulnerable to extinction due to:

- Large scale and constant destruction of the rainforest, partly due to the rapid expansion of the palm oil industry (Indonesia and Malaysia accounting for 80% of global production). Indonesia has one of the world's highest deforestation rates. From 1990 to 2005 the forest area was reduced by 24%. Recent estimates suggest that 98% of Indonesia's natural rain forest could be lost by 2022[1].
- Logging, resulting in destruction and fragmentation of forests: an estimated 73 to 88% of all timber logged in Indonesia is illegal[2]
- Bush meat hunting for food for rapidly increasing human population
- Hunting for the pet trade
- Poor law enforcement
- The large body size of the animal
- The long inter-birth interval (6 to 9 years)
- Living in low densities in large home ranges
- Being restricted to lowland forest areas and increasingly to small forest fragments

[1, 2] Statistics from Orangutan Foundation Indonesia Forest Facts (Updated January 2010).

Dresden

Research has established that 250 individuals is the minimum number for a viable population and, in 2007, there were only 6 such populations remaining in Sumatra, and 32 in the whole of Borneo; today, it is certain that these numbers have been reduced.

In the wild, orang utans are almost exclusively arboreal and are frequently solitary. Adults spend most of their life and time on their own. As the largest and heaviest arboreal mammal, the orang utan is not able to cover large distances in their habitat but they have to consume large amounts of food.

Orang utans have a complex social structure. Most commonly, a male and a female join one another in a so-called "consort ship", characterised by regular sex; a pair may travel together for days or weeks. There are two forms of sexually mature males – "flanged" and "unflanged". Flanged males are large adults with fully developed secondary sexual characteristics (hair coat, cheek flanges, throat pouches); they are mostly solitary, have overlapping territories with home ranges of several females and are sexually active; they do not tolerate other flanged males, but are tolerant towards unflanged males in their home ranges. The unflanged males, with undeveloped secondary sexual characteristics, are more similar in size to females and are more tolerant and social towards other males. The change from unflanged to flanged is influenced by social factors and may occur suddenly (within months) in sub adult males or later in life. Females have a preference for fully adult males and choose flanged males for sexual consorts, whereas matings with unflanged males take place mostly outside consorts.

Orang Utan Management in Zoos

As with giraffes, the EEP recommends taking full account of life in the wild and trying to esta-blish comparable conditions as far as possible.

The very slow rate or even zero rate of growth in the orang utan population in European zoos is of concern, even though the present population is healthy and stable.

Consequences for the management, care and enclosure design include:

- Females should have a choice between different (separated) males and when to be with or separated from the preferred male.
- Bigger and more flexible facilities with a variety of indoor and outdoor en-closures must be constructed.
- Close co-operation between nearby zoos with orang utans to enable more choice for females.

In the first decade of this century, amongst the zoos in this survey, major investment in new orang utan houses and enclosures has been made at Amnéville, Beauval, Chester, Colchester, Frankfurt, Hamburg, La Palmyre, Leipzig, Munich, Münster, Sosto and Vienna. The benefits to population increase from these and developments under construction are yet to be felt.

An outstanding example of a successful mixed species exhibit which takes account of the natural environment in which orang utans thrive is to be found in Hamburg: a very happy social group

Ex-Situ Conservation

Hamburg

of orangs can be viewed on several levels and their occasional interaction with the small- clawed otters is fascinating. The height, natural light, warmth and vegetation and water make these surroundings pleasurable for both animals and visitors. The information on the orang utan in the house (not perhaps as up to date as it should be and it would be even more alarming if it were) highlights how endangered these lovely animals are.

Since records on orang utan births started being kept about 60 years ago, in each of these 10 of the 80 zoos, Duisburg, Frankfurt, Berlin, Munich, Chester, Dresden, Arnhem, Stuttgart, Twycross and Zurich, over 20 orang utan births have successfully taken place.

Recent EEP policy should enable a faster population growth rate, provide for a closer imitation of the natural social system in the wild, improve the psychological wellbeing of orang utans in captivity and provide visitors with a more pleasing orang utan visit experience.

Conclusion

The work of the EEP co-ordinator and his/her species committee is very wide-ranging. This illustrates the tremendous efforts being made to continually improve the wellbeing of giraffes and orang utans in our zoos. The population is growing, life expectancy is increasing, and exhibits are being improved as a result of this work. This is typical of other species covered by EEPs.

CHAPTER 7

In-Situ Conservation

General Situation

The world's human population has nearly doubled in the past 40 years and will reach 7 billion by end 2011; many forecasts give figures approaching 9.5 billion by 2050. At the same time as this population explosion, people's expectations and achievements of higher living standards are driving an ever growing demand for resources of all kinds.

In short, there are, as the introduction to the WAZA Conservation Strategy 2005 so clearly states, "too many human beings consuming far too great a proportion of the Earth's natural resources to allow non-human species a share that secures their future. The predicted increase in human population and the pronounced inequality in distribution of wealth among and within nations are two of the major problems facing humankind and directly and indirectly the conservation of species and habitats".

There are many organisations dedicated to conservation in the wild. These include the best known WWF (World Wildlife Fund) and a variety of international, regional and national organisations as well as individual zoos. There is evidence of a lack of overall co-ordination and probably there are too many separate operations in the wild. There is encouraging evidence of more young people, particularly from developed countries, wanting to be actively involved in conservation work.

However, the big decisions affecting most of the areas concerned are dictated by finance, by major corporations and by national governments, against which conservationists in all organisations have to fight. In general, conservationists are winning some battles but are currently losing the war in the face of the fundamental forces referred to in the opening paragraph, population explosion and people's expectations and achievements of higher living standards.

Kenya

In-Situ Conservation

El Remanso Lodge,
Costa Rica

Nevertheless, the growing army of conservationists from around the world continue to increase their efforts to save species and habitats. Zoos are very much involved on two fronts: first, directly, by involvement in projects in the field and, secondly, indirectly, by raising zoo visitors' conservation awareness, encouraging them to spread the message of the desperate need to support conservation in every way from their personal choice of product purchase to the direct actions being taken to help in-situ conservation projects.

The Role of Europe's Zoos

All zoos in this survey subscribe to the WAZA/EAZA policy of helping in-situ conservation; some allocate a significant part of their revenue budget in money and personnel whilst others may not have the financial resources or agreement of their owners to do so. A few zoos, such as London, Frankfurt and Antwerp, belong to or are very closely associated with famous zoological societies, which are well-resourced financially and staffed with highly qualified enthusiasts. Several zoos, particularly in UK, include in the entrance price a voluntary donation to conservation work, nearly always accepted by the visitors. Many zoos have support organisations, such as "Friends of the Zoo", who also raise money for in-situ conservation projects.

All zoos are under financial pressures, particularly following the 2008-9 global financial crisis, and it would be unrealistic to expect zoos to prioritise expenditure on in-situ conservation over the day-to-day running and improvement of their own zoos.

There is a case for better and more effective use of in-situ conservation expenditure. There are many NGOs in the field, various zoos with projects in many countries, and frequently local Government organisations (e.g. Kenya Wildlife Service) tasked with similar work. In the two countries surveyed in this chapter, there is evidence of a lack of co-ordination between these conservation bodies. This problem is similar to that in other human activities, such as relief work in natural disaster situations. Whilst no one would wish to dampen the enthusiasm of dedicated individuals, the effectiveness of conservation effort needs to be maximised.

Europe's zoos, through EAZA, have launched a conservation project data base in which their member zoos can list their conservation projects with a view to co-ordination of effort - but there is considerable room for improvement in its uptake and effectiveness.

To be successful, effective in-situ conservation must take into account ecotourism, education locally, poverty relief, in some cases water supplies, and convincing the local population of the economic benefits to them of local wildlife and habitat conservation. Such overall involvement is beyond the resources of most individual zoos. Recognising this, some zoos either contribute to conservation organisations, such as Stiftung Artenschutz, or concentrate on one or two small and manageable projects where they can make a real difference.

Kenya

Population increase in tropical countries

The great majority of biodiversity in terms of animal and plant species exists in the tropical countries. The iconic species highlighted in the zoos in this book originate mostly from these countries.

Human population increase in the tropical countries accounts for most of the world's increase in the past 40 years and is expected to do so for the next 40 years.

The countries selected for the table below represent many of the areas from which iconic species originate and where numbers in the wild have been decimated in recent decades. They contain most of the "hotspots" for conservation efforts with which our zoos and other conservation organisations are involved.

The table illustrates the youthfulness of tropical Africa's population, typically with a median age of 18 compared with a global one of 29 and typically 40+ in Europe. During the period 1970-2010, the population of Germany increased by under 5% whilst that of Kenya increased by over 250%!

In-Situ Conservation

Population Developments in Selected Tropical Countries							
Country	% Pop Increase 1970-2010	Pop 1970 Millions	Pop 2010 Millions	Median Age 2009	Pop Density 2010	% Pop. Growth Rate 2010	Pop Est. 2025 Millions	Pop Est. 2050 Millions
Ivory Coast	292.9	5.6	22.0	19.4	68	2.4	30.8	47.2
Kenya	257.1	11.2	40.0	18.3	69	2.7	51.3	65.2
Uganda	248.5	9.7	33.8	15.5	140	3.4	53.4	91.3
Angola	239.3	5.6	19.0	17.3	15	2.5	27.4	42.3
Tanzania	226.0	13.8	45.0	17.5	48	3.0	67.4	109.5
DRC - Congo	211.0	21.8	67.8	16.5	29	2.9	101.4	166.2
Guinea	200.0	3.6	10.8	18.4	44	3.0	15.9	25.1
Cameroon	198.5	6.7	20.0	19.1	42	2.3	26.5	36.7
Madagascar	195.6	6.8	20.1	18.3	34	2.7	28.6	42.7
Nigeria	184.7	55.6	158.3	18.5	171	2.4	217.4	326.4
Ghana	172.7	8.8	24.0	20.4	101	2.2	31.8	44.6
Costa Rica	170.6	1.7	4.6	27.8	90	1.3	5.3	6.1
Malaysia	165.1	10.9	28.9	26.0	87	1.6	34.9	41.0
Mozambique	151.6	9.3	23.4	17.9	29	2.3	31.2	44.1
Philippines	143.5	38.6	94.0	23.0	313	2.1	117.6	140.5
Ecuador	140.7	5.9	14.2	25.2	50	1.6	16.6	18.6
Nepal	135.3	11.9	28.0	21.3	191	1.9	35.7	46.1
Peru	123.5	13.2	29.5	25.3	23	1.6	34.5	39.8
South Africa	119.8	22.7	49.9	24.7	41	0.9	54.4	57.4
India	114.6	553.9	1188.8	24.7	362	1.5	1444.5	1748.0
Colombia	112.6	21.4	45.5	26.5	40	1.4	53.5	61.3
Vietnam	108.7	42.6	88.9	27.9	268	1.2	103.2	113.7
Brazil	102.0	95.7	193.3	28.6	23	1.0	212.4	215.3
Morocco	100.6	15.9	31.9	25.8	71	1.5	36.6	41.2
Burma	94.9	27.4	53.4	27.6	79	0.9	61.7	70.8
Indonesia	92.6	122.3	235.5	27.9	124	1.4	273.2	309.4
Thailand	83.6	37.1	68.1	32.8	133	0.6	72.6	73.4
Sri Lanka	64.3	12.6	20.7	30.3	315	1.2	23.2	25.4
China	63.1	820.4	1338.1	33.8	140	0.5	1476.0	1437.0
Cuba	31.8	8.5	11.2	37.7	101	0.3	11.1	9.7
Germany	4.9	77.8	81.6	43.9	229	-0.2	70.7	71.5
UK	11.9	55.6	62.2	39.7	256	0.4	68.6	77.0
Turkey	105.6	35.8	73.6	28.0	94	1.2	85.0	94.7
World	85.6	3713.0	6892.0	28.9	51	1.2	8108.0	9485.0
Sources:	Population Reference Bureau. The Economist" Pocket World in Figures". 2010 and Wikipedia							
Notes:	Density = persons per sq. km; Projections 2025 and 2050 vary according to source. These are relatively high projections.							

Threats to Wildlife can be summarised briefly as follows:

- Human population increase, particularly in tropical countries
- Habitat conversion to provide increased agricultural land for local farming
- Deforestation to increase area for commercial export crops
- Deforestation due to logging activities
- "Bush meat" to provide food for local population
- Poaching, particularly of species with alleged "medicinal value"
- Poaching of species with wide commercial value (e.g. elephants, crocodiles)
- Collecting for the pet trade (e.g. parrots, macaws)
- Trophy hunting
- Mining and extraction industries
- Draining and diverting water from lakes and rivers for human requirements
- Diseases, sometimes arising from humans and their domestic animals
- Increased desertification, arising from deforestation and climate change
- Use of toxic chemicals (e.g. in farming)

The effects of climate change are evidently increasing and have a further adverse effect.

In-Situ Conservation - Case Study Costa Rica

Costa Rica is home to nearly 5% of the world's identified living species. Amazingly, this Central American country is, at 51,000 sq. km, only slightly larger than Switzerland. Small in size it's big on biodiversity having more than 850 bird species, representing about 10% of the global total and an extraordinary range of butterflies. Costa Rica also has rich tropical vegetation, and a large and diverse range of mammals, reptiles and amphibians.

When Columbus arrived more than 500 years ago, Costa Rica was entirely covered with forest; today more than two thirds of this has been lost but the remaining 30-35% is protected national park (25% of the country), reserve or privately owned protected land. Habitats include lowland tropical rainforests, lowland dry forests and highland and cloud forests – the central mountainous region has many peaks over 3,000 m. The highest at 3,820 m is just higher than Austria's 3,797 m Großglockner.

Costa Rica is arguably unique amongst the tropical nations with regard to conservation; it faces severe environmental threats but is probably the most active and successful in its conservation efforts. The country has a long history of interest and activity in conservation, enacting strict wildlife trade laws from 1970 onwards, being the first Central American country to sign and adhere to CITES and allocating 25% of its total land area to parks and reserves embracing a healthy variety of eco systems in the different areas of the country.

Nevertheless, despite all these advantages there are problems as much wildlife remains under threat and key species are in decline. The main constituents of the conservation scene in Costa Rica may be summarised as follows.

IN-SITU CONSERVATION

Strengths:

- Government owned national parks and reserves still cover 25% of the country's area, a proportion rarely matched in the tropical countries.

- There is a long history of local and international interest in biodiversity conservation with substantial support primarily from the USA. Establishments such as OTS (Organisation for Tropical Studies) are a good example.

- Ecotourism regarded as travel to destinations, usually exotic, to admire and enjoy wildlife in relatively undisturbed natural areas, is increasing and is particularly strong in Costa Rica. After Intel's local plant, ecotourism is the second biggest component of GDP in the country.

- The long-term political stability of the country since 1948 provides a particularly attractive background for inward investment, including ecotourism and conservation. This is very rare in tropical countries.

- A relatively well educated local population, generally appreciative and supportive of wildlife conservation, results from up to 25% of the national budget being allocated to education; this is aided by the neutrality of the country and absence of armed forces and military expenditure.

- An unusually high proportion of students and other young people are involved in biodiversity and related subjects. There is particularly strong wildlife heritage awareness in the educated younger generation evinced in guides in reserves and national parks.

- 40% of the population lives in the greater San José metropolitan area, thereby reducing population pressures on more remote and wildlife rich areas.

- Indigenous tribes, historically involved in hunting, constitute only about 0.8% of the country's population.

Weaknesses:

- Human population continues to increase at an alarming rate; it has multiplied by two and a half in past 30 years and is forecast to reach 7 million within 15 years; this due partly to large immigration from neighbouring Nicaragua.

- Lack of Government financial support for its national parks and reserves, particularly affects recruitment and retention of sufficient park rangers, as well as compensation of landowners for agreed land transfers to protected areas.

- Insufficient Government action on illegal deforestation by logging companies, farmers and developers, continues to be a significant problem.

- Corruption at many levels results in illegal poaching, hunting and deforestation.

- Action against poachers and illegal hunters can only take place if the person concerned is caught with the relevant dead animal, which rarely happens.

- There seems to be an absence of critical data on numbers, distribution and population trends of key wildlife species, including CITES Appendix 1 and 2 species.

Opportunities:

- Government could increase its financial support to its national parks and reserves, thereby increasing substantially the potential effectiveness of its conservation policies.
- Government should further encourage co-operation between willing private landowners to establish larger conservation areas. A successful example of this type of private reserve is in the Osa Peninsula where an existing private refuge of 1670Ha has the potential to be enlarged by a further 900Ha.
- Government should give financial support to conservation and relevant research organisations such as OTS (OET).
- Encouraged by actions such as those outlined above, more local and international volunteers could become involved in conservation related work.
- Improved facilities for Eco tourists in some national parks and reserves, such as Corcovado, should be provided but must be limited to ensure minimum disturbance to the local wildlife.
- Government to consider taking a more prominent conservation leadership role in Central America; cross-border national parks should be further considered.

Threats:

- Due to population increase and rising expectations, there is pressure for more agricultural land.
- Further habitat destruction takes place as a result of major commercial developments such as hotels, golf courses and other non-eco-friendly facilities.
- Additional major banana, pineapple and other commercial crop developments necessitate habitat destruction and soil pollution.
- Pressures on Government finances could result in further deforestation and reduction in national park and reserve areas in favour of major mining, agriculture or other large-scale commercial developments.
- Bribery and corruption increase as a result of poor salaries for rangers and others, together with higher prices offered by poachers and hunters. With diminishing numbers of most major mammals world-wide, prices of large cat furs, such as Jaguar and Ocelot, and bush meat animals, including Tapir and Peccary, are likely to rise.
- Climate change, together with major natural catastrophes, such as earthquakes and volcanic eruptions – Costa Rica has seven active volcanoes – could well have an adverse effect on the country's biodiversity.
- New discoveries of oil, gold or other valuable mineral resources could be at the expense of conservation areas.

Conclusion

Costa Rica is arguably the most successful tropical country in retaining very substantial bio-diversity and developing national parks and enacting conservation policies. It has several important advantages over other tropical countries and is rightly renowned for its wildlife and successful resultant ecotourism. Costa Rica is fortunate not to suffer major problems such as Chinese demand for ivory, rhino horn and tiger parts or desertification. Nevertheless, it is experiencing continued deforestation, reduction in already very low numbers of key mammal species, such as Jaguar, and on-going environmental threats, aggravated by a very substantial increase in the human population. There seems to be an increasing emphasis on tourist developments unrelated to ecotourism.

It is essential that the present forest habitat covering about one-third of the country should be retained and effectively protected.

It would seem that, if in-situ conservation cannot succeed in the longer term in Costa Rica, it is unlikely to succeed elsewhere in tropical countries.

In-Situ Conservation - Case Study Kenya

Kenya, a former British colony, has been an independent nation since 1963. Since independence, its population has increased from about 6 million to 40 million in 2010 with a forecast of 65 million by 2050. This population growth is typical of sub-Sahara Africa. Kenya lies on the equator; it has only two substantial rivers. Drylands with semi-desert like conditions cover two thirds of the country and are concentrated in the northern half. These are included in the so-called Rangelands, which cover about 85% of the country's land area. National parks and other protected areas account for about 11% of the total land area. Protected areas are owned by the government or other public bodies and therefore are subject to official laws. Non-protected areas differ in that any wildlife protection has to be effected by non-legal means such as financial incentives and, in practice, are more beneficial to wildlife conservation.

El Remanso Lodge,
Costa Rica

Kenya, although it has suffered from severe political crises (such as in 2008), has enjoyed a more benign and stable democratically elected Government situation than most other sub-Sahara African countries. The economy has been more buoyant and has attracted foreign investment, although mining and minerals play a much smaller role in Kenya and exported agricultural products a larger role than in most other African countries.

Tourism and Wildlife

Kenya is a leading tourist destination both for wildlife and coastal holidays. Nairobi, its capital, is a major city and airport hub. It is renowned for its national parks and reserves, particularly the Tsavos, Masai-Mara, and Amboseli as well as for Mount Kenya, the Aberdares, and Lake Naivasha, where large numbers of wildlife enthusiast tourists are regular visitors. Therefore, Kenya should be in a better position than most tropical countries to protect its wildlife.

National Wildlife Policy

The Kenya Wildlife Service (KWS) is the Government body tasked with developing and implementing wildlife policy in the country. There are 23 National Parks, 10 National Reserves and 4 other protected areas, accounting in total for about 11% of the total area of Kenya. Most of this area is publicly owned and there are a few small private reserves. KWS was established in 1990 and manages the biodiversity of the country, protecting and conserving the flora and fauna. KWS manages the National Parks and National Reserves. They are also involved in education, training and veterinary services in support of their aims and objectives. They have held several species workshops in recent years with the object of developing national strategies for key species. Much thorough and good work has been and continues to be achieved. However, KWS suffers from insufficient funding and institutional weaknesses. KWS' vision for 2030 is to have 2,500 Rhinos, 5,000 lions and an "optimal" number of elephants. However, these may well be optimistic objectives in the light of present numbers and the threats to wildlife affecting conservation.

Wildlife Developments

It is estimated that 70% of Kenya's wildlife has been lost in the past 30 years and possibly up to 90% in the past 50 years. Western, Russell and Cuthill in their study on the status of Kenya's wildlife up to ten years ago, estimate that Wildlife populations over a twenty year period to 1997 have declined by 58% in Mara NR, 63% in Tsavo NP and 78% in Meru NP.[1]

An extreme example is the decimation and near extinction of black rhinos in Tsavo, the largest national park area in Kenya, from more than 12,000 in 1960 to under 100 some 50 years later. All major species, including elephant, giraffe, lion, zebra, bongo, show large declines during this period.

During the same period, Kenya has lost much of its forest area, and desertification has increased.

[1] The Status of Wildlife in Protected Areas Compared to Non- Protected Areas of Kenya, David Western, Samantha Russell, Innes Cuthill - Plus One July 2009, Vol. 4 Issue 7 e6140.

In-Situ Conservation

Examples of recent trends in the population of charismatic species in Kenya:

Elephants: Kenya has one of the largest populations of elephants and special attention has been given to this species. In 1973, the estimated elephant population in Kenya was 167,000. Uncontrolled poaching decimated numbers to a probably under-estimated 16,000 by 1989. This tragic decline gave rise to the foundation of the Kenya Wildlife Service in the same year and by 1999 the estimated elephant population had increased to 27,000[2] and has remained at about 30,000 in recent years, with two-thirds living in the Tsavo ecosystem and the Laikipea/Samburu area. They continue to be threatened by poachers, particularly in the north from Somalia, and by extreme drought conditions. However, this is a relative recent success story!

Rhinos: The main population today of the Eastern Black Rhino is in Kenya. Their numbers have been decimated from an estimated 15,000 in 1970 to as few as 430 in 2001[3]. However, numbers have been increasing in recent years to perhaps 600 in 2008 but are still of great concern due to intense poaching activities; the remaining small populations require continual guarding.

Large Carnivores: The increasing numbers of livestock owners consider lions and leopards enemies to be killed; these large carnivores, particularly in times of drought, are forced to prey on domestic livestock, thereby provoking a major human-wildlife conflict. Efforts are being made in several practical ways to overcome these problems but progress is patchy. Today, there are effectively only three remaining viable populations of lions in Kenya, in the Maasai Mara, Tsavo and Laikipia; outside of the national parks, lions could be extinct within a few years. KWS is developing national strategies for Kenya's six large carnivore species – lion, cheetah, leopard, spotted hyena, striped hyena and African wild dog. There has been a dramatic decline in numbers of all these species in recent years. KWS's workshop on lions and spotted hyenas, for example, bringing together an impressive collection of experts and interested parties, concluded that –

- Lion population was estimated to be 2,010 in 2008 (having been 2,280 in 2004) and today is likely to be well under 2,000. The total numbers are divided fairly evenly between protected and non-protected areas.

- Spotted Hyena population is much less well known. In 1998, an estimate of 2,000-4,000 was generally accepted (Mills and Hofer). There has been a major reduction since then, particularly in non-protected areas. In protected areas, a 2008 estimate of 785 animals was used.

- Lions and spotted hyenas form a vital component of Kenya's natural ecosystems. They are also very important to the tourism industry. Their presence in an area is considered to be an indicator of its wild integrity (KWS Workshop 2010)

Giraffes: Kenya is the only country to have as many as three species of giraffe – Masai, Reticulated and Rothschild's. There has been a dramatic decline in Kenya's giraffe population, as in other African countries: the total estimated Africa-wide population reduction has been over 30% in past 10 years.

The Rothschild's giraffe is the second most endangered of the 9 known sub-species with less than 650 remaining in the wild, 60% of which are in Kenya's protected areas; only one area,

---

[2] Data from The Status of Kenya's Elephants 1990 -2002, C. Thouless, J. King, P.Omondi, P. Kahumbu and I. Douglas Hamilton

[3] Data from Rhino Resource Center from Dr Kees Rookmaaker

Ruma National Park, has 100+ individuals. Most populations are isolated from one another and are not interbreeding.

Reticulated giraffes are found widely in northern Kenya. Population data is incomplete but estimated to be 3,000-5,000 compared with an estimated 28,000 only ten years earlier. The Masai giraffe, which lives in southern Kenya, is faring relatively better but have declined; their numbers are currently being estimated.

The KWS organised workshop is currently developing the basis for a national strategy.

Antelopes: The largest antelope in Kenya is the bongo, which lives in forested areas and used to be widespread in Kenya's forests. Estimates from 30 - 40 years ago indicated a national population of more than 1,000; today, the number may be as low as 100[4], primarily in the Aberdares region (Lyndon Estes). Whilst the bongo may be an extreme, although very important, example, several species of larger antelopes have been reduced by at least 70% over the past 30-40 years in Kenya.

[4] Dr Lyndon Estes, Bongo specialist

Threats to Wildlife

As already mentioned, the most important factor is the dramatic increase in human population, augmented by immigration from neighbouring countries, particularly Somalia. The great majority of the population remains very poor and dependent on subsistence farming. The second key factor is water shortages throughout most of Kenya and these have become worse in recent years with severe droughts aggravating the situation even more.

It is therefore not surprising that wildlife populations are declining due to:

- Deforestation
- Bush meat trade
- Poaching
- Cattle and other farm animal intrusions into national parks and reserves
- Water abstraction (e.g. Lake Naivasha)
- Mining pollution
- Vegetable and flower production for export
- Major commercial projects (e.g. Qatari sugar cane project in Tana river delta)
- Uncontrolled use of toxic pesticides (e.g. Carbofurum as used in Furadon)
- Major increase in world prices of rhino horn and ivory
- Huge increase in numbers of Chinese working in Africa (72,000 in 2001 to 500,000 in 2006), further encouraging poaching of rhinos and elephants
- Global warming and climate change, producing longer severe droughts (e.g. in Amboseli NP 2009-10.

In-Situ Conservation

Main Challenges to Eradication of Bush Meat Trade

The East African Wildlife Society in its quarterly magazine "SWARA" reported at end 2008 that the main problems could be summarised as:

- Bush meat is cheaper than beef and is therefore a cheaper source of protein to urban and rural poor.2008 was a peak year for world food prices but 2011 has commenced with even higher prices. This remains the biggest single threat to many mammal species.
- Rising poverty and landlessness among communities living adjacent to wildlife rich areas.
- Rising incidences of human-wildlife conflict cases and lack of compensation.
- Inadequate wildlife laws do not deter bush meat poaching.
- Poor knowledge of wildlife laws leads to offences being categorised as misdemeanours.
- Weak law enforcement allows cartels to thrive.
- Civil police, rather than wildlife authorities, prosecute wildlife crimes.
- Serial poachers are treated as first-time offenders in wildlife crimes; most of them are able to pay the small fines imposed and quickly return to make easy money from illegal trade.
- KWS has alienated communities and private landowners outside protected areas, eading to resentment and hostility.

It is now commonplace to find bush meat being sold in villages and settlements bordering the Tsavo national parks and other protected areas.

Other Adverse Factors

Other factors, adversely affecting conservation of wildlife in Kenya:

- Granting of licences for commercial agricultural expansion and mining exploration.
- Major water abstraction and pollution
- Legal and illegal encroachment of national parks and reserves, including re-gazetting (reducing areas).
- Inability to compete financially with poachers, who are able to pay fines and bribe rangers and other officials - particularly relating to elephant and rhino
- Kenya has the disadvantage, at least at present, of bordering Somalia, from where many of the poaching gangs come. The conduit through Somalia for illegal ivory and rhino horn is also a major problem for the control of poaching.

Kenya Wildlife Conservation and Management Policy – Idealists versus Pragmatists

In an ideal world, many of us including myself would prefer to see wildlife fully protected with trophy hunting being banned and other forms of consumptive use of wildlife being illegal. However, in the real world, this may not only be impossible to implement and control but also may not be in the realistic interests of wildlife conservation. Our conservation mission needs to be focussed on maximum conservation of wildlife in practice.

Since 1977, Kenya has banned consumptive use of wildlife, with a few minor exceptions. In spite of this seemingly pro-conservation policy, Kenya's wildlife has declined since 1977 by an estimated 70% and continues to decline by at least 3% annually. The great majority (circa 70%) of wildlife still exists in the rangelands outside the formally protected areas; it is here in the rangelands that there is a battle between the conservation idealists and pragmatists, led by NGOs primarily from outside Kenya.

There is, unsurprisingly, a strong economic dimension affecting the loss of wildlife in the rangelands. Wildlife reductions are lower where paying tourists visit, lower where there is transparent revenue sharing between protected areas and surrounding communities, and even wildlife increases where landowners manage their own tourist ventures rather than relying on outside agents and tour operators. Frequently 90-95% of relevant wildlife tourist revenues go to the service providers at the expense of the local population in the wildlife areas concerned. It is hardly surprising that the financial returns from wildlife compare poorly with alternative farming uses.

Of the 500,000 sq. km of rangelands, only 5% is used for photo tourism. With the ban on consumptive use of wildlife, there is little incentive to avoid agricultural use of such land and to remove much of the wildlife which typically may reduce agricultural profits by 50%.

Kenya

51

IN-SITU CONSERVATION

These problems have been and are the subject of much debate within Kenya, particularly since 2004 when the Government set up an independent drafting team, National Taskforce on Wild-life Policy, which in 2007 produced a draft Wildlife (Conservation and Management) Policy. This recommended a basic change to the 1977 ban and recognised the need for economic incentives for landowners to husband and invest in wildlife conservation. This would enable a range of consumptive uses of wildlife to be reintroduced under strict controls.

At this point, the international animal welfare NGOs, including International Fund for Animal Welfare (IFAW), ActionAid and the US-based Humane Society, who oppose any consumptive use of wildlife – particularly wealthy sport hunters – lobbied intensively the President and the Government not to proceed with the draft Wildlife (Conservation and Management) Policy. They succeeded and a replacement Taskforce was set up, sympathetic to the views of these NGOs. The past 10 years have witnessed the increased influence of these NGOs. Many conservationists now consider that only the reintroduction of limited consumptive use of wildlife can reverse the disastrous continuing loss of Kenya's wildlife.[5]

Europe's Zoos and In-situ Conservation in Kenya

As far as Kenya is concerned, several zoos are involved with projects there. Examples include Grevy's Zebra, Black and Northern White Rhino, and Rothschild's Giraffe. Reintroductions of species such as the black rhino are showing some success provided that there is adequate ranger cover. This is more successful in privately owned protected areas, frequently fenced as well as patrolled.

Help takes the form of financial contributions, research projects, reintroduction of species, and professional European staff coming to Kenya to give additional support to the many well trained, educated and passionate Kenyans working hard for local conservation.

Many zoos have greatly improved their adult education information, stressing the threats to wildlife in countries such as Kenya, and clearly showing what individual European consumers can and should do to help conservation efforts through careful and selective purchasing of a very wide range of products.

Conclusion

There seem to be too many national and international conservation NGOs and other conservation organisations involved with Kenya's wildlife conservation; the Government organisations do not seem to be co-ordinating the efforts of all these well-meaning bodies and persons.

However, this is recognised within the conservation community and efforts are being made to overcome this problem, not least due to the rising concern over water supplies, which has rapidly moved up the agenda of key conservation problems.

The ultimate success of KWS's substantial and laudable efforts depends on the decisions of Government and politicians and, as in so many African countries, can change from time to time. In view of the relentless population increase, this will remain a great challenge and uphill struggle.

[5] I am indebted to the academic papers and website of Dr Mike Norton-Griffiths for the economic data and information in this section.

CHAPTER 8

Spotlight on Elephants

From my visits to and analysis of questionnaire responses from the 80 survey zoos, it is clear that the elephant is the most popular single mammal with zoo visitors. The elephant has a very special place in the zoo. Zoo Directors are personally involved, zoo curators and keepers regard elephant keeping as the most prestigious such position and more training is required than for any other animal in the zoo.

This charismatic species is fascinating for zoo visitors of all age groups. Children are intrigued by elephants' size, their water antics and their remarkably versatile trunks, the 40,000 muscles of which take some mastering by young elephants who have to learn empirically from older members of the herd just how versatile an appendage it is. The social dimension of an elephant herd appeals to our own caring and social instincts: the entire elephant group will be involved in the care of the calves and an elephant social group exhibits loyalty and social awareness. "An elephant never forgets" is an often heard phrase: Matriarch elephants remember water and feeding locations and, even in an 80 strong herd, have an awareness that a group member may be missing. Asian elephants are remarkable for their preparedness to be trained and to work with man. This intelligent animal responds particularly well to enrichment and intrigues us with an ability to move with surprising precision and delicacy and with communication skills both within the social group and with their human keepers.

Unsurprisingly, therefore, huge sums are being invested in new and improved elephant indoor and outdoor enclosures; no other species receives as much money and attention as elephants. The improvements since 2000 result from European and national legislation and/or guidelines as well as from pressure from animal rights and welfare organisations.

Basel

SPOTLIGHT ON ELEPHANTS

Some Basic Facts

• Survey Zoos holding Elephants in 2010:	Group A Zoos 26 out of 30
	Group B Zoos 35 out of 50
• Elephant as most popular mammal in zoo:	31 out of 61 zoos
• Elephant as one of top 5 most popular:	58 out of 61 zoos
• Total African elephants in survey zoos:	107 in 28 collections
• Total Asian elephants in survey zoos:	223 in 40 collections
• Average number of elephants per zoo:	Between 5 and 6
• Largest single investment in new facility:	EUR 37 million (Copenhagen)
• Investment in new facilities 2000-2010:	> EUR 150 million
• Investment plans 2011-2015:	> EUR 100 million
• Zoos with 10 or more elephants in 2010:	Berlin Tierpark, Chester, Emmen, Hamburg, Hanover, Cologne

Major new Elephant Houses have been built and opened 2005-2010 in Amersfoort, Copenhagen, Dublin, Hamburg, Heidelberg, Cologne and Leipzig. Poznan, not in my survey, has also opened a major new elephant house.

My estimate of further investment in new elephant facilities for 2011-2015 is at least EUR 100 million for 9 presently known projects. These total projects would then add a further 2 zoos (Planckendael, Riga) to the present 61 zoos with elephants.

Minimum Standards

The EU Council Directive 1999/22/EC of 29.03.1999 relating to the keeping of wild animals in zoos requires national governments to implement various relevant measures including "accommodating their animals under conditions which aim to satisfy the biological and conservation requirements of the individual species, inter alia, by providing species specific enrichment of the enclosures; and maintaining a high standard of animal husbandry with a developed programme of preventive and curative veterinary care and nutrition".

This Directive has been translated into national and, in some countries, regional legislation which requires action by all licensed zoos within varying timeframes. This has been and is the driver behind the massive investment in elephant facilities during recent years, and reflects increasing public concern for welfare of animals in captivity.

The translation of the EU Directive into national legislation has varied greatly within EU member states both in its detail and its deadlines for compliance. In Germany, for example, the "Haltungsrichtlinie für Elefanten" under statute (EG) 338/ 97 was issued on 24.10.2000 and covers in detail minimum sizes of indoor and outdoor facilities both for male and female elephants, water facilities, diet and feeding arrangements, climatic conditions and group sizes and structures.

These minimum standards, which are now exceeded by most leading zoos, are currently being revised upwards in response to recent elephant keeping experience and pressures from animal welfare and rights organisations.

Management and Keeping of Elephants

Just as important as the investment in much larger and better Elephant houses and outdoor enclosures is the intense attention being given to the management and keeping of elephants in zoos. This requires adequate training of elephant keepers as well as possible involvement of specialist elephant consultants. Following on from the EU Directive, this has resulted in very close co-operation between EAZA members holding elephants through the two EEPs (African and Asian elephants) and initiation of specialised elephant management and training courses. The two Elephant EEPs – African and Asian – organise Elephant Management workshops at various European zoo locations and have done so for several years. Artificial insemination of elephants, particularly African, is the subject of special programmes; Vienna Zoo was one of the first and a sperm bank has been set up at Zooparc Beauval.

The annual nine day duration First European Elephant Management School began in 2003 in Hamburg's Tierpark Hagenbeck. This commercially organised course, which is attended by keepers from many leading European and US zoos keeping elephants, has specialist international

Dresden

lecturers on topics including population genetics, social structure and herd dynamics, health and care issues, breeding and best birthing practice, translocation, exhibit design, enrichment and hands-on as against protected contact keeping. In addition, in-situ and ex-situ conservation issues are considered and discussed with speakers from in-situ areas. Practical sessions in the Hagenbeck elephant facilities are also included.

The new shorter Executive Elephant Management and Facility Design Course at Hamburg considers exhibit design to the benefit of the animal and the visitor, animal management and staff training, marketing impact, leisure architecture and master planning, feasibility study and concept development, philosophy development for a successful elephant management programme and in-situ and ex-situ conservation issues.

There are also elephant consultants active in the field, helping European zoos. One example of elephant management consultancy is provided by Alan Roocroft. He has been involved in advising zoos globally including major projects in Europe and USA, and is the author of many articles and papers on elephant management in zoos. His advice is based on new thinking, enabling zoo elephants to lead a better and longer life, discarding some traditional methods based on making life easier for zoo Directors and Keepers! Alan Roocroft recommends indoor natural substrates, usually sand to a good depth, 24-hour feeding strategies, use of exhibit furniture that encourages and enables natural body movement, such as kneeling, stretching and climbing, optimum utilisation of indoor space and avoidance of large and boring concrete areas. Outdoor enclosures, he emphasises, should be designed to be varied and encourage 24-hour activities.

The provision of substantial bathing facilities and humid conditions are really important for Asian elephants whilst mud areas are important for both Asian and African elephants. The question of hands-on as against protected contact is still an individual decision for the Zoo Director and his/her keepers who know the character of their elephants, although the tendency is increasingly towards protected contact not least due to health and safety issues and the absolute necessity to avoid the risk of accidents.

Mixed species exhibits, in general, are very popular with visitors and generally provide good animal enrichment. Although there is an exception at Borås Djurpark in Sweden, in Europe, to date, elephants are very rarely involved in mixed species exhibits even though in the wild they live with other mammals and birds. A major US zoo is currently experimenting with a mixed species exhibit involving African elephants with giraffes, zebras, ostriches and impalas which could result in similar experiments in European zoos.

Education and Conservation

In addition to the many positive developments in elephant enclosures and welfare, an increased focus on education and in-situ conservation programmes has taken place. Major new elephant houses, such as Copenhagen, incorporate very substantial educational activities and information. Leading zoos feature specific in-situ elephant programmes linked to the actual elephants being exhibited.

Copenhagen

The Special Place in the Zoo

Although elephant rides for children no longer take place, this species occupies a very special place in the zoo. They invariably have names, made known to the visitors, have birthdays and places of birth frequently included on signage, and other personal details of general interest; few other species are so treated. Elephant feeding by visitors, strictly controlled, takes place in several zoos, including Colchester and Münster. In Hamburg, elephant feeding is a major attraction for visitors; it also provides animal enrichment for the elephants.

In Copenhagen Zoo, for example, the genealogy of their (royal) elephants is noted in great detail, showing relocations from and/or relationships with other zoos – Chester, Rotterdam, Twycross, Plock and others – as well as in-house births. Certain zoos, such as Ljubljana and Rostock, have solitary old elephants who rule the roost in their zoos. In Ljubljana, their 44 year old Asian elephant, who has refused the company of other elephants, is very particular about having only male keepers and not having certain types of mammals and birds in neighbouring enclosures! There are many other examples of the particular individual likes and dislikes of elephants in our zoos.

SPOTLIGHT ON ELEPHANTS

Conclusion

Elephants are of great importance to our leading zoological gardens; out of 30 Group A zoos, only Frankfurt, Gelsenkirchen and London do not keep elephants. Nürnberg have active plans to revert to doing so as soon as possible. They are by far the most popular animal with visitors. Great progress has been made in improving their facilities and their overall wellbeing in the leading zoos in the past 10 years; at least as much again is likely to occur in the next 10 years. These developments are the zoos' response to those who argue that elephants (and other large mammals) should not be kept in zoos. Given really good indoor and outdoor facilities, and given the implementation of best practice in the management and keeping of elephants, there is no reason why the life of the well - kept and adored zoo elephants should not be the best for these wonderful animals.

Twycross

CHAPTER 9

Commercial and Marketing

All zoos in my survey are planning to invest in improved and new exhibits and facilities, as well as wishing to extend their educational and conservation programmes. Funding, whether from public or private sources, is the key issue. The present financial crisis, triggered by the speculation of banks in 2008, has impacted on all the leading zoological gardens increasing their difficulties in funding zoo projects. Therefore the importance and effectiveness of the zoos' commercial and marketing activities are even more intensely under the microscope.

The majority of zoos in my survey are led by a Zoo Director with a relevant zoological education and experience; a minority have a CEO with a commercial or financial background. Some zoos have appointed Commercial or Financial Directors to assist or even to work in parallel with traditionally qualified Zoo Directors. Each zoo's management structure will depend on the Zoo Director/CEO and reflect the actual personnel involved and funding available for senior posts.

Many of the zoos have made considerable progress in recent years through EU assistance which frequently requires matching funding from the zoo. Attracting more sponsors and donors has enabled greatly increased investment in zoos and allowed them to augment their 5 to 10 year plans.

Fund raising covers many aspects affecting net available financial resources, including extra revenue from gate receipts to catering, merchandising, sponsors, donors, animal adopters, supporters/friends of the zoo memberships and in-house cost reductions.

Gelsenkirchen

COMMERCIAL AND MARKETING

Example: Zoo Osnabrück

This Zoo, which has increased its visitor numbers steadily from 400,000 in 1996-98 to 850,000 in 2009, and likely soon to rise to 1,000,000, has systematically developed a commercial strategy over the past decade to finance an increasing amount of investment in new and improved facilities, including an expansion of the zoo site. Until 1999 visitor numbers had been static and fund raising minimal; the zoo was faced with increasing costs and declining municipal subsidies and investment funds. Action was taken, based on strategic analysis and resulting decisions on marketing, sponsoring, catering, energy use and internal financial controls carried out by the CEO/Commercial Director, Andreas Busemann, fully supported by the well respected and experienced Zoological Director, Dr. Susanne Klomburg.

At the outset, priority consideration was given to commercial sponsoring. Local relevant information was collected and analysed:

- Why do Companies donate to local cultural organisations? Is it for their public image or for customer reasons or for employee motivation or simply because the owner or CEO has a particular liking for or interest in a particular organisation?
- Where are such sponsors located? Are they local, regional, national or international?
- What types of Companies are mainly involving in sponsoring?
- Are sponsors mainly short-term or long-term sponsors?

Osnabrück

After analysing local and regional information, and carrying out surveys, a carefully devised and targeted campaign was carried out. This involved meetings, visits and invitations to the zoo. The CEO and his team have been and are constantly involved with networking, enabling sponsors to obtain maximum benefit from their support to the zoo, and generally bonding and keeping in close contact with the sponsors. The Friends of the Zoo organisation is also heavily involved with this work.

The main targeted potential sponsors come from companies in food and drink, financial services, insurance, and manufacturing industry.

The result has been that over EUR 7 million has been donated to the zoo plus a very significant value of freely donated goods and services by such sponsors from 120 different companies in the past 10 years and a regular annual income of about EUR 1 million is being received by the zoo for investment in new and improved facilities. The names of the sponsors are well publicised throughout the zoo, including all 120 being listed on the model giraffes at the entrance to the zoo.

Secondly, visitor surveys have been conducted and analysed professionally to assist in determining priorities and making the zoo increasingly attractive to repeat and new visitors. Overall visitor satisfaction rates, as in other survey zoos, are encouragingly high with typically 85% very satisfied and a further 14% satisfied. However, the important information is contained in responses to many detailed questions.

Indicated perceived weaknesses in:

- Route signage – way round the zoo
- Space given to certain species
- Ability to see certain animals
- Insufficient light to see certain exhibits and/or signage relating to them
- Difficult inclines for small children
- Catering choice and/or price (this, of course, is a common complaint elsewhere!)
- Cleanliness, particularly of toilets

With regard to space given to certain species, investment priorities have responded accordingly as with Chimpanzees (in new Takamanda since mid-2010), Bears (to move to new Taiga in 2011) and Pig-tailed Macaques (to have new home in 2011). These 3 projects required total investment of EUR 14 million, of which EU funds account for EUR 5 million.

With regard to catering, which should be an important income stream for the zoo, regular visitor surveys are conducted. Attention continues to be given to the main areas of complaint, such as choice of food and beverages, taste/quality, value for money, spaciousness, cleanliness, and staff friendliness, not least to children. Survey results are used in negotiations with catering sub-contractors and in-house management.

Admission receipts are the main source of income for the revenue budget. At the same time, visitor numbers are of critical importance to sponsors and to management, including the city council, which has ultimate responsibility. In Osnabrück, admission prices are determined by the Directors with a general policy of low and competitive prices to encourage maximum visitor numbers. Surveys of visitors are carried out to determine optimum entrance prices. In recent years, it has become clear that, as a result of major new African exhibits such as Samburu savannah mixed species and Takamanda with its new house and enclosures for chimpanzees, there has been a significant increase in the median acceptable price for single and annual entrance tickets.

Annual tickets are of particular importance, as they impact favourably both visitor numbers and catering and merchandising turnover. City zoos are in a strong position to increase sales of annual tickets but have difficult decisions to make in pricing relationship between daily and annual tickets. Zoo Osnabrück decided to slowly erode the price ratio to make annual tickets more attractive by freezing the annual ticket price whilst gradually increasing the daily ticket price. Sales of annual tickets have increased steadily from 1,200 in 1996 to 20,000 in 2009.

Marketing strategy is critical to ensure optimum use of very limited resources. Wherever possible, professional surveys and data are analysed to determine priorities for marketing spend. These include:

- Radio and Television. Every happening at the zoo of interest to the public is notified to the media, and followed up where important. Occasionally, the zoo can be involved in a free TV programme or news item, either on its own or with other zoos.

- Newspapers. Regular press releases are sent, interviews and open invitations are arranged, and coverage analysed.

- Advertising. Analysis of visitors' home locations and resulting penetration in various geographic areas, together with consideration of competitive attractions, enable area targeting to be optimised.

- Events. Special events at the zoo are of importance and are regularly reviewed and monitored in terms of their revenue generation.

- Anniversary Sponsorship. The 75th anniversary of the zoo's foundation, which takes place in 2011, is being used to offer 105 model Bears around the zoo at EUR 1500,- each for a 6-months rental period with 50% of the profits going to UNICEF.

Expenditure on energy is of major and increasing importance and concern. A new energy system was installed for the Takamanda development and is now being extended to all buildings in the zoo. This will reduce CO_2 emissions and be energy saving with a significant benefit to heating costs in the revenue budget. This results from a comprehensive analysis of energy use and priorities for change to more efficient and environmentally friendly forms of energy.

Chester

These activities form the backbone of the zoo's commercial and marketing activities. Management takes seriously the internationally recognised NPS (net promoter score) which currently stands at 74% for Zoo Osnabrück compared with an average of 16% for 400 organisations across 28 industries. Surveys now show a probable visitor return visit rate of 96% and a probable recommendation rate to family and friends of 92%. These are commendable figures that augur well for the zoo.

Example: Chester Zoo

Chester Zoo, owned by the North of England Zoological Society, a registered charity since 1934, has developed during the past 10 years to become the U.K's most visited wildlife attraction and has the largest animal collection in the country. Its European and international standing has risen substantially during this period. Its future plans are the most ambitious of any zoo in Europe, although these are currently having to be scaled down due to the U.K's financial situation.

Founded in 1931 by George Motteshead, Chester Zoo owns about 165 Ha of land of which 50 Ha are currently in use by the zoo. The founder followed the open zoo design principles of Carl Hagenbeck. The zoo is situated on the outskirts of Chester (population 80,000) and is about 35 km from Liverpool and 65km from Manchester; these major city conurbations with good motorway connections are therefore well within the catchment area and account for at least 50% of the zoo's visitors. Chester Zoo is the major paid visitor attraction in its area and there are no significant zoo competitors there. The population of the immediate catchment area is about 3 million and of the wider area up to 7 million.

Strategic Planning since 1995

Against this background, Prof. Gordon McGregor Reid, appointed in 1995 as CEO and subsequently Director-General, decided to investigate the possibilities and viability of dramatic expansion. He appreciated the increasingly competitive nature of the leisure industry and the imperative of maintaining attractiveness for visitors. Being independent of state financial assistance and receiving relatively little from commercial sponsors, Chester Zoo is dependent on visitors' expenditure on entrance fees, catering and retail.

Gordon Reid, who became highly respected within the international zoo community becoming President of WAZA (World Association of Zoos and Aquaria) in 2007, built up a strong management team and an organisation employing nearly 300 staff, including in-house catering and retail outlets. The post of Development Director was established within the top management.

Marketing, Public Relations (PR) and Publicity featured highly with staffing increased from 4 to 12 over the past 10 years. A major increase in investment in marketing activity took place in 2006, doubling the previous expenditure level. As a result, the zoo receives about EUR 3.5 million of publicity from its own PR activities. A high profile media presence including the television series from the zoo entitled "Zoo Days" (Granada Television) and television adverts during key holiday periods, has raised the public profile of the zoo. Zoo membership has been growing at about 8% annually to 36,000 at end 2010.

Visitor numbers increased from 760,000 in 1995 to 1,360,000 in the year before Gordon Reid's retirement in 2010. Revenues increased dramatically and current assets, excluding fixed assets, reached GBP 11 million (EUR 13.5 million) by 2010. Catering and retail now contribute GBP 700,000 (EUR 850,000) annually to the zoo's profits.

The „Super Zoo" - Natural Vision Project

Gordon Reid's highly ambitious vision has been to develop and build the biggest and best zoo not only in the U.K. but in the whole of Europe – the "Super Zoo" – planned to attract regularly at least 2 million visitors annually. Since 2005, the Development Director, Simon Mann, and his team have been charged with developing and realising the Natural Vision Project, involving an overall investment of at least GBP 250 million (EUR 300 million) over a possible 10 year period in up to 4 phases. Detailed planning approval was eventually granted by the local planning authority in November 2010 for what could be the largest investment by any single European zoo. Design consultants and market research consultants had been appointed at the outset; initial financial assistance for this preparation phase was provided by the North West Regional Development Authority (NWDA) after they were convinced of the regional importance of this project.

In addition, the Project provided for a 90-room 3-star themed hotel, to be built on site and to include conference and leisure facilities. In total, the whole project was expected to generate at least 500 additional jobs in the area, including those at the zoo, and to be the flagship project for tourism in the north-west of England.

The overall initial research effort, including major market surveys, reports and analyses, and meetings with public authorities and potential donors, was a very significant burden for an organisation of this size. The Project was based upon :

- Phase 1. Heart of Africa Biodome. Based on a Congo-Guinea rainforest, it is planned to provide an unique immersion visitor experience. Species include gorilla, chimpanzee, pygmy hippo, okapi, colobus and bongo. River ride and canopy walkway are planned to be included within possibly the largest zoo tropical building in Europe.

- Phase 2. African Savannah Grasslands, including river ride and elevated walkways, featuring giraffe, zebra, black rhino, warthog, roan antelope, lesser kudu, impala and ostrich are envisaged.

- Phase 3. Islands and Water. These could include sea lions, penguins, flamingos, hornbills, birds of paradise, as well as lemurs and fossa, and a large walk-through aviary.

- Phase 4. Asian Plains. Terraced grasslands and woodland backdrops, will be provided for Asian elephant herd, lion, cheetah, rhino, camel and onager.

Münster

COMMERCIAL AND MARKETING

An application for financial funding was submitted to the NWDA for up to GBP 40 million (EUR 48 million), representing 50% of estimated Phase 1 cost, and it was confidently anticipated that GBP 30 million (EUR 36 million) would be granted by end 2010 (with European Regional Development Fund help to NWDA). However, as a result of the U.K. financial situation and the change of national Government in May 2010, this was not finally confirmed. Now, all Regional Development Authorities (RDAs) are to be abolished and replacement arrangements are unlikely to be in place for the immediate future. As a result, Chester Zoo has withdrawn its application and decided to reconsider its plans and proceed using its own resources and borrowing facilities. For details see chapter 15.

It now seems likely that a redesigned project Phase 1, costing perhaps GBP 30 million (EUR 36 million), will proceed over a longer timescale, being finalised in 2011 for opening in 2015. The Zoo will continue to prioritise a major indoor attraction so as to increase visitor numbers in inclement weather periods. The revised project will still be one of the largest zoo projects in Europe in the next few years. The experience gained over the past 5 years will be of great help to the zoo in proceeding speedily with revised plans. Once the replacement arrangements for the NWDA are in place, possibly active in 2012, I would expect that some reduced financial assistance from public, including European, funds will help Chester Zoo with its modified Natural Vision Project.

Dr Mark Pilgrim, Director of Conservation and Education under Gordon Reid, now the well - respected successor as Director General, is overseeing a modified strategy. While the highest standards of animal welfare and guest experience continue to be the priority, far greater attention is being given to increasing revenue from catering and retail, with better choice of products, and to increasing funding from commercial sponsors. The impetus behind the Natural Vision Project will not be lost.

La Flecche

CHAPTER 10

Zoos Transformed -
What Can Be Achieved 1990-2010

The European zoo scene has been transformed in the past few decades. Traditionally, the city zoo focused on exhibiting the maximum number of species but often at the expense of their overall welfare. The scene is now one of fewer species, more space and infinitely better and more attractive indoor and outdoor enclosures, combined with a major focus on education and conservation.

All 80 zoos in this book have moved at varying paces in this direction. For this chapter, I have selected just four examples of outstanding achievement, two being publicly owned and two privately owned. There is widespread agreement that Vienna and Leipzig are leading examples of the most dramatic and successful transformations of publicly owned zoos; similarly, there is widespread admiration for what has happened at the privately owned Burgers' Arnhem and Colchester Zoos. Four different countries from the twenty one countries in the survey are re-presented in this chapter from material sufficient to constitute a book in its own right.

Tiergarten Schönbrunn (Vienna Zoo)

At the end of the 1980s, Vienna Zoo was in a poor state and failing to keep pace with the improvements taking place in many other major European zoos. Visitor numbers were static, staff morale was poor, a lack of infrastructure maintenance was evident and the reputation of the zoo was in decline. These problems were suddenly compounded by the accidental death of Madi, one of the zoo's two African elephants, much loved by the public. Madi's long time

Vienna

67

female elephant companion, Jumbo, was grieving distraught at finding herself alone. In spite of efforts to bring a new female elephant to Vienna quickly, it was more than two years before Kiwu finally arrived from Halle Zoo as a companion for Jumbo. The combined multiple mistakes of the zoo and the Government ministry responsible for the zoo became a public scandal, amplified by the media. This resulted in increasing pressure either to close the zoo or to relocate at least the larger animals to Donaupark in another part of the city.

Fortunately for the future of Tiergarten Schönbrunn, a leading politician, who later became Prime Minister of Austria, was passionately devoted to Vienna zoo; he still is. Dr Wolfgang Schüssel declared it essential to retain and improve the existing zoo, and to give it a new structure and organisation. Although he was Economics Minister in the Austrian Government at that time, he quipped famously "I've had enough of this bureaucratic jungle and that never again should any animal in Schönbrunn have to suffer as Jumbo had to".

The result was that Dr Schüssel, with the support of the three major political parties in Parliament, formed a new company, Schönbrunner Tiergarten GmbH, on 13.12.1991 and, having advertised widely and internationally for a new Zoo Director, appointed Dr Helmut Pechlaner, previously Zoo Director at Alpenzoo Innsbruck, as the new Zoo Director in Vienna. The new company replaced the Government Ministry as the owner of the zoo; this proved to be of fundamental importance to the future development and success of the zoo.

Helmut Pechlaner, on taking up his new post on 01.01.1992, declared that, by its 250th anniversary in 2002, Tiergarten Schönbrunn must again become the finest and most beautiful zoo in the world. To assist the new start for the zoo, the Government donated nearly EUR 15 million (ATS 200 million) to the new company. A new era had truly begun!

From the start, Helmut Pechlaner inspired and motivated his staff; a new enthusiasm, tempo and optimism replaced the previous malaise. Staff at every level were encouraged to come up with new ideas and a real team spirit was established. The Director's first priorities, thinking on behalf of the zoo's animals, were to improve their houses and enclosures. Bad enclosures were closed and others were provided with new ground materials – cambark, wood chippings, sand, earth, hay, straw as appropriate to the species – and were repaired and improved wherever possible. Benches were repaired, footpaths improved and attention to detail prevailed. All of these actions cost little but had a big positive effect on the animals, their keepers and visitors. In addition, the collection was examined and analysed, resulting in many animal exchanges with other zoos and the establishment of more breeding groups.

A combination of a lifelong love for animals with hard work and dynamic leadership enabled the new Zoo Director soon to declare that Tiergarten Schönbrunn will become the zoo for lucky animals. The transformation of the zoo was now well underway.

Even the zoo's animals joined the staff in promoting the zoo, restoring its image and raising money. A prime example was Nonja, the friendly Orang Utan, who became world famous as an artist. Her paintings were used on silk scarves, ties, credit cards and in countless publications; they were auctioned and featured in ORF programmes.

Vienna

The company soon established an Advisory Board (Beirat); Austria's best professional experts were invited to join. Keepers, frequently on exchanges, were sent to leading European zoos to gain expert experience. Well qualified curators were recruited and appointed for each major species group. Above all, a new management team was assembled with the key appointment in 1993 of Dr Dagmar Schratter, now the worthy successor of Helmut Pechlaner, as Deputy Director with zoological responsibility, and of Gerhard Kasbauer as Commercial Manager, a post he still holds today.

A further early aim was to enlarge the existing education component within the zoo. Training places were established for students and teachers with the declared intention of creating Austria's largest school! The Verein der Freunde des Tiergartens Schönbrunn (Friends of the Zoo) was also established and was rapidly to become a very important supporting organisation with up to 10,000 members, steadily growing in numbers and raising EUR 2.3 million in its first 12 years for the zoo.

Not surprisingly, these many positive developments attracted widespread media attention. Helmut Pechlaner was invited to many public events and became well known throughout the country and, subsequently, internationally. In 1993, WAZA (World Association of Zoos and Aquariums) held its conference in Vienna, at his invitation, and developed its first conservation strategy at this meeting. Already, there was a strong whiff of success in the air!

Donors and sponsors, private and commercial, started to appear already in 1992; these indicated the widespread support for and interest in reviving and transforming Tiergarten Schönbrunn. In that year, an anonymous local donor gave Dr Schüssel EUR 53,000 for the zoo, followed by another donor at Christmas that year giving EUR 73,000. Kronen Zeitung, a leading Vienna newspaper, raised EUR 36,000 in its widely publicised appeal for the zoo. ÖRF, the national radio and TV provider, and the press gave increasing and positive coverage to the newly revived zoo.

After taking care of the immediate priorities, Helmut Pechlaner and his team embarked on a Master plan, requiring large investments over the coming years. In addition to its initial funding, the company raised large sums from donors and supporters, as well as substantial financial assistance from the Government.

The total investment of about EUR 100 million over the following 15 years resulted in a huge overall improvement to the zoo's exhibits:

1993 Small Monkey House
1994 Big Cats Enclosures
1995 Tirolerhof
1996 Wolves Enclosure
1997 Elephant Park
1998 Waldrapp (Hermit) Ibis exhibit
1999 Bird House, Birds of Prey Volière, Gasthaus Tirolergarten
2001 Terrarium/Aquarium/Crocodile House, Butterfly House
2002 Humboldt's Penguins exhibit, Spectacled Bears enclosure
2003 Regenwald House, Koala Bears exhibit, Wustenhaus, Giant Pandas exhibit, Coati exhibit, Serau exhibit
2004 Polarium
2005 Haus der Schrecken
2006 Rhino House and enclosure
2009 ORANG.erie
2010 South America House and enclosure

Amongst more than 60 organisations, commercial sponsor companies have included Alcatel, Austrian Airlines, Esso, Microsoft, Nordsee, Nokia, SAP, Siemens and Swarovski.

During this period, all aspects of the zoo were systematically developed. These included an ever increasing involvement in in-situ conservation programmes in many tropical countries, participation in a large number of ex-situ EEPs and the development of education programmes for all ages.

For children, in particular, activities within the zoo were added such as parties, face painting, birthday celebrations, workshops and competitions of many types.

Vienna

Visitor numbers, steady at around 700,000 in the 1980s, increased rapidly, reaching 1,000,000 in 1994. Helmut Pechlaner declared early on that they should reach at least the level of Vienna's total population; this was achieved with 1,600,000 visitors in 2000, increasing to 2,000,000 in 2003 and 2,600,000 in 2008. No other European zoo can boast of such impressive growth figures. The aim of becoming Austria's most visited tourist and cultural attraction, as stated by Dr Schüssel, had been achieved.

A major component of the growth of visitor numbers after 2003 has been the addition of Giant Pandas; Vienna then joined Berlin and Madrid as the only European zoos with these rare and sought after animals. It was well known that very few zoos are able to obtain these animals from the Chinese Government; politics and money are involved, as the Giant Panda is regarded by the Chinese as being a very special, symbolic and valuable animal. Any zoo with such pandas must be involved in research and breeding programmes, and develop a close relationship with the Chinese authorities. Against this background, Dr Schüssel was still determined from the outset of the revived zoo to bring Giant Pandas to Tiergarten Schönbrunn. He used his ministerial and subsequently prime ministerial position to break through the bamboo curtain and achieve his objective. After 7 years' pressure from the Austrian Government, the breakthrough came at an UN organised high level meeting on world ethics, chaired by Kofi Annan the UN Secretary General, at the renowned Schlosshotel Fuschl. Dr Schüssel was seated next to the Chinese delegate who, after further pressure from the Austrian Premier, agreed to recommend to his Prime Minister that Vienna should now have a pair of pandas, able to breed. On the next day, 19.09.2002, the Chinese Premier phoned Dr Schüssel to inform him that his request has been granted, and the Austrian Parliament was informed accordingly. On 20.09.2002,

ZOOS TRANSFORMED

Wolfgang Schüssel and Helmut Pechlaner welcomed the Chinese Premier to Parliament and the required contract was signed.

In record time, the new outdoor enclosure and the rebuilt house were completed, ready for the arrival of the two celebrity animals on 14.03.2003. Helmut Pechlaner, accompanied by zoo vets and keepers, had accompanied Yang Yang and Long Hui on the flight to Vienna. On 19.03.2003, in front of more than 2000 specially invited guests, Dr Schüssel and Helmut Pechlaner officially opened the new exhibit. The Zoo Director proudly declared that he knew nearly all the panda zoo enclosures in the world and that his is the best and the most beautiful. He went on to assure the Chinese ambassador that Vienna's is the best quality enclosure and the best for breeding and for research. This statement was crowned with success on 23.08.2007 when Fu Long became the first naturally born Giant Panda in an European zoo. Three years later to the day Fu Long's brother, Fu Hu, which translates as Happy Tiger, was born.

Today, Tiergarten Schönbrunn is widely regarded as the best zoological garden in Europe. This reflects its very high standards of quality and care, the flair and unique atmosphere created by its wonderfully renovated historic Habsburg buildings, its excellent enclosure and building designs, and its delightful surroundings within the Schönbrunn parkland and woodland area. This superb zoo is also amongst the most involved in education, conservation and research, and therefore has an envied comprehensive excellence.

The two names Wolfgang Schüssel, a pre-eminent politician and statesman, and Helmut Pechlaner, the multi-talented and inspirational Zoo Director, will go down in the history books as the headline figures responsible for the dramatic turnround and transformation of this now magnificent zoological garden. However, they have been fortunate in recruiting a very able senior team, now led by the also exceptionally talented and capable Dagmar Schratter who is following well in the footsteps of her former Director. This zoo continues to improve, under her leadership, and the projects for the next few years suggest that its lead in Europe will continue. This is an inspirational success story. Twenty years of unremitting hard work and commitment to animal welfare and excellence have transformed a sad situation into one where all those associated with the zoo and the citizens of Vienna can be justly proud of a preeminent Zoological Garden which is a real pleasure to visit.

Zoo Leipzig

Zoo Leipzig was founded in 1878 as one of the many German 19th century zoological gardens established in major German cities. It established a high reputation, not least for its successful breeding of lions.

In the DDR period, Zoo Leipzig was the most important East German zoo. During the 1980s, the Zoo was the most important paid visitor attraction in Leipzig attracting about 1,300,000 visitors annually (1,560,000 at its peak). Despite the high visitor numbers, little was invested except in the centenary year of 1978; the standards became well out-of-date compared with

Leipzig
Gondwanaland

zoos in Western Europe at that time. There was little competition from other attractions, no public pressure for radical improvements and no regular investment funding available.

All this changed dramatically in 1989 with the fall of the Berlin Wall and German unification. Suddenly, Zoo Leipzig was faced with increasing competition from other attractions, the freedom of citizens to travel anywhere, rising expectations of zoo visitors and its owner, the city, faced with huge demands from every local service and facility. Zoo Leipzig was no longer the top priority of the city council although continually appreciated by the public. It became apparent that savings would have to be made and would result in zoo staff reductions and the introduction of a new organisation and modern accounting procedures. This was a major change to the management and staff, resulting in uncertainty about the future; the adjustment to the modern commercial world needed to take place and rapidly!

The first priorities were the removal of bad enclosures and replacing or repairing the rotten infrastructure, bringing retained exhibits up to standard and renovating historic buildings that were in a poor state of repair partly due to non-availability of relevant construction materials. During the early 1990s, visitor numbers declined sharply to about half the average level in the 1980s: in 1996 they were only 675,000. By then, however, some new developments were taking place with the opening of the Australia area and improvements to the Aquarium and the new Sea lions exhibit and more.

The appointment of the present Zoo Director, Dr. Jörg Junhold, in 1997 was a master stroke and proved a turning point in the fortunes of Zoo Leipzig. Jörg Junhold, who studied veterinary science at Leipzig university, as did his father, joined the US owned leading animal foodstuffs company, Effem GmbH, in 1992 and became its Market Activity Manager; in that position, he rapidly learnt much about Europe-wide and global marketing strategies and travelled throughout Germany. This experience was to prove of great value to the future development of Zoo Leipzig.

ZOOS TRANSFORMED

Also in 1997, the world famous Max-Planck-Institute (MPI), whose Institute of Evolutionary Anthropology had been established in Leipzig, offered to the City of Leipzig the possibility of building, together with the zoo, a world class Primate Centre both for the use of its scientific and research staff and students and for the benefit of the zoo. A short time before the appointment of the dynamic and ambitious new Zoo Director, the City Council agreed and the MPI's proposal was accepted and immediately commenced. The new primate centre became today's Pongoland (Pongo is Angolan for apes).

Historically Zoo Leipzig had established a reputation for keeping the great apes. Chimpanzees were kept from 1880; the first Orang-utan arrived from Hagenbeck Hamburg in 1894, Gorillas in 1905 and Bonobos in 1989. The Apes House of 1982 had no outdoor enclosures, allegedly due to lack of funding, and right up to 1997 the apes lived only in indoor and outdoor cages. This was to be solved by building a totally new house with spacious outdoor facilities.

The MPI established a separate department, Wolfgang Köhler Zentrum für Primatenforschung (WKZPF) a centre for primate research which was tasked with the joint development with Zoo Leipzig of Pongoland. The joint development committee called on experts from outside and also involved the zoo team under the Director. Every aspect of best practice in keeping the big apes was taken into account, as well as the needs of the students and the expectations of visitors.

The result was a massive investment of EUR 16.5 million in a tropical hall with 5 indoor enclosures totalling 1600 sq. m. and 5 outdoor enclosures covering nearly 3 Ha. These are designed to be suitable for groups of each of Gorillas, Chimpanzees, Bonobos and Orang-Utans and for breeding of each of the species. At the same time, they are designed to enable scientists and students to observe the apes clearly and comfortably. Research focuses on understanding the behaviour and thinking of the four species of great apes. There is a special focus on the chimpanzee. Researchers and students from the University of Leipzig and other universities internationally conduct their research projects here at Pongoland. The indoor and outdoor enclosures avoid any impression of the animals being in cages. The natural habitat and behavioural characteristics of each species has been taken into account. The visitor to Pongoland notices immediately the impact of this research and design in the naturally behaving primate groups. The tropical hall, which has a large triple layer foil membrane roof and panoramic glass windows to all enclosures, is temperature and humidity controlled and the enclosures have free areas with natural ground surfaces including living grass, which has not previously existed in apes' indoor facilities, and natural climbing features using natural tree trunks and branches. The spacious five outdoor enclosures, over 1.2 Ha in size, have also been carefully designed to reflect the individual species' requirements using natural materials and being separated from visitors by moats with raised walkways. For the Orang-utans, much higher climbing structures are provided and they also have a gibbon for company. The landscape includes hills and valleys, and many types of trees and vegetation.

Pongoland was opened in April 2001, four years after the MPI first contacted the City of Leipzig and the zoo with their proposals. It soon became recognised as the leading centre of its kind in Europe and has an international reputation for excellence in keeping primates.

Concurrently with Pongoland's development, the zoo was engaged with many improvements. Major developments included:

1997 Aquarium/Terrarium renovated

1997 New Australia exhibit

1997 New Meerkat exhibit

1997 New Rhino exhibit

1998 New Sea lion enclosure

1998 New Zoo Shop

1998 New Aviaries in Elephant House

1999 New Safari office and Children's Zoo facilities

2000 New Tortoise outdoor exhibit

The Zoo Director was in constant discussion with the City Council and had indicated his ideas for a radical Master Plan "Zoo of the Future" which required massive financial support and independence from day-to-day involvement of the City Council. After strenuous efforts by Jörg Junhold to convince the City Council, Zoo Leipzig GmbH was established on 01.08.2000 with an initial capital of EUR 1 million, owned by the City of Leipzig, but with its own constitution and supervisory board consisting of outside experts as well as key members of the City Council. With the opening of Pongoland in 2001, visitor numbers increased by over 50% over the year 2000 to nearly 1.2 million and they have grown by a further 50% again since then to nearly 1.8 million in 2007.

Leipzig

ZOOS TRANSFORMED

Leipzig

"Zoo of the Future" combines state-of-the-art enclosures and best possible conditions for the animals on show with active conservation in-situ and ex-situ and education for all ages. It aims to remove visible concrete, steel and other non-natural materials, to have moats rather than fences and to provide for mixed species groups as, for example, in the African savannah. The idea is to enable visitors to experience endangered species in their natural habitats and thereby convince the public of the need to support wildlife conservation and act accordingly.

Since 2000, the Zoo has opened many important and significant new or improved exhibits:

2001 Lion Savannah "Makasi Simba"

2002 Sloth Bear Ravine

2002 Entdeckerhaus Arche (Discovery Centre)

2003 Tiger Taiga

2004 Kiwara Savannah and House for Giraffe and other ungulates

2005 Asian Walk Through Volière

2006 Elephant Temple "Ganesha Mandir"

2007 Renovation of the former zoo director's house primarily as a Zoo School.

2009 Kangaroo Walk-Through Area

The zoo will be organised in six themed areas: 3 continental areas Africa, Asia and South America, the Founders' Garden (with the historical entrance area), and the two outstanding attractions Pongoland and Gondwanaland (the ancient joined up three present day continents). Visitors are to enjoy an unforgettable experience, and the Master Plan is scheduled to be completed by end 2015.

The Zoo Director is in regular discussion with his team and with outside organisations including architects, leisure experts, caterers and sponsors actual and potential. Zoo Leipzig has been able to obtain very substantial sponsors, classified as gold, silver and bronze, resulting from its continual success since 1997 and particularly its nationwide publicity, particularly through national television programmes such as Elefant, Tiger & Co and Tierärztin Dr. Mertens. Gold sponsors included Mercedes-Benz (Leipzig subsidiary), Ur-Krostitzer Brewery, Langnese Ice cream, Sparkasse Leipzig, Leipziger Volkszeitung and Stadtwerke Leipzig. Sponsors and donors are significant contributors to the zoo's annual revenue budget; this is quite exceptional for a zoo!

Jörg Junhold, who will be President of WAZA in 2011, continues to consider the role of the zoo in an age of global tourism and of increasing competitive attractions, the integration of zoo developments with conservation and education activities, and increasing further visitor numbers and financial support from sponsors, visitors and others arising from the opening of Gondwanaland in 2011.

Gondwanaland, which will cost EUR 67 million, will be the largest tropical hall in Europe's zoological gardens in 2011, spanning over 1.65 Ha and accommodating about 40 additional species of mammals, birds, reptiles, amphibians and fish with visitor viewing from boats or on foot in an unforgettable tropical forest designed to ensure visitors are well aware of what is happening to the world's rainforests and the consequences of man's destruction of them.

The opening of Gondwanaland, eagerly awaited by the entire European zoological community as well as the citizens and council of the City of Leipzig, the country as a whole and the media, will be the crowning achievement of 15 years of Jörg Junhold's leadership of Zoo Leipzig, together with his well- motivated and enthusiastic supporting team.

 The dramatic transformation of Zoo Leipzig into one of the world's leading zoological gardens, owes much to the visionary zeal and determination of the Director, who has managed to convince a major, but medium sized, German city and its politicians, as well as the media and the major sponsors and donors, of the significance and value of the "Zoo of the Future", together with the decision of the MPI to establish the outstation of the Institute of Evolutionary Anthropology in Zoo Leipzig.

The story of Zoo Leipzig over the last twelve years is another remarkable one illustrating what can be achieved when a motivated team is led by a Director who has the combination of zoological and commercial skill sets and who arrives on the scene at an opportune moment.

ZOOS TRANSFORMED

Burgers' Zoo - Arnhem

Burgers' Zoo, founded by Johan Burgers and opened in 1913, is the largest privately owned zoological garden in the Netherlands. It has remained in the ownership of the same family, now the Van Hooff family, throughout its history and receives no public funding assistance.
In the mid-1980s, the zoo faced a financial crisis, caused largely by large investment in necessary infrastructure projects, including an extensive central animal feed store facility and veterinary and animal hospital departments. These investments had no positive influence on income and visitor numbers.

At this time, the then Director, Antoon van Hooff, worked hard on his dream project of building and creating a tropical rainforest hall. This required not only expensive tropical trees and other vegetation, waterfalls and other water features, but also appropriate material for the demanding conditions of a very large translucent roof. The idea was to replicate the conditions of a tropical rainforest; at the time it was pioneering work as no such building existed in Europe and it was a huge challenge, not least with respect to the technical requirements of the roof. The initial roof on the then test hall which is now being used for Mangrove unsuitable actually collapsed in 1982. Eventually, the German manufacturer Höchst developed a suitable material which resulted in a successful roof being installed on the test hall.

Arnhem

Plans could then be drawn up for a large tropical hall, later known as "Bush", covering nearly 1.5 Ha of ground space. To realise this project, considerable loan finance was required. Sixteen banks in the Netherlands, Germany and UK were approached; none of them was prepared to provide finance for what was considered to be "too risky" a project. This response was not helped by many of the zoo's staff, who petitioned the owners not to go ahead with such a project! The turning point for the "Bush" project – and indeed for Burgers' Zoo – came in 1986 with the promise of EU funding assistance through the local provincial council; this covered up to 25% of the project cost. Thereafter, it was possible to obtain the remaining funds from local Dutch banks.

The Director's dream project could now be realised; the first large tropical rainforest building in Europe was successfully built and opened in 1988. It was and is central to the zoo's philosophy of exhibiting animals in their natural home surroundings to give both the animals and their visitors real pleasure of their being in as open and as natural landscapes as possible.

This proved to be an instant success and the gamble paid off! A further three large walk-through indoor buildings were to follow. The extent of these indoor visitor facilities shows not just a consideration for the animals exhibited but also an awareness of the needs of the visitors to Northern European zoos, particularly in the winter months. The public and the media showed immediate interest and the zoo's prospects were transformed, practically overnight! Visitor numbers increased from 800,000+ in late 1980s to 1.2 million in 1990 and steadily to 1.5 million by the late 1990s. Antoon van Hooff featured in many Dutch TV programmes, such as Ja, Natuurlijk and the zoo became world famous for its pioneering new developments commencing with Bush.

The stability and loyalty of the staff, the high level of applicants for every advertised zookeeper post and the appointment of the present highly respected zoo director, Dr Alex van Hooff, as Chairman of the Dutch Zoos Association (NVD) all testify to the current high standing of Burgers' Zoo in the Netherlands.

In total, about EUR 100 million has been invested by Burgers' Zoo during the past 20 years. The highlights are:

1988 Bush - Tropical rainforest, plus large restaurant

1992 Mangrove - S. E. Asian Mangrove swamp

1994 Desert - N. American desert. Largest desert hall in Europe.

2000 Ocean - S. E. Asian Coral sea with 8 million litres water. 2nd largest in the world.

2005 Safari - E. African savannah with walkways at different levels, Congress Hall, restaurant, Giraffe House and indoor viewing of extensive hoofstock facilities.

2008 Rimba - Malayan tropical rainforest species in natural surroundings.

Today, Burgers' Zoo is widely regarded as one of the best in Europe; it provides visitors with an original indoor experience, exhibits a delightful and comprehensive range of species and is heavily engaged in widely publicised in-situ conversation projects.

Many visitors will be looking forward to the zoo's centenary in 2013 which will be celebrated by the announcement of a further exciting major new project.

Colchester

There are several Group B privately owned zoos, particularly in France and UK, that have made remarkable progress during the past 20 years. One of these certainly is Colchester, situated 80 km north-east of London.

Founded in 1963, this was a relatively small and unknown zoo until its acquisition in 1983 by the present owners, the Tropeano family. During the past 20 years, it has been steadily developed into one of the UK's leading zoological gardens with a strong European reputation. This has occurred as a result of the dedicated leadership and full direct involvement of its main shareholder and Zoo Director, Dominique Tropeano, OBE. With a business background, he has steered the zoo through good and hard times and has developed the zoo and its education and conservation activities without any direct public financial support.

Basic Facts

In a difficult decade for the UK, the zoo has progressed in all spheres: visitor numbers have increased from 340,000 in 1990 to over 750,000 in 2010. In 1983 the zoo employed only 7 keepers and today it has 68 who care for an increased animal collection.

Colchester

Increase in Colchester's Collection 1984 to 2010				
	Number 1984	Species 1984	Number 2010	Species 2010
Mammals	206	76	404	94
Birds	205	52	232	57
Reptiles	67	23	121	31

The area of the zoo has increased from 17 to 25 Ha and EUR 30 million (GBP 25 million) has been invested 1990-2010 in new facilities

Milestones

1990 Site extended from 17 to 25 Ha

1998 Elephant House and enclosure (Kingdom of the Wild)

2001 Giraffe House and mixed species enclosure (Spirit of Africa)

2005 Sea Lion exhibit (Playa Patagonia)

2008 Dragons of Komodo

2009 Orangutan Forest

2010 Amur Leopards

Planned future exhibits include a Tropical Hall and various mixed species and walk-through exhibits.

The most recent of the new exhibits, the leopards at Ussuri Falls, and the Orang utan forest are good examples of advantageous use of zoo terrain and the modern zoo's focus on better and more attractive enclosures, combined with an emphasis on education and conservation.

Today, the collection at Colchester Zoo includes representatives of all of my "iconic species groups" of mammals, birds and reptiles.

Education and Conservation

In addition to enlarging the zoo and developing a first-class collection, there has been an impressive development in education and conservation, starting from near zero.

Zoos Transformed

Colchester

The zoo has developed all of the following in the last decade:

- An Education Centre with full-time staff and modern facilities which includes the Discovery and Learning Centre and is used by 30,000 school children annually
- Research projects, carried out primarily by university students, have become a major feature with at least 20 students involved annually
- Significant involvement in EAZA with Dominique Tropeano on the Council and Chair of their Technical Assistance and Welfare Committee until 2009
- Colchester Zoo's charitable organisation Action for the Wild was established in 2004 to provide substantial funding for in-situ projects, now totalling 11 such projects
- Umphafa, a private nature reserve now owned by the above charitable organisation, developed from 3 South African farms totalling 4500 Ha. Over EUR 200,000 has been invested, including land purchase and fencing costs, and staff provided. This reserve now accommodates over 20 mammal species, including giraffes and rhinos, many being transported from Colchester Zoo

Current Developments

Anthony Tropeano, Dominique's son, is now Zoological Director and responsible for the day-to-day running of the zoo. Whilst there is no great master plan there is a clear vision for future developments which include continuing steady investment to improve further the zoo with mixed species exhibits, to concentrate on highly endangered species and to improve further the overall visitor experience. In 2011, „Wilds of Asia" with 3 large, naturalistic, enclosures will open. This is a good example of a well-managed private zoo, with high level dedicated staff and a very special atmosphere where education and enjoyment are well combined. Colchester is making progress in all of the many aspects of a modern zoo's role – the visitor experience, education, research and conservation.

CHAPTER 11

Interesting Zoo Facts

Visitor Numbers

Arriving at fair and comparable visitor numbers is not straightforward; those listed below and elsewhere in the book include actual or estimated free entries, such as young children, use

Zoo	Country	Visitors (000)
BERLIN Zoo	GERMANY	3100
VIENNA	AUSTRIA	2500
STUTTGART Wilhelma	GERMANY	2400
ZURICH	SWITZERLAND	1800
LEIPZIG	GERMANY	1750
BASEL	SWITZERLAND	1700
COLOGNE	GERMANY	1700
HAMBURG Hagenbeck	GERMANY	1650
HANOVER	GERMANY	1600
PRAGUE	CZECH REPUBLIC	1600
ROTTERDAM	NETHERLANDS	1600
ARNHEM Burgers	NETHERLANDS	1520
MUNICH Hellabrunn	GERMANY	1500
CHESTER	UNITED KINGDOM	1360
ANTWERP	BELGIUM	1335
COPENHAGEN	DENMARK	1300
AMSTERDAM Artis	NETHERLANDS	1240
BARCELONA	SPAIN	1150
NUREMBERG	GERMANY	1080
ZSL LONDON	UNITED KINGDOM	1050
MADRID	SPAIN	1050
BERLIN Tierpark	GERMANY	1000
BUDAPEST	HUNGARY	1000
DUISBURG	GERMANY	1000
EMMEN	NETHERLANDS	1000
GELSENKIRCHEN	GERMANY	1000
FRANKFURT	GERMANY	1000
KARLSRUHE	GERMANY	1000
MÜNSTER	GERMANY	1000
DUBLIN	EIRE	950
RHENEN	NETHERLANDS	910
PAIRI DAIZA Paradisio	BELGIUM	900
MECHELEN Planckendael	BELGIUM	850
OSNABRÜCK	GERMANY	850
COLCHESTER	UNITED KINGDOM	750
LA PALMYRE	FRANCE	750
DRESDEN	GERMANY	740
LISBON	PORTUGAL	730
PARIS - Menagerie	FRANCE	720
WARSAW	POLAND	720

Zoo	Country	Visitors (000)
AMERSFOORT	NETHERLANDS	675
KRONBERG Opel	GERMANY	650
WROCLAW	POLAND	650
EDINBURGH	UNITED KINGDOM	645
AMNEVILLE	FRANCE	630
WUPPERTAL	GERMANY	630
AUGSBURG	GERMANY	580
HEIDELBERG	GERMANY	580
VALENCIA	SPAIN	575
ROSTOCK	GERMANY	555
BRISTOL	UNITED KINGDOM	550
DVUR KRÁLOVÉ	CZECH REPUBLIC	550
HELSINKI	FINLAND	550
KOLMÅRDEN	SWEDEN	550
ST AIGNAN BEAUVAL	FRANCE	550
TWYCROSS	UNITED KINGDOM	550
ROME	ITALY	540
PAIGNTON	UNITED KINGDOM	530
ZLIN	CZECH REPUBLIC	525
DORTMUND	GERMANY	520
MARWELL	UNITED KINGDOM	505
BUSSOLENGO	ITALY	500
SOSTO	HUNGARY	500
ZSL WHIPSNADE	UNITED KINGDOM	475
PLZEN	CZECH REPUBLIC	460
ODENSE	DENMARK	450
ERFURT	GERMANY	430
KREFELD	GERMANY	380
RIGA	LATVIA	375
BOJNICE	SLOVAKIA	370
MULHOUSE	FRANCE	350
HALLE	GERMANY	340
MAGDEBURG	GERMANY	330
TALLINN	ESTONIA	330
BELFAST	UNITED KINGDOM	300
BRATISLAVA	SLOVAKIA	300
LJUBLJANA	SLOVENIA	275
DOUE LA FONTAINE	FRANCE	250
ESKILSTUNA	SWEDEN	250
LA FLECHE	FRANCE	220

Interesting Zoo Facts

of annual or member cards and school visits. Rounded visitor numbers representing a good year in the past five years have been used. For most zoos listed, visitor numbers are tending to increase.

Zoo Area

This table shows the actual present area of the zoo or total belonging to the zoo. There may be small differences, depending on whether car parking, service areas, parts of rivers or lakes

Zoo	Country	Area (Ha)
ZSL WHIPSNADE	UNITED KINGDOM	260
BERLIN Tierpark	GERMANY	160
KOLMÅRDEN	SWEDEN	140
BRATISLAVA	SLOVAKIA	96
TALLINN	ESTONIA	89
DVUR KRALOVE	CZECH REPUBLIC	70
NUREMBERG	GERMANY	70
ERFURT	GERMANY	63
PRAGUE	CZECH REPUBLIC	60
PAIRI DAIZA Paradisio	BELGIUM	55
ZLIN	CZECH REPUBLIC	52
CHESTER	UNITED KINGDOM	50 +
MARWELL	UNITED KINGDOM	50
ARNHEM Burgers	NETHERLANDS	45
BUSSOLENGO	ITALY	45
ROSTOCK	GERMANY	42
BOJNICE	SLOVAKIA	41
DUBLIN	EIRE	40
MECHELEN Planckendael	BELGIUM	40
SOSTO	HUNGARY	40
WARSAW	POLAND	40
MUNICH Hellabrunn	GERMANY	36
EDINBURGH	UNITED KINGDOM	34
PAIGNTON	UNITED KINGDOM	34
WROCLAW	POLAND	33
BERLIN Zoo	GERMANY	32
ST AIGNAN BEAUVAL	FRANCE	30 +
GELSENKIRCHEN	GERMANY	30
MÜNSTER	GERMANY	30
STUTTGART Wilhelma	GERMANY	30
DORTMUND	GERMANY	28
ROTTERDAM	NETHERLANDS	28
KRONBERG Opel	GERMANY	27
LEIPZIG	GERMANY	27
ZURICH	SWITZERLAND	27
HAMBURG Hagenbeck	GERMANY	25
MULHOUSE	FRANCE	25
OSNABRÜCK	GERMANY	25
BELFAST	UNITED KINGDOM	24
COLCHESTER	UNITED KINGDOM	24

Zoo	Country	Area (Ha)
LISBON	PORTUGAL	24
WUPPERTAL	GERMANY	24
HELSINKI	FINLAND	23 +
AUGSBURG	GERMANY	22
COLOGNE	GERMANY	22
HANOVER	GERMANY	22
MADRID	SPAIN	22
RHENEN	NETHERLANDS	22
RIGA	LATVIA	22
PLZEN	CZECH REPUBLIC	21 +
LJUBLJANA	SLOVENIA	20 +
MAGDEBURG	GERMANY	20
EMMEN	NETHERLANDS	18 +
TWYCROSS	UNITED KINGDOM	18 +
AMERSFOORT	NETHERLANDS	18
AMNEVILLE	FRANCE	18
LA PALMYRE	FRANCE	18
ROME	ITALY	18
VIENNA	AUSTRIA	17 +
VALENCIA	SPAIN	16 +
DUISBURG	GERMANY	16
ZSL LONDON	UNITED KINGDOM	15
AMSTERDAM Artis	NETHERLANDS	14 +
DOUE LA FONTAINE	FRANCE	14
ESKILSTUNA	SWEDEN	14
KREFELD	GERMANY	14
LA FLECHE	FRANCE	14
BARCELONA	SPAIN	13 +
DRESDEN	GERMANY	13 +
KARLSRUHE	GERMANY	13
ANTWERP	BELGIUM	12 +
BASEL	SWITZERLAND	12 +
FRANKFURT	GERMANY	12
BUDAPEST	HUNGARY	11 +
COPENHAGEN	DENMARK	11 +
HEIDELBERG	GERMANY	10 +
HALLE	GERMANY	10
ODENSE	DENMARK	9 +
PARIS - Menagerie	FRANCE	6
BRISTOL	UNITED KINGDOM	5 +
	+ = Expansion Plans 2011 to 2020	

84

or unused areas are included. Several zoos have expanded their areas in recent years and some are planning to do so in the next 10 years, as indicated in the table below.

Several of the smaller area city zoos, such as Antwerp, Basel, Budapest and Copenhagen, have successfully landscaped and designed their sites to be able to give appropriate space to an impressive range of species including large mammals.

Date of Foundation

Zoo	Country	Foundation
VIENNA	AUSTRIA	1752
MADRID	SPAIN	1774
PARIS - Menagerie	FRANCE	1794
ZSL LONDON	UNITED KINGDOM	1828
DUBLIN	EIRE	1830
BRISTOL	UNITED KINGDOM	1835
AMSTERDAM Artis	NETHERLANDS	1838
ANTWERP	BELGIUM	1843
BERLIN ZOO	GERMANY	1844
HAMBURG Hagenbeck	GERMANY	1848
ROTTERDAM	NETHERLANDS	1857
FRANKFURT	GERMANY	1858
COPENHAGEN	DENMARK	1859
COLOGNE	GERMANY	1860
DRESDEN	GERMANY	1861
HANOVER	GERMANY	1865
KARLSRUHE	GERMANY	1865
WROCLAW	POLAND	1865
BUDAPEST	HUNGARY	1866
MULHOUSE	FRANCE	1868
BASEL	SWITZERLAND	1874
MÜNSTER	GERMANY	1875
LEIPZIG	GERMANY	1878
WUPPERTAL	GERMANY	1881
LISBON	PORTUGAL	1884
HELSINKI	FINLAND	1889
BARCELONA	SPAIN	1892
ROSTOCK	GERMANY	1899
HALLE	GERMANY	1901
MUNICH Hellabrunn	GERMANY	1911
ROME	ITALY	1911
NUREMBERG	GERMANY	1912
RIGA	LATVIA	1912
ARNHEM Burgers	NETHERLANDS	1913
EDINBURGH	UNITED KINGDOM	1913
PAIGNTON	UNITED KINGDOM	1923
PLZEN	CZECH REPUBLIC	1926
WARSAW	POLAND	1928
ZURICH	SWITZERLAND	1929
ODENSE	DENMARK	1930

Zoo	Country	Foundation
CHESTER	UNITED KINGDOM	1931
PRAGUE	CZECH REPUBLIC	1931
ZSL WHIPSNADE	UNITED KINGDOM	1931
RHENEN	NETHERLANDS	1932
BELFAST	UNITED KINGDOM	1934
DUISBURG	GERMANY	1934
HEIDELBERG	GERMANY	1934
EMMEN	NETHERLANDS	1935
OSNABRÜCK	GERMANY	1936
AUGSBURG	GERMANY	1937
KREFELD	GERMANY	1938
TALLINN	ESTONIA	1939
DVUR KRALOVE	CZECH REPUBLIC	1946
LA FLECHE	FRANCE	1946
AMERSFOORT	NETHERLANDS	1948
ZLIN	CZECH REPUBLIC	1948
LJUBLJANA	SLOVENIA	1949
STUTTGART Wilhelma	GERMANY	1949
MAGDEBURG	GERMANY	1950
DORTMUND	GERMANY	1953
BERLIN Tierpark	GERMANY	1955
BOJNICE	SLOVAKIA	1955
ESKILSTUNA	SWEDEN	1956
KRONBERG Opel	GERMANY	1956
MECHELEN Planckendael	BELGIUM	1956
ERFURT	GERMANY	1959
BRATISLAVA	SLOVAKIA	1960
DOUE LA FONTAINE	FRANCE	1961
COLCHESTER	UNITED KINGDOM	1963
TWYCROSS	UNITED KINGDOM	1963
KOLMÅRDEN	SWEDEN	1965
LA PALMYRE	FRANCE	1966
BUSSOLENGO	ITALY	1969
MARWELL	UNITED KINGDOM	1972
ST AIGNAN BEAUVAL	FRANCE	1980
AMNEVILLE	FRANCE	1986
PAIRI DAIZA Paradisio	BELGIUM	1994
SOSTO	HUNGARY	1996
GELSENKIRCHEN	GERMANY	2005
VALENCIA	SPAIN	2008

The table above, and the references elsewhere in this book, refers to the foundation or original opening date of the zoo, although it may not still be on its original site. Interestingly, of the 28 zoos founded before 1900, 15 were in the German speaking areas at that time. During the period 1945-1989, 8 zoos were established in the then Eastern European area. Only 2 of the 80 zoos in the survey, Gelsenkirchen and Valencia, have been opened since 2000.

Type of Ownership

Defining every zoo by an ownership type is not a straightforward exercise since some have complex shareholding structures. However, it seems that 60% of the zoos in this survey are publicly owned or controlled and that 40% are in the private sector.

For the public sector zoos, there is a general move towards the formation of separate, albeit municipally controlled, companies thereby providing more independence to the zoo, both in its day-to-day operations and in its future plans and investment.

Types of Ownership:

PUBLIC SECTOR

Direct Municipal (zoo directly responsible to City Council)	22
Indirect Municipal (zoo responsible to municipal controlled company)	15
Indirect Municipal (zoo resp. to municipal controlled public company)	6
Direct National Government (zoo directly responsible to Govt. Dept.)	2
Indirect Government (zoo responsible to Govt. controlled company)	1
Direct Regional Government (zoo directly resp. to Regional Govt.)	2
TOTAL	**48**

PRIVATE SECTOR

Charitable Zoological Society (independent)	8
Charitable Zoological Society (with public sector financial support)	6
Private Family Owned	4
Private Company non-profit	4
Private Company	8
Publicly quoted Company	2
TOTAL	**32**

There are major differences between countries. For instance, 90% of British zoos are privately owned whilst over 90% of the German zoos in the survey are publicly owned.

Friends of the Zoo

There are different forms of support organisations helping zoos. The two basic models are "Friends of the Zoo" and "Members of the Zoo" where such organisations exist. "Friends of the Zoo" are societies organised separately from the zoo's own staff but dedicated to supporting the zoo, particularly through fund raising. Typically, the society will have its own elected committee and chairperson, organise and run its own programme of meetings with speakers, arrange visits to other zoos, collect money for specific projects in its zoo, produce and circulate a newsletter or magazine to members, and have its own website. Some societies may be the channel through which corporate fundraising is organised.

"Friends of the Zoo" - Largest memberships:

- Zurich   35,000
- Stuttgart   24,000
- Vienna   10,000
- Münster   8,000
- Munich   7,000
- Rotterdam   6,500
- Duisburg   6,000
- Frankfurt   6,000
- Cologne   5,000

"Members of the Zoo", on the other hand, are generally supporter organisations attached to and organised by the zoo's staff, who have the benefit of annual cards, discounts at the zoo's catering and retail outlets, a zoo magazine and other forms of information, and sometimes discounts at other zoos.

"Members of the Zoo" - Largest memberships:

- Antwerp/Planckendael   200,000
- Barcelona   110,000
- London/Whipsnade   45,000
- Colchester   36,000
- Chester   35,000
- Arnhem   25,000
- Edinburgh   22,000
- Marwell   18,000
- Paignton   13,000
- Bristol   12,000

Annual or Season Tickets

Whilst these are particularly relevant for city zoos, which are the attraction of choice on a regular basis for large numbers of local residents, annual tickets are becoming increasingly popular and widely used. In part, this is due to a major reduction in the relative price of an annual and daily ticket in recent years. Many zoos have reduced this ratio from 5:1 down to 3:1 in an effort to greatly increase the number of annual ticket sales: these now represent excellent value for visitors. This has been very successful and resulted in doubling or more the annual ticket sales in recent years in several zoos.

The importance of increasing annual ticket sales lies in boosting overall visitor numbers – a key public indicator of the zoo's success – and increased catering and retail sales with direct financial benefit to the zoo. In addition, exposure to the vital conservation and education messages in the zoo is increased.

Apart from Members of the Zoo, direct sales of Annual Tickets are largest in:

- Copenhagen   150,000
- Vienna   125,000
- Rotterdam   120,000
- Hannover   100,000
- Emmen   100,000
- Amsterdam   80,000

Most Popular Zoo Mammals

I have asked each Zoo Director to name the 5 most popular mammals in his/her zoo with the visitors. Whilst responses are generally personal and subjective, they do seem to reflect the results of visitor surveys, where these exist, and general expectations.

For many zoos, they indicate "must have" species and the importance to the zoo of breeding such species if possible. This, again, is reflected in media interest.

Mammal Species	Zoos Holding	Most Popular Single Mammal		In Top 5 Most Popular Mammals	
Elephant	61	31	51%	58	95%
Gorilla	40	8	20%	32	80%
Giraffe	66	3	5%	48	73%
Lion	74	4	5%	50	68%
Chimpanzee	48	5	10%	32	67%
Tiger	65	6	9%	40	62%
Polar Bear	25	1	4%	15	60%
Orang utan	42	4	10%	24	57%
Sea Lion/Seal	60	5	8%	26	43%
Rhinoceros	51	1	2%	20	39%
Hippo/ pygmy Hippo	48	1	2%	17	35%
Meerkat	60	2	3%	11	18%
Black/Brown Bear	55	2	4%	10	18%

Largest Collections

My survey has looked at mammals, birds and reptiles. If amphibians, fish and invertebrates are counted as well, Berlin Zoo would have the largest collection of the 80 Zoos. There are several ways of deciding on the largest collections. I have taken, for this table, the number of different species of mammals, birds and reptiles, and then multiplied mammals x3, birds x2, and reptiles x1 to produce an overall score as follows.

Name of Zoo	Total Points	Mammals Number	Mammals Species	Birds Number	Birds Species	Reptiles Number	Reptiles Species
Pilzen	2081	1514	241	1845	505	1325	248
Berlin Tierpark	1453	1415	191	2425	389	537	102
Berlin Zoo	1318	1147	177	2481	355	485	77
Prague	1167	1200	169	1428	270	851	120
Pairi Daiza Paridisio	860	310	40	2800	320	1600	100
Stuttgart	827	655	114	1023	199	370	87
Budapest	817	780	108	1475	195	455	103
Wroclaw	774	551	105	624	149	806	161
Beauval	742	552	87	1513	215	314	51
Warsaw	686	399	65	1092	213	262	65
Cologne	682	501	66	1290	202	479	80
Lisbon	669	611	120	644	129	359	51
Rotterdam	631	1268	83	1343	145	648	92
Madrid	624	525	99	1195	117	350	93
Leipzig	618	446	88	738	146	215	62
Antwerp	599	333	77	703	150	337	68
Chester	599	1864	79	1138	155	230	52
Vienna	573	651	94	1186	116	326	59
Barcelona	572	727	88	698	108	432	92
Tallinn	572	984	95	601	120	145	47
Amsterdam	560	516	94	730	102	296	76

Nearly all zoos have been reducing their collection sizes in order to give more space to the remaining species; these reductions have been taking place over a period of time. In some instances, particularly where zoos are acquiring additional land or using hitherto empty space, small increases in the collection size are being seen.

Zoo Opening Hours

Although it is difficult to draw a line between "city zoos" and "non-city zoos", I have divided them into 62 city zoos and 18 non-city zoos for this analysis.

Of the 80 zoos in the survey, 1 city zoo (Eskilstuna) and 4 non-city zoos (Bussolengo, Doué-la-Fontaine, Kolmården and Pairi Daiza) are closed during winter months.

My analysis of zoo opening hours, taken from the zoo profiles in Chapter 12, is as follows –

	Summer		Winter	
	City zoos	Non-city zoos	City zoos	Non-city zoos
Open to visitors before 0900	9	2[1]	4	2[1]
Open to visitors before 0930	44	10	38	6
Open to vistors only 1000 or later	16	6	21	6
In Summer, open at least 9 hours	51	12		
In Summer, open less than 8 hours[2]	1	4		
[1] = Bojnice, Zlin				
[2] = London, Kolmården, Paignton, Twycross, Whipsnade				
Note. In some zoos, there are some longer opening hours in summer. This table is for all days throughout the season. In general, UK and Scandinavian zoos open later, typically at 1000. It should also be noted that some zoos allow visitors to remain as long as they like, even when the entrance kiosks are closed, particularly in summer.				

Bussolengo

CHAPTER 12

Star Rating of Iconic Species by Zoo

I discussed iconic species in Chapter 11. The iconic species in this table stem from that selection. The table is designed both to provide a guide to assist visitors who are interested in particular species and to give an overall view of the listed species being kept in each zoo.

The following points should be noted in the use of this information:

1. Zoos are placed by country in alphabetical order. **Group A Zoos** are listed in **bold letters** and Group B Zoos in standard letters.

2. Rating points are based on personal visits made 2008-2010, and are calculated to reflect the appropriateness and quality of the indoor and outdoor enclosure for the species both from the viewpoint of the animal and the visitor, and to take account of the number of animals on exhibit. Where a half point may have been recorded, I have rounded the rating points up.

3. Rating scores are 1 to 6, with 6 being the best. 0 signifies the zoo does not exhibit the species.

4. Where a zoo exhibits more than one type of animal in the animal column in the table (e.g. Ostrich, Rhea, Emu, Cassowary), the rating point used is for the best exhibit.

5. Where I fully anticipate that plans and finance are in place to improve the exhibit or add the species to the collection by 2020, this is shown with the symbol ↑ next to the number. The table is not necessarily comprehensive: a minority of zoos feel unable to discuss future developments.

6. Where a zoo is known to have a species which I have not yet marked, or which may be off exhibit, the symbol ? is used.

7. For those southern zoos with warmer climates, allowance has been made for less good indoor facilities.

8. Due to continual improvements and changes within zoos, it cannot be guaranteed that all the animals shown in this table will be on show at the time of any particular visit

9. Whilst acceptable standards for keeping many species are rising, special attention is being given to elephants, polar bears and sea-lions as mandatory higher minimum standards are being imposed in EU countries. This is reflected in many of the improvements expected during the next few years, as indicated in this table.

STAR RATING OF ICONIC SPECIES BY ZOO

Unusual Iconic Species

The following significant species are not included in the table as they are exhibited by very few zoos. These are listed below with the rating points in brackets.

1. The **Giant Panda** is presently exhibited in 3 Zoos – Vienna (6), Madrid (4), Berlin (2). Edinburgh will receive 2 Pandas in 2011. At least 3 other zoos are in discussion but, in view of the sensitivity of negotiations, are not mentioned here. Berlin is likely to have an improved exhibit before 2020.

2. The **Koala Bear** is presently exhibited in 7 Zoos – Beauval (4), Planckendael (4), Duisburg (3), Vienna (3), Edinburgh (2), Lisbon (2), Madrid (1). They are likely to be held in Budapest, Bussolengo, Dresden before 2020.

3. The **Dolphin** is presently exhibited in 7 Zoos – Kolmården (6), Nuremberg (6 from mid 2011), Duisburg (6), Lisbon (4), Barcelona (2), Madrid (2), Münster (2 but none after 2012). Barcelona and Madrid likely to have improved exhibits before 2020.

4. The **Manatee** is presently exhibited in 5 Zoos – Nuremberg (6 from mid 2011), Odense (5), Arnhem (4), Beauval (4), Berlin Tierpark (1). They are likely to be held in Wroclaw before 2020.

5. The **Giant Otter** is presently exhibited in 5 Zoos – Doué-la-Fontaine (6), Chester (5), Dortmund (5), Duisburg (5), Hamburg (4). Leipzig will show their animals in the Gondwanaland from 2011. They are likely to be held in Bussolengo and Madrid before 2020.

6. No zoo currently exhibits the **Walrus**. However, they will be exhibited in Hamburg from 2012.

Duisburg

Iconic Species		Elephant	Giraffe	Okapi	Lion	Tiger	Snow Leopard	Chimpanzee/Bonobo	Gorilla	Orang utan	Polar Bear	Hippo (bold)/Pygmy Hippo	Rhinoceros	Sea Lion/Seal	Gibbon/Siamang	Ringtail Lemur
AUSTRIA	VIENNA	4	2↑	0	4	5	0	0	0	6	2↑	4	5	4	6	6
BELGIUM	ANTWERP	2	1↑	1↑	1↑	1↑	0	3	3	0	0	4	0	3	2	1
BELGIUM	MECHELEN Planckendael	0↑	3	0	3	0	?	6	0	0	0	0	2	0	4	0
BELGIUM	PAIRI DAIZA	1↑	2↑	0	0↑	0↑	0	0	0	0↑	0	4↑	0	3	4	5
CZECH REPUBLIC	PRAGUE	1↑	4	0	3	3	0	0	4	5	3↑	2↑	0	6	4	6
CZECH REPUBLIC	DVUR KRALOVE	2	2	3	4	2	0	1	1	3	0	2	4	0	0	6
CZECH REPUBLIC	PLZEN	0↑	4	0	3	3	4	2	3	0↑	0	4	3	0	3	3
CZECH REPUBLIC	ZLIN	3	2	0	2	3	0	0	2	0	0	0	1	4	2	2
DENMARK	COPENHAGEN	6	4	2	3	3	0	3	0	0	1↑	6	4	5	3	2
DENMARK	ODENSE	0	2	0	3	5	0	6	0	0	0	0	0	2	0	3
EIRE	DUBLIN	6	2	0	3	3	3	4	1↑	1↑	0	4	4	2	4	2
ESTONIA	TALLINN	4	0↑	0	2	3	4	1	0	0	1↑	3	3	1	0	0
FINLAND	HELSINKI	0	0	0	3	5	6	0	0	0	0	0	0	3	0	0
FRANCE	AMNEVILLE	2	3	0	3	3	4	0	0↑	6	4	3	3	3	3	5
FRANCE	BEAUVAL	4	3	2	3	4	2	3	4	3	0	0↑	3	4	0	5
FRANCE	DOUE LA FONTAINE	0	2	0	6	6	6	0	0	0	0	4	3	0	4	0
FRANCE	LA FLECHE	3	1↑	0	2	2	0	2	0	0	5	1	0↑	0	2	2↑
FRANCE	MULHOUSE	0	0↑	0	2	2	4	0	0	0	1↑	0	0	2	3↑	5
FRANCE	LA PALMYRE	2	2	0	2	2	6	6	6	3	3	3	1	3	3	2
FRANCE	PARIS - Menagerie	0	0	0	0	0	0	0	0	2↑	0	0	0	0	0	0
GERMANY	BERLIN Tierpark	2	4	0	2	3	2	0	0	0↑	4	0	2	0	5	6
GERMANY	BERLIN Zoo	3	3	3	4	4	0	4	4	4	3	6	3	5	4	0
GERMANY	DUISBURG	3	3	0	3	2	0	0	4	3↑	0	4	2	2	1↑	0
GERMANY	FRANKFURT	0	2↑	2	3	4	0	5	5	5	0	1↑	1	4	5	1
GERMANY	GELSENKIRCHEN	0	4	0	5	0	0	6	0	6	6	4	3	6	0	0
GERMANY	HAMBURG Hagenbeck	6	2↑	0	2	4	0	0	0	6	0↑	0	0↑	3↑	0	4
GERMANY	HANOVER	5	3	0	3	4	0	1	4	1	6	4	3	4	4	1
GERMANY	KARLSRUHE	2↑	3↑	0	2↑	0	1↑	2	0	0	5	2↑	0	5	0	0
GERMANY	COLOGNE	6	2↑	2	3	4	4	5	3	3	0	6	1↑	2↑	4	0
GERMANY	LEIPZIG	6	5	2	4	4	1↑	6	6	6	0	0↑	4	5	6	5
GERMANY	MUNICH Hellabrunn	3↑	1↑	0	2	4	5	4	4	4	5	0	1↑	2	4	4
GERMANY	MÜNSTER	2↑	1↑	0	1↑	3	0	3	4	5	0	0	3	3	0	4
GERMANY	NUREMBERG	0↑	3↑	0	5	4	4	0	4	0	4	0	4	4↑	3	0
GERMANY	STUTTGART Wilhelma	1↑	2	3	1↑	2	0	2↑	2↑	2↑	2	1	1↑	2	2	0
GERMANY	AUGSBURG	1	4	0	3	2	0	2	0	0	0	0	0	4	3	5
GERMANY	DORTMUND	0	5	0	2	3	0	0	0	5	0	0	3	3	5	0
GERMANY	DRESDEN	3	5	0	4	0	1↑	0	0↑	2↑	0	0	0	0↑	0	6
GERMANY	ERFURT	1↑	1↑	0	4	0	0	0	0	0	0	0	0	0	2	0↑
GERMANY	HALLE	3	0	0	3	3	0	4	0	0	0	3	0	2	0	0
GERMANY	HEIDELBERG	5	0↑	0	2↑	4	0	2↑	2↑	1	0	0	0	3	0	0

STAR RATING OF ICONIC SPECIES BY ZOO

Iconic Species Table		Elephant	Giraffe	Okapi	Lion	Tiger	Snow Leopard	Chimpanzee/Bonobo	Gorilla	Orang utan	Polar Bear	Hippo (bold)/Pygmy Hippo	Rhinoceros	Sea Lion/Seal	Gibbon/Siamang	Ringtail Lemur
GERMANY	KREFELD	1↑	0	0	0	4	3	1↑	1↑	2↑	0	1	1	2	1	0
GERMANY	KRONBERG Opel	1↑	5	0	0	0	0	0	0	0	0	3↑	0↑	0	2	0
GERMANY	MAGDEBURG	1↑	4	0	3	4	4	3!	0!	0	0	0	4	0	1	3
GERMANY	OSNABRÜCK	2	4	0	3	2!	0	6	0	2↑	1↑	0	2↑	3	2	0
GERMANY	ROSTOCK	2↑	0	0	3	0	4	1	1↑	1↑	2↑	0	0	5	0↑	1↑
GERMANY	WUPPERTAL	4	0	2↑	4	5	3	2↑	4	5	2↑	0	0	2	5	0
HUNGARY	BUDAPEST	3↑	4	0↑	2↑	2	0	0	5	3	2	2	2	4	2	4
HUNGARY	SOSTO	3	3	0	2	3	2↑	0	3	5	2	4	4↑	2	5	4
ITALY	BUSSOLENGO	0	2	0↑	4	6	6	3↑	0↑	0	0	5	5	0	0	5
ITALY	ROME	1↑	2	0	3	1↑	0	4	0	?	0	1	0	2	0	3
LATVIA	RIGA	0↑	5	0	2	3	0	0	0	0	1	1	0	2	0	3
NETHERLANDS	AMSTERDAM Artis	1↑	3↑	0	1	0	0	3	3↑	0	1	0	0	3	3	4
NETHERLANDS	ARNHEM Burgers	3	5	0	6	5	0	3	4↑	0↑	0↑	4	5	2	4	5
NETHERLANDS	EMMEN	3	3	0	0↑	5	0	0	0	0	0	2	2	4	4	4
NETHERLANDS	ROTTERDAM	4	5	3	2	3	0	0	4	0	5	3	3	5	5	0
NETHERLANDS	AMERSFOORT	4	3	0	2	2	0	2↑	0	0	0	0	3	0	2	3
NETHERLANDS	RHENEN	2	2	0	3	4	0↑	0	0!	3	4	0	0	6	4	4
POLAND	WARSAW	4	2↑	0	3	2	2	6	6	0	0!	5	3	3!	3	4
POLAND	WROCLAW	1↑	1↑	0	2	2	0	3	0	1	0	1↑	0!	3!	6	6
PORTUGAL	LISBON	1↑	1	3	3	4	3	4	3	3	0	2	2	2	4	3
SLOVAKIA	BOJNICE	1↑	0	0	1↑	0	0	0	0	3	0	0	0	0	2	0
SLOVAKIA	BRATISLAVA	0↑	1↑	0	2	2	0	4↑	0↑	5	0	1	2↑	0	1↑	1
SLOVENIA	LJUBLJANA	1	3	0	1	2	0	1	0	0	0	0	0↑	2	2	0
SPAIN	BARCELONA	1↑	1↑	0	1	2	0	4	3	1	0	5	2	3↑	2	2
SPAIN	MADRID	2↑	2	0	1	1	0	2↑	4	2	0	1↑	2↑	2	2	3
SPAIN	VALENCIA	5	5	0	4	0	0	4	5	0	0	6	4	0	0	6
SWEDEN	ESKILSTUNA	0	0	0↑	3	5	0	0	0	0	0	5	0↑	0	4	0
SWEDEN	KOLMÅRDEN	2	4	0	4	6	4	4	4	0	0	0	4	6	4	0
SWITZERLAND	BASEL	2↑	2	2	4	0	4	4↑	4↑	4↑	0	5↑	4	2	0	4
SWITZERLAND	ZÜRICH	2↑	0↑	0	5	5	5	0	3	2	0	2	2↑	3	5	4
UNITED KINGDOM	CHESTER	5	3	3↑	2	3↑	0	4↑	0↑	5	0	0↑	3	2	4	3↑
UNITED KINGDOM	ZSL LONDON	0	1	2	5	3↑	0	0	4	0	0	2	0	0	4	2
UNITED KINGDOM	BELFAST	2↑	3	0	2	5	0	3	3	0	0	0	0↑	3	3	3
UNITED KINGDOM	BRISTOL	0	0	2	6	0	0	0	4↑	0	0	2	0	5	3	4
UNITED KINGDOM	COLCHESTER	2	2	0	3	4	0	3	0	4	0	2	2	4	0!	3
UNITED KINGDOM	EDINBURGH	0	0	0	3	2	0	6	0	0	0	2	2	3	0	2
UNITED KINGDOM	MARWELL	0	4	3	0	4	5	0	0↑	0↑	0	1↑	2	0	4	4
UNITED KINGDOM	PAIGNTON	3	3	0	4	3	0	0	3	3	0	0	3	0	3	0
UNITED KINGDOM	TWYCROSS	4↑	1↑	0↑	1↑	0	5	2↑	3	2	0	0	0	2	1	2
UNITED KINGDOM	ZSL WHIPSNADE	4	3	0	5	5	0	5	0	0	0	2	4	3	0	4
TOTAL ZOOS EXHIBITING SPECIES		61	66	17	74	65	30	50	40	42	25	48	51	60	57	56

Iconic Species Table		Spider Monkey	Colobus	Meerkat	Zebra	Penguin	Ostrich/Rhea/Emu/Cassowary	Pelican	Flamingo	Maccaw	Birds of Prey	Crocodile/Alligator	Komodo Dragon	Giant Tortoise	Anaconda/Python
AUSTRIA	VIENNA	0	0↑	4	3	6	4	5	4	3	4	6	0	6	6
BELGIUM	ANTWERP	2	1	5	3	5	0	3	1	1	2	4	6	0	2
BELGIUM	MECHELEN Planckendael	0	0	0	3	0↑	4	3	2	2	4	0	0	0	3
BELGIUM	PAIRI DAIZA	0	0↑	2	3↑	3	6	6	6	5	5	3	0	3	3
CZECH REPUBLIC	PRAGUE	5	5	2	2	4	4	5	5	3↑	6	5	3	6	4
CZECH REPUBLIC	DVUR KRALOVE	0	2	5	6	0	4	6	2	2	?	2	0	0	2
CZECH REPUBLIC	PLZEN	2	4	0	5	2	5	5	3	0	1	3	0	0	3
CZECH REPUBLIC	ZLIN	2	0	0	2	3	5	4	4	4	5	5	0	0	1
DENMARK	COPENHAGEN	2	0	0	4	1↑	3	3	1↑	4	3	3	0	0	4
DENMARK	ODENSE	0	0	0	2	6	4	5	5	3	0	1	0	6	1
EIRE	DUBLIN	3	0	2	2	3	2	0	3	1	0	2	0	0	2
ESTONIA	TALLINN	0	0	1	0↑	0	4	3	3	2	2	3	0	0	2
FINLAND	HELSINKI	0	0	0	0	0	?	0	?	2	?	3	0	0	2
FRANCE	AMNEVILLE	5	0	2	3	2↑	3	4	4	4	6	3↑	0↑	0↑	2↑
FRANCE	BEAUVAL	4	3	2	4	6	4	4	4	3	3	2	0	2	3
FRANCE	DOUE LA FONTAINE	6	0	0	2	2	0	0	6	2	6	2	0	0	2
FRANCE	LA FLECHE	6	1↑	1	2	1↑	2	2	4	2↑	0	1	0	0	1
FRANCE	MULHOUSE	2!	0	0	3	3	3	3	2	3	3	1	0	0	0
FRANCE	LA PALMYRE	0	3	2	4	4	4	6	5	5	6	4	0	2	3
FRANCE	PARIS - Menagerie	0	0	0	0	0	4	0	4	2	3	3	0	1	2
GERMANY	BERLIN Tierpark	0	0	0	3	3	4	6	3	3	4	3	0	4	4
GERMANY	BERLIN Zoo	0	0	3	4	5	3	6	5	?	5	3	0	2	5
GERMANY	DUISBURG	0	4	6	2	2	3	3	3	2	4	3	0	0	0
GERMANY	FRANKFURT	1	1	2	2↑	2↑	3	2	?	?	4	4	0	0	3
GERMANY	GELSENKIRCHEN	0	0	5	3	0	3	4	2	0	3	0	0	0	0
GERMANY	HAMBURG Hagenbeck	0	0	0	2↑	2↑	4	4	6	5	0	6	0	4	4
GERMANY	HANOVER	0	0	3	4	3	4	6	2	4	5	0	0	0	2
GERMANY	KARLSRUHE	3	0	3	2↑	4	2	3	3	3	?	0	0	0	2
GERMANY	COLOGNE	0	1	6	3	4	3	6	6	?	5	6	0	0	2
GERMANY	LEIPZIG	0	0	5	6	3	4	4	4	1	4	4	0↑	0↑	2
GERMANY	MUNICH Hellabrunn	3	0	0	4↑	2↑	4	4	4	2	?	4	0	6	4
GERMANY	MÜNSTER	0	6	3	6	3	6	4	5	4	3	3	0	0	2
GERMANY	NUREMBERG	0	0	0	4↑	5	6	4	6	4	3	2	0	0	?
GERMANY	STUTTGART Wilhelma	2	0	4	2	2	2	4	4	2	3	4	0	0	2
GERMANY	AUGSBURG	0	0	4	3	5	2	5	4	0	0	0↑	0	0	2
GERMANY	DORTMUND	0	0	2	4	5	4	0	4	1	2	3	0	0	2
GERMANY	DRESDEN	0	5	0	4	3	4	4	3	3	5	4	0	3	2
GERMANY	ERFURT	4	0	6	4	0	6	0	4	2	4	3	0	0	3
GERMANY	HALLE	0	0	4	3	4	3	4	?	2	4	5	0	0	3
GERMANY	HEIDELBERG	0	0	4	2↑	0	0	2	3	2	5	0↑	0	3	*?

Iconic Species Table -1-		Spider Monkey	Colobus	Meerkat	Zebra	Penguin	Ostrich/Rhea/Emu/Cassowary	Pelican	Flamingo	Maccaw	Birds of Prey	Crocodile/Alligator	Komodo Dragon	Giant Tortoise	Anaconda/Python
GERMANY	KREFELD	0	4	0	3	3	3	0	4	4	0	4	0	1	3
GERMANY	KRONBERG Opel	0	0	2	5	0	0	3	?	0	0	1	0	0	1
GERMANY	MAGDEBURG	0	0↑	6	4	2	0	4	4	2	4	0	0	0	2
GERMANY	OSNABRÜCK	4	0	3	4	3	4	3	4	2	2	3	0	3	3
GERMANY	ROSTOCK	0	0	5	4	1	2	6	4	0	?	2	0	0↑	0↑
GERMANY	WUPPERTAL	1	0	4	2	6	5	?	2	1	3	2	0	0	1
HUNGARY	**BUDAPEST**	0	0	6	2↑	4	3	4	3	4	4	2	0	0	3
HUNGARY	SOSTO	0	4	3	6	3	3	6	3	3↑	0	4	5	0	3
ITALY	BUSSOLENGO	0	0	2	3	0↑	5	6	4	2	4	3	0!	4	3
ITALY	ROME	0	0	0	2	0↑	4	3	3	0	3	4	0	0	3
LATVIA	RIGA	0	0	2	2	0	2	3	3	2	1	3	0	3	1
NETHERLANDS	**AMSTERDAM Artis**	2↑	0	3	4	4	4	5	?	1	6	4	0	2	3
NETHERLANDS	**ARNHEM Burgers**	0	0	6	5	3↑	0	3	3	2	4	3	0	0	4
NETHERLANDS	**EMMEN**	3	4	5	3	6	4	3	6	4	0	4	0	0	4
NETHERLANDS	**ROTTERDAM**	0	4	4	5	6	3	2	3	?	5	5	4	4	3
NETHERLANDS	AMERSFOORT	0	0	5	3	4	6	0	4	2	3	2	0	0	0
NETHERLANDS	RHENEN	0	0	4	3	3↑	2	4	3	3	5	4	0	2	4
POLAND	WARSAW	0	0	2	3↑	3	4↑	4	4	3	3	3	0	0	3
POLAND	WROCLAW	0	2	1	3↑	0↑	3↑	3	3	3	4	2!	0	3	2
PORTUGAL	LISBON	4	3	4	2	2	0	2	2	2	2	3	1	0	1
SLOVAKIA	BOJNICE	0	2	0	4	0	4	4	2	1	4	1	0	0	2
SLOVAKIA	BRATISLAVA	0	1	4	1↑	0	3	4	4	1	2	0	0	0	0
SLOVENIA	LJUBLJANA	0	0	0↑	2	0↑	5	3	0↑	2	3	0!	0	0	1
SPAIN	**BARCELONA**	3	0	2	2↑	3	2	4	4	3	2	3	5	1	3
SPAIN	**MADRID**	0	1	3	2	2	3	5	5	1	3	3	0	1	2
SPAIN	VALENCIA	0	0	4	5	0	5	3	3	0	0	5	0	0	3
SWEDEN	ESKILSTUNA	3	0	4	0	0	4	0	2	0	0	4	6	1!	3
SWEDEN	KOLMÅRDEN	0	0	6	4	6	5	0	0	?	?	5	0	0	4
SWITZERLAND	**BASEL**	4	0	4	4	3	3	6	6	0	0	6	0	0	3
SWITZERLAND	**ZÜRICH**	0	0	0	2!	3!	5	0	3!	3	?	4	0	5	3
UNITED KINGDOM	**CHESTER**	4	0	3	2	4	3	3	4	3	6	4↑	3↑	2	2
UNITED KINGDOM	**ZSL LONDON**	2	3	4	1	3!	3	5	4	2	5	3	6	5	3
UNITED KINGDOM	BELFAST	3	3	3	3	3	2	5	3	2	4	0	0	0	0
UNITED KINGDOM	BRISTOL	0	0	4	0	4	3	3	3	3	0	3	0	4	3
UNITED KINGDOM	COLCHESTER	2	2	4	2	2	2	3	2	2	3	4	5	0	3
UNITED KINGDOM	EDINBURGH	0	0	0	4	6	0	0	2	0	0	2	0	0	0
UNITED KINGDOM	MARWELL	0	4	4	4	3	4	0	2	0	0	3	0	0	2
UNITED KINGDOM	PAIGNTON	3	4	4	4	0	5	5	3	?	0	3	0	3	3
UNITED KINGDOM	TWYCROSS	1	1	3	0↑	2	3	4	3	2	0	1	0	2	0
UNITED KINGDOM	ZSL WHIPSNADE	0	0	3	3	4	3	0	2	0	?	2	0	0	1
TOTAL ZOOS EXHIBITING SPECIES		30	27	60	74	61	72	66	78	68	63	69	10	30	71

CHAPTER 13

Ranking Lists

Introduction

Ranking lists, always controversial, are now commonplace in all types of business activity; they serve as useful benchmarks to the organisations concerned as well as being of real interest to their customers. They always have their limitations and represent a moment in time.

Zoo Ranking Lists

These do appear occasionally in various publications. To my knowledge, none existing take account of a very wide range of factors relevant to zoos; I have tried to produce unique ranking lists which do justice to the most important work of modern zoos.

My Ranking Lists

The marks are derived from individual scores against 26 different factors which are then grouped into three different areas of activity – visitor factors, education and conservation, and commercial and organisation. The marks have been derived from an analysis of the responses to a zoo questionnaire with 86 questions, interviews with individual zoo directors, published information and extensive zoo visits. The quality of information available obviously varies; also changes and improvements are continually taking place. The weighting of factors acknowledges that the customers, visitors and sponsors, are of first importance and that the primary goals of education and conservation are funded primarily by the zoo's customers.

Omissions

My ranking lists use a wide spectrum of core zoo activities but do not take account of catering and retail outlets, events and shows, children's zoos and playgrounds, transport and car parking, zoo opening hours, and research work. Zoos are aware of the importance of all these factors but, apart from academic research which could constitute a further detailed study in its own right, I feel these aspects are difficult to compare meaningfully and are best suited to evaluation from visitor satisfaction surveys which the best zoos take seriously.

Ranking List Results

As is typical of many ranking lists, many of the marks are very close. Some zoos are very high on one and very low on another of the lists. The situation is dynamic and will change as some zoos invest and improve more quickly than others. I have tried to take account of on-going improvements in allocating significant marks for Master Plans and investment plans, together with the likelihood of funding availability for the years to 2020.

The 4 Ranking Lists

All four ranking lists divided into two sections – Group A and Group B zoos – and are:

- Visitor Factors (Animal collection, animal houses and enclosures, design, landscaping, vegetation, ambience, enclosure signage).   108 marks (48.9% of total)
- Education and Conservation Factors (Zoo school, numbers of school pupils, university students, in-situ and ex-situ conservation)   35 marks (15.8% of total)
- Commercial and Organisation Factors (Visitor numbers and trends, investment past and future, staffing, zookeeper training, marketing, publicity, master plan, friends of the zoo, admission ticket prices, management)   78 marks (35.3% of total)
- Overall Ranking List, combining all of the above three lists.

Anthony Sheridan, Dr. Dagmar Schratter (Zoo Director), Dr. Helmut Pechlaner (former Zoo Director), Dr. Reinhold Mitterlehner (Federal Minister)

Trophy Awards

On the basis of my work on ranking lists I have awarded a trophy to the best of the many excellent zoological gardens in Europe. Vienna has won the trophy for the best Group A zoo in 2009 and 2011.

In 2011, I introduced an additional trophy for the leading Group B Zoo which was awarded to Beauval.

Ranking Order - Total - Group A

	Group A 30 Zoos	1 million+ visitors	Visitor Factors	Education and Conservation	Commercial and Organisation	TOTAL ALL ITEMS
			108	35	78	221
1	VIENNA	AUSTRIA	87	30	69	186
2	LEIPZIG	GERMANY	79	22	70	171
2	ZURICH	SWITZERLAND	77	30	64	171
4	BERLIN ZOO	GERMANY	87	17	66	170
5	BASEL	SWITZERLAND	78	23	61	162
5	CHESTER	UNITED KINGDOM	76	31	55	162
5	COLOGNE	GERMANY	75	25	62	162
8	ROTTERDAM	NETHERLANDS	82	29	50	161
9	ARNHEM Burgers	NETHERLANDS	84	20	53	157
10	HAMBURG Hagenbeck	GERMANY	75	20	60	155
10	PRAGUE	CZECH REPUBLIC	77	24	54	155
12	MUNICH Hellabrunn	GERMANY	79	24	51	154
13	ANTWERP	BELGIUM	63	32	56	151
13	COPENHAGEN	DENMARK	69	26	56	151
13	HANOVER	GERMANY	70	19	62	151
13	STUTTGART Wilhelma	GERMANY	74	19	58	151
17	FRANKFURT	GERMANY	69	30	51	150
18	MÜNSTER	GERMANY	74	23	52	149
19	AMSTERDAM Artis	NETHERLANDS	69	26	52	147
19	NUREMBERG	GERMANY	72	23	52	147
21	BUDAPEST	HUNGARY	74	22	48	144
22	DUISBURG	GERMANY	73	18	47	138
23	EMMEN	NETHERLANDS	72	20	45	137
24	ZSL LONDON	UNITED KINGDOM	58	33	44	135
25	BERLIN TIERPARK	GERMANY	72	14	48	134
26	BARCELONA	SPAIN	64	25	40	129
27	GELSENKIRCHEN	GERMANY	66	8	54	128
28	MADRID	SPAIN	67	19	38	124
29	DUBLIN	EIRE	60	16	45	121
29	KARLSRUHE	GERMANY	58	16	47	121

Ranking Order - Total - Group B

	Group B 50 Zoos	500,000+ visitors	Visitor Factors	Education and Conservation	Commercial and Organisation	TOTAL ALL ITEMS
			108	35	78	221
1	ST AIGNAN BEAUVAL	FRANCE	81	25	36	142
2	OSNABRÜCK	GERMANY	68	19	51	138
3	AMNEVILLE	FRANCE	74	26	35	135
4	KOLMÅRDEN/Tropicarium	SWEDEN	71	18	45	134
5	LISBON	PORTUGAL	73	24	36	133
5	VALENCIA	SPAIN	76	20	37	133
7	WUPPERTAL	GERMANY	73	18	41	132
8	BRISTOL	UNITED KINGDOM	63	32	35	130
8	COLCHESTER	UNITED KINGDOM	64	23	43	130
8	PAIGNTON	UNITED KINGDOM	64	30	36	130
8	PAIRI DAIZA Paradisio	BELGIUM	66	14	50	130
12	MECHELEN Planckendael	BELGIUM	55	22	50	127
12	WARSAW	POLAND	73	15	39	127
14	ZSL WHIPSNADE	UNITED KINGDOM	63	26	37	126
15	ROSTOCK	GERMANY	60	14	51	125
16	BUSSOLENGO	ITALY	67	19	36	122
17	DRESDEN	GERMANY	64	10	47	121
17	EDINBURGH	UNITED KINGDOM	53	24	44	121
19	PLZEN	CZECH REPUBLIC	65	14	40	119
20	RHENEN	NETHERLANDS	66	18	34	118
21	HEIDELBERG	GERMANY	61	20	36	117
22	LA PALMYRE	FRANCE	72	14	30	116
22	TWYCROSS	UNITED KINGDOM	52	22	42	116
24	DORTMUND	GERMANY	64	17	33	114
24	DOUE LA FONTAINE	FRANCE	67	25	22	114
26	DVUR KRÁLOVÉ	CZECH REPUBLIC	64	16	33	113
26	MARWELL	UNITED KINGDOM	56	23	34	113
26	ZLIN	CZECH REPUBLIC	65	13	35	113
29	ERFURT	GERMANY	54	13	44	111
30	WROCLAW	POLAND	54	11	45	110

Ranking Order - Total - Group B

			Visitor Factors	Education and Conservation	Commercial and Organisation	TOTAL ALL ITEMS
	Group B 50 Zoos	**500,000+ visitors**	**108**	**35**	**78**	**221**
31	SOSTO	HUNGARY	61	11	37	109
32	BELFAST	UNITED KINGDOM	63	15	30	108
33	MAGDEBURG	GERMANY	60	11	35	106
34	AMERSFOORT	NETHERLANDS	56	16	33	105
35	AUGSBURG	GERMANY	61	12	30	103
36	KREFELD	GERMANY	52	13	35	100
37	ESKILSTUNA	SWEDEN	57	15	27	99
37	KRONBERG OPEL	GERMANY	48	14	37	99
37	ODENSE	DENMARK	55	7	37	99
37	ROME	ITALY	60	11	28	99
41	TALLINN	ESTONIA	50	12	36	98
42	HELSINKI	FINLAND	45	18	34	97
43	HALLE	GERMANY	58	10	28	96
44	MULHOUSE	FRANCE	48	21	23	92
45	RIGA	LATVIA	43	9	35	87
46	LA FLECHE	FRANCE	59	5	20	84
47	BOJNICE	SLOVAKIA	44	14	25	83
48	BRATISLAVA	SLOVAKIA	40	12	27	79
49	PARIS Menagerie	FRANCE	44	11	23	78
50	LJUBLJANA	SLOVENIA	40	6	30	76

Ranking Order - Visitor Factors

	Group A 30 Zoos	1 million+ visitors	108
1	BERLIN ZOO	GERMANY	87
1	VIENNA	AUSTRIA	87
3	ARNHEM Burgers	NETHERLANDS	84
4	ROTTERDAM	NETHERLANDS	82
5	LEIPZIG	GERMANY	79
5	MÜNCHEN Hellabrunn	GERMANY	79
7	BASEL	SWITZERLAND	78
8	PRAGUE	CZECH REPUBLIC	77
8	ZURICH	SWITZERLAND	77
10	CHESTER	UNITED KINGDOM	76
11	COLOGNE	GERMANY	75
11	HAMBURG Hagenbeck	GERMANY	75
13	BUDAPEST	HUNGARY	74
13	MÜNSTER	GERMANY	74
13	STUTTGART Wilhelma	GERMANY	74
16	DUISBURG	GERMANY	73
17	BERLIN TIERPARK	GERMANY	72
17	EMMEN	NETHERLANDS	72
17	NUREMBERG	GERMANY	72
20	HANOVER	GERMANY	70
21	AMSTERDAM Artis	NETHERLANDS	69
21	COPENHAGEN	DENMARK	69
21	FRANKFURT	GERMANY	69
24	MADRID	SPAIN	67
25	GELSENKIRCHEN	GERMANY	66
26	BARCELONA	SPAIN	64
27	ANTWERP	BELGIUM	63
28	DUBLIN	EIRE	60
29	KARLSRUHE	GERMANY	58
29	ZSL LONDON	UNITED KINGDOM	58

Group B 50 Zoos	500,000+ visitors	
1	ST AIGNAN BEAUVAL	FRANCE	81

	Group B 50 Zoos	500,000+ visitors	
1	ST AIGNAN BEAUVAL	FRANCE	81
2	VALENCIA	SPAIN	76
3	AMNEVILLE	FRANCE	74
4	LISBON	PORTUGAL	73
4	WARSAW	POLAND	73
4	WUPPERTAL	GERMANY	73
7	LA PALMYRE	FRANCE	72
8	KOLMÅRDEN/Tropicarium	SWEDEN	71
9	OSNABRÜCK	GERMANY	68
10	BUSSOLENGO	ITALY	67
10	DOUE LA FONTAINE	FRANCE	67
12	PAIRI DAIZA Paradisio	BELGIUM	66
12	RHENEN	NETHERLANDS	66
14	PLZEN	CZECH REPUBLIC	65
14	ZLIN	CZECH REPUBLIC	65
16	COLCHESTER	UNITED KINGDOM	64
16	DORTMUND	GERMANY	64
16	DRESDEN	GERMANY	64
16	DVUR KRÁLOVÉ	CZECH REPUBLIC	64
16	PAIGNTON	UNITED KINGDOM	64
21	BELFAST	UNITED KINGDOM	63
21	BRISTOL	UNITED KINGDOM	63
21	ZSL WHIPSNADE	UNITED KINGDOM	63
24	AUGSBURG	GERMANY	61
24	HEIDELBERG	GERMANY	61

	Group B 50 Zoos	500,000+ visitors	
24	SOSTO	HUNGARY	61
27	MAGDEBURG	GERMANY	60
27	ROME	ITALY	60
27	ROSTOCK	GERMANY	60
30	LA FLECHE	FRANCE	59
31	HALLE	GERMANY	58
32	ESKILSTUNA	SWEDEN	57
33	AMERSFOORT	NETHERLANDS	56
33	MARWELL	UNITED KINGDOM	56
35	MECHELEN Planckendael	BELGIUM	55
35	ODENSE	DENMARK	55
37	ERFURT	GERMANY	54
37	WROCLAW	POLAND	54
39	EDINBURGH	UNITED KINGDOM	53
40	KREFELD	GERMANY	52
40	TWYCROSS	UNITED KINGDOM	52
42	TALLINN	ESTONIA	50
43	KRONBERG OPEL	GERMANY	48
43	MULHOUSE	FRANCE	48
45	HELSINKI	FINLAND	45
46	BOJNICE	SLOVAKIA	44
46	PARIS Menagerie	FRANCE	44
48	RIGA	LATVIA	43
49	BRATISLAVA	SLOVAKIA	40
49	LJUBLJANA	SLOVENIA	40

Ranking Order - Education and Conservation

	Group A 30 Zoos	1 million+ visitors	35
1	ZSL LONDON	UNITED KINGDOM	33
2	ANTWERP	BELGIUM	32
3	CHESTER	UNITED KINGDOM	31
4	FRANKFURT	GERMANY	30
4	VIENNA	AUSTRIA	30
4	ZURICH	SWITZERLAND	30
7	ROTTERDAM	NETHERLANDS	29
8	AMSTERDAM Artis	NETHERLANDS	26
8	COPENHAGEN	DENMARK	26
10	BARCELONA	SPAIN	25
10	COLOGNE	GERMANY	25
12	MUNICH Hellabrunn	GERMANY	24
12	PRAGUE	CZECH REPUBLIC	24
14	BASEL	SWITZERLAND	23
14	MÜNSTER	GERMANY	23
14	NUREMBERG	GERMANY	23
17	BUDAPEST	HUNGARY	22
17	LEIPZIG	GERMANY	22
19	ARNHEM Burgers	NETHERLANDS	20
19	EMMEN	NETHERLANDS	20
19	HAMBURG Hagenbeck	GERMANY	20
22	HANOVER	GERMANY	19
22	MADRID	SPAIN	19
22	STUTTGART Wilhelma	GERMANY	19
25	DUISBURG	GERMANY	18
26	BERLIN ZOO	GERMANY	17
27	DUBLIN	EIRE	16
27	KARLSRUHE	GERMANY	16
29	BERLIN TIERPARK	GERMANY	14
30	GELSENKIRCHEN	GERMANY	8

Group B 50 Zoos	500,000+ visitors	
1	BRISTOL	UNITED KINGDOM	32
2	PAIGNTON	UNITED KINGDOM	30
3	AMNEVILLE	FRANCE	26
3	ZSL WHIPSNADE	UNITED KINGDOM	26
5	DOUE LA FONTAINE	FRANCE	25
5	ST AIGNAN BEAUVAL	FRANCE	25
7	EDINBURGH	UNITED KINGDOM	24
7	LISBON	PORTUGAL	24
9	COLCHESTER	UNITED KINGDOM	23
9	MARWELL	UNITED KINGDOM	23
11	MECHELEN Planckendael	BELGIUM	22
11	TWYCROSS	UNITED KINGDOM	22
13	MULHOUSE	FRANCE	21
14	HEIDELBERG	GERMANY	20
14	VALENCIA	SPAIN	20
16	BUSSOLENGO	ITALY	19
16	OSNABRÜCK	GERMANY	19
18	HELSINKI	FINLAND	18
18	KOLMÅRDEN/Tropicarium	SWEDEN	18
18	RHENEN	NETHERLANDS	18
18	WUPPERTAL	GERMANY	18
22	DORTMUND	GERMANY	17
23	AMERSFOORT	NETHERLANDS	16
23	DVUR KRÁLOVÉ	CZECH REPUBLIC	16
25	BELFAST	UNITED KINGDOM	15

Group B 50 Zoos	500,000+ visitors	
25	ESKILSTUNA	SWEDEN	15
25	WARSAW	POLAND	15
28	BOJNICE	SLOVAKIA	14
28	KRONBERG OPEL	GERMANY	14
28	LA PALMYRE	FRANCE	14
28	PAIRI DAIZA Paradisio	BELGIUM	14
28	PLZEN	CZECH REPUBLIC	14
28	ROSTOCK	GERMANY	14
34	ERFURT	GERMANY	13
34	KREFELD	GERMANY	13
34	ZLIN	CZECH REPUBLIC	13
37	AUGSBURG	GERMANY	12
37	BRATISLAVA	SLOVAKIA	12
37	TALLINN	ESTONIA	12
40	MAGDEBURG	GERMANY	11
40	PARIS Menagerie	FRANCE	11
40	ROME	ITALY	11
40	SOSTO	HUNGARY	11
40	WROCLAW	POLAND	11
45	DRESDEN	GERMANY	10
45	HALLE	GERMANY	10
47	RIGA	LATVIA	9
48	ODENSE	DENMARK	7
49	LJUBLJANA	SLOVENIA	6
50	LA FLECHE	FRANCE	5

RANKING LISTS

Ranking Order - Commercial and Marketing

	Group A 30 Zoos	1 million+ visitors	78
1	LEIPZIG	GERMANY	70
2	VIENNA	AUSTRIA	69
3	BERLIN ZOO	GERMANY	66
4	ZURICH	SWITZERLAND	64
5	COLOGNE	GERMANY	62
5	HANOVER	GERMANY	62
7	BASEL	SWITZERLAND	61
8	HAMBURG Hagenbeck	GERMANY	60
9	STUTTGART Wilhelma	GERMANY	58
10	ANTWERP	BELGIUM	56
10	COPENHAGEN	DENMARK	56
12	CHESTER	UNITED KINGDOM	55
13	GELSENKIRCHEN	GERMANY	54
13	PRAGUE	CZECH REPUBLIC	54
15	ARNHEM Burgers	NETHERLANDS	53
16	AMSTERDAM Artis	NETHERLANDS	52
16	MÜNSTER	GERMANY	52
16	NUREMBERG	GERMANY	52
19	FRANKFURT	GERMANY	51
19	MUNICH Hellabrunn	GERMANY	51
21	ROTTERDAM	NETHERLANDS	50
22	BERLIN TIERPARK	GERMANY	48
22	BUDAPEST	HUNGARY	48
24	DUISBURG	GERMANY	47
24	KARLSRUHE	GERMANY	47
26	DUBLIN	EIRE	45
26	EMMEN	NETHERLANDS	45
28	ZSL LONDON	UNITED KINGDOM	44
29	BARCELONA	SPAIN	40
30	MADRID	SPAIN	38

Group B 50 Zoos	500,000+ visitors	
1	OSNABRÜCK	GERMANY	51
1	ROSTOCK	GERMANY	51
3	MECHELEN Planckendael	BELGIUM	50
3	PAIRI DAIZA Paradisio	BELGIUM	50
5	DRESDEN	GERMANY	47
6	KOLMÅRDEN/Tropicarium	SWEDEN	45
6	WROCLAW	POLAND	45
8	EDINBURGH	UNITED KINGDOM	44
8	ERFURT	GERMANY	44
10	COLCHESTER	UNITED KINGDOM	43
11	TWYCROSS	UNITED KINGDOM	42
12	WUPPERTAL	GERMANY	41
13	PLZEN	CZECH REPUBLIC	40
14	WARSAW	POLAND	39
15	KRONBERG OPEL	GERMANY	37
15	ODENSE	DENMARK	37
15	SOSTO	HUNGARY	37
15	VALENCIA	SPAIN	37
15	ZSL WHIPSNADE	UNITED KINGDOM	37
20	BUSSOLENGO	ITALY	36
20	HEIDELBERG	GERMANY	36
20	LISBON	PORTUGAL	36
20	PAIGNTON	UNITED KINGDOM	36
20	ST AIGNAN BEAUVAL	FRANCE	36
20	TALLINN	ESTONIA	36

Group B 50 Zoos	500,000+ visitors	
26	AMNEVILLE	FRANCE	35
26	BRISTOL	UNITED KINGDOM	35
26	KREFELD	GERMANY	35
26	MAGDEBURG	GERMANY	35
26	RIGA	LATVIA	35
26	ZLIN	CZECH REPUBLIC	35
32	HELSINKI	FINLAND	34
32	MARWELL	UNITED KINGDOM	34
32	RHENEN	NETHERLANDS	34
35	AMERSFOORT	NETHERLANDS	33
35	DORTMUND	GERMANY	33
35	DVUR KRÁLOVÉ	CZECH REPUBLIC	33
38	AUGSBURG	GERMANY	30
38	BELFAST	UNITED KINGDOM	30
38	LA PALMYRE	FRANCE	30
38	LJUBLJANA	SLOVENIA	30
42	HALLE	GERMANY	28
42	ROME	ITALY	28
44	BRATISLAVA	SLOVAKIA	27
44	ESKILSTUNA	SWEDEN	27
46	BOJNICE	SLOVAKIA	25
47	MULHOUSE	FRANCE	23
47	PARIS Menagerie	FRANCE	23
49	DOUE LA FONTAINE	FRANCE	22
50	LA FLECHE	FRANCE	20

Odense

Rhenen

CHAPTER 14

How Will These Zoos Look in 2020?

In looking ahead, I have asked each Zoo Director about their Master Plan or equivalent, preferably up to 2020. The response has been predominantly positive and encouraging although in a minority of cases zoos have not been able to give a forward view either because no such plan exists or because, if it does, it cannot be disclosed. In any event, circumstances can change and no plans can be considered absolutely fixed for the next ten years.

I have endeavoured to forecast what is likely to happen on the basis of the information I have gathered and taking account of the financial and funding situation at each zoo. This also assumes that there will be no major catastrophe during this decade that would greatly affect zoos' plans.

All zoos need to invest in major new and improved facilities progress momentum in this decade being driven by:

1) The requirement from EU and national legislation to meet new minimum standards under which many species can be kept in zoos.

2) A necessity to remain competitive with other visitor attractions in the area. This may require major new attractions on a regular basis.

3) Pressures of "Friends of the Zoo" and other supporter organisations for improvements, frequently supported by their ability to raise funds.

4) Requests of visitors, often registered in visitor surveys and supported by zoo management, to improve conditions for certain species.

The financing of the new investments will come from many different sources; every zoo is different and will have its own investment funding mix. EU financial assistance is most likely in those countries that joined the EU most recently.

My estimate is that the 80 zoos in this survey will invest in excess of EUR 1.5 billion during 2010-2020 – an average of at least EUR 150 million per year and an average of EUR 18.75 million per zoo over the decade.

Only zoos that have given me sufficient information are included. They are listed in order by country under Group A (25) and then Group B (29) zoos.

Vienna

Following major new openings in 2009-10, Tiergarten Schönbrunn's plans up to 2015 include the renovation and improvement of the Monkey House (which also includes new species such as Colobus Monkeys), followed by much improved and enlarged Polar Bear enclosures, and then the enlargement and remodelling of the Giraffe exhibit. Thereafter, there could be an enlargement of the zoo, possibly to include new exhibits for large European mammal species in natural surroundings and/or an African savannah exhibit. Such an investment programme would keep Vienna at the forefront as a top zoo.

Antwerp

After completion of the present major project for Lions and other species, there will be corresponding improvements for Tigers and Leopards. An even larger investment will be made in developing the recently acquired and demolished 32 residential houses, probably enabling much better provision for the Elephants, Giraffes and Okapis. Monkeys presently without outdoor enclosures are expected to get these facilities. Other present species will also receive improved houses and enclosures. In total, this will be a major transformation of this zoo.

Prague

Work on new Elephant and Hippo Houses and enclosures are due to commence soon. These are likely to be followed by improvements for Polar Bears and indoor and outdoor facilities for the addition of Indian Rhinos. A major new Aviary/Volière is being added. There is adequate space for the addition of further species to an already very good collection.

Copenhagen

Following the walk-through Flamingo Aviary with free fly Flamingos, Ibis and Spoonbills, due to open in 2011, and the exciting Arctic Ring project for Polar Bears, Arctic Bird species and others, due to open in 2012, there may be a pause after several years of major investment. Chimpanzees and Brown Bears are likely to have priority in the next improvement phase, followed by the possible addition of Orang Utans requiring a new house and outdoor enclosure.

Berlin Tierpark

It is too soon to speculate on the details of a new Master Plan for Tierpark due to be released in 2011. There is an immediate programme for renovation and improvement of the Alfred Brehms House from 2012: its separate internal tropical free fly area will be renovated and the big cats are likely to see improvements to their outdoor enclosures. A new South-east Asia House, particularly featuring orang utans and gibbons is expected to be completed by 2014. It is likely that there will be new ideas for future changes and improvements, taking account of the character of the large parkland area ideally suited to mixed species ungulates which would increasingly differentiate Tierpark from Zoo Berlin. There is an appreciation of the need to reduce reliance on subsidies from the City.

Berlin Zoo

For the next 5 years, the renovation and major improvement of the old Bird House is the biggest project, which follows completion of the present improvement project for Orang-utans. Other likely major projects will improve facilities for Rhinos (only one species to remain here)

Berlin

and Tapirs, Bears other than Polar Bears and various small cat species. The Children's Zoo can expect improvements. I would not be surprised to see a new pair of Giant Pandas in a fine new enclosure well before 2020. This zoo always needs to spend large sums on historic buildings and monuments, as it has done recently on Giraffe, Antelope and Zebra houses; the famous entrance gates and restaurant are likely to benefit.

Cologne

Following the opening of the spacious and exciting Hippodom for Hippos and Crocodiles in 2010 to celebrate the Zoo's 150th birthday, a new Master Plan 2020 has been developed and recently publicised; this involves major investment of at least EUR 100 million spread over a probably longer period. The zoo expects to add 1.5 Ha soon. In 2012, there will be a new exhibit for Giant Anteaters. The zoo is gradually to be reorganised into a GEO-Zoo with Africa, Asia and South America being the main areas. Several enclosures are planned for improvement and an African savannah for the Giraffes, Rhinos and Antelopes, combining the present out-door areas for the Giraffes and Impalas, Rhinos and Bison and providing a new Rhino House, possibly using the former Elephant House is anticipated before 2020. Amongst new species additions, the Warthog is likely to have priority. In the longer term, an exciting "KlimArktis" development will include Walruses. Many other exciting new houses are being planned.

Duisburg

Current projects include a new exhibit for Spectacled Bears, possibly to be joined by Coatis, and the new Children's Zoo. Ruffed Lemurs will also be enjoying the excellent walk-through area of the Ring-Tailed Lemurs. The present outlook is for modest non-municipal funds only to be available for investments. Priority is expected to be given to major improvements for apes, baboons and other monkey species, followed by improvements for other species at the zoo. By 2020, it is hoped that additional space will be added for a substantial new European fauna and flora area.

Frankfurt

Following the firm decision a few years ago for Frankfurt Zoo to remain on its present site, a major new development plan is in place. The very fine Borgori Apes House and outdoor enclosures, opened in 2009, and the new exhibit under construction for the Spectacled Bears with a new main entrance are the initial major projects. These are likely to be followed by a new Penguin exhibit and an African savannah including better provision for their Giraffes. By 2020, I would not be surprised to see a new Hippo house and enclosure and a possibly improved Grzimek House. It can reasonably be expected that this zoo will have overcome a considerable backlog of modernisation by 2020.

Hamburg

The exciting and innovative Eismeer project, to be opened in 2012, includes 700m of visitor walkways through a 3-level visitor immersion exhibit with cliff rocks and landscaped Arctic enclosures for Polar Bears, Sea-lions, Walruses (a first amongst the surveyed zoos), King and Humboldt's Penguins and other marine birds. A new Australia House will open in late 2011. Improvements to existing exhibits, including a new Giraffe House, are likely to be the next priorities. Major new developments prior to 2020 may well include the addition of Rhinos, requiring a new House and enclosure, and the opening of a new South America House, which will add further species. This zoo will remain in the forefront of innovative new developments.

Karlsruhe

This zoo has embarked on the biggest investment programme in its history, which will transform Zoo Karlsruhe; most of it should be completed to celebrate the 150th birthday of the zoo and the 300th anniversary of the city of Karlsruhe in 2015 which will coincide with special celebrations in the city. At present, new enclosures are being opened in the Lauterberg sloping area for Snow Leopards, Red Pandas, Coatis and several other species, to be followed by a new African savannah exhibit over several years. The zoo is being substantially extended on the northern side; the former "Tullabad" sports centre is being acquired and will be transformed into the "Exotenhaus" tropical hall which will include Vivarium, Education Centre, Children's Zoo and provision for many existing and new species of mammals, birds, reptiles and amphibians. After 2015, it is planned to build a new Elephant House and enclosure and to improve

Münster

indoor and outdoor facilities for the Lions and Hippos. New exhibits for Camels, Gazelles and other mammals may well be included. These are exciting times at Zoo Karlsruhe following on from the major developments for Polar Bears, Sea-lions and Penguins in recent years!

Leipzig

The opening of the eagerly awaited 1.65 Ha Tropical Hall, Gondwanaland, in mid-2011 will be a further milestone in the zoo's wonderful recent history. This will add a further 40 species, including Pygmy Hippos, Komodo Dragons, Tapirs and Servals. The visitor experience in this EUR 67 million development will be unique and will include an indoor boat journey in the tropics. Further investment is planned to complete by end 2015 the "Zoo of the Future" with its 6 themed areas described in detail in Chapter 10.

Münster

Top priority is being given to investment in an Elephant Park and accommodation for a bull Elephant to establish a breeding group with completion scheduled by 2014. Major improvements for the zoo's Giraffes and Lions are expected to follow, whilst earlier priority is being given to the Leopards. After 2015, one can expect a new Tropical Hall to be planned with opening before 2020.

Munich

The GEO-Zoo concept, which started here, is fundamental to the new plans for major improvements. Major investment is planned, commencing with the new Humboldt's Penguin exhibit to be opened early in 2011 and extending to the King Penguins in the Polarium the following year. Small clawed Otters are to be added. Improvements to the Children's Zoo and Aquarium are also planned. The next phase will concentrate on improvements for the Giraffes which are to be relocated to a new House and savannah enclosure near the Isar Gate: here they will be joined by the Zebras and African Antelope species. The space vacated in the Elephant House when the Giraffes are relocated will provide a major improvement for the zoo's Elephants. Thereafter, improvements for the Rhinos, who will become sole occupants of their house, and for the Tapirs, who will require a new house, are likely to be priorities. I would expect all of these improvements to take place by 2016 and for further exciting additions and improvements to follow thereafter.

Nuremberg

The large and exciting Laguna (Dolphins/Manatees) project, due to open in summer 2011, will include a second Sea-Lion exhibit, a Butterfly House and some important mammal additions as well as new catering and events facilities. Thereafter, due to the cost of this project, smaller projects such as for Spectacled Bears and Polecats, as well as improvements to the Giraffe House, are planned to follow. I anticipate that, before 2020, a new Elephant House will have opened with a large Africa savannah area, including opportunities for Elephants and Rhinos to bathe and mix with other species, stretching back to the present Giraffe and Zebra outdoor enclosures. With all this is in place, Tierpark Nürnberg would be a truly fantastic visitor attraction.

How Will These Zoos Look in 2020?

Stuttgart

Wilhelma's Master Plan concentrates on major improvements for existing species, better organisation as a GEO-Zoo, and collection priority for endangered species. The ambitious development programme envisages opening the new Gorilla and Bonobo exhibit in 2012, followed by a remodelling of the present Apes House to give much improved facilities for the Orang-Utans and Gibbons. The present Elephant enclosure for the 3 elderly female Elephants is to be improved before the major new project for a new Elephant House and much larger enclosure for an elephant herd, possibly during 2013-15. A new Indian Rhino exhibit, using the present Elephant enclosures, will follow. Other species likely to receive new or improved facilities by 2020 include Lions, Leopards, Drills, Lemurs and Tapirs. Such a programme would transform and update Wilhelma.

Budapest

Many historic buildings have been beautifully restored and improved in 2010, including the old Giraffe House, old Buffalo House and what is now the Australia House. Planned additions to the collection include Okapis in the old Giraffe House and Koalas in the Australia House. The major "Magic Mountain" project, providing a Magic of Life exhibit, a Museum and an interactive live Science exhibition, will open in 2011. The Zoo plans to acquire the neighbouring 6.5 Ha Amusement Park which will eventually increase the zoo's area to over 17 Ha. First priority will then be given to a new Elephant Park for a breeding herd. Many other improvements are planned to ensure that Budapest Zoo remains amongst the best in Europe.

Amsterdam

Artis, which is in the process of implementing its 10-year Master Plan, has the largest current investment programme of the Dutch zoos in this survey. The re-opening of the remodelled historic Ape and Bird Houses will take place in mid-2011 with walkthrough exhibits. The reconstructed Pheasantry Volière will also open in 2011. Major new developments planned to be completed by 2015 include a new Jaguar exhibit, dual and enlarged facilities for two separate Gorilla groups, Penguin underwater viewing, major redevelopment of house and enclosures for Lions and other feline species, followed by the biggest project, the new Elephant House and enclosure for a breeding Elephant herd in the new 1.7 Ha zoo extension. By 2020, Artis' aim of having innovative and modern facilities for its animals, whilst retaining its 19th century foundation monuments, should be realised.

Arnhem

The financial crisis has delayed the opening of another eagerly awaited innovative major exhibit at Burgers' Zoo, which will celebrate its centenary in 2013. The slightly delayed project, which may well open in 2015, can be expected to concentrate on Arctic species including Polar Bears. I also expect to see the return to the collection of much loved Orang-Utans in an exciting new house and enclosure.

114

Emmen

Emmen

This zoo, which was renowned for its innovative exhibits in the 1990s, is in transition due to the plans to move the entire zoo to the Es site on the edge of the city. At least EUR 200 million is required to implement the very ambitious and exciting project, the go-ahead for which depends on Emmen City's ability to raise sufficient funding. A decision is expected later in 2011. The present city centre site will be used at least until 2015; at least one new exhibit, commencing with Lions in 2011, should be opened each year until then.

If the zoo does relocate, the plan is to build and develop an entirely new zoo that would again be sufficiently different and innovative to attract very large numbers of visitors from long distances. It would be organised in climatic zones – tropical, desert, arctic – and have adventurous and exciting exhibits including, at the outset, a very large Tropical Hall housing, amongst others, Elephants and Orang-Utans, both of which would have very interesting outdoor facilities accessed by visitors in various ways. The new zoo would concentrate on visitor immersion of animals in natural surroundings. High mature trees and expensive vegetation would be part of the zoo on this presently rather open site. The plans indicate a very interesting and attractive visitor experience.

Barcelona

The Spanish financial crisis has directly affected this municipal zoo, and the timing of implementation of its Master Plan. In the short term, new Volières for birds of prey are to be added and concentration on enlarging the collection of Sahel species.

The key to implementation of the Master Plan is the availability of the new separate 5 Ha site for marine species, which will involve the transfer of dolphins, sea-lions and other species. The space vacated on the zoo site, together with an extra 3 Ha will enable the zoo to reorganise into 3 main GEO areas (Africa, Asia, South America) and gradually make the necessary improvements to existing exhibits. The excellent vegetation would be used to develop forest type enclosures. Priority will be given to a new Elephant House and enclosure for a breeding group of Elephants. The next main development will be an African savannah for a large mixed species exhibit.

It is impossible to give a timetable at present for funding availability. I would expect part of the above to be open before 2020 and many minor improvements to be made in the next few years. Full implementation would transform this zoo. Both the zoo and the planned marine site will remain under the same ownership and management.

Madrid

Plans are in place for an increased annual investment in new and improved facilities for the next 3 years. Following the 2009 covered enlargement to the elephant enclosure, a major extension to both the Elephant House and enclosure will take place in 2012-13 to provide for a breeding group. The present Master Plan also provides for a new Hippo House and a new Chimpanzee House with visitor entry. An extended Children's Zoo and further much needed improvements to the Bears' enclosures should be completed by 2013. Amongst several new species, it is planned to add Giant Otters to the collection. By 2020, this zoo should be very greatly improved.

Basel

Basel Zoo has a Master Plan to 2020. This zoo has solid independent financial backing, enabling it to make realistic and realisable plans for major investment projects within given timescales. Presently, the "Zolli" is redeveloping and improving the enclosures for the Gorillas, Orang-utans and Chimps; this very large project will provide excellent outdoor enclosures with viewing through panoramic windows. As usual for this zoo, the limited ground area is to be very well used with a multi-storey exhibit with new enclosures for Squirrel, Spider and Howler Monkeys on the top level. This exciting exhibit is to open in 2012.

Thereafter, priority will be given to larger facilities for their Elephants and Hippos, which will also involve an additional 1 Ha for the zoo. It would not be a big surprise if, by 2020, Giant Pandas appeared here, especially if China continues to increase its captive population of these animals. In any event, the "Zolli" will remain in the forefront of the leading European zoos.

Zurich

Zürich Zoo has a Master Plan to 2020 and, like Basel, has very solid financial backing to realise its ambitious plans. Today, the Pantanal, the new South America exhibit, is under construction and due to open early in 2012. The new House and 2Ha of enclosures will provide superb accommodation for Giant Anteaters, Tapirs, Capybaras and Squirrel Monkeys. Flamingos will also feature, with a substantial lake included. The next major project will be for a new Penguin exhibit near the main entrance, opening in 2013. The largest new investment will be in the new Elephant Park and House for a breeding herd; this will rival the best in Europe and is due to open in 2014. There will also be a new hoofstock exhibit.

Zurich

The renovation and improvement of the Aquarium is expected by 2016. Thereafter, the major project is for a new African savannah which will include the greatly missed Giraffes with a new house, living together with Rhinos, Zebras and various Antelopes. By 2020, Zürich Zoo will be at the very forefront of our zoos.

Chester

As part of its revised Master Plan, which it hopes to implement during 2014-2024, Chester Zoo is exploring a new zonal approach. The intention is to create bold, immersive environments that link the zoo's conservation programmes to a range of animal species in natural landscapes. There is a single common theme in this approach.

The first such zone, known as "Endangered Islands", will feature the delicate habitats and diverse ecosystems of Madagascar, the Mascarenes, the Philippines and possibly other island groups. This exciting exhibit, which will comprise a series of show houses and will include a boat ride and underwater viewing, is scheduled to open in 2014. Projected species include both species of Orang-utans, Sumatran Tigers, Komodo Dragons, several Lemur species, Macaques and Crocodiles. A further large zonal exhibit is likely to follow before 2020.

In addition, a "Cheshire heritage" zone, with linked attractions including native wildlife areas, will be developed around the beautiful 19th century manor house in the zoo.

Planckendael

The major new exhibit under construction is the 3Ha Elephant House and enclosure for a new breeding herd of Asian Elephants, linked to Kerala (India), with visitor walk-through, due to open in 2012. A new exhibit for Humboldt's Penguins is due to open in 2013. Meanwhile, the recently opened (2008) African savannah is developing further. There are plans for further species additions with mixed species exhibits wherever possible.

Pairi Daiza

This zoo, previously Parc Paradisio, was founded as a Bird Park in 1994. Whilst it retains an outstanding bird collection and exhibits, it is rapidly developing into a comprehensive zoo.

The new Australasia area, including Kangaroo and large Volière walk-throughs, will open in 2011, together with Phase 1 of the new Africa area, adding Cheetahs and Colobus Monkeys to the collection. Phases 2 and 3 will follow within 3 years and will include a new Elephant House and enclosure, improved Hippo House and add Lions, Rhinos, Crocodiles and various antelope species to the collection. Other new exhibits during 2011-12 include Chinese Alligators in the splendid Chinese area of the zoo, and Coastal Encounter for Flamingos and sea birds. Longer term plans include "The Great North" Arctic exhibit.

This is a truly exciting development phase in an unusual zoo which showcases animals in their human cultural setting.

Plzen

Following the opening of major new African and Asian exhibits, covering 25% of the zoo's area in 2010, this zoo is likely to develop further before 2020. The major new project, involving a 13.5 Ha extension to the zoo site, is the South-east Asia project which provides for a new Elephant House, adding Indonesian Elephants together with Orang-utans and other Indonesian species. Visitors would view these species from boats in appropriate surroundings. This will be the crowning achievement of the zoo and fulfil the dreams of the Director before 2020.

Zlin

First priority for this zoo, in order to fulfil its Master Plan, is the acquisition of 15 Ha of neighbouring land to develop the zoo as a GEO-Zoo. Ethiopia Phase 1 for Gelada Baboons, Hyrax and Bird Volière opens in 2011. Phase 2 for Greater Kudu, Striped Hyena, Meerkats and other species is due to open in 2013. This will be followed by a Stingray exhibit and a new walk-through exhibit "Tonle Sap" for South-east Asian mammals and birds, due to open in 2015. In the following 5 years, I would expect major new investment in an Aquarium, Hippo exhibit and a new large African savannah area. This zoo's development is particularly encouraging, considering its low population catchment area.

Odense

This zoo has made good progress recently, especially with the impressive Oceanium including Penguin House, Tropical House and Kiwara developments. The present 5-year plan to 2013 includes a new African savannah, Fishbone Bay for marine species, and a major active learning Science Zoo to be built on municipally owned land adjoining the zoo. There is sufficient land to enable the zoo to add major species, requested by the visitors, particularly Elephants and Bears.

Odense

Tallinn

Implementation of the zoo's Master Plan has been relatively slow, particularly during the financial crisis. Following the opening of the Elephant House for pachyderms in 2008, new Snow Leopard and Amur Tiger exhibits have been opened. A major project, to begin as soon as funding is available, is a new 7 Ha African savannah. It will include a new Giraffe House and will also accommodate Zebras, Kudus and other antelope species. Also planned are a new Polar Bear enclosure and improved enclosures for Brown Bears, Wolves and several monkey species. I would expect all of these to be opened by 2020, together with the new Main Entrance building including a new Zoo School, conference centre, restaurant and offices.

Amneville

This zoo opens a significant new exhibit every year and has detailed plans for the next 5 years. The new larger Humboldt's Penguins exhibit opened in 2011 and will be followed by the new South America House, including the addition of Giant Anteaters to the collection, also in 2011. The next major project, which involves an additional 1 Ha, is a new Gorilla House, based on the ideas of the recently opened Orang-utan House, with 3 outdoor enclosures. This is to be followed by the new Kodiak Bear exhibit and improvements for the Brown Bears and Children's Zoo. By 2016, it is expected that Komodo Dragons will be added to the impressive reptile collection in a new Vivarium. Amnéville will remain amongst the top zoos in France.

La Fleche

Following the recent addition of Giant Anteaters, new exhibits for Ocelots, White Lions, and African and South American mixed species exhibits, and the opening of "Nocturama", the zoo's Master Plan provides for considerable investment in improved facilities for existing animals, including the breeding group of Giraffes in a new mixed species African savannah. A new addition will be White Rhinos and a new Vivarium. A hotel is to be built.

Dortmund

Whilst funding for new investments remains very limited at present, there are ambitious plans for further improvements to this zoo. Following several significant projects in the past 3 years, including the new Clouded Leopard exhibits, the zoo is currently building new facilities for Gaurs and Amur Leopards and in the Children's Zoo. The major projects likely to open in the next few years are a new House and facilities for the zoo's logo species, the Giant Anteater, and a large new Sea-lion exhibit possibly with other aquatic species.

Dresden

This zoo has developed well in the past 5 years and is likely to continue to do so, given the support of the City Council. However, it requires additional land from the neighbouring Grosser Garten municipal park and this is difficult.

Dresden Zoo is awaiting availability of Koalas for its 2010 opened Prof-Brandes House. A new Snow Leopard exhibit opens in 2011, to be followed by a new Patagonia exhibit and Black Bears in 2012-13. The old monkey house will be replaced to provide new accommodation for monkey species. The Orang-utan House will be replaced and, in the longer term, it is hoped that Gorillas will be added to the collection. More outdoor enclosure space for the Elephants is also required when more zoo space becomes available. All of the above could be completed by 2020.

Dortmund

Erfurt

This zoo has developed well recently and has an ambitious Master Plan for the next 5+ years. The major project, due to commence in 2011 to open in 2013 is the new Elephant House with nearly 2 Ha enclosure, suitable for a breeding group. The African savannah, partly opened in 2010, should be completed by 2012. Meanwhile, a walk-through Lemur exhibits and improved facilities for Siamangs and Cheetahs are planned for 2011-12. Thereafter, the old Elephant House will be converted for use by Giraffes and Zebras. Major improvements are planned for the reptile and nocturnal areas of this same house. It is hoped to add Giant Anteaters to the recently opened South America Pampas area. The big project towards 2020 is a large new Tropical Hall, to be located opposite the Kangaroo exhibits, with a separate roadside public entrance. This zoo on an exciting site is scheduled to become amongst the leading German zoos.

Heidelberg

Following the opening in 2010 of the admirable new Elephant House and enclosure, there are several smaller improvements and exhibits scheduled for 2011 including Small-clawed Otters and Binturongs and a new Aqua Terrarium for Madagascan species in the Africa House. New aviaries will house existing and new species. Also, the Chimpanzees' new outdoor enclosure will open before 2012. In 2012, the new Lion enclosure and a large new enclosure for Meerkats and Porcupines will open.

Major new projects from 2013 will include a new enclosure for Gorillas and an African savannah, depending on availability of the extra 2.5 Ha promised for the zoo. This major new development will include a Giraffe House and make provision for Zebras and several Antelope species. By 2020, I anticipate seeing Crocodiles added to the collection.

Kronberg

The building of the new Elephant House at the Opel-Zoo will commence in 2011 and should be open, with improved enclosure, in 2012; this exciting development will accommodate a breeding group and be of great interest to the greater Frankfurt area. During the following years, an improved Hippo facility will be built and Rhinos are expected to be added to the collection. Improvements for other species are also planned. This decade will be a milestone for the Opel-Zoo.

Magdeburg

There has been considerable new development in implementation of the Master Plan "Vision 2006+" during the past 2 years, commencing with the impressive spacious multifunctional entrance building (2009) followed by the Amazon House (2009) and Africambo 1 (2010). The African savannah area is being completed. The next main project is renovation of the Apes House and provision of an outdoor Chimpanzees' enclosure. Gorillas might be added to the collection at that time. The biggest project in the zoo's history will be Africambo 2, which will include a new Elephant House and enclosure, suitable for a breeding group, and uniquely a mixed exhibit of Rhinos and Colobus Monkeys. These should all be opened by end of 2015. Thereafter, the zoo is likely to increase its collection steadily and to improve enclosures for existing species. By 2020, this zoo will be transformed.

Osnabrück

Following the opening of Takamanda (2010), the zoo's 75th anniversary in 2011 will be marked by the opening of the Taiga project for Polar/Mixed Bears, Bison, Wolves, Lynx, Raccoons, Wolverines and Silver Foxes in a 1.5 Ha new exhibit. Pig-tailed Macaques will also enjoy a new exhibit in 2011. Thereafter, a major new North America area, together with Bird and Owl Volières, will be developed 2013-17, followed by a new South-east Asia exhibit, including Tigers and Gibbons, to be completed by 2020. This zoo goes from strength to strength.

Rostock

The Master Plan 2020 envisages a major transformation in this zoo. A new Wapiti exhibit will open in 2011. Work has started on the ground-breaking Darwineum project, which will be by far the biggest in the zoo's history, and will open in 2012-13. This exciting project will provide generous space inside and outside for large breeding groups of Gorillas and Orang-utans, accompanied by Gibbons, and accommodate other monkey species, Ring-Tailed Lemurs, Giant Tortoises and various bird and reptile species. Educational and service facilities will be included. Thereafter, priority will be given to new Polar Bear enclosures, the long awaited addition of Giraffes with a new house and Amur Tigers. With all this in place by 2020, Rostock will become a major European zoo.

Wuppertal

Wuppertal

Following major improvements and exciting new openings in recent years, the zoo is constrained by the well-publicised financial problems of the city. The investment plans to 2013 envisage major improvements to the Okapi house and enclosures, new outside enclosure for the Bonobos and a new Volière. The Polar Bears' exhibit is to be substantially enlarged and improved and a major project for the fine small cat species will follow.

Sosto

Following on from the zoo's milestone opening in 2010 of the Indonesian tropical house, the Gorilla exhibit and the African Savannah, a new Australia exhibit will open in 2011. Thereafter, the immediate priorities are to improve many exhibits and to establish breeding groups wherever possible. It is hoped that much larger visitor numbers can be attracted through the new indoor facilities and having all year opening. More indoor facilities are planned, including a Tropical Bird House, South America House and Butterfly House, all of which should be open by 2020. The collection will continue to expand with the planned addition of Black Rhinos – the third Rhino species here – and Spectacled Bears. This zoo is steadily raising its European profile.

Bussolengo

Italy's leading zoo has ambitious plans; following the considerable improvements and investments in 2010, the adjacent safari park should be fully integrated with the zoo by 2013. The reorganisation into GEO-Zones will continue. Priority will be given to building new indoor facilities to enable the zoo to offer all year opening. Initially, I expect the new Chimpanzees' House, open to visitors, will appear within two years, possibly including space for Gorillas which the Zoo intends to add to its collection. Other additions in the longer term could include Koalas, Komodo Dragons and Okapis, all of which will require indoor accommodation. By 2020, I expect to see more of the missing popular species, including Penguins, Giant and Small clawed Otters, and Giant Anteaters. This zoo will become an increasingly popular visitor attraction, not least for the millions of tourist visitors to Verona and Lake Garda.

Rome

Significant investment is now taking place and Bioparco's strategic plan for 10 years is in place. There is a large backlog of improvements to be made. During 2011-12, new areas for Gibbons and Tamarins are being built and the Orang-utans' and Mangabeys' enclosures are to be modernised and extended. Sea Lions and Penguins will also benefit from new investment. Major projects to follow include a new Aquarium and complete renovation of several historic buildings including Tigers' House and ex-Egyptian House for elephants. Investment has increased to at least EUR 7 million annually. On this basis, Rome Zoo should be making steady and significant progress.

Riga

The financial crisis, which has hit Latvia particularly hard, has delayed the zoo's major project, planned to be open for the zoo's centenary in 2012 but now more likely in 2013-14; this is a new Elephant House and enclosure, enabling Elephants to return after a 10-year absence at Riga Zoo. A project to complete the African savannah, with indoor facilities for Zebras, Antelopes and Ostriches, is more likely to be opened in 2012. There are plans to invest in major improvements to some very poor exhibits, such as Bears and Hippos. I believe that all of these vital projects will have been completed before 2020, thereby making this a much more interesting and attractive zoo.

Amersfoort

The new Master Plan is being finalised with improved enclosures for Chimpanzees taking priority in the immediate future. The zoo will continue to develop its distinctive character. Before 2020, there will be several major developments, probably including an unusual themed Indonesian House incorporating strong educational and adventure components as well as adding Komodo Dragons and other interesting species. There is also likely to be a large European mammals' exhibit in an unusual immersion exhibit.

Warsaw

In recent years, this zoo has improved greatly with substantial investments having been made in new Apes and Hippo houses since 2008. Up to 2013, there will be a new rehabilitation

Warsaw

centre for wild birds, a CITES reptile centre and a Paludarium added to the collection. Further ahead, Warsaw Zoo intends to open an African savannah to bring together their Giraffes, Zebras, Antelopes and Ostriches, to build an Oceanarium and to provide new enclosures for various species, including Polar and Brown Bears. The longer term project is to build a Butterfly House.

Wroclaw

Wroclaw is starting work now on the largest investment ever made in a Polish zoo, namely the Africarium/Oceanarium, due to open in 2014. This ground breaking project, amongst the very largest in Europe, will include a tropical hall of 14,000 m2. Various African ecosystems will be zoned and house many species including Nile Hippos and Crocodiles, Sharks, South African Seals and Penguins, Manatees, Talapoin Monkeys and Aardvarks.

The Zoo plans to add 5 Ha soon to develop an African savannah. In 2011-12, Red Pandas are being added and Squirrel Monkeys will have a moated island exhibit. Thereafter, Indian species including Rhinos, Langurs and Muntjacs will be added. In the longer term and probably before 2020, the major project will incorporate a boat ride in a South-east Asian outdoor exhibit including Elephants and Gibbons. This zoo has great plans and an exciting future.

Bojnice

This year, the Zoo will commence work on the EUR 8 million programme to improve infrastructure to enable the zoo to progress significantly with its animal houses and enclosures. This initial work also includes a new environmental education centre and signage and other information being modernised. Thereafter, the zoo's priorities, likely to be in place by 2020, include a new Carnivores House and major improvements to the Elephant House and outdoor enclosure. New facilities for Brown Bears and other large European mammals are also to be expected. Major Government financial restrictions are delaying much needed investment.

Bratislava

Following the opening of the impressive new Apes House in 2010, the old Chimpanzee/Gibbon House is due to be reconstructed this year so as to accommodate the Chimpanzees, temporarily housed in the new Apes House. Then, Gorillas can be introduced into the new Apes House and Gibbons can join the Orang-utans already there.

Subject to the present severe financial situation easing, the planned new Africa complex, including a new Giraffe House and a savannah for Giraffes, Rhinos, Zebras and Antelopes, should follow. The largest project likely to be completed by 2020 is a new Elephant House and enclosure. Before then, many improvements to the present exhibits will have taken place.

Ljubljana

A very ambitious Master Plan was completed in late 2007 but lack of funding has prevented any of this being implemented. The plan provides for a complete transformation of the zoo into 6 GEO-Zones and service areas, involving the addition of an extra 15 Ha of adjoining land; it would enable the zoo to meet EU standards and provide for larger, mixed species, exhibits. Species to be added to the present collection include Rhinos, Meerkats, Coatis, Penguins, Crocodiles and Flamingos. Subject to funding, the Plan could be fully implemented within 6 years. At present, it seems that a first phase may commence in the near future and much can be expected to be open to visitors by 2020.

Bristol

Bristol Zoo has Master Plans, involving large investments, for each of its two sites – Bristol Zoo Gardens (BZG) and National Wildlife Conservation Park (NWCP)
The BZG Master Plan provides for its limited site to be developed into 3 main zones – tropical forest, mountain and riverine – which will accommodate largely existing species in exciting new exhibits, focussing on visitor engagement with environmental and conservation issues. The Gorilla House will be modified to only house Gorillas. All of these changes can be expected to be completed by 2020.
The NWCP, a 55 Ha site, is located about 10 km from BZG. Development planning permission has been granted to implement the Master Plan which provides for various habitat areas – forest, savannah and grassland – representative of Africa, Asia and Latin America, and a few major indoor exhibits. It is planned to introduce large mammal species absent from BZG. At present, funding is being sought; given the foreseeable financial situation, it is likely that only an initial phase of the ambitious Master Plan will be in place before 2020 but this could easily change!

Twycross

Following the opening of "Himalaya", including its Snow Leopards, and of "Uda Walawa" and its new Asian Elephant enclosure in 2010, Twycross Zoo is planning to continue to invest large sums in new and improved exhibits over the next 5 years. These include a new Chimpanzee House with enclosures to bring together the various Chimpanzee groups in the zoo, a large new exhibit for Lions and Hyenas, a new Giraffe enclosure, a replacement Elephant House to include Bull's accommodation, and completion of the waterways project. Longer term, one can expect further species additions, including Tigers, and improvements to many of the present enclosures. By 2020, the zoo will have implemented much of its Master Plan and visitor numbers are expected to increase very substantially.

Conclusion

The second decade of this century will definitely witness a further great improvement in Europe's leading zoological gardens. These further advances should increase the effectiveness of these organisations as education and conservation platforms: they should counter the anti-zoo lobby and further awaken Europe's citizens to the enormous threats to biodiversity in the wild.

CHAPTER 15

Other European Zoos of Special Significance

Introduction

The 80 zoos in my survey meet carefully stated requirements. There are a further 200 + zoos within EAZA and many more not meeting EAZA requirements.

Amongst those within EAZA, there are some smaller, highly specialised, zoos of major importance to the European zoo community due to their renowned breeding, education and conservation reputations. I have selected five of these for special mention and inclusion in this book. They all breed and supply rare species to other European zoos. All five zoos are privately owned and all are worth a visit. All of these zoos, except Apenheul, are open throughout the year.

Nordens Ark, Sweden

100,000+ visitors   www.nordensark.se

Situated in beautiful and dramatic Swedish west coast scenery 120 km north of Gothenburg, this zoo specialises in threatened species from Nordic climate zones. The zoo occupies a fraction of the 380 Ha estate, comprising forest, rocky hillsides and lakes, and is owned by a non-profit conservation foundation, established in 1988 and supported by the Swedish royal family. Apart from the wetland house with its tropical amphibian collection, there are few formal animal houses; animal shelters are provided in large natural enclosures. The limited range of mammals includes Amur Tigers and Leopards, Snow Leopards, Red Pandas, Przewalski Horses, Maned Wolves and European carnivores. Various birds of prey, including those re-introduced in Sweden from here, are amongst the 90 species in the zoo.

This zoo enjoys a very high reputation in the zoo world, particularly for its research, conservation and education work. It has its own hotel and conference centre.

Durrell Wildlife Conservation Trust, Jersey Zoo, Jersey

100,000+ visitors   www.durrell.org

Situated in the largest of the Channel Islands, this zoo is identified with the late Gerald Durrell and his tireless conservation efforts. It is primarily a conservation centre, specialising in highly endangered species living in tropical islands and highlands, being involved in active re-introduction where possible. Islands particularly associated with Durrell projects include Madagascar, Mauritius, St. Lucia and Montserrat.

The zoo occupies 17 Ha of varied landscaped parkland and water gardens with wooded areas. The limited range of larger mammals amongst the 28 exhibited species include Orang Utans, Gorillas, Gibbons, Macaques, Lemurs and Maned Wolves. There are over 100 species of birds, reptiles and amphibians. Major exhibits are Jewels of the Forest (Asian birds), Cloud Forest (South American mixed species), Gaherty Reptile and Amphibian Centre, Kirundy Forest (Madagascar), Central Valley and Discovery Desert. The Tamarins and Marmosets, some of which are free in a small wooded area, and the Orang utans and Gibbons in their spacious and well designed outdoor enclosures, are particularly memorable. Guided Tours and Animal Talks are of the highest order. Durrell's Organic Farm, established in 1976, provide the animals with chemical free foods.

OTHER EUROPEAN ZOOS

Howletts and Port Lympne Wild Animal Parks, England UK

230,000+ visitors and 170,000+ visitors   www.totallywild.net

Situated in Kent, South-east England, these associated zoos belong to the Aspinall family, having been founded by the late John Aspinall. They are dedicated primarily to conservation work, particularly in Java, Gabon, DRC Congo and Madagascar. John Aspinall's dream was to own a park where wild animals would be protected, bred and returned to safe areas in the wild; this was realised with the acquisition of Howletts (40 Ha) and Port Lympne (160 Ha). Enclosures in both zoos are large but there are few indoor facilities.

Howletts, with 52 mammal species, specialises in primates, felids and African Elephants and is renowned for its Gorillas with the largest collection in Europe, supplying many other zoos from its successfully breeding groups as well as reintroducing them into Gabon and elsewhere. Javan Leopards and Langurs, and Clouded Leopards are other unusual strengths. The site is generally flat with some fine mature trees.

Port Lympne, situated near the coast, is partly open hillside and partly wooded with a manor house and extensive flower gardens. It has a fine safari park area, concentrating on African hoofstock, which is visited with guides in covered safari vehicles. The 73 mammal species include Rothschild's Giraffes, Grants Zebras, Black Rhino, African Elephants, Barbary Lions, Amur Tigers, Gorillas and many antelope species.

These are not zoological gardens, but are very worthwhile visiting and are highly regarded within the zoo community for their strengths in many threatened mammal species.

Weltvogelpark Walsrode, Germany

350,000+ visitors   www.weltvogelpark.de

Situated to the north of Hanover in the Lüneberger heathlands, this world famous Bird Park has over 4000 birds of 700 species, several of them not to be seen elsewhere. Walsrode sets the standards for breeding birds in Europe, holds most of the European Studbooks and supplies most of the zoos in this survey. It houses birds from all climate zones and all continents. Walsrode is heavily involved in many bird conservation projects, particularly in Madagascar.

The zoo, which has only a few non-bird species, occupies a delightful 36 Ha site, also renowned for its rhododendron, azalea and other flowering shrub gardens, with landscaped areas including many mature deciduous trees.

Indoor houses include the fine Taman Burong (Indonesia) House, in which a great variety of tropical birds fly amongst delightful vegetation, and the Lori House with 40 species in lush tropical vegetation .Other indoor exhibits include an extensive range of African birds. There is a strong link with the Bali Bird Park. A very large indoor enclosure is used in summer for bird shows and demonstrations. Particular attractions include Penguins, Pelicans, Shoebills and Scarlet Ibis (50% of Europe's zoos have stock of this species from here).

This is a must-see zoo for all bird enthusiasts and the vegetation is truly beautiful too. It is likely to develop further under its new owners.

Apenheul Primate Park, Netherlands

400,000+ visitors   www.apenheul.nl

Situated near Apeldoorn, 80 km east of Amsterdam, Apenheul – literally Apes' home or safe haven – is a unique zoo, famous for its wonderful collection and breeding record of apes, monkeys and lemurs. Established in 1971, Apenheul was the first zoo to create large scale walk through areas with South American monkeys. The 46 species of mammals, most of which are primates live in a 12 Ha wooded park area. The monkeys are either free to roam and mingle with visitors or live on moated wooded islands;, they can choose between interaction with visitors, who are not allowed to feed or pet them, or take refuge and forage in their forest trees. The monkeys have the choice of initiating contact and patient visitors can expect some of the 100 squirrel monkeys to jump on their shoulders.

Apenheul is famous for its social groups of Lowland Gorillas, Orang utans and Bonobos and successfully breeds these species. The Orang utans exhibit, opened in 1999, is unique in occupying 4 islands with hundreds of posts of tree trunks and 10 km of ropes and nets. Together with six indoor rooms, the islands interconnect giving the Orang utans different exploration routes. The gorilla troop is one of the largest in European zoos and lives on a spacious wooded island. Visitors can watch from a grandstand the natural behaviour of these apes and listen to regular commentaries by the keepers. The Apenheul commitment to in-situ conservation and high standards of animal welfare is visible throughout the park.

This zoo is closed between November and March.

Beauval

Beauval

CHAPTER 16

Sub-Regional and National Zoo Associations

Introduction

EAZA (European Association of Zoos and Aquaria), whose headquarters are in Amsterdam, is the regional association of over 300 collections to which all of the zoological gardens in this survey belong. EAZA, with a significant administrative staffing, promotes co-operation for furthering regional collection planning and wildlife conservation, particularly through EEPs (see Chapter 6), and education. EAZA contributes to international meetings and discussions and advises, as required, the European Union and other European representative committees and organisations.

All sub-regional and national associations, referred to in this chapter, belong to EAZA, and appoint representatives of their countries to the EAZA Council. Zoos can only become members of EAZA after a thorough screening procedure including inspections.

Whilst EAZA has begun to include collections in non-European countries, such as Israel, UAE and Kazahstan, references in this book refer only to European zoological gardens.

www.eaza.net

National and Sub-regional Associations

The two largest organisations to which over 50 % of the 80 zoos belong are BIAZA and VDZ. In this survey, out of 80 Zoos, 30 are members of VDZ (17 Group A and 13 Group B) and 11 are members of BIAZA (3 Group A and 8 Group B).

BIAZA (British + Irish Association of Zoos and Aquariums)

BIAZA is the professional organisation representing the zoo and aquarium community in Britain and Ireland. Founded in 1966, it is a conservation, education and scientific wildlife charity, with about 100 full members, including almost all of the significant zoos and aquariums. Its HQ is at ZSL London Zoo, and has a full time Executive Director, Dr. Miranda Stevenson, and assisting staff. Its aims are to lead and support its members to:

- Inspire people to help conserve the natural world
- Participate in effective co-operative conservation programmes
- Deliver the highest quality environmental education, training and research
- Achieve the highest standards of animal care and welfare in zoos, aquariums and in the wild

Its membership includes many associate members connected with the zoo and aquarium community. Visitors to all of these institutions total around 24 million annually, of which nearly 8 million visit the 11 zoos in this survey.

BIAZA Council consists of 18 members from different collections, and 4 main committees. An annual meeting, held at different members' locations, and several conferences are organised by BIAZA each year. A comprehensive annual report and quarterly magazine are published. Awards in several categories are presented to members in recognition of their achievements. BIAZA is active in promoting member interests to and liaising with UK Government departments, in particular the Department for Environment, Food and Rural Affairs (DEFRA) and directly with politicians, including an annual Parliamentary reception with members and guests.

www.biaza.org.uk

VDZ (Verband Deutscher Zoodirektoren e. V.)

The VDZ is the association of the German speaking area Zoo Directors, which has evolved from annual meetings of Central European Zoo Directors commencing in 1887 at Antwerp. It is the oldest such zoo association in the world. Today, it has about 67 full members from 49 zoos in Germany, 5 in Austria, 4 in Switzerland and 1 in Estonia; in earlier years, there have been members from zoos in neighbouring countries including Czech Republic, Hungary and Poland, all of which now have their own associations.

The legal domicile is in Berlin but the present Director, Dr. Peter Dollinger, is based in Bern. The Executive Board always includes a member from Austria and from Switzerland. The annual meeting takes place in a different member zoo and is well attended by the membership, which also includes additional honorary and associate members including well respected retired Zoo Directors. Members are expected to have appropriate academic qualifications. The President, Vice-President and Treasurer are elected for 3 years' term of office.

VDZ has a magazine "Der Zoologischer Garten", published from Tierpark Berlin. All members except for Gelsenkirchen (membership pending) are also EAZA full members and most also belong to WAZA. All the major zoos in these countries are members. Total visitor numbers are about 40 million annually and therefore are by far largest in Europe. In my survey, 6 out of top 10 and 12 out of top 20 Group A Zoos are VDZ members. There are estimated to be 60 million visitors to all types of zoos and aquaria in Germany.

VDZ aims and policies follow those of EAZA and WAZA. VDZ also works closely with the DTG (Deutsche Tierpark Gesellschaft e.V.), founded in 1976 and representing mostly smaller German zoos and with the DWV (Deutscher Wildgehegeverband e.V) and with the small Austrian (OZO) and Swiss (SASZ) zoo associations.

www.zoodirektoren.de

NVD (Nederlandse Vereniging van Dierentuinen)

The NVD Dutch Zoo Association, founded in 1966, has 15 members including all the major Dutch zoos. Total zoo attendance is about 10 million annually, a very high figure in proportion to the Dutch population! Their office is in Amsterdam zoo with a full-time Director, Mrs. Marielle van Aggelen.

NVD, which is a membership based umbrella organisation, has a chairman, treasurer and secretary and 2 other committee members, all drawn from member zoos. NVD co-ordinates education, training, marketing, national campaigning, conservation, research and relations with the Dutch Government. Through the Dutch Zoo Conservation Fund, to which its members contribute financially, NVD is involved in specific in-situ conservation projects (e.g. lowland tapirs in Brazil and Grevy's zebra in northern Kenya and Somalia).

All NVD members are full EAZA members and most are also WAZA members. In my survey, 2 of the top 10 and 3 of the top 20 Group A zoos are NVD members.

www.nvddierentuinen.nl

ANPZ (Association Nationale des Parcs et Jardins Zoologiques) and SNDPZ (Syndicat National des Directeurs de Parcs Zoologiques Français)

The ANPZ, founded by privately owned French zoos, is open to membership from all French zoos meeting appropriate standards. Its aim is to assist zoos in their development, to represent member zoos at international meetings, to develop implementation of WAZA/EAZA conservation strategy, to work on conservation programmes and to help to improve the conservation education of visitors to members' zoos.

The SNDPZ is a non-profit organisation dedicated to the training of Zoo Directors and managers in various fields, including zoo biology, legislation, ethics and environment. SNDPZ organises congresses, symposia and training within zoos. Membership of SNDPZ is open to both private and public sector zoos. SNDPZ assists members in becoming EAZA and/or WAZA members.

There are 43 member collections of these 2 organisations, of which 32 are EAZA members. In my survey, 7 of the 50 Group B Zoos are members, including 2 in the top 10.

www.sndpz.fr

AIZA (Asociación Ibérica de Zoos y Acuarios)

The Spanish and Portuguese Zoos Association was founded in 1988; a separate Portuguese association has been founded recently. Membership includes 34 Spanish and 5 Portuguese collections. About 16 million people, including 3 million children, visit member zoos and aquariums annually; very large numbers visit the aquariums and other marine collections in Spain. The Management Board comprises 9 from member zoos and the secretarial office is at Barcelona Zoo. All main zoos, except for Lisbon, are members. Out of 39 AIZA members, 12 are EAZA members. The aims of AIZA follow the policy of EAZA but implementation of the EU Directive 1999/22/CE on minimum standards is delegated to regional authorities and is slow and patchy. AIZA represents the interests of its members in contacts with the relevant Ministry of Environment and is involved in national and regional negotiations. AIZA co-ordinates education and conservation activities, veterinary and zookeeper training standards in member institutions, relations with the media and representation at national and international level.

www.aiza.org.es

UCSZ (Unie Ceskych a Slovenskych Zoologickych Zahhrad)

The Union of Czech and Slovak Zoological Gardens has 19 members, of which 15 are Czech zoos and 4 are Slovak zoos; these include all the larger and more important zoos in both countries. About 7 million visitors – 6 million of which are in the Czech Republic – visit these zoos annually. In the Czech Republic, 4 of the top 10 most visited attractions in the country were to member zoos. 15 of the 19 members are also EAZA members and 12 are also WAZA members. UCSZ, which publishes a comprehensive annual report, operates through a members' Council, with 7 specialist committees and 15 individual animal species groups. In addition, there is a CEAF organisation, which brings together the individual zoos' "Friends of the Zoo" organisations.

UCSZ is very active in promoting in-situ conservation projects and reintroductions, not least in their own countries.

Within EAZA, UCSZ members have 3 members on Council, 2 EEP Co-ordinators and are involved in 12 ESBs. In my survey, 1 zoo is in Group A and 5 are in Group B.

www.zoo.cz

PZS-SZG Polish Zoological Society, Directors of Polish Zoological Gardens + Aquariums

Founded in 1960, this Association includes the 15 most important zoological collections in Poland, of which 9 are members of EAZA. The Zoos are visited by over 3 million visitors annually with Warsaw having the largest number of visitors. A comprehensive annual report is published, giving very detailed information on each member zoo, its collection, and involvement in EEPs, ESBs and latest developments. There is a close working collaboration between Polish zoos. The Association is also involved in education and conservation issues, as well as relations with the Polish Government.

The members' zoos are all founded in the 20th century with the exceptions of Wroclaw (Breslau) and Poznan (Pozen). 2 zoos in Group B are included.

www.zoo.lodz.pdi.net

FHZ Federation of Hungarian Zoos (Magyar Állatkertek Szövetsége)

Founded in 1983, the FHZ has 11 member zoos plus one environmental NGO. Out of the 11 zoos 6 are EAZA members.

The oldest member and the first zoo in Hungary is Budapest Zoo, founded in 1866, the other members were founded between 1958 and 1989. The total number of visitors in member zoos is circa 3 million.

There is a presidium of 3 elected officials, chairman, vice-chairman and secretary. Members are united in their ethical guidelines and commitment to education and conservation. The activity of the federation concentrates on exchange of information, development of education, conservation, and on administration and training of keepers and other professional staff and also joint promotion of member zoos.

FHZ co-operates with the Danish Ministry of Rural Development to ensure members' compliance with standards to be met as per EU Directive 1999/22/CE and applied in Hungary under strict and detailed standards listed in a ministerial decree approved in 2007. There are no additional standards of the FHZ because the government standards have been developed through a long participatory process deeply involving FHZ. Hungarian standards provide data for the animal facilities as well as for the requirements about licensing, qualification of zoo staff and collection planning and its approval by authorities.

In my survey, two members, Budapest and Sosto, are included and both are rated highly in the Group A and B zoos respectively.

The Federation has a website, almost exclusively in Hungarian with links to all members.

www.zoo.hu

DAZA Danish Association of Zoos and Aquaria

DAZA is the national federation to which all of the most important collections belong. There are 16 members of which 9 are major zoos and 7 are aquaria. They attract 4 million visitors annually, representing an exceptionally high percentage of Denmark's population.

There is a committee of 5 Zoo Directors with an elected chairman. Members are united in their ethical guidelines and commitment to education, conservation and research. The activity of the federation concentrates on exchange of information, development of education, conservation and research, and on administration, marketing and visitor services.

DAZA co-operates with the Danish Justice Ministry to ensure members' compliance with standards to be met as per EU Directive 1999/22/CE and applied in Denmark under standards approved on 12.12.02. High standards are expected of all members and there are detailed rules on this subject.

www.daza.dk

SDF Svenska Djurparksföreningen (Swedish Association of Zoos and Aquaria)/SAZA

SAZA was established in 1991 and has 21 full members and 5 associated members. Their office is at Kolmården Zoo.

In Sweden, the history of zoological parks and aquaria is recent and less renowned than in most other parts of Europe. Today, SAZA members consist of well managed and increasingly visited parks scattered across a country where space is still less of an issue compared to elsewhere in Europe. Swedish Zoos are EAZA members, participating in EEPs with Eskilstuna and Kolmården being involved in the largest number. Due to the harsh climatic conditions for much of the year, several Swedish zoos specialise in native wildlife and exotic fauna of temperate and arctic origin. SAZA members are developing breeding programmes for endangered Nordic wildlife, linked to in-situ conservation.

SAZA aims to improve the professionalism of its members and to support their task in meeting prime objectives of conservation of biological diversity, support for education and research, and conveying information to the public. SAZA is also involved in collaboration both internally and internationally.

They are also involved with co-operative in-situ conservation projects, including Amur tiger and Cross-river gorilla.

www.svenska-djurparksforeningen.nu

UIZA Unione Italiana Giardini Zoologici e Acquari

UIZA is the Italian national association with 11 full members and 5 honorary individual members. Its headquarters is in Rome. Membership includes several leading Italian zoos and aquaria with an estimated 3 million visitors annually.

UIZA is particularly concerned with representing their members at national level, in promoting conservation, research and educational activities within their membership and endeavouring to have implemented the requirements of the EU Directive 1999/22/CE.

www.uiza.org

OZO Österreichische Zoo Organisation

OZO is the Austrian scientific organisation for leading Austrian zoos and aquaria; it has 7 members including 5 zoos. Its prime aim is education and support for wildlife and biodiversity. OZO co-operates with the implementation of wildlife protection projects and with breeding and research projects. It is involved with the training of keepers and others concerned with animal keeping. It supports officials concerned with wildlife subjects.
OZO members must meet modern standards for animal keeping and disseminate appropriate information to their visitors. Membership criteria include high quality of animal keeping, competent leadership with relevant animal related qualifications, a well established education programme and engagement in conservation research activities.
OZO promotes common pass tickets for member zoos, and is involved in co-operative in-situ conservation projects such as Bearded vulture (Bartgeier) and Przewalski horse.

www.ozo.at

ZOOSCHWEIZ Association of Swiss Scientific Zoos

Zooschweiz is a small organisation, similar to OZO, with its office in Berne. It has 5 member zoos, and aims and objectives similar to OZO, but does not offer common entrance tickets to its member zoos nor has it direct involvement in in-situ conservation projects.

www.zoos.ch

Vienna

CHAPTER 17

Individual Zoo Profiles

Introduction

No two zoos are the same: that is one of the pleasures of visiting zoological gardens. In these individual zoo profiles I have used a common format for the information about each of the 80 zoos in this survey; all possible care has been taken with the compilation of the information which was sent to each zoo for verification. However, the zoo scene is not a static one and visitors should use the zoo's web site or contact the zoo to ensure that any matter of particular importance to them applies on the day of their visit. All the zoos have web sites: many of them are excellent and provide extensive visitor information, news of new zoo arrivals, animal births, events in the zoo and conservation projects.

Unsurprisingly, Zoo variety makes presenting some of the information fairly difficult. The profiles are designed to be both a useful guide for visitors, prior to possibly checking entrance prices and some other items on the zoo's website before visiting, and to give some comparisons between zoos.

Opening Hours

Most city zoos are open throughout the year, and have fixed opening hours which can vary between summer and winter, often linked to summer and winter times that run with the change of the clocks. For enthusiastic zoo visitors, it is an advantage to visit relatively early or late in the day as several species are more active then; city zoos are mainly open by 09.00 for much of the year and some allow visitors to remain until dusk. Other zoos may have longer summer visiting hours, perhaps linked to school holidays. In many zoos, the last time for ticket purchase at the gate may be one hour earlier than the zoo's quoted closing time.

Entrance Prices

The free entry age limit for children varies considerably from under 2 to under 6. Concessions for free or reduced price entries also vary widely but usually include pensioners and disabled visitors with their carers. Annual or season tickets are widespread and are often beneficial for visitors wishing to visit a zoo at least three times annually. In a few cases, these can be valid for

Zoo Co-operation: Mutual Concessions

Two examples of free or reduced admission charges for annual card holders to other zoos in this survey (Zoo Co-operation: Mutual Concessions) are as follows:

- Germany, NRW (Nordrhein-Westfalen): Dortmund, Duisburg, Gelsenkirchen, Cologne, Krefeld, Münster, Wuppertal
- British Isles: Belfast, Bristol, Chester, Colchester, Dublin, Edinburgh, Marwell, Paignton, Twycross

free or reduced price entry to certain other zoos. For tourists, there are frequently city tourist cards which will include discounted entry to the zoo. There are also wide variations in family entrance tickets. Some zoos, including the majority of those in the UK, include a voluntary contribution to conservation in their published prices. Prices shown are those applicable at the beginning of 2011.

Catering Facilities

I have included only the most important catering outlets. All zoos have small cafés and kiosks though these may only be open in summer. Zoo owned facilities are those managed, staffed and owned by the zoo. A few zoos have invested in new hotel facilities such as Beauval, Hamburg and Kolmården and others are likely to do so.

Dogs on Leads

Some zoo Directors believe the presence of visitors' dogs provides "animal enrichment" to their zoo animals; others are more concerned about health and safety issues and do not allow visitors' dogs to enter the zoo.
Where dogs are permitted, most zoos charge for the dog's day or annual ticket. Dogs must be kept on short leads and are generally not allowed into animal houses: outside there will be water and a tethering point.

Signage on Exhibits

Any language, other than the zoo's native one, indicates that there is at least summary information apart from the name of the species on display. The signage star rating refers to the quality and comprehensiveness of the signage, three stars being the best. Like all organisations, zoos are involved in continuous improvement. Many may have made improvements to the signage since my last visit.

Zookeeper Talks

These reflect actual commentaries with good information on the species concerned and are not just animal feeding times, although these two activities can be combined.

Friends of the Zoo Organisation

This refers to the presence of a "Friends of the Zoo" or direct equivalent, meaning an independently run and organised society, having its own elected officers and arrangements, frequently including its own magazine, programme of meetings, fund raising activities for its zoo, and visits to other zoos.
Members of the Zoo or of the Zoo's zoological society, on the other hand, are an integral part of the zoo's administration and are organised through the zoo's staff. Their benefits frequently include a magazine, annual entrance tickets, and discounts in the zoo's catering and retail outlets.

Volunteers

These are unpaid assistants, helping zoo staff at the busiest times of the year. They are frequently either committed and knowledgeable students or retired people, and are involved with visitor guiding, exhibit surveillance and supplementing the work of keepers.

Extent of Indoor Exhibits

Those animal houses open to visitors are included and give an indication not just of interesting exhibits but of possibilities in poor weather zoo visiting.

Star Attractions

These are my personal selection of exhibits that are particularly good in comparison with those in other zoos; they are generally 6 or 5 star rated in Chapter 12. For smaller zoos with more limited collections, they might exceptionally include a few with 4 star rating.

Dublin

Cologne

DIERENPARK AMERSFOORT

Contact

Name	DierenPark Amersfoort
Address	Barchman Wuytierslaan 224, 3819AC Amersfoort, NL
Phone	+31 (0)33 422 7100
Fax	+31 (0)33 422 7101
Email	info@dierenparkamersfoort.nl
Website	www.dierenparkamersfoort.nl

Opening Hours

Open every day of the year
March to September   09.00 to 18.00
October to February   10.00 to 17.00

Entrance Prices 2011

	EUR
Adult	18.50
Child 3 - 12	15.50
Child Under 3	Free
Annual Card - Single Adult	57.50
Annual Card - Child	50.00
Concessions: over 65s	

Transport Access

Car	A1 then A28
Car Park	Yes, at Zoo EUR 6.50 per day
Bus	70
Nearest Station	Amersfoort central station, 20 minutes' walk to zoo

Ownership of Zoo   Private Company   100% Family owned

Area of Zoo   18 Ha

Date of Foundation   1948

Visitor Numbers   675.000

DIERENPARK AMERSFOORT

Animal Inventory at 31.12.2009

	Number	Species
Mammals	350	56
Birds	197	46
Reptiles	38	11
Amphibians	4	1
Fish	1217	8

Facilities

Catering (zoo owned):
Restaurants, Café, Kiosks, Picnic Place - Parkrestaurant de Olifant,
Restaurant de Boerderij, Grand Café de Berenhof
Retail (zoo owned): 2 Zoo shops
Children´s Zoo: Yes   Children´s Playground: Yes

Dogs

Allowed on leads: Yes   Kennel Facilities: No

Feeding by Visitors

Strictly prohibited

Shows, etc

Yes, Close encounters with snakes and tarantulas, Dinobos - Dinosaurs

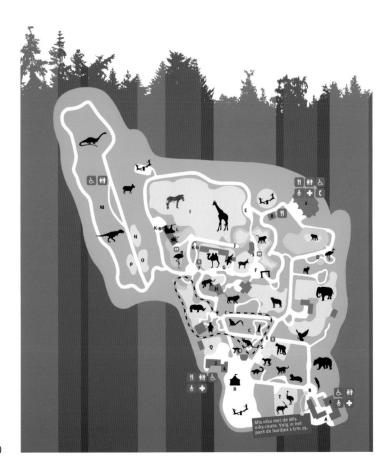

Plan (2009)

DIERENPARK AMERSFOORT

Education

Zoo keeper talks: Yes
In Summer 5 opportunities per day – see daily programme
Zoo School/Education Centre: No, but private guided education tours
Biodiversity Centre: No
Zoo Guidebook: No
Signage on Exhibits: Dutch   Star Rating: *

Friends of the Zoo

No

Volunteers

Yes, circa 70 for story-telling and guided tours.

General Site Description

The zoo is situated on a well wooded flat site with good vegetation and water features in some areas. A distinguishing feature, which young children enjoy, is a labyrinth formed from footpaths bordered with varieties of vegetation which can be found in the original part of the zoo. The ethnic STAD DER OUDHEID (Ancient City) development provides an interesting themed area.
The 2010 elephant house is unusual in design: the indoor and outdoor enclosures replicate one another to give the elephants continuity of feel and for most of the year the elephants are free to choose their location.
Story-telling linking animals to their local people is a special feature in this lovely zoo.

Indoor Exhibits

Elephant House, Night, Rhino House, Museum

Star Attractions

Elephants, Night, Meerkats, Penguins, Spotted Hyenas, Flamingos, Baboons, Manchurian Cranes, Ostriches/Scimitar Oryx, Geoffrey's Cats

Time required

whole zoo: 4 - 5 hours   star attractions: 1 - 2 hours

ZOO D'AMNÉVILLE

Contact

Name	Zoo d'Amnéville
Address	1, rue du Tigre, Centre Thermal et Touristique 57360 Amnéville, F
Phone	+33(0) 3 87 70 25 60
Fax	+33(0) 3 87 71 41 45
Email	zoo.amneville@wanadoo.fr
Website	www.zoo-amneville.com

Opening Hours

Open every day of the year
April to September 09.30 to 19.30
October to March 09.00 to Dusk

Entrance Prices 2011

	EUR
Adult	27.00
Child 3 - 11	22.00
Child Under 3	Free
Annual Card - Adult	108.00
Annual Card - Child	88.00

Transport Access

Car	A4 exit Amnéville or A31 exit Mondelange, then follow Amnéville
Car Park	Yes, at Zoo and Centre Thermal et Touristique Free of Charge
Nearest Station	Hagondange 3 Kms away

Ownership of Zoo Private Company 100% Parc Zoologique d' Amnéville Co-operative

Area of Zoo 18 Ha

Date of Foundation 1986

Visitor Numbers Circa 630.000

Animal Inventory at 02.06.2010

	Number	Species
Mammals	501	76
Birds	707	123
Reptiles	406	82
Amphibians	0	0
Fish	0	0

Zoo d'Amnéville

Facilities

Catering (zoo owned):
Restaurants, Café, Kiosks, Picnic Place - La Terrasse, Pizzeria, La Sandwicherie
Retail (zoo owned): Zoo shop
Children's Zoo: Yes   Children's Playground: Yes

Dogs

Allowed on leads: No   Kennel Facilities: No

Feeding by Visitors

Permitted where safe and appropriate

Shows, etc

Yes, Birds of Prey, Parrots and Sea Lions

Education

Zoo keeper talks: Yes
Zoo School/Education Centre: Yes
Biodiversity Centre: Yes
Zoo Guidebook: Yes, EUR 6,00
Signage on Exhibits: French and some German   Star Rating: **

ZOO D'AMNÉVILLE

Friends of the Zoo No

Volunteers No

General Site Description Situated adjacent to a Sports and Entertainment complex, with shared car parking, this is a very pleasant zoological garden with good tree cover and fine, varied vegetation including plentiful bamboo. There are some good water features in parts of the zoo. There is good conservation information and excellent visibility of the animals in their enclosures. There are exciting new additions planned each year. Buildings, except for the large, impressive 2008 Orang Utan House, are not noteworthy. The Vivarium houses a particularly interesting reptile collection.

Indoor Exhibits Orang Utan House, Elephant House, Rhino House, Vivarium, Giraffe House

Star Attractions Orang Utans and Small Claw Otters, Polar Bears, Spider Monkeys, Wild Cats, Ring Tailed Lemurs, Tigers, Gibbons, Marmosets, Birds of Prey Show, Leopards, Siamangs, Crested Cranes, Capuchin Monkeys, Fishing Cats

Time required whole zoo: 8 hours   star attractions: 3 hours

Contact

Name	Natura Artis Magistra/ Amsterdam Zoo	
Address	Plantage Kerklaan 38-40, 1018 CZ Amsterdam, NL	
Phone	+31(0) 20 523 3400	
Fax	+31(0) 20 523 3419	
Email	info@artis.nl	
Website	www.artis.nl	

Opening Hours

Open every day of the year
Summer April to October   09.00 to 18.00
Winter November to March 09.00 to 17.00
June to August   the zoo is open until Dusk

Entrance Prices 2011

	EUR
Adult	18.95
Child 3-9	15.50
Child under 3	Free
Annual Card - 1st Adult	72.50
Annual Card - 2nd and each Child	42.50
Concessions: 65+, Disabled Visitors	

Transport Access

Navi	Sat Nav 9292 ov.nl
Car	Plantage Middenlaan
Car Park	Yes, at Zoo EUR 8.00 per 6 hours and then EUR 4 per hour
Boat	Artis Zoo Express from Rederij Lovers
Tram	9 from Central Station, 10, 14
Nearest Station	Amsterdam Central

Ownership of Zoo

Private Foundation Non Profit   100% Natura Artis Magistra
Royal Zoological Society with financial support from Amsterdam City Council

Area of Zoo

14 Ha

Date of Foundation

1838

Visitor Numbers

Circa 1,200,000

Animal Inventory at 31.12.2009

	Number	Species
Mammals	516	94
Birds	730	102
Reptiles	270	74
Amphibians	170	15
Fish	1706	251

Facilities

Catering (sub-contract):
Restaurants, Café, Kiosks - The Two Cheetahs Restaurant , Butterfly House Café, Flamingo Café, Mobile Kiosks - restored traditional Dutch Style
Retail (zoo owned): Zoo shop
Children's Zoo: Yes, Children's Farm   Children's Playground: Yes

Dogs

Allowed on leads: No   Kennel Facilities: No

Feeding by Visitors

Strictly prohibited

Shows, etc

Yes, Zoological Museum, Diorama, Planetarium

Education

Zoo keeper talks: Yes, 10+ daily
Zoo School/Education Centre: Yes
Biodiversity Centre: To be opened in old Museum Building
Zoo Guidebook: Yes
Signage on Exhibits: Dutch and English   Star Rating: **

Friends of the Zoo

No, but Annual Card Holders are Members of ARTIS   circa 80,000

Volunteers   Yes, Circa 150

General Site   A famous old city zoological and botanical garden, Artis is situated in the ol-
Description   dest Amsterdam city park: it is a haven of peace and tranquillity in the middle
                      of the city. Artis has more than 800 trees, primarily deciduous, representing
                      over 200 species and some beautifully planted gardens. The zoo is laid out on
                      a grid structure and has fine vegetation and historic buildings. A Planetarium,
                      a Biodiversity Centre and a Zoological Museum are all on the site. Another
                      interesting feature of this zoo is its large collection of invertebrates which will
                      form part of the planned Micro Zoo.

                      In the last few years, there have been some highly imaginative developments,
                      such as the Butterfly House. The zoo is engaged in the major renovation of its
                      historic buildings, including the old Monkey House and Bird House which will
                      reopen in 2011 with new walk through exhibits. Artis is proceeding with the use
                      of its site extension.to give larger mammals more space. These major invest-
                      ments will transform Artis to a 21st Century Zoo whilst retaining the character
                      and history of the 19th Century origins.

Indoor Exhibits   Butterfly Pavilion, Jungle by Night, Small Mammals House, Elephant House,
                      Aquarium Gorilla House, Primate House, Giraffe House, Reptile House, Chim-
                      panzee House, Bird House, Insectarium/ Planetarium, Borneo House - Crocodiles

Star Attractions Butterfly Pavilion, African Savannah, Griffin Vulture, South American Pampas,
                      Ring Tailed Lemur Walk Through, Pelicans, White Cheeked Gibbon, Racoons,
                      Penguins, Aquarium, Prairie Dogs

Time required   whole zoo: 5 - 7 hours   star attractions: 2 hours

Contact

	Name	Antwerp Zoo
	Address	Koningin Astridplein 26
		2018 Antwerp, B
	Phone	+32(0) 3 202 4540
	Fax	+32(0) 3 202 4547
	Email	info@zooantwerpen.be
	Website	www.zooantwerpen.be

Opening Hours

Open every day of the year

May, June and September	10.00 to 18.00
July and August	10.00 to 19.00
October, March and April	10.00 to 17.30
November to February	10.00 to 16.45

Entrance Prices 2011

	EUR
Adult	19.50
Child 3-17	17.00
Child under 3	Free
Annual Card - Adult	93.00
Annual Card 2 Adults and children under 18	164.00
Concessions: 60+, Disabled Visitors and their Carers, Planckendael Combi Ticket	

Transport Access

The zoo is next to Antwerp Central Station

Car	Follow signs to Central Station/Zoo
Car Park	Yes, Public Car Parks within 5 minutes' walk
Buses	Any bus to Central Station
Trams	Any tram to Central Station
Nearest Station	Antwerp Central 1 minutes' walk

Ownership of Zoo

Private Foundation Non Profit   100% KMDA,
Royal Zoological Society of Antwerp with financial support from
Antwerp Council and Flanders Regional Government

Area of Zoo

11,5 Ha

Date of Foundation

1843

Visitor Numbers

Circa 1,335,000

Animal Inventory at 31.12.2009

	Number	Species
Mammals	333	77
Birds	703	150
Reptiles	337	68
Amphibians	526	48
Fish	2751	245

Facilities

Catering (zoo owned):
Restaurants, Café, Kiosks, Picnic Place -
Restaurant Flamingo, Grand Café Paon Royal
Retail (zoo owned): Zoo shop
Children's Zoo: Yes   Children's Playground: Yes

Dogs

Allowed on leads: No   Kennel Facilities: No

Feeding by Visitors

Strictly prohibited

Shows, etc

Yes, Sea Lion Show and Planetarium Exhibition

Education

Zoo keeper talks: Yes, see programme in zoo
Zoo School/Education Centre: Yes
Biodiversity Centre: No
Zoo Guidebook: No
Signage on Exhibits: Flemish, French and English   Star Rating: *

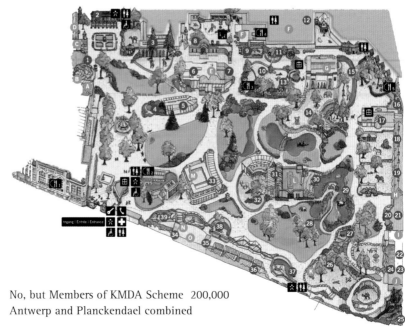

Friends of the Zoo

No, but Members of KMDA Scheme   200,000
Antwerp and Planckendael combined

Volunteers

Yes, Circa 40

General Site Description

A fine old established Zoological garden, adjacent to the city's main railway station and the Queen Elizabeth Hall for which KMDA is responsible. Well maintained historic buildings and mature trees characterise the site. The zoo has a current development programme involving exciting new enclosures for the lions, tigers and leopards as well as a site extension.

Indoor Exhibits

Elephant and Giraffe House, Monkey House, Tropical House, Aquarium, Apes House, Reptile House, Bird House, Planetarium, Hippo House, Nocturnal House

Star Attractions

Komodo Dragon, Pygmy Marmosets, Nocturnal House, Golden Headed Lion Tamarins, Penguins, Blue Duikers, Red Pandas, Iguanas, Coatis, Monitor Lizards

Time required

whole zoo: 4 - 6 hours   star attractions: 1 - 2 hours

Contact

Name	Burgers' Zoo Arnhem
Address	Antoon van Hooffplein 1, 6816 SH Arnhem, NL
Phone	+31 (0)26 44 24 534
Fax	+31 (0)26 44 30 776
Email	info@burgerszoo.nl
Website	www.burgerszoo.nl

Opening Hours

Open every day of the year
Summer April to October   09.00 to 19.00
Winter November to March 09.00 to 17.00

Entrance Prices 2011

	EUR
Adult 10 - 64	18.50
Child 4 - 9	16.50
Child Under 3	Free
Annual Card - Single Adult	50.00
Annual Card - Child	45.00
Annual Card – Family Range of prices	135.00 to 299.00
Annual Card holders are automatically Members of the Zoo and have reduced price entry to other Dutch NVD Zoos.	
Concessions: over 65s, combi-ticket for Zoo and Dutch Open Air Museum.	

Transport Access

Car	A12 Arnhem Noord then signposted to zoo
Car Park	At Zoo EUR 3.00
Bus	3 from Arnhem Central Station –check it goes to Burgers' Zoo; 13 during holiday season
Nearest Station	Arnhem Central Station

Ownership of Zoo

Private, 100% Family Van Hooff

Area of Zoo

45 Ha

Date of Foundation

1913

Visitor Numbers

Circa 1,520,000

Animal Inventory at 31.12.2009

	Number	Species
Mammals	529	57
Birds	1160	138
Reptiles	223	32
Amphibians	286	17
Fish	2447	153

Facilities

Catering (zoo owned):
Bush Restaurant – tropical theme, Desert Restaurant – Texan Mexican Theme,
Safari Restaurant – African theme, Park Restaurant – Dutch Theme, Penguin
Corner - Café
Retail (zoo owned): Zoo shop
Children's Zoo: No   Children's Playground: Yes, Burgers' Adventure playground

Dogs

Allowed on leads: No   Kennel Facilities: No

Feeding by Visitors

Strictly prohibited

Shows, etc

No, but there are guided zoo tours

Education

Zoo keeper talks: No
Zoo School/Education Centre: No
Biodiversity Centre: No
Zoo Guidebook: Yes, EUR 3,00
Signage on Exhibits:: Dutch, German, English, French
Star Rating: ***

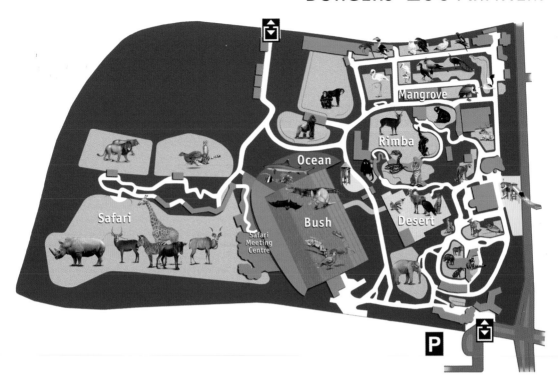

Friends of the Zoo	No. Members of the Zoo are Annual Card holders with various benefits
Volunteers	No, but circa 60 Trained IVN Tour Volunteers give Zoo Tours
General Site Description	Situated in a naturally wooded area, the zoo has good water features and has been enhanced by extensive planting of fine vegetation and many rocks and boulders. This very fine zoological garden is spacious, well landscaped, organised in habitat zones and has room for expansion. Animals are, as far as possible, exhibited in their natural habitat following Hagenbeck design and eco principles.
Indoor Exhibits	BUSH Rain Forest, Monkey House, OCEAN Aquarium, Apes House, MANGROVE Tropical Swamp Forest, DESERT...
Star Attractions	BUSH, Lions, Coati, OCEAN, Tigers, Sun Bears and Binturong, MANGROVE, Leopards, Small Clawed otters, DESERT, Siamangs, Flamingos, African Savannah, Meerkats, Chimpanzees
Time required	whole zoo: 6 - 8 hours star attractions: 3 - 5 hours

ZOO AUGSBURG

Contact

	Name	Zoologischer Garten Augsburg GmbH
	Address	Brehmplatz 1,
		86161 Augsburg, D
	Phone	+49(0) 821 567149-0
	Fax	+49(0) 821 567149-13
	Email	info@zoo-augsburg.de
	Website	www.zoo-augsburg.de

Opening Hours

Open every day of the year

November to February	09.00 to 16.30
March and October	09.00 to 17.00
April, May and September	09.00 to 18.00
June to August	09.00 to 18.30

Entrance Prices

	EUR	EUR
Summer/Winter	Mar to Oct	Nov to Feb
Adult	8.00	6.00
Child 3-15	4.00	3.00
Child under 3	0.00	0.00
Family Ticket Book 4 x adult & 6 x child	44.00	44.00
Dog	2.50	2.00
Annual Card - Adult	35.00	
Annual Card – Child 3-15	15.00	
Annual Card – Zoo & Botanic Garden	50.00	
Concessions: students, over 65s, disabled, armed services personnel and families on Friday Family Days.		

Transport Access

	Car	A8 Exit Augsburg East or Augsburg West then B300Car
	Park	Yes, at zoo Free of Charge
	Bus	32 from Augsburg Hbf or Königsplatz to Zoo/Botanic Gardens
	Nearest Station	Augsburg Hbf

Ownership of Zoo

Municipal Company, Zoologischer Garten Augsburg GmbH
99.2% City of Augsburg, 0.8% Private Individuals

Area of Zoo

22 Ha

Date of Foundation

1937

Zoo Augsburg

Visitor Numbers   Circa 580,000

Animal Inventory at 31.12.2009

	Number	Species
Mammals	421	50
Birds	857	178
Reptiles	134	34
Amphibians	68	14
Fish	0	0

Facilities

Catering (sub-contract):
Restaurant, Café, Kiosks, Picnic Place - Zoo Gaststätte, Halbzeit Bistro
Retail (sub-contract): Zoo shop, Minature Railway
Children's Zoo: Yes, Elephant rides can be booked
Children's Playground: Yes

Dogs

Allowed on leads: Yes   Kennel Facilities: No

Feeding by Visitors

Strictly prohibited except birds and goats from food dispensers in the zoo

Shows, etc

No

Education

Zoo keeper talks: Yes - at feeding of South African Fur Seal twice daily.
Zoo School/Education Centre: Yes
Biodiversity Centre: No
Zoo Guidebook: Yes, EUR 3,50
Signage on Exhibits:: German   Star Rating: **

Friends of the Zoo

Yes, Freundeskreis Augsburger Zoo
Membership at 31.12.2009 – Circa 500

Volunteers

No

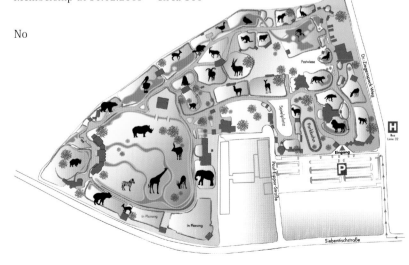

General Site Description

A pleasant site with lakes and good water features particularly for birds and good tree cover in some areas. Augsburg Zoo has a pleasant, calm atmosphere. The new Walk Through Ring Tailed Lemur Exhibit with its fine trees, water features and vegetation is a true delight.

Indoor Exhibits

Elephant and Chimps House, Tiger House, Giraffe House, Reptile House, Lion House, Tropichalle (Bird House)

Star Attractions

African Savannah, Penguins, Fennec Foxes, Ring Tailed Lemur Walk Through, Bird House, Beavers, Takins, Coatis, Bird Lake, Pelicans, Baboons, Lions, Maned Wolves

Time required

whole zoo: 4 - 6 hours   star attractions: 2 hours

ZOO BARCELONA

Contact
	Name	Parque Zoologico de Barcelona
	Address	Parc de la Ciutadella s/n,
		08003 Barcelona, E
	Phone	+34(0)93 2256 780
	Fax	+34(0)93 2213 853
	Email	zoobarcelona@bsmasa.es
	Website	www.zoobarcelona.com

Opening Hours

Open every day of the year

Summer 15/05 to 15/09	10.00 to 19.00
Spring and Autumn 16/09 to 31/10 and 16/03 to 14/05	10.00 to 18.00
Winter 01/11 to 15/03	10.00 to 17.00

Entrance Prices 2011

	EUR
Adult	16.50
Child 3-16	9.90
Child under 3	Free
Annual Card - Adult	34.00
Annual Card - Family	72.00
Concessions: students, 65+ and disabled visitors, Annual Card holders are Zoo Club Members	

Transport Access

Car	Follow signs to Citadel Park
Car Park	Charged City Car Park in vicinity of Zoo
Bus	14,17,36.39,40,41,45,51,57,59,100,141,157
Tram	T4 Ciutadella-Vila Olimpica
Metro	L4 and L1
Nearest Station	Estació de França

Ownership of Zoo   Municipal, 100% Barcelona City Council

Area of Zoo   13 Ha

Date of Foundation   1892

Visitor Numbers   Circa 1,150,000

Animal Inventory at 31.12.2009

	Number	Species
Mammals	727	88
Birds	698	108
Reptiles	432	92
Amphibians	202	18
Fish	149	12

Facilities

Catering (sub-contract):
Restaurant, Café, Kiosks, Picnic Place - Restaurant La Granja
Retail (sub-contract): Zoo shop - Botiga Tienda, Minature Railway
Children´s Zoo: Yes, Pony Rides   Children´s Playground: Yes

Dogs

Allowed on leads: No   Kennel Facilities: No

Feeding by Visitors

Strictly forbidden

Shows, etc

Yes. Dolphins and Sea Lions.

Education

Zoo keeper talks: Yes
Zoo School/Education Centre: Yes
Biodiversity Centre: No
Zoo Guidebook: Yes
Signage on Exhibits:: Spanish, Catalan, EnglishStar Rating: *

Friends of the Zoo

No, but Zoo Club Membership at 31.12.2009 - Circa 100,000. Members of the Zoo Club are Annual Card holders with various benefits

Volunteers

Yes, Circa 50

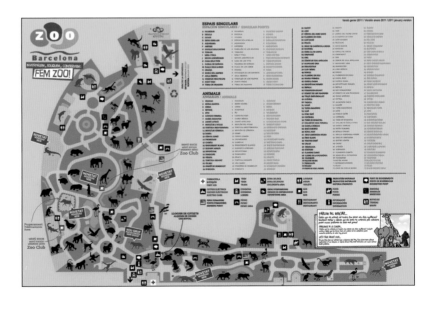

General Site Description

Barcelona is a city centre zoo situated on a level site conveniently within the Citadel Park. It's a true city zoological garden with well-established tree cover, Mediterranean vegetation and lovely botanical displays. The zoo offers visitors a remarkably comprehensive collection: although enclosures are somewhat variable there's a programme for improvement and plans to relocate the aquatic mammal species to a new site, thereby giving the remaining species in the zoo additional space. The recently opened award winning Komodo Dragon Exhibit is particularly noteworthy.

Indoor Exhibits

Dolphinarium, Aviary, Terrarium Reptile House, Monkey House

Star Attractions

Komodo Dragons, Sea Lions, Spider Monkeys, Chimpanzees, Otters, Aviary, Gorillas, Pygmy Hippos

Time required

whole zoo: 5 - 6 hours   star attractions: 2 - 3 hours

ZOO BASEL

Contact

Name	Zoo Basel
Address	Binningerstr. 40, CH-4011, Basel, CH
Phone	+41(0) 61 295 3535
Fax	+41(0) 61 281 0005
Email	zoo@zoobasel.ch
Website	www.zoobasel.ch

Opening Hours

Open every day of the year

May to August	08.00 to 18.30
September, October, March and April	08.00 to 18.00
November to February	08.00 to 17.30

Entrance Prices 2011

	CHF
Adult	18.00
Child 6-16	7.00
Child under 6	Free
Young Person 16 - 25	12.00
Family Day Ticket – Parents and their Children under 20	39.00
Annual Card - Adult	80.00
Annual Card – Child and Young Person 6 to 25	40.00
Annual Card – Family Parents and their children under 20	140.00
Concessions: 62+, Mondays except holidays	

Transport Access

Car	A2 CH or A5 Exit Basel Süd
Car Park	Yes, at Zoo Main Entrance and Car Parks at Heuwaage
Bus	34 and 36 to Zoo Stop Dorenbach
Tram	1, 8 to Zoo Stop Bachletten, 2 to Zoo Stop Dorenbach, 10 and 17 to Zoo Stop
Nearest Station	Basel SBB, 10 minutes walk

Ownership of Zoo   Private Non Profit Company, 1000+ shareholders

Area of Zoo   12 Ha

Date of Foundation   1874

Visitor Numbers   Circa 1,700,000

Animal Inventory at 31.12.2009

	Number	Species
Mammals	382	65
Birds	671	90
Reptiles	254	37
Amphibians	35	9
Fish	3219	294

Facilities

Catering (Zoo Owned):
Restaurant, Café, Kiosks - Restaurant à la carte (first class), Selbstbedienung Restaurant (Self Service Restaurant), Die Cafeteria
Retail (Zoo Owned): Zoo shop
Children's Zoo: Yes, Special Attraction „Kinderzolli", direct contact with animals in spacious enclosures. Children 8+ allowed to help daily
Children's Playground: Yes

Dogs   Allowed on leads: No   Kennel Facilities: No

Feeding by Visitors   Strictly prohibited

Shows, etc   Yes, in Etosha House.

Education

Zoo keeper talks: Yes
Zoo School/Education Centre: Yes
Biodiversity Centre: Yes - Bionics Centre
Zoo Guidebook: Yes, CHF 7.00
Signage on Exhibits::German, French Star Rating: **

Friends of the Zoo

Yes, Verein der Freunde des Zoologischen Gartens Basel. Membership at 31.12.2009 – Circa 3000

Volunteers

Yes, Circa 50

General Site Description

The "Zolli", as Zoo Basel is known locally, is one of the most beautiful zoos in Europe. Situated in the middle of the city close to the main station, it is a delightful city centre oasis. It is a wonderfully designed zoological garden with well-established trees, gardens and varied vegetation. The space has been exceptionally well used and landscaped to provide beautiful perspectives on the enclosures. There is a good use of water features and period buildings are well restored and maintained. Attention to design detail is evident throughout the zoo even in the pathways. Local wildlife is well represented by the storks, herons and squirrels frequenting the zoo. The large number of indoor exhibits is impressive. The remarkable Vivarium, which houses 75% of all species living in this zoo, is truly a zoo within the zoo. Built on four levels, creating a thematic circular world tour, it covers an impressive range of reptiles, amphibians, fish and coral reefs. The Apes' enclosures are being greatly improved and extended and will reopen in the Summer of 2012.

Indoor Exhibits

Vivarium, Apes House, Elephant House, Etosha House, Hippos House, Primates House, Gamgoas House, Giraffe and Antelopes House, Bird House, Australia House, Rhino House Children's Zoo House...

Star Attractions

Vivarium, Squirrel Monkeys, African Hunting Dogs, Hippos, Ring Tailed Lemur, Woolly Monkeys, Ostriches, Cheetahs, Grant's Zebras, Fish Otters, Indian Rhino, Nile Crocodile, Flamingos, White Pelicans, Somali Wild Asses, Crocodiles, Etosha House – Love Birds, Weaver Birds and Bee Eaters and many other exhibits, Gorillas, Chimpanzees and Orang Utans from 2012

Time required

whole zoo: 6 - 8 hours   star attractions: 2 - 3 hours

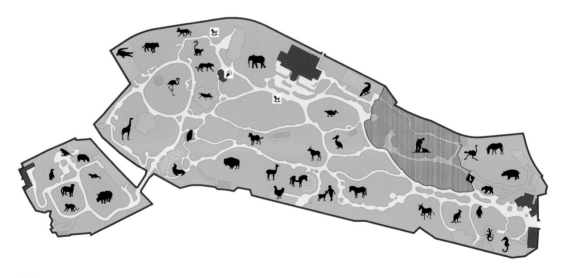

Contact

Name	Zooparc de Beauval
Address	41110 St Aignan sur Cher, F
Phone	+33(0) 2 54 75 5000
Fax	+33(0) 2 54 74 4001
Email	infos@zoobeauval.com
Website	www.zoobeauval.com

Opening Hours

Open every day of the year
All Year   09.00 to dusk

Entrance Prices 2011

Entrance Prices 2011	EUR
Adult	22.00
Child 3-10	16.00
Child Under 3	Free
Dogs	Free
Annual Card - Adult	66.00
Annual Card – Child 3-10	48.00
Concessions: disabled visitors in wheelchairs	

Transport Access

Car	A10/A71/A85 Exit St Aignan
Car Park	Yes, at Zoo Free of Charge
Nearest Station	St Aignan sur Cher

Ownership of Zoo

Private 100% Family Delord

Area of Zoo

30 Ha

Date of Foundation

1980

Visitor Numbers

Circa 550,000

Animal Inventory at 31.12.2009

	Number	Species
Mammals	552	87
Birds	1513	215
Reptiles	314	51
Amphibians	108	11
Fish	1770	98

Facilities

Catering (Zoo Owned):
Hotel, Restaurant, Café, Kiosks, Picnic Place - Hotel and Restaurant Les Jardins de Beauval, Restaurant – Le Tropical, Creperie La Roseraie
Retail (Zoo Owned): 2 Zoo shops
Children's Zoo: Yes, Children's Farm   Children's Playground: Yes

Dogs

Allowed on leads: Yes   Kennel Facilities: No

Feeding by Visitors

Strictly prohibited, except at Children's Farm

Shows, etc

Yes, March to November Birds of Prey and Sea Lions

Education

Zoo keeper talks: Yes, April to September throughout the day. See daily programme for 12 different opportunities..
Zoo School/Education Centre: Yes
Biodiversity Centre: No
Zoo Guidebook: Yes, Euro 25.00
Signage on Exhibits:: French   Star Rating: ***

Friends of the Zoo   No

Volunteers   No

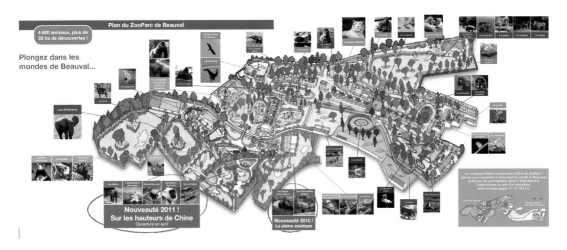

General Site Description

Situated to the south of the attractive Loire valley area east of Tours, Beauval Zoo has a particular charm and flair and evinces some creative investment and a uniformly high exhibit standard. The site has varied topography, good matures trees and vegetation and some lovely water features. On entering the zoo the walk along the duck river is quite enchanting. Signage and message boards are attractive and informative. The animal collection is impressive with the cat, primate and bird families particularly well represented.

Indoor Exhibits

Apes House, Gorillas and Manatees, Tropical Birds House, Elephant House, Australia House, Vivarium, Tropical Aquarium

Star Attractions

White Tigers, Ring Tailed Lemurs, Racoons, Tree Kangaroos, Elephants, Spotted Hyenas, Penguins, Manatees, African Savannah, Giant Anteaters, Tropical Bird House, Gorillas, Asian Plain, Koalas, Flamingos

Time required

whole zoo: 6 - 8 hours   star attractions: 2 - 3 hours

Contact

Name	Belfast Zoological Gardens
Address	Antrim Road,
	Belfast BT36 7PN, UK
Phone	+44(0) 28 9077 6277
Fax	+44(0) 28 9037 0578
Email	info@belfastzoo.co.uk
Website	www.belfastzoo.co.uk

Opening Hours

Open every day of the year

April to September	10.00 to 19.00
October to March	10.00 to 16.00

Entrance Prices 2011

	GBP	GBP
	Oct to Mar	Apr to Sep
Adult	7.10	8.90
Child 4–17	3.60	4.70
Child under 4	Free	Free
Annual Card - Adult	25.70	27.00
Family Day Ticket 2 Adults and 2 Children	19.10	24.50
Annual Card – Child	12.75	13.40
Annual Card – Family	72.00	75.60
Concessions: 60+ and disabled visitors are free of charge		

Transport Access

Navi	Sat Nav BT36 7NP
Car	From North M2 Junction 4 and from the South M1 then M2
Car Park	Yes, at Zoo Free of Charge
Bus	1A, 1B, 1C, 1D, 1E, 1F, 1G, 2A
Nearest Station	Whiteabbey 3 miles away

Ownership of Zoo

Municipal 100% Belfast City Council

Area of Zoo

24 Ha / 55 acres

Date of Foundation

1934

Visitor Numbers

Circa 300,000

BELFAST ZOO

Animal Inventory at 31.12.2009

	Number	Species
Mammals	360	67
Birds	380	63
Reptiles	32	13
Amphibians	3	2
Fish	12	1

Facilities

Catering (sub-contract):
Restaurant, Café, Kiosks, Picnic Place - Lion's Den Restaurant, Percy's Picnic Pitstop
Retail (Zoo Owned): Zoo shop - Zoovenir
Children's Zoo: No   Children's Playground: Yes

Dogs

Allowed on leads: No   Kennel Facilities: No

Feeding by Visitors

Strictly prohibited

Shows, etc

No

Education

Zoo keeper talks: No
Zoo School/Education Centre: Yes
Biodiversity Centre: No
Zoo Guidebook: Yes
Signage on Exhibits:: English   Star Rating: **

Friends of the Zoo

Yes. Membership at 31.12.2009 - Circa 220

Volunteers

Yes, through Friends of the Zoo

BELFAST ZOO

General Site Description	Located on Cave Hill and overlooking the Belfast Lough with fine views, this attractive hilly site has a dramatic rocky backdrop. There is a good variety of indigenous trees, shrubs and plants. Some paths are fairly steep but the overall site is well suited to a fine Zoological Garden. Buildings are primarily from 1990-2000.
Indoor Exhibits	Tropical Rain Forest, Apes House, Elephant and Giraffe House, Monkey House
Star Attractions	Spectacled Bears, Lemurs, Tigers, Temmincks Golden Cat, Fossas, Coatis, Tree Kangaroos, Pudus, Walk Through Bird Park, Gorillas, Chimpanzees, Tamarins/Goeldi's Monkeys
Time required	whole zoo: 6 hours star attractions: 2 - 3 hours

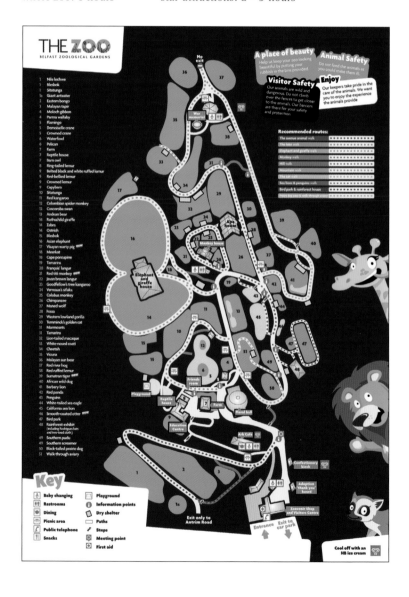

TIERPARK BERLIN
DER HAUPTSTADT ZOO

Contact

Name	Tierpark Berlin Friedrichsfelde
Address	Am Tierpark 125,
	10319 Berlin, D
Phone	+49(0) 30 515 310
Fax	+49(0) 30 512 4061
Email	info@tierpark-berlin.de
Website	www.tierpark-berlin.de

Opening Hours

Open every day of the year
20 March to 24 October   09.00 to 18.00
25 October to 19 March   09.00 to 17.00

Entrance Prices 2011

Entrance Prices 2011	EUR
Adult	12.00
Child 5-15	6.00
Child under 5	0.00
Dogs	0.00
Annual Card - Adult	58.00
Annual Card - Child 5-15	28.00
Annual Card - Family 2 Adults and 3 Children	120.00
Concessions: school children, students, apprentices and disabled visitors	

Transport Access

Car	Berlin - Lichtenberg - Friedrichsfelde, Alt -Friedrichsfelde/ Am Tierpark/ Treskow Allee Waldow Allee
Car Park	Yes, at Zoo EUR 4.00
Bus	296, 396 and 194
Tram	M17, 27, 37
Nearest Station	Tierpark - Linie U5

Ownership of Zoo

Municipal/Company - 100% Berlin Zoo AG. Circa 2800 shareholders, Land Berlin holds 1 golden share. Tierpark Berlin Friedrichsfelde GmbH is a wholly owned subsidiary of Zoo Berlin AG

Area of Zoo   160 Ha

Date of Foundation   Founded 1954, opened 1955

Visitor Numbers   Circa 1,000,000

TIERPARK BERLIN

Animal Inventory at 31.12.2009

	Number	Species
Mammals	1415	191
Birds	2425	389
Reptiles	537	102
Amphibians	39	4
Fish	1228	128

Facilities

Catering (sub-contract):
Restaurant, Cafeteria, Kiosks, Picnic Place - Café im Tierpark
Retail (sub-contract): Zoo shop
Children's Zoo: Yes, large variety of farm, domestic and other animals
Children's Playground: Yes

Dogs

Allowed on leads: Yes   Kennel Facilities: No

Feeding by Visitors

Strictly prohibited

Shows, etc

History of Berlin Zoos in Schloss Friedrichsfelde planned 2011

Education

Zoo keeper talks: No
Zoo School/Education Centre: Yes
Biodiversity Centre: No
Zoo Guidebook: Yes, EUR 4.00
Signage on Exhibits:: German   Star Rating: **

Friends of the Zoo

Yes, Freunde Hauptstadtzoos
Fördergemeinschaft von Tierpark und Zoo Berlin e. V.
Membership at 31.12.2009 - Circa 1500

Volunteers Yes

General Site Description At 160ha, this is the second largest zoo site in this survey. The generally flat site was once part of the neoclassical Friedrichfelde Palace which now belongs to the Tierpark and has recently been sympathetically renovated. Formal planted gardens lead up to and surround the palace. The site is predominantly open but has some beautiful mature trees and wooded areas and some good water features particularly in the Palace area. Of special note are the large enclosures for hoofstock.

Indoor Exhibits Alfred Brehms House - large cats/ tropical birds and flying fox, Giraffe House, Pachyderms House - elephants, rhinos and manatees, Crocodile Hall, Monkey House, Reptile House

Star Attractions Gelada Baboons, Polar Bears, Rock Hyrax, Pelicans, Giraffes, Camels, Gibbons, Tigers, Turtles, Birds of Prey Volière, Lemur Walk Through, Fruit Bats

Time required whole zoo: 8 - 10 hours star attractions: 3 hours

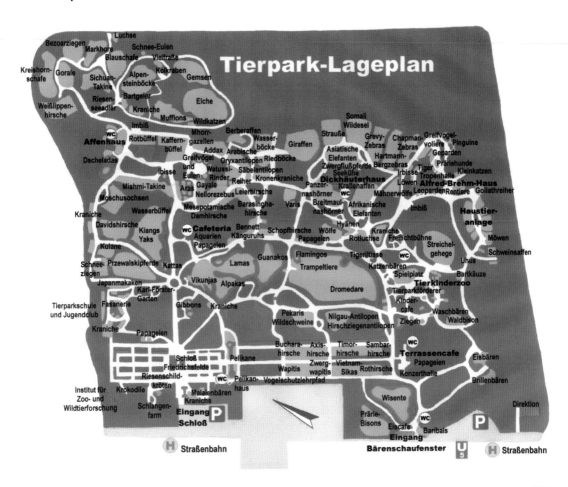

ZOO BERLIN
DER HAUPTSTADT ZOO

ZOO AQUARIUM BERLIN
DER HAUPTSTADT ZOO

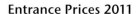

Contact

Name	Zoologischer Garten Berlin
Address	Hardenbergplatz 8
	10787 Berlin, D
Phone	+49(0) 30 25 4010
Fax	+49(0) 30 25 401 255
Email	info@zoo-berlin.de
Website	www.zoo-berlin.de

Opening Hours

Open every day of the year

April to September	09.00 to 19.00
October to March	09.00 to 17.00
Aquarium All Year	09.00 to 18.00

Entrance Prices 2011

	Zoo	Zoo and Aquarium
	EUR	EUR
Adult	13.00	20.00
Child 5-15	6.50	10.00
Child under 5	Free	Free
Family Card - 1 Adult and Children	22.00	33.00
Family Card - 2 Adults and Children	35.00	50.00
Annual Card - Adult	60.00	90.00
Annual Card - Child 5-15	30.00	45.00
Annual Card - Adult and Children	77.00	115.00
Annual Card - 2 Adults and Children	122.00	180.00
Concessions: students, apprentices, unemployed, disabled visitors and their carers		

Transport Access

Car	Budapesterstrasse/Kurfürstendamm
Car Park	Parkhaus Nürnberger Straße & Parkhaus Budapester Straße
Bus	Terminal Zoologischer Garten 15 Lines
Metro	Zoologischer Garten U2 and U9
Nearest Station	S Bahn Zoologischer Garten

Ownership of Zoo

Municipal/Company - 100% Berlin Zoo AG. Circa 2800 shareholders, Land Berlin holds 1 golden share.

Area of Zoo

32 Ha

Date of Foundation

Founded 1841 Opening 1844

Visitor Numbers

Circa 3,100,000

Animal Inventory at 31.12.2009

	Number	Species
Mammals	1147	177
Birds	2481	355
Reptiles	485	77
Amphibians	435	46
Fish	5434	511

Facilities

Catering (sub-contract):
Restaurant, Cafeteria, Kiosks, Picnic Place - Das Hauptrestaurant, Waldschänke, Bistro Aquarium & Kiosk
Retail (sub-contract): Zoo shop
Children's Zoo: Yes   Children's Playground: Yes

Dogs

Allowed on leads: No   Kennel Facilities: No

Feeding by Visitors

Strictly prohibited

Shows, etc

No

Education

Zoo keeper talks: No, but several opportunities to see animals being fed - see daily programme
Zoo School/Education Centre: Yes
Biodiversity Centre: No
Zoo Guidebook: Yes, EUR 4.00
Signage on Exhibits:: German   Star Rating: **

Friends of the Zoo

Yes, Freunde Hauptstadtzoos
Fördergemeinschaft von Tierpark und Zoo Berlin e. V.
Membership at 31.12.2009 - Circa 1500

Volunteers

Yes

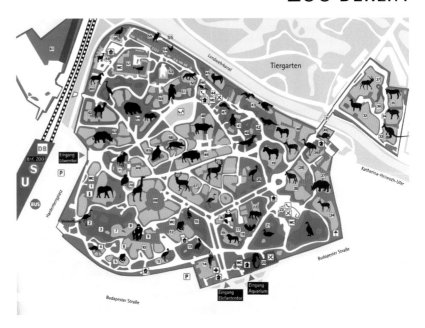

General Site Description

This famous zoo is a really delightful classical zoological garden with fine mature tree cover and well maintained gardens. The zoo has good water features and vegetation, well designed and varied enclosures and the feel of an oasis of calm in a major capital city. Europe's largest animal collection is housed here often in historical listed buildings which have been well restored. It's the birthplace of Knut and you can see 50 pairs of breeding herons who have made the zoo their home.

Indoor Exhibits

Aquarium, Apes and Monkeys House, Elephant House, Rhino and Tapir House, Giraffe House, Penguin House, Hippo House, Bird House

Star Attractions

Hippos, Tigers, Elephants, Pygmy Hippos, Lions, Beavers, Chimpanzees, Walk Through – Shore Birds, King Penguins, Gorillas, Walk Through – Water Birds, Pelicans, Orang Utans, Small Claw Otters

Time required

whole zoo: 10 hours   star attractions: 4 hours

BOJNICE ZOO

Contact

Name	Zooloogická Záhrada Bojnice
Address	Zámok a okolie 6
	97201 Bojnice, SK
Phone	+421(0) 465 40 29 75
Fax	+421(0) 465 40 32 41
Email	zoobojnice@zoobojnice.sk
Website	www.zoobojnice.sk

Opening Hours

Open every day of the year

February	08.00 to 16.00
April to August	08.00.to 18.00
September, October, March and April	08.00 to 17.00
November to January	08.00 to 15.00

Entrance Prices 2011

	Summer / EUR	Winter / EUR
Adult	3.00	2.50
Child 4-15	1.50	1.00
Child under 4	Free	Free
Concessions: Students, Over 65s, Disabled Visitors		

Transport Access

Car	E75 Bratislava –Trencin and then E572 Trencin - Bojnice
Car Park	Yes, at Zoo Charged
Bus	Bus Stop 600m from Zoo Entrance
Nearest Station	Prievidza Town 3 Kms

Ownership of Zoo   Government, 100% Ministry of Environment

Area of Zoo   41 Ha (21 Ha in use)

Date of Foundation   1955

Visitor Numbers   Circa 370,000

Animal Inventory
at 31.12.2009

	Number	Species
Mammals	350	80
Birds	536	136
Reptiles	446	49
Amphibians	55	15
Fish	599	85

Facilities   Catering (sub-contract):
                         Restaurant, Cafeteria, Kiosks, Picnic Place
                         Retail: Zoo shop
                         Children's Zoo: Yes, including small rodent house
                         Children's Playground: Yes

Dogs	Allowed on leads: No Kennel Facilities: No
Feeding by Visitors	Strictly prohibited
Shows, etc	No
Education	Zoo keeper talks: No Zoo School/Education Centre: Yes Biodiversity Centre: No, but planned in new development. Zoo Guidebook: Yes, EUR 5.00 Signage on Exhibits:: Slovak Star Rating: *
Friends of the Zoo	No
Volunteers	No
General Site Description	A fine undulating site with substantial areas of deciduous and coniferous trees, large natural rock features but with limited water supply. Fine view of the neighbouring Bojnice castle. The small planted areas in the zoo are those formerly belonging to the castle. There is a contrast between the 20th Century fenced outdoor enclosures and the much more attractive 21st Century open moated outdoor enclosures which give a pleasant perspective. The zoo is in the early stages of major improvement through new investment.
Indoor Exhibits	Elephant House, Primate House, Vivarium
Star Attractions	Orang Utans, Greater Kudu, Mountain Goats, Hartmann's Zebra, Guanaco, Llama, Sarus Crane, Bongo, Rhea, Blackbuck, Steller's Sea Eagle, Cassowary
Time required	whole zoo: 3 - 4 hours star attractions: 1 - 2 hours

Contact

	Name	Zoo Bratislava
	Address	Mlynská Dolina 1,
		84227 Bratislava, SK
	Phone	+421(0) 265 42 28 48
	Fax	+421(0) 265 42 18 68
	Email	zoo@zoobratislava.sk
	Website	www.zoobratislava.sk

Opening Hours

Open every day of the year
April to October   09.00 to 19.00
November to March   10.00 to 16.00

Entrance Prices 2011

	Summer	Winter
	EUR	EUR
Adult	4.30	3.30
Child 3-15	2.70	2.00
Child under 3 and disabled visitors	Free	Free
Family Day Ticket 2 Adults and 2 Children	12.60	
Book of 10 Adult Tickets	33.50	
Book of 10 Child Tickets	20.00	
Annual Card – Parents	33.20	
Annual Card – Child 3-6	6.65	
Concessions: Over 65s, Special Needs Visitors, Students		

Transport Access

Car	Follow brown signs to Dino Park Zoo from CR highway
Car Park	Yes, at Zoo Free of Charge
Bus	30,31,32 from Bratislava Main Station and 37,39,92 to Stop Zoo
Nearest Station	Bratislava Main Station

Ownership of Zoo   Municipal, 100% Bratislava
City Council

Area of Zoo   96 Ha

Date of Foundation   1960

Visitor Numbers   Circa 300,000

Animal Inventory at 31.12.2009

	Number	Species
Mammals	698	88
Birds	209	45
Reptiles	48	20
Amphibians	0	0
Fish	90	8

Facilities

Catering (sub-contract):
Cafés, Picnic Place - 5 Cafés
Retail (sub-contract): Zoo shop
Children´s Zoo: Yes   Children´s Playground: Yes

Dogs

Allowed on leads: No   Kennel Facilities: No

Feeding by Visitors

Strictly prohibited

Shows, etc

Dino Park

Education

Zoo keeper talks: Yes, opportunities daily May to September –
see programme in Zoo
Zoo School/Education Centre: Yes
Biodiversity Centre: No
Zoo Guidebook: No, not at present
Signage on Exhibits:: Slovak   Star Rating: **

Friends of the Zoo

No

Volunteers

Yes, Circa 2

ZOO BRATISLAVA

General Site Description	A very large hilly site within the city with mature tree cover. Although a small river runs through the lower part of the zoo, there is a distinct water shortage elsewhere. A large part of the zoo is presently unused but there are plans for an African savannah in the future. The great apes house, opened in 2010, is a milestone in the zoo's history as it provides the first very fine indoor facility.
Indoor Exhibits	Great Apes House, Tiger House, Lion House, Leopard and Jaguar House, Bird House
Star Attractions	Orang Utans, Gibbons, Ruffed Lemurs, Chimpanzees, Meerkats, Racoons, Flamingoes, Pelicans, Turtles
Time required	whole zoo: 4 - 6 hours star attractions: 1 - 2 hours

Contact

	Name	Bristol Zoo Gardens
	Address	Clifton,
		Bristol BS8 3HA, UK
	Phone	+44(0)117 974 7300
	Fax	+44(0)117 973 6814
	Email	information@bristolzoo.org.uk
	Website	www.bristolzoo.org.uk

Opening Hours

Open every day of the year, except Christmas Day

Summer: Late March to Late October 09.00 to 17.30

Winter: Late October to Late March 09.00 to 17.00

Summer BST and Winter GMT - follow dates for clock change

Entrance Prices 2011

	GBP
Daily Ticket Prices Include a 10% Voluntary Conservation Donation	
Adult	14.00
Child 3-14	8.50
Child under 3 and Carers of Disabled Visitors	Free
Family Day Ticket - 2 Adults and 2 Children	40.50
Annual Card - Adult	50.00
Annual Card - Child	20.00
Annual Card – Joint 2 Persons	80.00
Concessions: students, over 60s, disabled visitors and their carers	
Annual Card Holders are entitled to free entry at reciprocal zoos	

Transport Access	Car	M5 Junction 17 A4018 Follow Brown Tourist signs to Zoo in Clifton area of Bristol. M4/M32 Follow signs for Clifton and Zoo
	Car Park	North Car park at Zoo every day £3 per day
		West Car Park – overflow car park on College Road £3 per day
	Bus	8 or 9 to Zoo's Main Entrance
	Nearest Station	Clifton Down Station - 10 minute walk to Zoo, Bristol Temple Meads Station then 8 or 9 Bus to Zoo
	Bicycle	Bicycle Racks at Zoo

Ownership of Zoo   Registered Charity, 100% Bristol, Clifton & West of England Zoological Society Limited

Area of Zoo   5 Ha / 12 acres

Date of Foundation   1835

Visitor Numbers   Circa 550,000

Animal Inventory at 31.12.2009

	Number	Species
Mammals	465	57
Birds	520	74
Reptiles	208	46
Amphibians	253	15
Fish	2144	126

Facilities

Catering (sub-contracted):
Restaurant, Café, Kiosks, Picnic Place - The Coral Café
Retail (zoo owned): Zoo shop
Children's Zoo: Yes
Children's Playground: Adventure Playground - ZooRopia
Adults GBP 7.50 Children GBP 6.40: ZooRopia provides an adventure playground allowing adults and children over 5 to swing alongside the apes – harnesses and training provided.

Dogs   Allowed on leads: No
Kennel Facilities: No

Feeding by Visitors   Strictly prohibited.
Except Lorikeet Feeding
in Forest of Birds

Shows, etc   Yes

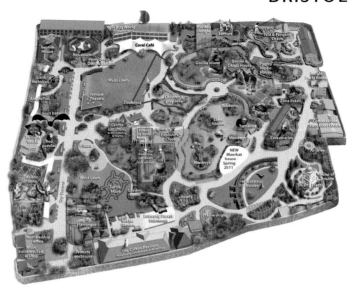

Education

Zoo keeper talks: Yes, 10 daily - see website or information in zoo for daily programme. Keeper talks or animal encounters every 30 minutes between 11.00 to 16.00 daily
Zoo School/Education Centre: Yes
Biodiversity Centre: No
Zoo Guidebook: Yes. GBP 3.00
Signage on Exhibits:: English   Star Rating: **

Friends of the Zoo

No, but Annual Membership Scheme
Membership at 31.12.2009 – Circa 12,000

Volunteers

Yes, Circa 280

General Site Description

Despite its small area, Bristol zoo is a delight: it has a truly garden atmosphere as it is set in award winning gardens which give a sense of space, colour and good perspectives. The site is flat and manageable. Many exhibits, such as Seal and Penguin Coasts, evince really good planning. A new Meerkat Enclosure opens in 2011.
The zoo was the home of, Alfred, the only gorilla in the UK (1930 to 1938), and of the first Gorilla born in the UK in 1971.
Though Bristol is the smallest of the zoological gardens surveyed by geographical size, a visit here is a great pleasure.

Indoor Exhibits

Monkey Jungle, Twilight World, Okapi House, Reptile House, Bug World, Gorilla House, Aquarium, Butterfly House, Forest of Birds

Star Attractions

Asian Lions, Penguins, Lemur Walk Through, Prairie Dog, Fur Seals, Red Panda, Giant Tortoise, Keas

Time required

whole zoo: 5 hours   star attractions: 2 hours

BUDAPEST
ZOO

BUDAPEST ZOO

Contact

Name	Budapest Zoo and Botanical Gardens
Address	H - 1146 Budapest, H
	Állatkerti krt. 6-12.
Phone	+36 (0) 1 273 4900
Fax	+36 (0) 1 273 4986
Email	titkarsag@zoobudapest.com
Website	www.zoobudapest.com

Opening Hours

Open every day of the year, except 24/12 and 31/12

January, February, November, December	09.00 to 17.00
March, April, September, October	09.00 to 18.00
May, June, July, Augus	09.00 to 19.00

Entrance Prices 2011

Entrance Prices at 01.04.2010	HUF
Adult	1,990
Child 2-14	1,390
Child under 2	Free
Students' Ticket	1,390
Family - 2 Adults and 2 Children	5,700
Additional Child on Family Ticket	980
Discounts with Budapest Card	27%
Palm House and Aquarium Free with zoo ticket	

Transport Access

Car	100 m from Heroes' Square (Hösök tere)
Car Park	Street Parking only in vicinity
Trolley Bus	Red coloured trolley-bus No.72, 75, 79 to stop Állatkert (Zoo).
Bus	Blue coloured bus No. 20E, 30, 30A, 105 to stop Hösök tere (Heroes' Square)
Metro Stations	200 m to M1 Yellow Underground to Szécheny Furdo

Ownership of Zoo   Municipal, 100% Budapest City Council

Area of Zoo   11 Ha

Date of Foundation   1866

Visitor Numbers

Circa 1,000,000
Number 1 Paid Attraction
in Budapest

Animal Inventory at 31.12.2009

	Number	Species
Mammals	780	108
Birds	1,475	195
Reptiles	455	103
Amphibians	561	32
Fish	2,753	282

Facilities

Catering (sub-contract):
Restaurant, Cafeteria, Kiosks, Picnic Place
Retail (zoo owned): Zoo shop
Children's Zoo: Yes, including superb Hamsters Exhibit
Children's Playground: Yes, an outdoor playground and the indoor Zoo Camp
and Playhouse.

Dogs

Allowed on leads: No   Kennel Facilities: No

Feeding by Visitors

In general not allowed, except from dispensers in zoo for certain species

Shows, etc

Yes - Regular art, photo, ethnographic and science exhibitions. In Summer, Meet
the Animals Encounters every 30 minutes. Magic Mountain Museum of Life

Education

Zoo keeper talks: Yes
Zoo School/Education Centre: Yes
Biodiversity Centre: Yes
Zoo Guidebook: Yes
Signage on Exhibits:: Hungarian, English   Star Rating: *

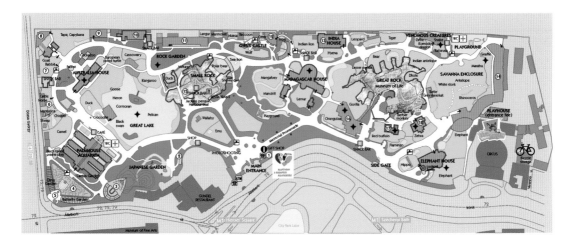

Friends of the Zoo   Yes. Membership at 31.12.2009 – Circa 2,700

Volunteers   Yes. Number of Volunteers at 31.12.2009 – Circa 70

General Site Description   Budapest Zoo is a traditional city zoological and botanical garden, with several fine, sympathetically restored, historic listed buildings. Wonderful vegetation includes 2000 plant species and many historic tree species. The Bonsai collection in a lovely setting is intriguing. The Palm House, the largest tropical garden in Hungary, is delightful. The great rock is a particularly striking feature and is the largest of its kind in European zoos. The collection size, the number of substantial indoor exhibits and feel of the site belies the zoo's relatively small size: it has a very special atmosphere and is a real pleasure to visit. There are plans to extend the site at a future date.

Indoor Exhibits   Savannah House, Palm House and Aquarium, Butterfly House, Old Elephant House, Crocodile House, Buffalo House, Old Giraffe House, South America House, House of Venom, Madagascar House, Monkey House, Gorilla House, Australia House, Insectarium, Orang Utan House, India House, Indonesia House

Star Attractions   Gorillas, Great Pond - Pelicans and Waterfowl, Japanese Garden - Bonsai Collection, Red Pandas, South America Volière, Prevost's Squirrel, Meerkats, Madagascar House - Lemurs, Two Toed Sloth, Mandrills, Australia House, Tortoises, Mangabeys, African Savannah - Giraffes, Barbirussas, Palm House - Toucans, Marmosets

Time required   whole zoo: 6 - 8 hours   star attractions: 3 - 4 hours

PARCO NATURA VIVA

Contact

Name	Parco Natura Viva	
Address	Localita Figara 40,	
	37012 Bussolengo, Verona, I	
Phone	+39 045 71 70 113	
Fax	+39 045 67 70 247	
Email	info@parconaturaviva.it	
Website	www.parconaturaviva.it	

Opening Hours

Open early March to End November	
Early March to End November	09.00 to 18.00
December, January and February	Closed

Entrance Prices 2010

	May to Oct	Mar, Apr and Nov
	EUR	EUR
Adult	19.00	17.50
Child 3-12	16.00	14.00
Child under 3	Free	Free
Annual Card - Adult	45.00	
Annual Card – Child	35.00	
Annual Card – Family 2 Adults, 2 children	105.00	
Price for Safari Park Entry with Vehicle carrying up to 9 persons	18.00	

Transport Access

Car	A4 From West Exit Peschira From East Exit Verona Nord
Car Park	Yes, at Zoo. No charge
Bus	Bus to Zoo from Verona Porta Nuova Station
Nearest Station	Verona Porta Nuova

Ownership of Zoo   Private Company. 100% parco Natura Viva - Garda Zoological Park srl

Area of Zoo   45 Ha

Date of Foundation   1969

Visitor Numbers   Circa 500,000

Animal Inventory at 31.12.2009

	Number	Species
Mammals	487	78
Birds	640	126
Reptiles	306	40
Amphibians	0	0
Fish	152	37

Facilities

Catering (sub-contract):
Restaurant, Cafeteria, Kiosks, Picnic Place - Simba Restaurant, Panda Bar
Retail (sub-contract): Zoo shop - Natura Shop
Children's Zoo: Yes   Children's Playground: Yes

Dogs

Allowed on leads: No   Kennel Facilities: Yes, no charge

Feeding by Visitors

Strictly Prohibited

Shows, etc

Yes. Dino - Extensive Dinosaur Park

Education

Zoo keeper talks: No, but Guides available.
Zoo School/Education Centre: Yes
Biodiversity Centre: No
Zoo Guidebook: Yes. EUR 8.00
Signage on Exhibits: Italian Star Rating: **

Friends of the Zoo   No. Planned for future.

Volunteers   Planned for future.

General Site Description

This developing zoo combines a zoological garden with an adjoining safari park: from 2013 these two aspects will be integrated and Viva Natura will be purely a zoological garden with no drive through Safari section. The zoo is situated on an attractive, diverse, undulating site in a beautiful region near to Lake Garda. The diverse parkland combines savannah, woodland and sloping areas with Mediterranean vegetation and good water and rock features: this varied terrain is well used to provide attractive and naturalistic enclosures.
A delightful feature in the park is the happy sound of 500 plus green parrots nesting in trees in the zoo. There are also free flying storks and herons.
This steadily developing and improving zoo is being organised on GEO -Zoo principles.

Indoor Exhibits   Tropical House – mammals, reptiles, and birds

Star Attractions

Tropical House, Red Pandas, Squirrel Monkeys, Wild Parrots, Snow Leopards, Ring Tailed Lemurs, Tapirs and Rheas, Père David's Deer, Amur Tigers, Ruffed Lemurs, Wolves, Green Iguana, Barbary Macaques, Lynx, Pelicans, Mixed Species Exhibit - of Rhino, Hippo and Nyala, Dino/Extinction area

Time required   whole zoo: 8 hours   star attractions: 3 hours

CHESTER

CHESTER ZOO

Contact

	Name	Chester Zoo
	Address	North of England Zoological Society, Cedar House, Caughall Road, Upton-by-Chester, Chester. CH2 1LH, UK
	Phone	+44 (0)1244 380 280
	Fax	+44 (0)1244 371 273
	Email	info@chesterzoo.org
	Website	www.chesterzoo.org

Opening Hours

Open every day except 25th & 26th December

Low Season: November, December, January, February	10.00 to 16.00
Mid Season: March, April, September, October	10.00 to 17.00
High Season: May, June, July, August	10.00 to 18.00

Entrance Prices

	Low-Season	Mid-Season	High-Season
	GBP	GBP	GBP
Daily Ticket Prices include a 10% Voluntary Conservation Donation			
Adult	13.60	15.95	16.90
Child 3 - 15	9.90	10.95	12.45
Under 2s	Free	Free	Free
Family Ticket Book - 2 Adults and 2 Children	41.50	49.50	55.55
Concession Price	12.05	14.15	15.25
Concessions: Students, Seniors, Disabled Visitors and Carers and Visitors who cycle to Zoo.			

Transport Access

Navi	Sat Nav Post Code CH2 1EU
Car Park	Extensive Free Parking at Main Entrance
Bus	Chester City Centre Bus Exchange
Tram	First Bus Service Nr 1 from Chester City Centre Bus Exchange, every 15 minutes Monday to Saturday and half hourly on Sunday
Nearest Station	Chester Mainline Station and then free Rail Link to Chester City Centre Bus Exchange
Cycle	Cycle Paths to Zoo and 15% discount for visitors arriving by bike

Ownership of Zoo

Registered Charity, 100% North of England Zoological Society

Area of Zoo

50 Ha / 120 acres

Date of Foundation

1931

CHESTER ZOO

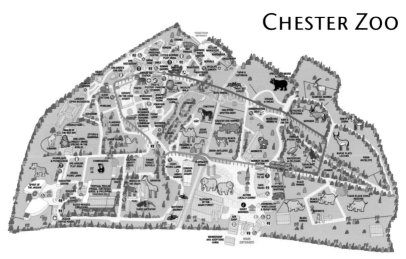

Visitor Numbers   Circa 1,360,000

Animal Inventory at 31.12.2009

	Number	Species
Mammals	1864	79
Birds	1138	155
Reptiles	230	54
Amphibians	577	24
Fish	3829	80

Facilities   Catering (zoo owned):
Restaurant, Café, Kiosks, Picnic Place - Oakfield Manor, Ark Restaurant,
Café Tsavo, Jaguar Coffee House, Acorn Pub – Summer Only
Retail (zoo owned): 2 Shops Ark Zoo Shop and Fountains Shop
Children´s Zoo: No
Children´s Playground: Yes - 3 including adventure Playground

Dogs   Allowed on leads: No   Kennel Facilities: No

Feeding by Visitors   Strictly Prohibited

Shows, etc   Various exhibitions in Joseph Banks Room

Education   Zoo keeper talks: Yes, organised at specific times on certain days.
Zoo School/Education Centre: Yes
Biodiversity Centre: No
Zoo Guidebook: Yes. GBP 6.00
Signage on Exhibits: English   Star Rating: **

Friends of the Zoo   No, but Members of Chester Zoo, Circa 35,000

Volunteers   Yes. Circa 30. 400 in high season.

CHESTER ZOO

General Site Description

Although a rather flat site with partial tree cover, it has been converted to a delightful zoological garden with good water features. Outdoor enclosures are generally spacious and without obvious barriers, providing an excellent visitor experience. Buildings, many of which are recent, are functional.

The gardens include beautiful examples of artistic specialised landscape work which include Andes and Asian gardens, grasses display, fountains lawn with bedding plants, a sunken garden and a Roman garden. There is also a local wildlife garden.

A lovely combination of zoological and botanical highlights combines to make Chester Zoo the leading UK zoological garden and the UK's second biggest paid visitor attraction.

Indoor Exhibits

Elephant House, Secret World of the Okapi, Butterfly House, Realm of the Red Ape, Tropical Realm - reptiles and birds, Monkey House, Spirit of the Jaguar, Tsavo Rhino Experience, Aquarium, Chimpanzee House, Fruit Bat Forest

Star Attractions

Elephants, Giant Otters, Rodriguez Bats, Jaguars, Coati and Spectacled Bears, Hornbills, Condors, Orang Utan and Small Claw Otter, Marmosets and Tamarins, Gibbons, Babirussa and Small Claw Otter, Lion Tailed Macaque

Time required

whole zoo: 6 - 8 hours   star attractions: 3 - 4 hours

COLCHESTER ZOO

Contact

	Name	Colchester Zoo
	Address	Maldon Road, Stanway,
		Colchester, Essex CO3 0SL, UK
	Phone	+44(0)1206 331 292
	Fax	+44(0)1206 331 392
	Email	enquiries@colchester-zoo.co.uk
	Website	www.colchester-zoo.com

Opening Hours

Open every day except Christmas Day

November to February	09.30 to 16.30
March, September and October	09.30 to 17.00
April to August	09.30 to 18.00

Entrance Prices 2011

Prices include a voluntary GBP 1.00 donation to Action for the Wild Charity Mid, Peak and Winter Prices apply – Mid Prices are given here (others +/- 12%)	
	GBP
Adult	16.00
Child 3-14	10.00
Child under 3	Free
Annual Card - Adult	43.00
Annual Card - Child 3-14	27.00
Concessions: students, over 60s, disabled visitors and their carers, advance purchase e tickets	
Annual Card Holders are entitled to free entry at reciprocal zoos	

Transport Access

Navi	Sat Nav CO3 0SL
Car	A12 Junction 26 A1124 and follow brown elephant signs
Car Park	Free Parking at Colchester Zoo
Bus	Colchester Bus Station Stand 9 for various bus services according to season
Nearest Station	Colchester Main Station 10 minute taxi ride
Bicycle	Cycle Racks at Zoo

Ownership of Zoo

Private. 100% Colchester Zoo Limited owned by the Tropeano Family

Area of Zoo

24 Ha / 60 acres

Date of Foundation

1963

Visitor Numbers

Circa 750,000

Animal Inventory at 16.07.2010

	Number	Species
Mammals	403	88
Birds	220	47
Reptiles	117	30
Amphibians	50	6
Fish	1144	69

Facilities

Catering (sub-contract):
Restaurant, Café, Kiosks, Picnic Place - Café Um Phafa – main restaurant
Retail (zoo owned): Colchester Zoo Ark Shop, Acacia Shop, Tanganyika Road Train
Children's Zoo: Yes   Children's Playground: Yes

Dogs

Allowed on leads: No   Kennel Facilities: No

Feeding by Visitors

Strictly Prohibited. Keeper supervised elephant and giraffe feeding each afternoon

Shows, etc

Yes

Education

Zoo keeper talks: Yes, 50 opportunities daily – see information in zoo for daily programme. Keeper talks or animal encounters between 10.30 to 16.30 daily.
Zoo School/Education Centre: Yes, including Discovery Centre
Biodiversity Centre: No
Zoo Guidebook: Yes. GBP 2.99
Signage on Exhibits: English   Star Rating: ***

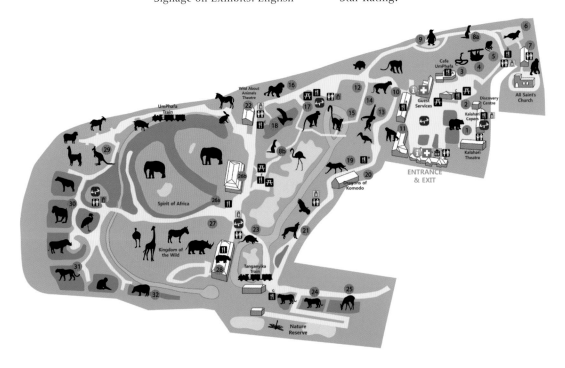

Friends of the Zoo No but Annual Membership Scheme
Membership at 31.12.2009 – Circa 36,000

Volunteers Yes. Circa 15.

General Site Description Colchester Zoo is on a steep hilly site which has been advantageously used in enclosure design to give varied perspectives on the animals. A great deal of thought has been put into the facilities and enclosure vegetation for the animals exhibited. Throughout the Zoo there is good varied vegetation and there are several good water features. Extensive and interesting information is well displayed.
A yellow easier route is provided for wheelchair and pushchair users: it avoids the steepest hills. Another thoughtful feature of the zoo is the extensive use of covered walkways around many enclosures. The zoo is divided into 7 zones: Beginning Zone, Aquatic Zone, Valley Zone, Lakelands, Kidz Zone, African Zone and The Heights.
Colchester Zoo's Action for the Wild Charity has purchased a 5,000 Ha reserve in Kwa Zulu Natal, South Africa and several formerly indigenous species have been successfully reintroduced to the area: many are breeding well and information in the zoo features this conservation project.

Indoor Exhibits Orang Utan House, Chimps House, Elephant House, Worlds Apart - Reptiles, Giraffe and Rhino House, There are extensive covered areas for viewing many species.

Star Attractions Amur Leopards, Orang Utans, Giant Anteaters, Meerkats, Mandrills, Margays, Binturongs, Tamarins and Marmosets, Cattle Egrets

Time required whole zoo: 6 - 8 hours star attractions: 3 hours

KÖLNER ZOO

COLOGNE ZOO

Contact

Name	Kölner Zoo/Cologne Zoo
Address	Riehler Straße 173, 50735 Köln, D
Phone	+49(0) 221 778 50
Fax	+49(0) 221 778 5111
Email	info@koelnerzoo.de
Website	www.koelnerzoo.de

Opening Hours

Open every day of the year

Summer Mid-March to Mid-October	09.00 to 18.00
Winter Mid-October to Mid-March	09.00 to 17.00
Aquarium - All Year	09.00 to 18.00

Entrance Prices 2011

Zoo plus Aquarium	EUR
Adult	15.00
Child 4-14	7.50
Child Under 4	Free
Annual Card - Adult	75.00
Annual Card - Child	45.00
Annual Card – Family 2 Parents and 2 children	200.00
Concessions: students, pensioners, disabled visitors and their carers	
On Mondays (except holidays) and after 16.00 daily reduced price entry Annual Card holders qualify for NRW discount	

Transport Access

Car	From South: A3/A4, then Köln Centrum, then zoo signposted
	From North: A1/A57, then Köln Centrum, then zoo signposted
Car Park	Yes, at Zoo Daily Charge EUR 3.00
Bus	140 to Stop Zoo/Flora or Zoo Express from Domplatz
U-Bahn	Nr. 18 to Zoo/Flora

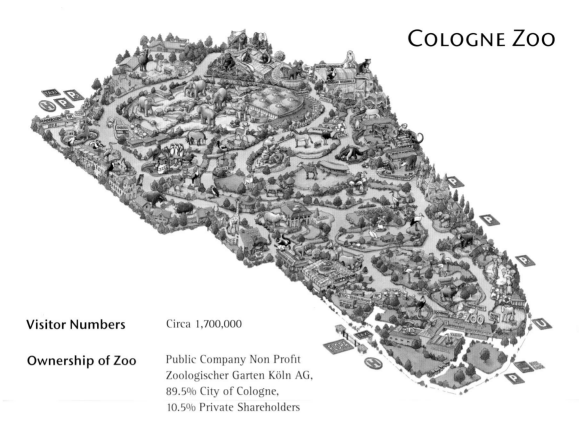

COLOGNE ZOO

| **Visitor Numbers** | Circa 1,700,000 |

| **Ownership of Zoo** | Public Company Non Profit
Zoologischer Garten Köln AG,
89.5% City of Cologne,
10.5% Private Shareholders |

Area of Zoo   20 Ha plus 1.5 Ha being added

Date of Foundation   1860

Animal Inventory at 31.12.2010

	Number	Species
Mammals	501	66
Birds	1290	202
Reptiles	479	80
Amphibians	318	37
Fish	5550	234

Facilities

Catering (zoo owned):
Restaurant, Cafeteria, Kiosks, Picnic Place - Zoo Restaurant, Café Kunterbunt, Imbiss am Elefantenpark, Zebrasserie
Retail (zoo owned): Zoo shop - Zoovenirs (Run by Friends of the Zoo)
Children's Zoo: No, in planning stage   Children's Playground: Yes

Dogs   Allowed on leads: No   Kennel Facilities: Yes

Feeding by Visitors   Strictly prohibited

Shows, etc   Sea Lion Show, Bird show, History of Cologne Zoo Exhibit

COLOGNE ZOO

Education Zoo keeper talks: Yes, 7 opportunities daily – see daily programme in Zoo
Day and Night Tours
Zoo School/Education Centre: Yes
Biodiversity Centre: No
Zoo Guidebook: No
Signage on Exhibits: German Star Rating: ***

Friends of the Zoo Yes, Die Freunde des Kölner Zoos e. V. Membership at 31.12.2009 – Circa 5,000

Volunteers Yes, Circa 75

General Site Description Köln is a very fine city zoo located close to the banks of the Rhine. There are many fine mature trees and attractive gardens. The elephant park is large, spacious, high-tech and one of the most impressive in the survey; it covers 2.5Ha. There are over 25 primate species. The Aquarium includes a Terrarium and Insectarium. There is an excellent atmosphere in the zoo. Visitors have very good visibility onto imaginative exhibits which give the animals natural habitats and there are some unusual varieties of shrubs and plants.

Indoor Exhibits Elephant House, Tropenhaus (Rainforest). Apes House (Urwaldhaus), Hippodom (Hippos and Crocodiles), Old Elephant House, Giraffe House, Aquarium, Madagascar House, South America House

Star Attractions Asian Elephants, Bonobos, Red Pandas, Baboons, Hippos, Meerkats, White Lipped Tamarins, Bird Volières, Crocodiles, Racoons, Tapirs/Capybaras, Pelicans, Cheetahs, Fish Otters, Ring Tailed Madagascan Mongooses, Flamingos, Socorro Doves, Marabous

Time required whole zoo: 6 - 8 hours star attractions: 3 - 4 hours

Contact	Name	Zoo København / Copenhagen Zoo
	Address	Roskildevej 38, 2000 Frederiksberg, DK
	Phone	+45 (0) 72 200 200
	Fax	+45(0) 72 200 2193
	Email	zoo@zoo.dk
	Website	www.zoo.dk

Opening Hours

Open every day of the year

November to March	10.00 to 16.00
April, May, September, October	10.00 to 17.00
June to August	10.00 to 18.00/ 21.00

Entrance Prices 2011

	Mar to Oct / DKK	Nov to Feb / DKK
Adult	140.00	110.00
Child 3-11	80.00	50.00
Annual Card - Adult	440.00	
Annual Card - Child	275.00	
Concessions: 65+, students, disabled visitors and their carers		
Annual card also gives free entry to 3 other Danish Zoos		

Transport Access

Car	From Copenhagen Centre Vesterbrogade/Roskildevej
Bus	6A, 28
Nearest Station	Copenhagen Central Station

Ownership of Zoo   Private Foundation. Non-profit trust foundation with government support and patron HRH Prince Consort, Zoologisk Have København

Area of Zoo   11 Ha

Date of Foundation   1859

Visitor Numbers   Circa 1,300,000

Animal Inventory at 16.07.2010

	Number	Species
Mammals	597	65
Birds	471	82
Reptiles	242	44
Amphibians	383	22
Fish	442	15

Facilities

Catering (zoo owned):
Restaurant, Café, Kiosks, Picnic Place - Restaurant Provianten, Café Karen Blixen
Retail (zoo owned): Zoo shop
Children's Zoo: Yes, a special feature: it includes Pony Track and Farm Experience
Children's Playground: Yes

Dogs

Allowed on leads: No   Kennel Facilities: No

Feeding by Visitors

Strictly Prohibited.

Shows, etc

Yes. Birds of Prey Display. Daily events 11.00 to 15.30, Feeds, demonstrations and encounters – see daily programme

Education

Zoo keeper talks: Yes
Zoo School/Education Centre: Yes, Fine Zoo School
Biodiversity Centre: No
Zoo Guidebook: Yes. DKK 45.00
Signage on Exhibits: Danish and some English   Star Rating: *

Friends of the Zoo

No, but Members and Sponsors Club (open to annual card holders and sponsors)

Volunteers   No

General Site Description

Copenhagen Zoo provides a fine example of a traditional city zoological garden and makes superb use of a relatively small site bisected by a main road and bordering a large natural royal park. The generally flat site has mature deciduous trees and good vegetation. The zoo is exceptionally clean, has a thoroughly attractive feel and evinces good environmental awareness.. Major investment over the last decade has produced some excellent quality buildings and the historic listed buildings are well renovated and maintained.
The new Flamingo Exhibit will open in 2011 and this will be followed in 2012 by Arctic Ring. It may be possible to extend the site in the future.

Indoor Exhibits

Elephant House, Giraffe House, Farm Animals House, Hippo House, Butterfly House, World of Primates, Scarlet Ibis House, Reptile House, The Living Night, Tropical Birds and Reptile House, Ape Jungle

Star Attractions

Asian Elephants, Seals , Giraffes, Hippos, Macaws, Loris, Tropical House, Tamarins, Tasmanian Devils, African Savannah, Scarlet Ibis

Time required   whole zoo: 6 - 8 hours   star attractions: 3 - 4 hours

ZOO DORTMUND

Contact

	Name	Zoo Dortmund
	Address	Mergelteich Str. 80, 44225 Dortmund, D
	Phone	+49(0) 231 502 8581
	Fax	+49(0) 231 712 175
	Email	zoo@dortmund.de
	Website	www.zoo-dortmund.de

Opening Hours

Open every dax of the year

16 March to 15 October	09.00 to 18.30
16 October to 15 February	09.00 to 16.30
16 February to 15 March	09.00 to 17.30

Entrance Prices 2011

	EUR
Adult	7.50
Child 4-17	4.00
Children under 4	Free
Annual Card - Adult	45.00
Annual Card - Child	24.00
Annual Card – Family	120.00
Concessions: Friends of the Zoo, Students, Dortmund Social Pass Holders, Armed Forces Personnel	
Annual Card Holders qualify for NRW Partner Zoos discount	

Transport Access

Car	Autobahnring Exit Dortmund Süd or B236/B1/B54
Car Park	Yes, at Zoo Free of Charge Weekdays, EUR 1.00 Sundays and Holidays
Bus	438,440,443,447,449,450,518
Tram	U49 Direction Hacheney
Nearest Station	Dortmund - Tierpark

Ownership of Zoo   Municipal. 100% Stadt Dortmund

Area of Zoo   28 Ha

Date of Foundation   1953

Visitor Numbers   Circa 520,000

**Animal Inventory
at 16.07.2010**

	Number	Species
Mammals	773	72
Birds	458	80
Reptiles	49	16
Amphibians	53	9
Fish	142	20

Facilities

Catering (sub-contract):
Restaurant, Café, Kiosks, Picnic Place - Restaurant Kronen am Zoo, Waldschänke
Retail (sub-contract): Zoo shop
Children's Zoo: Yes   Children's Playground: Yes

Dogs

Allowed on leads: No   Kennel Facilities: No

Feeding by Visitors

In general NOT allowed - except in petting zoo under supervision

Shows, etc

No

Education

Zoo keeper talks: Yes
Zoo School/Education Centre: Yes
Biodiversity Centre: No
Zoo Guidebook: Yes. EUR 1.00
Signage on Exhibits: German   Star Rating: **

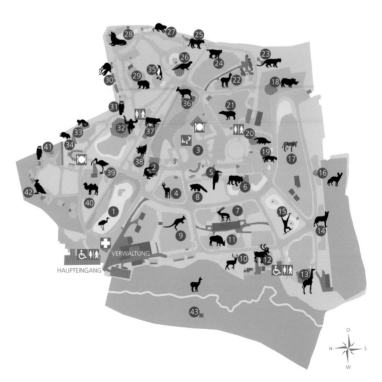

ZOO DORTMUND

Friends of the Zoo   Yes, Zoofreunde Dortmund e. V.   Membership at 31.12.2009 – Circa 400

Volunteers   Yes, Number at 31.12.2009 - Circa 12

General Site Description   Splendidly set in delightful woodland and parkland area which was formerly a manor site, Dortmund Zoo is on the edge of the city. The zoo has a fine selection of deciduous and coniferous trees which are informatively labelled. Dortmund has a notable Giant Anteater exhibit: the zoo holds the European Studbook and is heavily involved in breeding and conservation of this endearing species. The zoo is very clean and well-arranged and the signage to help you navigate the zoo is good.

Indoor Exhibits   Rumah Hutan – Tropical House, Giraffe House, Amazon House, Rhino House, Tamandua House, Otter House, Lion and Tiger House

Star Attractions   Orang Utans, Jaguarundis, Giant Otters, Owls Walk Through, Giraffes , Lynx, Penguins, Bat-Eared Foxes, Giant Anteaters, Siamangs, Flamingos, Cormorants, African Savannah, Bush Dogs

Time required   whole zoo: 6 - 8 hours   star attractions: 2 - 3 hours

BIOPARC
ZOO DE DOUÉ LA FONTAINE

ZOO DE DOUÉ-LA-FONTAINE

Contact

Name	BIOPARC Zoo de Doué-la-Fontaine
Address	Rue de Cholet,
	49700 Doué-la-Fontaine, FR
Phone	+33(0) 2 41 59 18 58
Fax	+33(0) 2 41 59 25 86
Email	infos@zoodoue.fr
Website	www.zoodoue.fr

Opening Hours

Open February to October

April, May, June and September	09.00 to 19.00
October, February and March	10.00 to 18.30
July and August	09.00 to 19.30

Entrance Prices 2011

	EUR
Adult	17.50
Child 3-10	12.00
Child Under 3	Free
Annual Card - Adult	32.00
Annual Card – Child 3-10	22.00
Annual Family Card 2 Adults and 2 Children	95.00
Concessions: Disabled Visitors	

Transport Access

Car	A65 Exit Saumur then 20 kms to zoo signposted
Car Park	Yes, at Zoo Free of Charge
Bus	From Saumur station to zoo
Nearest Station	Saumur

Ownership of Zoo   Private, 100% Family Gay

Area of Zoo   14 Ha

Date of Foundation   1961

Visitor Numbers   Circa 250,000

Animal Inventory at 16.07.2010

	Number	Species
Mammals	211	37
Birds	500	42
Reptiles	33	10
Amphibians	0	0
Fish	0	0

Facilities	Catering (zoo owned): Restaurant, Snack Bar, Kiosks, Picnic Place – Restaurant/ Bar – Le Camp des Girafes, panoramic restaurant, Le Calao – snack bar Retail (zoo owned): Zoo shop – La Boutique du BIOPARC Children's Zoo: No Children's Playground: No
Dogs	Allowed on leads: No Kennel Facilities: No
Feeding by Visitors	Strictly prohibited except for "Le goûter des girafes" and "La ferme africaine" sheep and goats
Shows, etc	No
Education	Zoo keeper talks: Yes, opportunities throughout the day – see daily programme in zoo Zoo School/Education Centre: Yes Biodiversity Centre: No Zoo Guidebook: No Signage on Exhibits: French and English Star Rating: **

ZOO DE DOUÉ-LA-FONTAINE

Friends of the Zoo   No

Volunteers   No

General Site Description   Close to the Loire valley, Doué BIOPARC has an interesting and unusual historic setting. Established in what were previously former open cast sand pits, excavated at different levels, the zoo has introduced lush semi tropical vegetation and several waterfalls. There are cavernous rocky enclosures, which provide really memorable experiences including Europe's largest aviary, a dramatic walk-through enclosure covering over a hectare, it's a wonderful exhibit of South American birds, and a great walkthrough with birds of prey. A feature of the zoo possibility for spectacular natural close encounter with several iconic species.

Indoor Exhibits   Vivarium

Star Attractions   Lions, Red Panda, Giant Otters, Birds in the Great Aviary, Tigers, Ruffed Lemurs, Vultures, Leopards, Spider Monkeys, Red Ibis, Snow Leopards, Tamarins, Flamingos

Time required   whole zoo: 4 - 6 hours   star attractions: 2 - 3 hours

 ZOO DRESDEN

Contact

Name	Zoo Dresden GmbH
Address	Tiergartenstraße 1, 01219 Dresden, D
Phone	+49(0)351 47 80 60
Fax	+49(0)351 4 78 06 60
Email	info@zoodresden.de
Website	www.zoo-dresden.de

Opening Hours

Open evey day of the year

Summer	08.30 to 18.30
Spring and Autumn	08.30 to 17.30
Winter	08.30 to 16.30

Entrance Prices 2011

	EUR
Adult	10.00
Child 3-16	4.00
Child under 3	Free
Family Card Adults and up to 4 children	24.00
Annual Card - Adult	29.00
Annual Card - Child	18.00
Annual Card – Family 2 Adults, 4 children)	70.00
Concessions: students, apprentices, disabled visitors and Dresden card holders	
Reduced Adult Entry Price Mondays – except holidays	
Annual Card Holders - reduced entry to Berlin, Berlin Tierpark, Leipzig, Rostock and Munich Hellabrunn Zoos	

Transport Access

Car	A4 Dresden Altstadt then B170 South and Signposted to Zoo
Car Park	Opposite Zoo
Bus	75
Tram	9, 13
Nearest Station	Dresden Hbf

Ownership of Zoo

Municipal Company,
Zoo Dresden GmbH,
100% Stadt Dresden

Area of Zoo

13 Ha

Date of Foundation

1861

Visitor Numbers

Circa 740,000

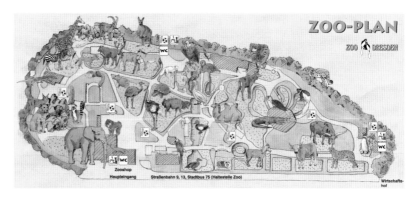

Animal Inventory at 16.07.2010

	Number	Species
Mammals	433	72
Birds	622	110
Reptiles	107	35
Amphibians	34	12
Fish	496	61

Facilities

Catering (sub-contract):
Restaurant, Café, Kiosks, Picnic Place - Drumbo's Welt, Pinguin Café
Retail (sub-contract): Zoo shop
Children's Zoo: Yes   Children's Playground: Yes

Dogs

Allowed on leads: No   Kennel Facilities: Yes, Charge of EUR 2.50

Feeding by Visitors

Strictly prohibited

Shows, etc

No

ZOO DRESDEN

Education

Zoo keeper talks: Yes, 10 opportunities – see daily programme in zoo
Zoo School/Education Centre: Yes
Biodiversity Centre: No
Zoo Guidebook: Yes
Signage on Exhibits: German   Star Rating: **

Friends of the Zoo

Yes, Zoo Freunde Dresden e. V.   Membership at 31.12.2009 – Circa 400

Volunteers

No

General Site Description

Situated on the edge of the large, well known city oasis, Dresdner Großer Garten, Dresden Zoo is a fine, established zoological garden with mature trees, floral displays and varied vegetation. Developing from a traditional strength in impressive volières, substantial new buildings for large mammals have been opened in the last five years, culminating in the 2010 Professor Brandes-Haus which will have the addition of Koalas when they become available.
In conjunction with plans to expand the collection, it is hoped that more space will become available to the zoo. Dresden Zoo is the home of Max, the famous 4.7 m long crocodile, who arrived in the zoo in 1958 when he was only 0.6 m.

Indoor Exhibits

Professor Brandes-Haus, Orang Utan House, Africa House, Terrarium

Star Attractions

Professor Brandes-Haus - especially Colobus, Macaques, Woolly Monkeys, Tamarins, Africa House - Elephants and Mandrills, Giraffes, Banded Mongooses, Ring Tailed Lemurs Walk Through, Lions, Dholes, Bird Volière, Red Pandas, Arctic Foxes

Time required

whole zoo: 4 - 6 hours   star attractions: 2 hours

D U B L I N

Contact	
Name	Dublin Zoo
Address	Phoenix Park, Dublin 8, IRL
Phone	+353(0) 1 474 8900
Fax	+353(0) 1 671 1660
Email	info@dublinzoo.ie
Website	www.dublinzoo.ie

Opening Hours

March to September	09.30 to 18.00
February and October	09.30 to 17.00
November to January	09.30 to 16.00

Entrance Prices 2011

	EUR
Adult	15.00
Child 3-16	10.50
Child under 3	Free
Family Day Ticket 2 Adults and 2 Children	43.50
Family Day Ticket 2 Adults and 3 Children	49.00
Family Day Ticket 2 Adults and 4 Children	52.00
Annual Card – Adult	100.00
Annual Card – Family	160.00
Concessions: Students, Over 60s, Special Needs Visitors	

Transport Access

Car	R101, then North Road then Signposted
Car Park	In Phoenix Park, free of charge
Bus	Nos 10, 10A, 25, 25A, 26, 66, 66A, 66B, 67, 67A, 68, 69
Nearest Station	Heuston Station

Ownership of Zoo Registered Charity. 100% The Zoological Society of Ireland. Land property of Irish Government

Area of Zoo 40 Ha

Date of Foundation 1830

Visitor Numbers Circa 950,000

Animal Inventory at 16.07.2010

	Number	Species
Mammals	204	38
Birds	174	26
Reptiles	71	24
Amphibians	9	2
Fish	0	0

Facilities

Catering (sub-contract):
Restaurant, Café, Kiosks, Picnic Place - Meerkat Restaurant - has window into Meerkat habitat, Cafés and Kiosk, Ice cream delivery bicycles in Summer
Retail (zoo owned): Zoo shop
Children's Zoo: Yes, Family Farm   Children's Playground: Yes

Dogs

Allowed on leads: No   Kennel Facilities: Yes, Charge of EUR 2.50

Feeding by Visitors

Strictly prohibited

Shows, etc

Yes

Education

Zoo keeper talks: Yes, March to September up to 10 Keeper Talks per day from 11.30 to 2.30
October to February at weekends only
Zoo School/Education Centre: Yes
Biodiversity Centre: Yes, Learning and Discovery Centre
Zoo Guidebook: Yes, EUR 2.00
Signage on Exhibits: English   Star Rating: *

Friends of the Zoo

No, but Annual Card Holder Membership
Membership at 31.12.2009 – Circa 12,500

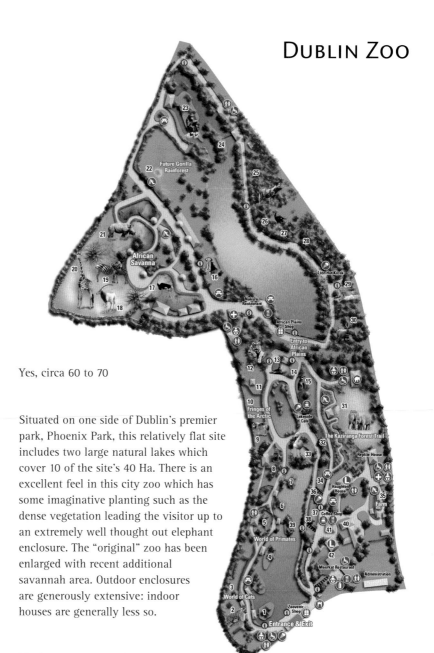

DUBLIN ZOO

Volunteers

Yes, circa 60 to 70

General Site Description

Situated on one side of Dublin's premier park, Phoenix Park, this relatively flat site includes two large natural lakes which cover 10 of the site's 40 Ha. There is an excellent feel in this city zoo which has some imaginative planting such as the dense vegetation leading the visitor up to an extremely well thought out elephant enclosure. The "original" zoo has been enlarged with recent additional savannah area. Outdoor enclosures are generously extensive: indoor houses are generally less so.

Indoor Exhibits

Elephant House, South America House, Lion and Tiger House, Tropical Bird House, Rhino and Hippo House, Orang Utan House, Roberts House, Chimps, Gorilla, Reptile House

Star Attractions

Elephants, Mangabey, Red Ruffed Lemur, Rhino, Siamang, African Hunting Dog, Waldrapp Ibis, Bird Lake, Grey Wolf, Penguins

Time required

whole zoo: 6 hours   star attractions: 2 - 3 hours

Contact

Name	Zoo Duisburg	
Address	Mülheimer Straße 273,	
	47058 Duisburg, D	
Phone	+49(0) 203 305 590	
Fax	+49(0) 203 305 5922	
Email	info@zoo-duisburg.de	
Website	www.zoo-duisburg.de	

Opening Hours

Open every day of the year
March to October   09.00 to 17.30
November to February   09.00 to 16.00
Visitors can remain in the zoo until dusk

Entrance Prices 2011

	Zoo	Zoo + Dolphinarium
		EUR
Adult	11.00	14.50
Child 3-16	5.50	7.00
Child under 3	Free	Free
Family - 1 Parents and up to 3 children	15.00	20.00
Family - 2 Parents and up to 3 children	23.50	32.00
Annual Card – Adult	40.00	50.00
Annual Card - Child	20.00	25.00
Annual Card – Family 1 Parent and up to 3 children	60.00	75.00
Annual Card – Family 2 Parents and up to 3 children	75.00	90 00
Concessions: students, pensioners, disabled visitors and their carers, armed services personnel Annual Card Holders qualify for a NRW Partner Zoos discount		

Transport Access

Car	A3/A40 Exit DU – Kaiserberg
Car Park	Yes, at Zoo EUR 2.50
Tram	901 to Zoo/Uni
Nearest Station	Duisburg Hbf and then Tram

Ownership of Zoo

Municipal Company, Zoo Duisburg AG, 72% City of Duisburg, 25.1% Zoo-Förderverein, 2.9% Private Shareholders

Area of Zoo

16 Ha

Date of Foundation

1934

Visitor Numbers

Circa 1,000,000

Animal Inventory at 16.07.2010

	Number	Species
Mammals	467	79
Birds	628	79
Reptiles	145	22
Amphibians	7	3
Fish	745	76

Facilities

Catering (sub-contract):
Restaurant, Cafeteria, Kiosks, Picnic Place - Restaurant Waldschänke
Retail (sub-contract): 2 Zoo shops
Children's Zoo: Yes   Children's Playground: Yes

Dogs

Allowed on leads: No   Kennel Facilities: No

Feeding by Visitors

In general not allowed but keeper supervised feeding at stated times for certain species.

Shows, etc

Zoo Museum, Dolphinarium

Education

Zoo keeper talks: Yes, in Elephant House and Apes and Monkey House
Zoo School/Education Centre: Yes
Biodiversity Centre: No
Zoo Guidebook: Yes, EUR 2,00
Signage on Exhibits: German   Star Rating: ***

Friends of the Zoo

Yes, Verein der Freunde des Duisburger Tierpark e. V.
Membership at 31.12.2010 – Circa 6,000

Volunteers	Yes, Circa 12
General Site Description	Known as the A3 Zoo because the Motorway runs in a cutting through the site, Duisburg Zoo uses a well screened leafy pedestrian bridge to join the east and west halves of the zoological garden. Bordering the Duisburg Urban Forest on the northern edge of the city, the zoo has good vegetation and many mature deciduous trees. In the majority of the enclosures immense effort has gone into incorporation of rocks and water features and the use of cambark as a naturalistic base. Mixed species exhibits are developed and monitored wherever possible. Duisburg's twin town is Wuhan and the zoo's Chinese Garden is both a delight and an explanation to the visitor of the significance, allegory and symbolism of a Chinese garden.
Indoor Exhibits	RWE Dolphinarium, Elephant House, Koala House, Aquarium, Giraffe House, Ape and Monkey House, Rio Negro Tropical Hall, Carnivore House, Reptile House
Star Attractions	Dolphins, Ring Tailed Lemur Walk Through, Wombats, Koalas, Meerkats, Echidnas, Fossas, Raccoons, King Colobus, Coatis, Gorillas, Two Toed Sloths, Tamanduas, Tamarins, Toucans, Giant Otters, Manchurian Cranes, Sarus Cranes
Time required	whole zoo: 5 - 7 hours star attractions: 2 - 3 hours

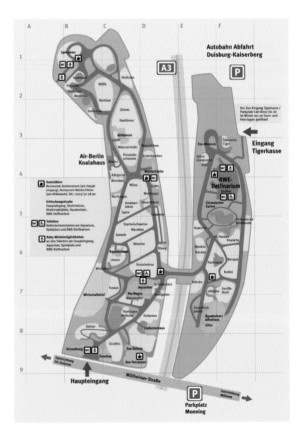

ZOO DVÛR KRÁLOVÉ

Contact
Name	Zoo Dvûr Králové
Address	Stefanikova 1029,
	54401 Dvûr Králové Nad Labem, CZ
Phone	+420(0) 499 329 515
Fax	+420(0) 499 320 564
Email	zoo.dk@zoodvurkralove.cz
Website	www.zoodvurkralove.cz

Opening Hours
Open every day of the year
May to October   09.00 to 18.00
November to April   09.00 to 16.00

Entrance Prices 2011

	CZK
Adult	110.00
Child 3-16	50.00
Child under 3	Free
Family Day Ticket 2 Adults and 2 Children	340.00
Dog	65.00
Annual Card – Adult	2,000.00
Annual Card – Family	1,500.00
Concessions: Over 65s, Disabled Visitors, School Children and Students Prices include Safari Bus Trip	

Transport Access
Car	National Roads 299 and 300 then signposted
Car Park	Yes, at Zoo free of charge
Bus	Normally during opening hours Bus from Dvûr Králové Nad Labem Station
Nearest Station	Dvûr Králové Nad Labem Station 3.5 Kms

Ownership of Zoo
Non Profit Company. 100% Hradec Králové Region

Area of Zoo
70 Ha including Safari area of 26 Ha

Date of Foundation
1946

Visitor Numbers
Circa 550,000

Animal Inventory at 31.12.2010

	Number	Species
Mammals	729	85
Birds	615	122
Reptiles	197	47
Amphibians	82	10
Fish	299	58

Facilities

Catering (sub-contract):
Hotel, Safari Lodges and Caravan Park, Restaurant, Kiosks, Hotel Safari and Safari Camp, Restaurant U Lemura
Retail (sub-contract): Zoo shop
Children's Zoo: Yes, Trains, horse drawn carriages and pony rides in fine weather
Children's Playground: Yes

Dogs

Allowed on leads: Yes   Kennel Facilities: No

Feeding by Visitors

Strictly prohibited

Shows, etc

Dinosaur World
Evening African Safari with commentary - 1 hour, June to September
Mammouth
Animal Encounter at 15.00 in Summer

Education

Zoo keeper talks: 7 Opportunities daily in Summer - see daily programme in zoo
Zoo School/Education Centre: Yes
Biodiversity Centre: No
Zoo Guidebook: Yes, CZK 55.00
Signage on Exhibits: Czech Star Rating: *

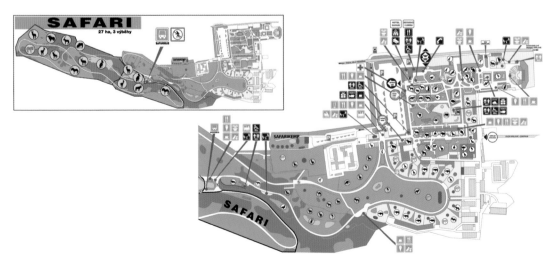

Friends of the Zoo
Yes, Natura Viva Civic Association for Fundraising, Conservation and Education - Circa 10 members

Volunteers
No

General Site Description
Dvûr Králové zoo is renowned for having the largest collection of giraffes, zebras and other African ungulates and for excellent breeding success of these species: stock emanating from this zoo can be seen in many European zoos and visitors can see impressive herds here both in the Safari and Zoo areas. The zoo's philosophy is one of minimum barriers so there's excellent visibility of the exhibits. The site is somewhat open and lacking in water in most areas but there are some very attractive planted shrubberies in the main area. Local craftsmanship is in evidence in painted signs in the zoo and particularly in the very impressive animal murals in the new Safari lodges.

Indoor Exhibits
World of Birds, Carnivore House, Tropical Swamp House, World of Water House Pygmy Hippo House, African Savannah House, Lion House, Meerkat House, Primate House, Golden Lion Tamarin House

Star Attractions
African Ungulates, Ringtail Lemurs, Lions, African Savannah, Meerkats, Cape Ground Squirrels, Javan Langurs, Marmosets, Bat Eared Foxes

Time required
whole zoo: 6 - 8 hours   star attractions: 2 - 3 hours

EDINBURGH ZOO

Contact
Name	Edinburgh Zoo
Address	RZSS 134 Corstophine Road
	Edinburgh EH12 6TS, UK
Phone	+44(0)131 334 9171
Fax	+44(0)131 314 0384
Email	info@edinburghzoo.org.uk
Website	www.edinburgh zoo.org.uk

Opening Hours

Open every day of the year

April to September	09.00 to 18.00
October and March	09.00 to 17.00
November to February	09.00 to 16.30

Entrance Prices 2010

Daily Ticket Prices Include a 10% Voluntary Conservation Donation	
	GBP
Adult	15.50
Child 3-15	11.00
Child under 3	Free
Family Day Ticket 2 Adults and 2 Children	47.70
Family Day Ticket 2 Adults and 3 Children	57.60
Family Day Ticket 1 Adult and 2 Children	33.70
Family Day Ticket 1 Adult and 3 Children	43.60
Annual Membership Card - Adult	56.00
Annual Membership Card - Child	30.00
Concessions: Groups, Students, Seniors, Disabled Visitors and Carers	

Transport Access
Navi	Sat Nav EH12 6TS
Car	Edinburgh Zoo is on A8 Corstophine Road
Car Park	Parking at Edinburgh Zoo GBP 4 per day
Bus	Lothian Buses 12,26,31 and Citylink 900,909 and 904
Nearest Station	Edinburgh Waverley Station and Edinburgh Haymarket
Bicycle	Cycle Route Carrick Knowe

Ownership of Zoo

Registered Charity. 100% The Royal Zoological Society of Scotland

Area of Zoo

34 Ha/ 83 acres

Date of Foundation

1913

Visitor Numbers

Circa 645,000

Animal Inventory at 31.12.2010

	Number	Species
Mammals	442	77
Birds	463	60
Reptiles	57	13
Amphibians	32	6
Fish	5	1

Facilities

Catering (zoo owned):
Jungle Café, Penguin Café, Stripes – Summer only, Picnic facilities
Retail (zoo owned): Zoo shop, Hilltop Safari Bus
Children's Zoo: No   Children's Playground: Yes

Dogs

Allowed on leads: No   Kennel Facilities: No

223

Feeding by Visitors   Strictly prohibited

Shows, etc   Yes, Penguin Parade is a special feature at 14.15

Education   Zoo keeper talks: Yes, 9 opportunities per day between 11.15 and 16.30 - see programme in zoo
Zoo School/Education Centre: Yes
Biodiversity Centre: No
Zoo Guidebook: Yes
Signage on Exhibits: English   Star Rating: **

Friends of the Zoo   No, but Annual Membership Scheme (RZSS)
Membership at 31.12.2010 – Circa 21,000

Volunteers   Yes, Circa 115

General Site Description   On a very hilly site, 1 in 12 in parts, affording fine views, Edinburgh zoo is a pleasant mixture of well laid out gardens and vegetation and extensive paddocks with some tree cover and a few water features.
Exceptional extensive penguin pools are home to nearly 200 penguins of 3 species. Edinburgh zoo also affords the only UK opportunity to see Koalas.
The recent Chimpanzees' Budongo Trail has very large indoor and outdoor enclosures and includes exceptional education and conservation information.

Indoor Exhibits   Budongo Trail - Chimps, Pygmy Hippo House, Rhino House, Living Links - Primates, Monkey House, Koala House, Magic Forest - Small Mammals, Camel House

Star Attractions   Chimpanzees, Squirrel Monkeys, Southern Pudus, Small Clawed Otters, Sun Bears, Capuchin Monkeys, Ratels (Honey Badger), Penguins – King, Gentoo and Rockhopper, Jaguars, Pallas Cats, Grey Owl

Time required   whole zoo: 6 - 8 hours   star attractions: 2 - 3 hours

DIERENPARK EMMEN

Contact

Name	Dierenpark Emmen
Address	Hoofdstraat 18
	7811 EP Emmen, NL
Phone	+31(0) 591 850 855
Fax	+31(0) 591 850 851
Email	info@ zoo-emmen.nl
Website	www.zoo-emmen.nl

Opening Hours

Open every day of the year

March, April, May and October	10.00 to 17.00
June , July, August	10.00 to 18.00
September	10.00 to 17.30
November to February	10.00 to 16.30

Entrance Prices 2011

	EUR
Adult	19.50
Child 3-9	17.00
Child under 3	Free
Annual Card - Adult	48.75
Annual Card - Child	28.90
Annual Card 2 Adults and 2 Children	155.30
Concessions: 65+ and disabled visitors and some winter price reductions Price includes Yucatan Children's play area	

Transport Access

Car	Emmen Town Centre
Car Park	Yes, at Zoo
Nearest Station	Emmen 10 minutes' walk, signposted to zoo

Ownership of Zoo

Private Foundation Non Profit. Noorderdierenpark B.V. – private/ public, 100% Shares City of Emmen

Area of Zoo

12 Ha Emmen Centre,
6 Ha Emmen Es

Date of Foundation

1935

Visitor Numbers

Circa 1,000,000

Animal Inventory
at 31.12.2009

	Number	Species
Mammals	474	44
Birds	502	47
Reptiles	124	27
Amphibians	857	6
Fish	4000	74

Facilities

Catering (zoo owned):
Restaurants, Café, Kiosks, Restaurant t Pariljoen, Het Safari Restaurant, De Olifant Café

Retail (zoo owned): Zoo shop
Children's Zoo: Yes and children's theatre
Children's Playground: Yes, plus inclusive entrance to large indoor Yucatan Playworld in Emmen Es

Dogs

Allowed on leads: No   Kennel Facilities: No

Feeding by Visitors

Strictly prohibited

Shows, etc

Yes, Biochron and Butterfly House

Education

Zoo keeper talks: Yes, at least 3 opportunities daily - see programme in zoo
Zoo School/Education Centre: Yes, but arrangements for schools are made through the marketing department
Biodiversity Centre: Yes, Biochron
Zoo Guidebook: Yes, EUR 3.00
Signage on Exhibits: Dutch, German and English   Star Rating: **

Friends of the Zoo

No, but Circa 80,000 Annual Card Holders are Members of the Zoo

Volunteers

Yes, Circa 70

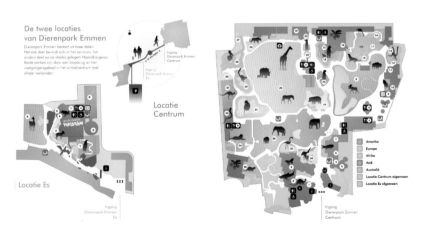

DIERENPARK EMMEN

General Site Description

The zoo is on two different sites about 500 metres apart. There is a plan to relocate many species from the central to the new site. The central site is a wonderful zoological garden with excellent vegetation and water features, well landscaped and providing an oasis in the city centre. Visitors can get close to animals frequently in mixed species exhibits and in convincing natural surroundings. The Humboldts Penguin exhibit is quite outstanding, the finest in all 80 surveyed zoos and a truly amazing visitor experience. The free roaming Squirrel Monkeys are a special attraction. A new Lion exhibit will open in Summer 2011.

Indoor Exhibits

Savannah Building, Tropical House, Monkey House, Africa House, Asia House, Elephant House, Americasa, Oasis House, Butterfly House

Star Attractions

Penguins, Meerkats, Tropical Butterflies, Sharks, Kodiak Bear, Baboons, Monitor Lizards, Squirrel Monkeys, Amur Tigers, Wood Bison/ Moose, Rhinoceros Iguanas, Elephants, Small Claw Otters, Bird Volière, Ring Tailed Lemurs, Naked Mole Rats, Crocodiles

Time required

whole zoo: 6 - 8 hours   star attractions: 3 - 4 hours

Zoo Erfurt

Contact	Name	Thüringer Zoopark Erfurt
	Address	Am Zoopark 1, 99087 Erfurt, D
	Phone	+49(0) 361 751 880
	Fax	+49(0) 361 751 8822
	Email	zoopark@erfurt.de
	Website	www.zoopark-erfurt.de

Opening Hours

Open every day of the year

April to October	09.00 to 18.00
November to March	10.00 to 16.00

Entrance Prices 2011

	Zoo	Aquarium
		EUR
Adult	7.00	2.00
Child 3-18	3.50	1.00
Child under 3	Free	Free
Family - 2 Parents and their children	17.50	5.00
Dog	1.50	Free
Annual Card - Adult	22.00	14.00
Annual Card - Child	11.00	7.00
Annual Card Family - 2 Parents and their children	52.00	
Concessions: disabled visitors and their carers, holders of City of Erfurt social identity card		

Transport Access

Car	A71 Exit 8 or A4 Exit Erfurt Centrum Erfurt Roter Berg and signposted to Zoopark
Car Park	Yes, at Zoo Free of Charge
Tram	5
Nearest Station	Hbf and then Tram 5 to Zoo

Ownership of Zoo

Municipal
100% City of Erfurt

Area of Zoo

62.5 Ha

Date of Foundation

1959

Visitor Numbers

Circa 430,000

Animal Inventory at 31.12.2009

	Number	Species
Mammals	388	59
Birds	160	32
Reptiles	144	50
Amphibians	68	13
Fish	2455	286
The Aquarium of the Zoopark is 4 Kms away		

Facilities

Catering (sub-contract):
Restaurant, Cafeteria, Kiosks, Picnic Place, Zoogaststätte Weinberghaus, Bistro Hakuna Matata
Retail (sub-contract): Zoo shop
Children's Zoo: Yes   Children's Playground: Yes

Dogs

Allowed on leads: Yes   Kennel Facilities: No

Feeding by Visitors

In general, Strictly Prohibited but permitted for some species where indicated

Shows, etc

No

Education

Zoo keeper talks: Yes, various opportunities - see daily programme in zoo
Zoo School/Education Centre: Yes
Biodiversity Centre: No
Zoo Guidebook: No
Signage on Exhibits: German   Star Rating: **

Friends of the Zoo

Yes, Verein der Zoopark Freunde in Erfurt e. V.
Membership at 31.12.2009 – Circa 600

Volunteers   No

General Site Description

This recently improved Zoo park is situated on the Roten Berg hillside on the northern edge of Erfurt in the countryside. Recent planting near the entrance area has created an extremely attractive welcome to visitors to the zoo.
The policy of the zoo is to develop walk through exhibits wherever possible and the landscape and space is conducive to this: this enables visitors to see many of the animals at extremely close quarters. The last five years have seen major improvements and new animal houses, including the new African Savannah and Lemur Walk Through.2011 will see the opening of new Cheetah and other enclosures. Built in 1861, Erfurt Zoo's Thüringer farmhouse provides a real understanding of a typical local farmstead and the animals used in agriculture.

Indoor Exhibits

Lion House, Elephant House, Rhino House, Monkey House, Giraffe House

Star Attractions

Lions, Wallaby Walk Through, Flamingos, Rhinos, South America Pampas Walk Through, American Bison, Meerkats, Mesapotamian Fallow Deer Walk Through, Bat Eared Foxes, Spider Monkeys, Macaque Walk Through, Siberian Weasels, African Savannah, Snowy Owls

Time required

whole zoo: 4 - 6 hours   star attractions: 2 hours

PARKEN ZOO ESKILSTUNA

Contact

	Name	Parken Zoo Estkilstuna
	Address	Parken Zoo I Eskilstuna AB, 631 86 Eskilstuna, S
	Phone	+46 (0) 16 10 01 00
	Fax	+46 (0) 16 10 01 14
	Email	info@parkenzoo.se
	Website	www.parkenzoo.se

Opening Hours

The Zoo is only open May to September

May to June	10.00 to 17.00
June to August	10.00 to 18.00
August and September	10.00 to 17.30

Entrance Prices 2011

		SEK	
		27/06 to 14/08	07/05 to 26/06 and 15/08 to 18/09
Adult		200.00	170.00
Child 3-17		150.00	120.00
Child under 3		Free	Free
Annual Card - Adult		330.00	
Annual Card - Child		240.00	

Transport Access

Car	Eskilstuna signposted Parken Zoo
Car Park	Yes, at Zoo SEK 40.00 daily
Buses	Local bus from Eskilstuna Station
Nearest Station	Eskilstuna

Visitor Numbers

Circa 255,000 (500,000 for whole complex)

Ownership of Zoo

Municipal. Parken Zoo i Eskilstuna AB, 100% City of Eskilstuna

Area of Zoo

14 Ha

Date of Foundation

1956

Animal Inventory at 31.12.2010

	Number	Species
Mammals	165	47
Birds	70	6
Reptiles	96	24
Amphibians	270	16
Fish	68	13

Facilities

Catering (zoo owned):
Cafés, Kiosks, Picnic area - Themed outlet cafés and kiosks
Retail (zoo owned): Zoo shop
Children's Zoo: Yes   Children's Playground: Yes

Dogs

Allowed on leads: No   Kennel Facilities: No

Feeding by Visitors

Strictly prohibited

Shows, etc

No

Education

Zoo keeper talks: Yes, 15 opportunities daily in summer - see programme in zoo
Zoo School/Education Centre: Yes
Biodiversity Centre: No
Zoo Guidebook: No
Signage on Exhibits: Swedish   Star Rating: **

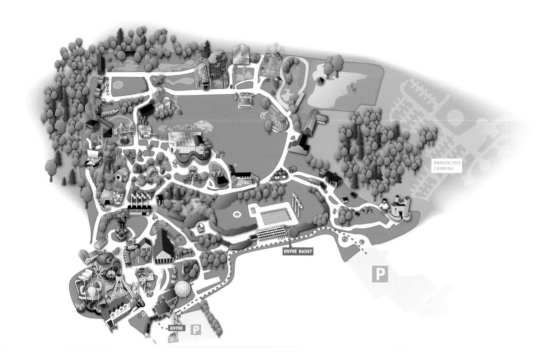

Friends of the Zoo	No, but Fan Club (commercial sponsors) and Company Strategic Co-operation Club
Volunteers	No
General Site Description	Part of an entertainment and sports complex, this fine zoological garden has many mature trees and good vegetation including a great display of rhododendrons and azaleas. There are fine outdoor enclosures .Cat species exhibits are especially strong. This is an unfortunate site combination of attractions for a zoo enthusiast as the entertainments complex detracts from a calm and natural atmosphere in parts of the zoo.
Indoor Exhibits	Amazon House, Leopard House, Reptile House, Komodo Dragon House
Star Attractions	White Tiger, Pallas Cat, Pygmy Hippo, Clouded Leopard, Sand Cat, African Wild Dog, Puma, Red Panda, Komodo Dragon, Amazon House
Time required	whole zoo: 4 - 5 hours star attractions: 2 - 3 hours

ZOO FRANKFURT
Tiere erleben - Natur bewahren

Contact

Name	Zoologischer Garten Frankfurt
Address	Bernhard-Grzimek-Allee 1, 60316 Frankfurt, D
Phone	+49(0) 69 212 337 35
Fax	+49(0) 69 212 378 55
Email	info.zoo@stadt-frankfurt.de
Website	www.zoo-frankfurt.de

Opening Hours

Open every day of the year
Summer - April to October   09.00 to 19.00
Winter - November to March   09.00 to 17.00
Summer and Winter times follow change of clocks

Entrance Prices 2011

	EUR
Adult	8.00
Child 6-17	4.00
Child Under 6	Free
Family Ticket - 2 Parents and their children	20.00
Annual Card - Adult	60.00
Annual Card – Child 6-17	25.00
Annual Card Combi - Adult with Palmengarten & Senkenberg Museum	90.00
Annual Card Combi - Child with Palmengarten & Senkenberg Museum	40.00
Annual Card Combi - Adult with Opel Zoo	80.00
Annual Card Combi - Child with Opel Zoo	32.00
Concessions: students, pensioners, disabled visitors and their carers, armed services personnel, last Saturday in the month, Frankfurt Card Holder	

Transport Access

Car	A661 Exit 13 or 14 and signposted to zoo
Car Park	Yes, Car Parks near Zoo: Zoopassage, City Ost, Mousonturm and Klinik Rotes Kreuz
Bus	31
Tram	14
U Bahn	U6 and U7 to Zoo
Nearest Station	Frankfurt Hbf then U Bahn

Ownership of Zoo   Municipal   100% City of Frankfurt

Area of Zoo   12 Ha

Date of Foundation   1858

Visitor Numbers   Circa 1,000,000

**Animal Inventory
at 31.12.2009**

	Number	Species
Mammals	1319	89
Birds	382	91
Reptiles	377	68
Amphibians	187	29
Fish	1580	178

Facilities

Catering (sub-contract):
Restaurants, Café, Kiosks - Sombrero Restaurant
Retail (zoo owned): Zoo shop (Opening summer 2012)
Children's Zoo: Yes   Children's Playground: Yes

Dogs

Allowed on leads: No   Kennel Facilities: No

Feeding by Visitors

Strictly prohibited

Shows, etc

South African Fur Seals - Daily 11.00 and 15.30, Penguins -Daily 10.45 and 15.45, Crocodiles - Thursday 15.15, Tropical Rain in Exotarium - daily 11.30 and 15.30, Big Cats - Please pay attention to the information at the enclosures
Please pay attention to the announcements on www.zoo-frankfurt.de!

Education

Zoo keeper talks: Yes, several opportunities daily in conjunction with feeding
Zoo School/Education Centre: Yes
Biodiversity Centre: No
Zoo Guidebook: Yes, EUR 3.50
Signage on Exhibits: German   Star Rating: *

Friends of the Zoo

Yes, Zoologischer Gesellschaft Frankfurt von 1858 e. V.
Membership at 31.12.2009 – Circa 6,000

Volunteers

Yes, Circa 50 - 100

General Site Description

At the entrance to this renowned historic zoo is the impressive Dominant Society House, home of the Frankfurt Zoological Society and the Zoo Management and Administration. In this city oasis, visitors will first come to a large lake with fountains surrounded by formal landscaped gardens. The famous Professor Dr Bernhard Grzimek was director of this zoo from 1945 to 1974. The two exceptional exhibits are the famous Grzimek House with its comprehensive collection of nocturnal species and the new well designed Borgori-Wald with its spacious indoor and outdoor enclosures. Uncertainty about the continuing future of the zoo on its current site has prevented investment until recently. Now the zoo's location continuity is assured, investment in new and improved facilities is proceeding and has commenced with the bears.

Indoor Exhibits

Grzimek House – Nocturnal House, Exotarium – Lower Vertebrates & Invertebrates, Giraffe House, Borgori-Wald – Primates & more, Rhino/Hippo House, Cat Jungle, Faust Bird House, Monkey House

Star Attractions

Grzimek House, Borgori Wald – (Gorillas, Orang Utans, Bonobos, Colobus), Aye-ayes, Fossas, Pied Herons, Kiwis, Echidnas Sumatran Tigers, Tamarins, White Cheeked Gibbons

Time required

whole zoo: 4 - 5 hours   star attractions: 2 - 3 hours

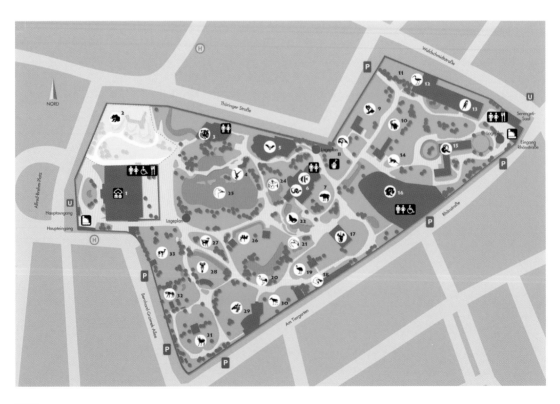

ZOOM GELSENKIRCHEN

Contact

	Name	Zoom Erlebniswelt Gelsenkirchen
	Address	Bleckstraße 64,
		45889 Gelsenkirchen, D
	Phone	+49(0) 209 954 50
	Fax	+49(0) 209 954 5121
	Email	info@zoom-erlebniswelt.de
	Website	www.zoom-erlebniswelt.de

Opening Hours

Open every day of the year

April to September	09.00 to 18.30
October and March	09.00 to 18.00
November to February	10.00 to 17.00

Entrance Prices 2011

	Summer	Winter
		EUR
Adult	16.50	11.50
Child 4-12	11.00	7.50
Child Under 4	Free	Free
Dog	4.50	3.50
Annual Card - Adult	56.00	
Annual Card - Child	34.00	
Annual Card - Dog	20.00	
Concessions: students, 65+, disabled visitors and their carers, armed services personnel; Annual Card holders qualify for NRW discount		

Transport Access

Car	A42 Exit 18 Grimbergstraße and signposted to Zoo
	A2 Exit 7 B227 or Exit 6 B226 and signposted to the zoo
Car Park	Yes, at Zoo EUR 3.50 per day
Trams	301
Nearest Station	Gelsenkirchen Hbf and Regional Bf Zoo

Ownership of Zoo

Limited Companiy Municipal. GEW Gesellschaft für Energie und Wirtschaft GmbH 100% City of Gelsenkirchen

Area of Zoo

30 Ha

Date of Foundation

2005 - formerly Ruhr Zoo founded 1949

Visitor Numbers

Circa 1,000,000

Animal Inventory at 31.12.2009

	Number	Species
Mammals	340	45
Birds	232	37
Reptiles	109	16
Amphibians	0	0
Fish	0	0

Facilities

Catering (zoo owned):
Restaurants, Café, Kiosks, Picnic Place - RyoKan Seeterrassen Restaurant, Alaska Diner, Pangung Tropengarten Restaurant, Afrika Lodge, Grimberger Hof
Retail (zoo owned): Zoo shop - ZOOM
African Savannah Boat Ride included in Zoo entry price
Alaska Ice Adventure Ride included in Zoo entry price
Children's Zoo: Yes
Children's Playground: Yes, exceptional facility: Indoor - Drachenland Asian themed, Outdoor - Adventure Playgrounds

Dogs

Allowed on leads: Yes, max. of 1 dog per person   Kennel Facilities: No

Feeding by Visitors

Strictly prohibited, Exception: special exhibitions under supervision

Shows, etc

Yes, African Queen and Alaska Ice Adventure

Education

Zoo keeper talks: Yes, various opportunities - see daily programme in zoo
Zoo School/Education Centre: Yes
Biodiversity Centre: No
Zoo Guidebook: Yes, EUR 2.00
Signage on Exhibits: German   Star Rating: *

Friends of the Zoo

No

Volunteers

No

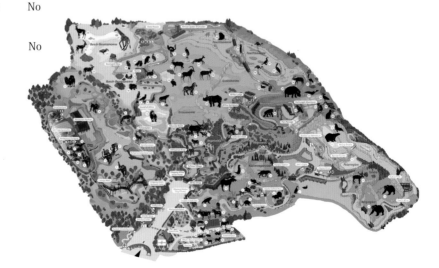

ZOOM GELSENKIRCHEN

General Site Description

Zoom Erlebniswelt is built on the site of the earlier Ruhr Zoo and is an adventure zoo divided into three distinct zones, Alaska, Africa and Asia. Major investment in huge water features, hills and vegetation creates a natural representative habitat in each of these zones. The Alaska Zone has information about the relationship between the indigenous population and the native animals of the region. The zoo is strong on mixed species exhibits for example the Zebras and Antelopes exhibit. The indoor animal houses are not generally accessible to visitors but a notable exception is the new „ELE Tropenparadies", an impressive tropical hall with over 100 species of Asian plants and large indoor facilities for orang utans with small clawed otters. Outdoor facilities are spacious and cleverly designed in such a way as to obviate the need for apparent barriers.

Indoor Exhibits

„ELE Tropenparadies", Africa Jungle Hall

Star Attractions

Serengeti View with Giraffes, Brown Bears, Meerkats, Pavian City, Polar Bears, Prevost's Squirrels, „ELE Tropenparadies", Kodiak Bears, Servals, Orang Utans, Lions, Sea Lions, Chimpanzees, Hippos, Langurs

Time required

whole zoo: 6 - 7 hours   star attractions: 3 - 4 hours

Contact

Name	Zoo Halle	
Address	Fasanenstraße 5A,	
	06114 Halle/Saale, D	
Phone	+49(0) 345 520 3300	
Fax	+49(0) 345 520 3444	
Email	office@zoo-halle.de	
Website	www.zoo-halle.de	

Opening Hours

Open every day of the year
Summer April to October   09.00 to 18.00 or 19.30 at weekends
Winter November to March 09.00 to 17.00

Entrance Prices 2011

	EUR
Adult	8.50
Child 4-17	3.50
Child under 4	Free
Family - 1 Parent and up to 3 children	11.50
Family - 2 Parents and up to 3 children	19.50
Dog	2.00
Annual Card - Adult	45.00
Annual Card - Child	20.00
Concessions: Students, Pensioners, Disabled Visitors and their Carers, Armed Services Personnel and Halle Pass Holders	

Transport Access

Car	B6 North Side of Halle and signposted to zoo
Car Park	Yes, at Zoo EUR 9.00 per day
Tram	3 and 12
Nearest Station	Halle Hbf and then S-Bahn Direction Trotha

Ownership of Zoo

Municipal   Zoologischer Garten Halle GmbH
100% City of Halle

Area of Zoo

9.5 Ha

Date of Foundation

1901

Visitor Numbers

Circa 340,000

Animal Inventory at 31.12.2010

	Number	Species
Mammals	387	59
Birds	604	106
Reptiles	87	25
Amphibians	31	4
Fish	470	48

Facilities

Catering (sub-contract):
Restaurants, Cafeteria, Kiosks, Picnic Place - Restaurant Villa Einzug,
Bergterrassen, Biergarten bei den Bären
Retail (zoo owned): Zoo shop
Children's Zoo: Yes, particularly strong on interactive media play and learning opportunities
Children's Playground: Yes

Dogs

Allowed on leads: Yes   Kennel Facilities: No

Feeding by Visitors

Strictly prohibited, except for specified domestic species using food from dispensers in zoo

Shows, etc

Sea Lions

Education
Zoo keeper talks: Yes, 3 opportunities – see daily programme in zoo
Zoo School/Education Centre: Yes, environmental Education Centre
Biodiversity Centre: No
Zoo Guidebook: Yes, EUR 3.00
Signage on Exhibits: German   Star Rating: **

Friends of the Zoo
Yes, Verein der Förderer und Freunde des Halleschen Bergzoo e. V.
Membership at 31.12.2009 – Circa 60

Volunteers
No

General Site Description
Halle Zoo is known locally as the Berg Zoo because of its situation on the Reilsberg on the northern side of the city. The zoo has several listed historic buildings which have been built in the regional style and which give character to the site. The zoo is particularly clean and orderly and the difficult hilly site has been attractively planted with flowers and shrubs. The zoo's motto is "fine but small" and is totally apposite.
The recently built crocodile house is rightly renowned. The zoo has an option on a further 1.5 Ha of wooded land.

Indoor Exhibits
Crocodile House, Chimpanzee House, Small Animal House, Elephant House, Monkey House, Pygmy Hippo House, Carnivore House, Squirrel Monkey House

Star Attractions
Crocodiles, Squirrel Monkeys, Marmosets, Bird Volière, Alligators, White Faced Sakis, Turtles, Bird House Walk Through, Penguins, Tamarins, Pelicans, Vulture Volière, Southern Pudu, Chile Flamingos, Monitor Lizards, Opossum

Time required
whole zoo: 4 - 5 hours   star attractions: 1 - 2 hours

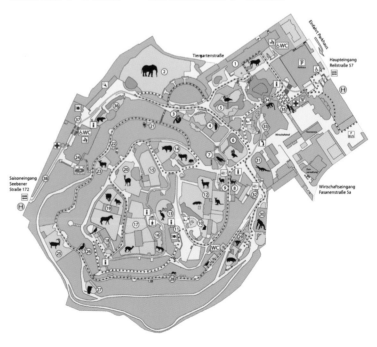

TIERPARK HAGENBECK

Contact	Name	Tierpark Hagenbeck GmbH, Hamburg
	Address	Lokstedter Grenzstraße 2, 22572 Hamburg, D
	Phone	+49(0) 40 53 00 33-0
	Fax	+49(0) 40 00 33-341
	Email	info@hagenbeck.de
	Website	www.hagenbeck.de

Opening Hours

Open every day of the year

06 March to 30 June	09.00 to 18.00
July and August	09.00 to 19.00
01 September to 24 October	09.00 to 18.00
25 October to 05 March	09.00 to 16.30
Christmas Eve and New Year's Eve	09.00 to 13.00

Entrance Prices 2011

				EUR
		Zoo	Zoo & Aquarium	Aquarium Only
Adult		17.00	27.00	14.00
Child 4-16		12.00	18.00	10.00
Child under 4		Free	Free	Free
Family Ticket - 2 Adults & 2 children		53.00	80.00	43.00
Family Ticket - 2 Adults & 3 children		61.00	90.00	49.00
Annual Card - Adult		90.00	145.00	70.00
Annual Card - Child		50.00	90.00	45.00

Transport Access	Car	A7 from N or S Exit Hamburg Stellingen signposted to zoo
	Car Park	Parkhaus am Haupteingang EUR 3.50
		Parkplatz am Gazellenkamp EUR 3.50/day Summer only
	Bus	22, 39,181,281 to stop Hagenbecks Tierpark
	U-Bahn	Linie U2 to Hagenbecks Tierpark
	Nearest Station	Hamburg Hbf

Ownership of Zoo

Private Company, Carl Hagenbeck GmbH
Tierpark Hagenbeck is a family run non-profit organisation

Area of Zoo

25 Ha Zoo and 0.8 Ha Aquarium

Date of Foundation

1848 Hagenbeck Company, 1907 Tierpark Hagenbeck

Visitor Numbers

Circa 1,650,000

Animal Inventory at 31.12.2009

	Number	Species
Mammals	647	61
Birds	790	112
Reptiles	171	44
Amphibians	17	2
Fish	11067	144

Facilities

Accomodation and Catering (zoo owned):
Hotel, Restaurant, Café, Kiosks, Picnic Place - Tierpark Hotel (the Award Winning Lindner Park - Hotel has 158 Rooms), Flamingo Lodge Restaurant (open in Summer, spacious, lovely view of Africa panorama), Restaurant am Spielplatz (open in Winter with views over lake and Japanese island), Café in Orang Utan House (with views of orangs and small clawed otters), Various Kiosks
Retail (zoo owned): 2 shops open in Summer, 1 shop (by main gate) open in Winter
Children's Zoo: Yes, Pony and Trap Rides EUR 2.00 for circa 10 minutes
Children's Playground: Yes

Dogs

Allowed on leads: No   Kennel Facilities: No,

Feeding by Visitors

Supervised Elephant feeding with zoo approved food from zoo shop
Supervised Giraffe Browse – zoo provided acacia browse
Baboons with food from Zoo shops

Shows, etc

Dinosaurier, Occasional special zoo evenings in Summer

Education

Zoo keeper talks: Yes, several opportunities daily see programme in Zoo
Tropen-Aquarium: Feeding of Crocodiles and Sharks twice weekly
Zoo School/Education Centre: Yes
Biodiversity Centre: No, but zoo school next to Elephant House open to all visitors
Zoo Guidebook: No
Signage on Exhibits: German   Star Rating: ***

Friends of the Zoo

Yes, Verein der Freunde des Tierparks Hagenbeck e. V. Membership at 31.12.2009 – Circa 2,600

Volunteers

Yes, Scouts from Verein der Freunde des Tierparks Hagenbeck e. V. – Circa 20

General Site Description

This historic zoo, which provides a beautifully landscaped oasis in the city, has a rich variety of beautifully managed deciduous and coniferous trees and extensive water and rock features. The zoo has a special feel for three reasons. First, the founder, Carl Hagenbeck, pioneered the "naturalistic" exhibit avoiding obvious barriers and creating the impression that the visitor has been allowed into the species' own realm. Modern Zoos are greatly indebted to his ideas. Secondly, architectural features, such as the Thai Sala and the Japanese bridge, add interest and character and provide cultural awareness. Thirdly, the perspectives and sight lines incorporated in the 1907 design are exceptional. Routing signs for visitors are particularly clear. A further delight is that muntjac, mara and water fowl are roaming freely in the park.

The Orang Utan House and the Tropen-Aquarium, which is on three levels, are outstanding exhibits. Eismeer is a new major investment. This project is well underway and will be an exhibit of polar bears, sea lions, walruses, penguins and sea birds and information; it will be open to visitors in 2012.

Indoor Exhibits

Orang Utan House, Tropen-Aquarium, Mandrill House, Lion House, Elephant House, Giraffe House, Giant Otter House, Coati House, Bird House, Macaw House, Kangaroo House

Star Attractions Zoo

Orang Utans and Small Clawed Otters, Storks, Elephants, Coatis, Flamingos, Caiman Lizards, Chinese Leopards, Giant Otters, Macaws, Village Weavers, Kamtschatka Bears, Emerald Tree Boas, Onagers, Barbary Sheep

Star Attractions Aquarium

Ring Tailed Lemurs, Boas, Turtles, Hai-Atoll Marine Tank, Nile Crocodiles, Pythons, Flying Foxes

Time required

whole zoo: 6 - 8 hours   star attractions: 3 - 4 hours

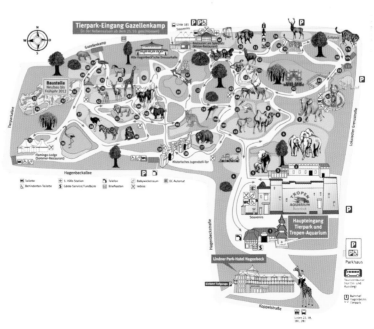

ZOO HANNOVER

Contact

	Name	Erlebnis-Zoo Hannover
	Address	Adenauerallee 3,
		30175 Hannover, D
	Phone	+49(0) 511 280 74 163
	Fax	+49(0) 511 280 74 212
	Email	info@zoo-hannover.de
	Website	www.zoo-hannover.de

Opening Hours

Open every day of the year

March to October	09.00 to 18.00
November to March	10.00 to 16.00

Entrance Prices 2011

	Summer	Winter
		EUR
Adult	23.00	16.00
Child 3-5	13.00	10.00
Child under 3	Free	Free
Child 6-17	16.00	13.00
Dog	9.00	9.00
Annual Card - Adult	79.00	
Annual Card - Child 3-17	57.00	
Annual Card - Family 2 Adults and their children	169.00	
Annual Card - Dog	54.00	

Concessions: pensioners, disabled visitors and their carers
Entrance Prices include Sambesi boat rides, etc

Transport Access

Car	From A7 Exit 60 to A37 to B6 and signposted to zoo
	From A2 Exit 47 to A37 to B3 and signposted to zoo
Car Park	Yes, at Zoo, Daily Charge EUR 3.50
Bus	128 and 134
Nearest Station	Hannover Hbf

Ownership of Zoo

Regionlal/Municipal
Zoo Hannover GmbH
96% Hannover Region,
4% Zoofreunde Hannover

Area of Zoo

22 Ha

Date of Foundation

1865

Visitor Numbers

Circa 1,600,000

Animal Inventory at 31.12.2010

	Number	Species
Mammals	625	88
Birds	617	81
Reptiles	65	16
Amphibians	10	2
Fish	2067	38

Facilities

Catering (zoo owned): Restaurants, Cafeteria, Kiosks, Picnic Place - Gasthaus Meyer, Mullewapp -"Tante Millis Futtertrog", Bauer Meyers Spieker, Jungle Palace-Wok Station and Palast Bistro, Meyers Inn and Beergarden, Café Kifaru, Yukon Bay-"Market Hall", Pasteria "Mamma Mia", Eiscafé Luigi Amarone
Retail (zoo owned): 5 Zoo shops - Smith and Johnson Trading Station, Bazaar, Yukon Store, Waldemars Wundertüte and Tatzi Tatz Wunderland
Sambesi Boat trips from April to October are included in entrance price
Children´s Zoo: Yes, includes Helme Heine's Mullewapp and Petting Zoo
Children´s Playground: Yes, several including Adventure Playground "Brodelburg"

Dogs

Allowed on leads: Yes   Kennel Facilities: No

Feeding by Visitors

Strictly prohibited - except in Children's Zoo using food from the zoo shop

Shows, etc

Yes, Show arena – see daily programme, Elephant Show, Seals and Sea Lions, Farmer Meyer's Animal Show

Education

Zoo keeper talks: Yes, up to opportunities daily – see programme in zoo
Zoo School/Education Centre: Yes
Biodiversity Centre: No
Zoo Guidebook: Yes, EUR 9.95
Signage on Exhibits: German   Star Rating: *

Friends of the Zoo   Yes, Zoofreunde Hannover e. V.   Membership at 31.12.2009 - Circa 700

Volunteers   No

General Site Description   Hannover's Adventure Zoo is not a traditional zoological garden but it has an exciting and interesting atmosphere. It now incorporates 7 theme worlds – the Zambesi Landscape, Gorilla Mountain, Indian Jungle Palace, the Neidersachsen Meyer's Farm, Mullewapp Children's Land, Australian Outback and Yukon Bay Landscape. Each world transports the visitor to an appreciation of the area concerned. Themed enclosures include the substantial and unusual Jungle Palace in which the elephant herd lives (a record 5 elephant births recorded here in 2010) and the impressive new Yukon Bay development which incorporates wave machines in the enclosures of the polar bears and sea lions. The 4 Ha Sambesi area provides an excellent visitor experience: the boat trip around the large lake affords good visibility of all those exhibits bordering the lake shore. Attractively planted vegetation represents plant species typical of different world zones. The zoo specialises in interesting mixed species exhibits.

The zoo is also famous for a wide choice of themed restaurants and retail outlets with regional specialities. It is also well known for hosting over 1000 external events in up to 10 locations within the zoo including the beautiful Indian Palace Hall.

Indoor Exhibits   Urwaldhhaus (Apes), Tropical House, Giraffe House, Monkey House, Hippo House, Henry's Underwater World, Mouse House

Star Attractions   Yukon Bay (Polar Bears, Sea Lions, Timber Wolves), Hippos, Sambesi (African Savannah), Elephants, Penguins, Two Toed Sloths, Gorilla Mountain, Wombats, Pelicans, Marmosets, Birds of Prey Volière, Red Pandas, Lorikeets, Meyer's Farm

Time required   whole zoo: 6 - 8 hours   star attractions: 3 - 4 hours

ZOO HEIDELBERG

Contact

	Name	Zoo Heidelberg
	Address	Tiergartenstraße 3, 69120, Heidelberg, D
	Phone	+49(0) 6221 645 50
	Fax	+49(0) 6221 645 588
	Email	info@zoo-heidelberg.de
	Website	www.zoo-heidelberg.de

Opening Hours

Open every day of the year

April to September	09.00 to 19.00
October and March	09.00 to 18.00
November to February	09.00 to 17.00

Entrance Prices 2011

	EUR
Adult	8.00
Child 3 - 17	4.00
Child under 3	Free
Dog	Free
Annual Card - Adult	40.00
Annual Card - Child	15.00
Annual Card - Family 2 Parents and their children	80.00
Concessions: students, pensioners, disabled visitors and their carers	

Transport Access

Car	A5/A656 and signposted to Zoo
Car Park	Yes, at Zoo and Parkhaus at Uniklinik adjacent to zoo 2,00 EUR for 5 Hours
Bus	31 and 32 from Hbf
Nearest Station	Heidelberg Hbf

Ownership of Zoo

Non Profit Company
Tiergarten Heidelberg gGmbH
99% City of Heidelberg,
1% Geheimrat Prof. Dr. Carl
Bosch Erben und Verein der
Tiergartenfreunde e. V.

Area of Zoo

10 Ha

Date of Foundation

1933 but opened 1934

Visitor Numbers

Circa 580,000

Animal Inventory at 31.12.2009

	Number	Species
Mammals	594	63
Birds	472	95
Reptiles	51	8
Amphibians	5	2
Fish	276	4

Facilities

Catering (sub-contract):
Restaurants, Cafeteria, Kiosks, Picnic Place - Restaurant Fody's Arena
Retail (zoo owned): Zoo shop
Children's Zoo: Yes   Children's Playground: Yes, several

Dogs

Allowed on leads: Yes, but not in Houses   Kennel Facilities: No

Feeding by Visitors

Strictly Prohibited, except where zoo dispensers are by enclosure

Shows, etc

The Secret Small Stars of Heidelberg Zoo, Animal Encounter at 12.00 daily Bird
Flight Demonstration - at 15.00 in good weather
Sea Lion Show at 11.00 and 16.00 but not Fridays

Education

Zoo keeper talks: Yes, several opportunities daily at feeding times – see daily
programme in zoo
Zoo School/Education Centre: Yes
Biodiversity Centre: No
Zoo Guidebook: Yes, EUR 2.50
Signage on Exhibits: German and English   Star Rating: **

Friends of the Zoo

Yes, Tiergartenfreunde Heidelberg e. V.   Membership at 31.12.2009, Circa 400

Volunteers

Yes, Circa 40

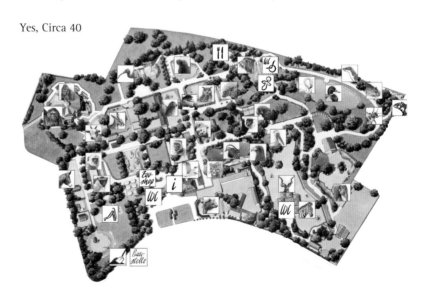

ZOO HEIDELBERG

General Site Description

On the edge of the University city of Heidelberg, this Zoological Garden has a pleasant feel: it has good vegetation, information and is strong on animal enrichment. The new elephant house and enclosure provides an excellent facility. There are plans to extend the site by 2.5 Ha to add an African Savannah which will ensure giraffes can be exhibited in the zoo.

Indoor Exhibits

Elephant House, Carnivore House, Apes House, Monkey House

Star Attractions

Elephants, Weasels, Seaside Bird Exhibit, Red Pandas, Prairie Dogs, Keas, Leopard Cats, Meerkats, Sea Eagles, Sumatran Tigers, Asian Golden Cats

Time required

whole zoo: 3 - 4 hours   star attractions: 1 - 2 hours

Contact

	Name	Korkeasaari/Helsinki Zoo
	Address	Korkeasaari–Högholmen, 00099 Helsinki, FIN
	Phone	+358(0) 9310 1615
	Fax	+358(0) 9310 37902
	Email	info@hel.fi
	Website	www.korkeasaari.fi

Opening Hours

Open every day of the year except 24/12

May to August	10.00 to 20.00
April and September	10.00 to 18.00
October to March	10.00 to 16.00

Entrance Prices 2011

	EUR
Adult	10.00
Child 6-17	5.00
Child under 6	Free
Family Ticket – 2 Adults and 3 Children 6-17	30.00
Annual Card – Adult	40.00
Annual Card – Child	16.00
Annual Card – Family 2 Adults and 3 Children 6-17	70.00
Concessions: students, 65+, unemployed, disabled visitors and their carers	
It is possible to buy a combined ferry and zoo entrance ticket on the ferry	

Transport Access

Car	Via Itävaylä, Kulossari, Mustikkamaa
Car Park	on the nearby recreation island
Bus	11 and ferry (May to Sept)
Nearest Station	Central Station 20 minutes
Boat (May to Sept)	Kauppatori Ferry from the pier in front of the Presidential Palace

Ownership of Zoo   Municipal   100% City of Helsinki

Area of Zoo   23 Ha

Date of Foundation   1889

Visitor Numbers   Circa 550,000

Animal Inventory at 31.12.2008

	Number	Species
Mammals	209	43
Birds	198	40
Reptiles	71	29
Amphibians	107	13
Fish	9	4

Facilities

Catering (sub-contract):
Restaurants, Cafeteria, Cafés, Kiosks, Picnic area - Restaurant Pukki, Safari Café and Watchman's Cottage
Retail (sub-contract): 2 Zoo shops - Safari and Korkeasaari
Children's Zoo: No   Children's Playground: Yes

Dogs

Allowed on leads: No   Kennel Facilities: No

Feeding by Visitors

Strictly prohibited

Shows, etc

No

Education

Zoo keeper talks: Yes, several opportunities – see daily programme in zoo
Zoo School/Education Centre: Yes
Biodiversity Centre: No
Zoo Guidebook: Yes, EUR 3.00
Signage on Exhibits: Finnish and Swedish   Star Rating: ***

Friends of the Zoo

Yes, Membership at 31.12.2009 - Circa 40

Volunteers

Yes, Circa 70

HELSINKI ZOO

General Site Description	This is an interesting island site within the Helsinki harbour waterway system. There is a bridge connection from the mainland to the island and most visitors use bus and ferry to reach the zoo. The island is rocky and hilly with limited tree cover. A great effort has been made with the planting of trees and shrubs and there are over 1000 plant species in the zoo. Helsinki zoo concentrates on exhibiting species from the northern and temperate zones.
Indoor Exhibits	Africasia House, Amazonia House, Borealia Building (Finnish Fauna)
Star Attractions	Snow Leopards, Otters, Amur Tigers, European Mink, Pallas Cats, Takin, Forest Reindeer
Time required	whole zoo: 4 - 5 hours star attractions: 1 - 2 hours

Zoo Karlsruhe

Contact

	Name	Zoo Karlsruhe
	Address	Ettlinger Straße 6, 76137 Karlsruhe, D
	Phone	+49(0) 721 133 6801
	Fax	+49(0) 721 133 6809
	Email	office@zoo.karlsruhe.de
	Website	www.karlsruhe.de/zoo

Opening Hours

Open every day of the year

February, March and 16-31 October	09.00 to 17.00
April and 1-15 October	09.00 to 17.30
May to September	08.00 to 18.00
November to January	09.00 to 16.00

Entrance Prices 2011

Zoo plus Stadtgarten	EUR
Adult	6.50
Child 6-15	3.00
Child Under 6	Free
Annual Card - Adult	30.00
Annual Card - Child	21.00
Concessions: Students, Pensioners, Disabled Visitors and their Carers, and Armed Services Personnel	

Transport Access

	Car	A5 or A8 Karlsruhe Mitte to Centrum/ Hbf
	Car Park	Yes, Festplatz, Hbf and Luisenstraße Car Parks
	Trams	S1, S4, S11, S41 to Hbf
	Nearest Station	Karlsruhe Hbf - Karlsruhe Zoo is opposite the Hbf Main Entrance

Ownership of Zoo

Municipal   100% City of Karlsruhe

Area of Zoo

9.5 Ha plus 3.5 Ha being added 2011
18 Ha Tierpark Oberwald

Date of Foundation

1865

Visitor Numbers

Circa 1,000,000

Animal Inventory at 31.12.2009

	Number	Species
Mammals	310	52
Birds	528	61
Reptiles	27	9
Amphibians	12	2
Fish	25	4

Facilities

Catering (zoo owned):
Restaurant, Cafeteria, Kiosks, Picnic Place - Zoo Terrassen Restaurant, Café an der Wolfanlage (Café Karle), Schuler Gastronomie
Retail (sub-contract): Zoo shop
Children's Zoo: Yes   Children's Playground: Yes

Dogs

Allowed on leads: No, except in Tierpark Oberwald
Kennel Facilities: No

Feeding by Visitors

Strictly prohibited, but allowed in Children's zoo

Shows, etc

No

Education

Zoo keeper talks: Yes, Elephants - see programme in zoo for times
Zoo School/Education Centre: Yes
Biodiversity Centre: No
Zoo Guidebook: Yes, EUR 1.00
Signage on Exhibits: German   Star Rating: *

Friends of the Zoo

Yes, Zoofreunde Karlsruhe e. V.
Membership at 31.12.2009 - Circa 185

ZOO KARLSRUHE

Volunteers

No

General Site Description

Karlsruhe Zoo forms part of the Zoo and Stadtgarten and provides a city centre oasis of 22 Ha. The zoo has recently invested in attractive new enclosures to exhibit Polar Bears, Sea Lions and Penguins. The zoo will celebrate its 150th anniversary in 2015 and in preparation for this there are several exciting new developments. These include the conversion of the Tullabad Centre to Exotica, a multi- faceted zoological and educational experience which will extend the range of species exhibited.
In addition to good water facilities, the zoo has the advantage of the wooded Lauterberg hillside, a lovely natural setting for many species but particularly the snow leopards.

Indoor Exhibits

Elephant and Hippo House, Giraffe House, Carnivores House, South America House, Apes House

Star Attractions

Polar Bears, Snow Leopards, Flamingos, Sea Lions, Persian Gazelles, Tierpark Oberwald, Penguins, Red Pandas

Time required

whole zoo: 4 - 5 hours
star attractions: 2 hours

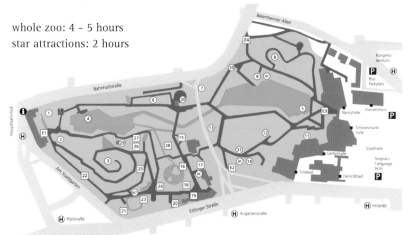

KOLMÅRDENS DJURPARK

Contact

Name	Kolmårdens Djurpark/ Kolmården Zoo
Address	61892 Kolmården, S
Phone	+46 (0) 11 24 9000
Fax	+46(0) 11 24 9040
Email	info@kolmarden.com
Website	www.kolmarden.com

Opening Hours

The Zoo and the Safari Park are open May to September

May to September   10.00 to 17.00*

*For seven weeks, late June to mid - August the Zoo and Safari Park are open until 18.00

The Tropicarium is open every day of the year

January to December   10.00 to 15.00

Entrance Prices 2011

		SEK
	Zoo and Safari Park Combined	Tropicarium
Adult	295.00	100,00
Child 3-12	185.00	60,00
Child under 3	Free for under 3s	Free for under 4s
Annual Card - Adult	590.00	290.00
Annual Card - Child	390.00	170.00
The above prices are dependent on visitors using their own vehicle in the Safari Park. Zoo Bus for Safari Park is SEK 30.00 per person		
Concessions: Students, 65+, Disabled Visitors and their Carers		

Transport Access

Car	E4 Exit signposted Kolmården
Car Park	Yes, Free
Nearest Station	Kolmården Station

Ownership of Zoo

Private Limited Company   Scandinavian Parks and Resorts Company Limited

The Tropicarium is owned by a separate company

Area of Zoo

172 Ha; 140 Ha (Zoo), 32 Ha (Safari Park)

Date of Foundation

1965

Visitor Numbers

Zoo and Safari Park Circa 550,000

Tropicarium Circa 130,000

KOLMÅRDENS DJURPARK

Animal Inventory at 31.12.2010

	Zoo and Safari Park		Tropicarium	
	Number	Species	Number	Species
Mammals	650	62	30	5
Birds	103	19	45	17
Reptiles	4	1	180	40
Amphibians	0	0	30	13
Fish	0	0	500	115

Facilities

Accomodation and Catering (zoo owned):
Hotel, Restaurant, Cafeteria, Kiosks, Picnic area -
Vildmarkshotellet and Restaurant, 7 Cafés throughout the zoo
Retail (zoo owned): 7 Zoo shops themed according to zoo areas
Children's Zoo: Yes, includes a substantial children's farm
Children's Playground: Yes, including the World of Bamse and Wild Camp

Dogs

Allowed on leads: No   Kennel Facilities: No

Feeding by Visitors

Strictly prohibited

Shows, etc

Yes, Birds of Prey Show, Dolphin Show, Seal Show, Animal Planet Exhibition

Education

Zoo keeper talks: No
Zoo School/Education Centre: Yes, Zoo School includes option for overnight accommodation
Biodiversity Centre: No
Zoo Guidebook: Yes
Signage on Exhibits: Swedish   Star Rating: **

KOLMÅRDENS DJURPARK

Friends of the Zoo	No
Volunteers	No
General Site Description	Kolmården's collection is the largest in Sweden and is different from any other in this survey. Kolmården's zoological offering is unusually complex as it comprises three separate entities, Kolmården Zoo Park, Kolmården Safari Park and Tropicarium. The Tropicarium is under separate ownership but is at the main entrance to the zoo park.
	The Zoo Park is set in natural mainly coniferous wooded and rocky landscape typical of the area and adjoining the coast. It is partly sloping and provides a delightful natural setting for many species.
	The Safari Park, adjacent to the Zoo Park is also in a mixed forest and rocky landscape. As well as African and Asian savannah species, there is a Scandinavian fauna area.
	There are several particularly fine outdoor enclosures. The Dolphin exhibit is spectacular and in Summer, night visits are an option.
Indoor Exhibits	Marine World (includes Dolphins), Great Ape House, Kolosseum (Pachyderms), Tiger World
Star Attractions - Zoo and Safari Park	Dolphins, Snow leopards, Meerkats, Wolves, Seals, Amur Tigers, Wolverines, Lynx, Penguins, Brown Bears, Dholes, Lions in Safari Park
Star Attractions - Tropicarium	Alligators, Rattlesnakes, Iguanas, Marmosets, Water Dragons
Time required	whole zoo: 6 - 8 hours star attractions: 4 - 5 hours

Contact

Name	Zoo Krefeld
Address	Uerdingerstraße 377, 47800 Krefeld, D
Phone	+49(0) 2151 955 20
Fax	+49(0) 2151 955 233
Email	info@zookrefeld.de
Website	www.zookrefeld.de

Opening Hours

Open every day of the year
Summer May to September   08.00 to 20.00
Winter October to April   09.00 to 17.00

Entrance Prices 2011

	EUR
Adult	8.50
Child 3-16	4.00
Child Under 3	Free
Family – 1 Parent and up to 4 children	15.00
Family – 2 Parents and up to 4 children	22.00
Dog	2.00
Annual Card - Adult	30.00
Annual Card - Child	15.00
Annual Card – Family 1 Parent and up to 4 children	60.00
Annual Card – Family 2 Parents and up to 4 children	75.00
Concessions: students, pensioners, disabled visitors and their carers Annual Card holders qualify for NRW discount	

Transport Access

Car	A57 Exit 13 and signposted to Zoo
Car Park	Yes, at Zoo, Free
Tram	042 and 043 from Hbf to Stop Grotenburg/Zoo
Nearest Station	Krefeld Hbf

Ownership of Zoo

Non Profit Company   Zoo Krefeld gGmbH
74.9% City of Krefeld, 25.1% Zoofreunde Krefeld

Area of Zoo   14 Ha

Date of Foundation   1938

Visitor Numbers   Circa 380,000

ZOO KREFELD

**Animal Inventory
at 31.12.2008**

	Number	Species
Mammals	336	64
Birds	425	96
Reptiles	85	14
Amphibians	35	4
Fish	400	20

Facilities

Catering (sub-contract):
Restaurant, Cafeteria, Kiosks, Picnic Place - Restaurant Grotenburg Schlösschen

Retail (zoo owned): Zoo shop
Children's Zoo: Yes   Children's Playground: Yes

Dogs

Allowed on leads: Yes, but not in Tropical Houses   Kennel Facilities: No

Feeding by Visitors

Strictly prohibited

Shows, etc

Sea Lions

Education

Zoo keeper talks: Yes, in Summer only. 5 opportunities daily – see daily programme

Zoo School/Education Centre: Yes, *Forscherhaus*
Biodiversity Centre: No
Zoo Guidebook: Yes, EUR 3.50
Signage on Exhibits: German   Star Rating: *

Friends of the Zoo

Yes, Zoofreunde Krefeld   Membership at 31.12.2009 – Circa 3,000

Volunteers

Yes, Circa 30

ZOO KREFELD

General Site Description

This pleasant zoological garden is bordered by a rather dominant Krefeld Football Stadium. It has good mature tree cover and several fine water features. The three tropical houses built more than ten years ago helped establish the zoo as a leading one in Germany at that time. The zoo has a good collection and a good reputation for breeding endangered species. Krefeld Zoo specialise in unusual South American species such as the striking and interesting tamandua anteater. A current building project is much needed outdoor enclosures for their great apes.

Indoor Exhibits

Pachyderm House, Tropical Bird House, Tropical Apes House, South America Rainforest House

Star Attractions

South America Rainforest House, Tigers, Tree Kangaroos, Bat-eared Foxes, Tropical Birdhouse, Red Pandas, Colobus, Butterfly Garden, River Otters, Flamingos

Time required

whole zoo: 4 - 5 hours   star attractions: 1 - 2 hours

OPEL - ZOO KRONBERG

Contact

	Name	Opel - Zoo Kronberg
	Address	Königsteinerstraße 35, 61476 Kronberg, D
	Phone	+49(0) 6173 3259 030
	Fax	+49(0) 6173 78 994
	Email	info@opel-zoo.de
	Website	www.opelzoo.de

Opening Hours

Open every day of the year

Summer   08.00 to 18.00

Winter   09.00 to 17.00

During Hessen's School Summer Holiday the Zoo is open for an additional hour until 19.00

In Opel Zoo visitors can stay in the zoo after these times if it is not yet dusk

Entrance Prices 2011

	EUR
Adult	10.50
Child 3-14	6.50
Child Under 3	Free
Dog	0.50
Annual Card - Adult	40.00
Annual Card - Child	15.00
Concessions: disabled visitors and their carers Annual card combined with Frankfurt Zoo also available	

Transport Access

Car	B455 between Kronberg and Königstein
Car Park	Yes, at Zoo, Free
Bus	917 from Kronberg Bahnhof in direction Falkenstein
Nearest Station	Kronberg Hbf

Ownership of Zoo

Non Profit Private Foundation 100% Von Opel Hessische Zoostiftung

Area of Zoo

27 Ha

Date of Foundation

1956

Visitor Numbers

Circa 650,000

Animal Inventory at 31.12.2009

	Number	Species
Mammals	384	56
Birds	231	58
Reptiles	179	27
Amphibians	149	11
Fish	229	29

Facilities

Catering (sub-contract):
Restaurant, Cafeteria, Kiosks, Picnic Place - Restaurant Lodge at Main Entrance,
Zoo Restaurant Sambesi
Retail (zoo owned): Zoo shop
Children's Zoo: Yes, and pony and camel rides   Children's Playground: Yes

Dogs

Allowed on leads: Yes   Kennel Facilities: No

Feeding by Visitors

Visitors may feed animals, unless there are signs to indicate that this is not permitted. Food must be supplied by the zoo (mainly carrots and dried food) although visitors can donate food at the zoo entrance.

Shows, etc

Yes , Exhibition in Hessischer Bauernhof

Education

Zoo keeper talks: No
Zoo School/Education Centre: Yes
Biodiversity Centre: No
Zoo Guidebook: Yes, EUR 3.50
Signage on Exhibits: German   Star Rating: **

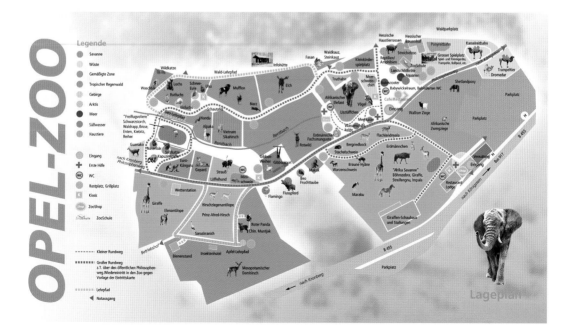

Friends of the Zoo Yes, Freunde+Förderer des Opel-Zoo e. V.   Membership at 31.12.2009 - Circa 70

Volunteers No

General Site Description Situated to the northwest of Frankfurt, the Opel Zoo is on a sloping site with fine views of the Taunus region. Stones and rocks have been attractively used as enclosure barriers giving visitors and excellent of generally generous enclosures. Although the site is natural countryside and lacks natural water features, great attention has been given to the footways and there has been imaginative planting.

Indoor Exhibits Giraffe House, Reptile House, Elephant House, Aquarium (in zoo school)

Star Attractions Giraffes, Nyala, Walk Through Volière, Zebras, Mountain Reedbucks, African Savannah, Mesopotamian Fallow Deer

Time required whole zoo: 3 - 4 hours   star attractions: 1 - 2 hours

LA FLÈCHE

Zoo de la Flèche

Contact

Name	Zoo de la Flèche
Address	72200 La Flèche, F
Phone	+33(0) 2 43 48 19 19
Fax	+33(0) 2 43 48 19 18
Email	info@zoo-la-fleche.com
Website	www.zoo-la-fleche.com

Opening Hours

Open every day except 25/12 and 01/01

April, May, June and September	09.30 to 18.00
July and August	09.30 to 19.00
October to March	10.00 to 17.30

Entrance Prices 2011

	EUR
Adult	18.50
Child 3-11	15.00
Child Under 3	Free
Annual Card - Adult	54.00
Annual Card - Child 3-11	43.50
Concessions: Students, and Disabled Visitors	

Transport Access

Car	A 11 Exit Durtal or Sablè
Car Park	Yes, at Zoo, Free of Charge
Nearest Station	Le Mans

Ownership of Zoo   Private   100% Da Cunha Company

Area of Zoo   14 Ha

Date of Foundation   1946

Visitor Numbers   Circa 220,000

**Animal Inventory
at 31.12.2009**

	Number	Species
Mammals	167	51
Birds	156	43
Reptiles	45	19
Amphibians	0	0
Fish	0	0

Facilities

Catering (zoo owned):
Grill, Café, Snack Bar, Kiosks, Picnic Area - La Bananaraie (grill), Clementine's Cafè, Casa Piazza
Retail (zoo owned): Zoo shop
Children's Zoo: Yes, La Minie-Ferme   Children's Playground: Yes

Dogs

Allowed on leads: No   Kennel Facilities: No

Feeding by Visitors

Strictly prohibited

Shows, etc

Yes, from April to September, Birds of Prey, Marine World, Parrot Jungle

Education

Zoo keeper talks: Several opportunities – see daily programme in zoo
Zoo School/Education Centre: No
Biodiversity Centre: No
Zoo Guidebook: Yes, EUR 5.00
Signage on Exhibits: French   Star Rating: ***

Friends of the Zoo

No

Volunteers

No

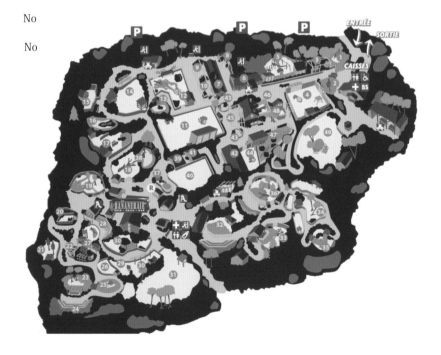

General Site Description	This site has fine vegetation and several waterfalls and other water features particularly well used in a good polar bear exhibit. There is plentiful use of bamboo and good outdoor enclosures, especially for the spider monkeys who enjoy the use of mature trees. Indoor houses with visitor access are very limited.
Indoor Exhibits	Vivarium
Star Attractions	Polar Bears, Spider Monkeys, Grizzly Bears, Sakis/Marmosets, Brown Bears, Coatis, White Lions, Red Pandas
Time required	whole zoo: 4 - 5 hours star attractions:1 - 2 hours

Contact

	Name	Zoo de la Palmyre
	Address	6 Avenue de Royan, 17570 Les Mathes, F
	Phone	+33(0) 5 46 22 46 06
	Fax	+33(0) 5 46 23 62 97
	Email	admin@zoo-palmyre.fr
	Website	www.zoo-palmyre.fr

Opening Hours

Open every day of the year
April to September   09.00 to 19.00
October to March   09.00 to 18.00

Entrance Prices 2011

	EUR
Adult	15.00
Child 3-12	11.00
Annual Card - Adult	45.00
Annual Card - Child	33.00

Transport Access

Car	A10 Exit 35 Saintes from North, Exit 37 Mirambeau from South
Car Park	Yes, at Zoo, Free of Charge
Bus	Jul to Sept from Royan Station
Nearest Station	Royan Station

Ownership of Zoo

Private
100% Private Family -
Majority Patrick Caillé

Area of Zoo   18 Ha

Date of Foundation   1966

Visitor Numbers   Circa 750,000

ZOO DE LA PALMYRE

Animal Inventory at 31.12.2009

	Number	Species
Mammals	800	67
Birds	686	33
Reptiles	110	16
Amphibians	0	0
Fish	0	0

Facilities

Catering (zoo owned): Kiosks and Picnic Place
Retail (zoo owned): Zoo shop
Children's Zoo: No   Children's Playground: No

Dogs

Allowed on leads: No   Kennel Facilities: No

Feeding by Visitors

Strictly prohibited for monkeys and apes but in general visitors are permitted to feed large herbivores where safe with appropriate food from zoo dispensers.

Shows, etc

Yes, April to October, Sea Lion Show and Parrot Show

Education

Zoo keeper talks: No
Zoo School/Education Centre: No, but Education Workshops
Biodiversity Centre: No
Zoo Guidebook: Yes, EUR 5.00
Signage on Exhibits: French   Star Rating: **

Zoo de la Palmyre

Friends of the Zoo   No

Volunteers   No

General Site Description   La Palmyre's Atlantic costal setting is extremely attractive: the site has sandy soil and numerous sea pines as well as some mature trees. The zoo also has a stunningly colourful entrance exhibit of flamingos under weeping willows with cascading water. There is a good atmosphere for visitors, 90% of whom are tourists. The zoo has a one way system, is well signposted and laid out and is very clean. Feeding large herbivores with food from dispensers in the zoo is, unusually, widely permitted with the effect that the exhibited animals are curious about the visitors and can usually be seen at close quarters. The recently-built Great Apes exhibit is especially memorable.

Indoor Exhibits   Great Apes House, Reptile House, Tamarin House, Bats House, Monkey House, Lemur and Capuchin House

Star Attractions   Gorillas, Red Panda, African Savannah, Orang Utans, Flamingos, Bats House, Chimpanzees, Pelicans, Red Ibis, Macaws, Griffon Vulture

Time required   whole zoo: 5 - 6 hours   star attractions: 2 - 3 hours

Der Natur auf der Spur.

Contact

Name	Zoo Leipzig
Address	Pfaffendorfer Straße 29, 04105 Leipzig, D
Phone	+49(0) 341 59 33 500
Fax	+49(0) 341 59 33 303
Email	office@zoo-leipzig.de
Website	www.zoo-leipzig.de

Opening Hours

Open every day of the year

May to September	09.00 to 19.00
October and April	09.00 to 18.00
November to March	09.00 to 17.00

Entrance Prices 2011

		EUR
	To 30.06.2011	From 01.07.2011
Adult	13.00	17.00
Child 4-14	9.00	10.00
Family Ticket - 2 Parents and their children	34.00	43.00
Annual Card - Adult	60.00	65.00
Annual Card - Child	40.00	40.00
Annual Card – Family 2 Parents and their children	155.00	165.00
Free admission for under 4s, disabled visitors and their carers Concessions for Students, Pensioners, Disabled Visitors, Armed Services Personnel, Leipzig Card Holders and Leipzig Pass Holders		

Transport Access

Car	From A9 Exit Leipzig West and follow signs to Zentrum and then follow signs to Zoo From A14 Exit Leipzig Mitte and then follow signs to
Zoo Car Park	Yes, at Zoo, Day Charge EUR 4.50
Tram	Linie 12 to Gohlis-Nord to Stop Zoo
Nearest Station	Leipzig Hbf

Ownership of Zoo

Municipal
Zoo Leipzig gGmbH,
100% City of Leipzig

Area of Zoo

27 Ha

Date of Foundation

1878

Visitor Numbers

Circa 1,750,000

Animal Inventory at 31.12.2009

	Number	Species
Mammals	446	88
Birds	738	146
Reptiles	215	62
Amphibians	35	11
Fish	2551	386

Facilities

Catering (sub-contract):
Restaurant, Cafeteria, Kiosks, Picnic Place - Kiwara Lodge Restaurant, Teichcafé Kandler, Restaurant Marché in Founders' Garden, Urwalddorf, Hacienda Las Casas Restaurant, Marché Patakan in Gondwanaland (from July 2011)
Retail (zoo owned): 3 Zoo shops
Children's Zoo: Yes   Children's Playground: Yes

Dogs

Allowed on leads: No   Kennel Facilities: No

Feeding by Visitors

Strictly prohibited

Shows, etc

Yes

Education

Zoo keeper talks: Yes, several opportunities – see daily programme in zoo
Zoo School/Education Centre: Yes
Biodiversity Centre: Yes, Entdeckerhaus Arche
Zoo Guidebook: Yes, German and English, EUR 3.50
Signage on Exhibits: German   Star Rating: **

Friends of the Zoo

Yes, Freundes- u. Förderkreis des Zoologischen Gartens Leipzig e. V.
Membership at 31.12.2009 - Circa 500

Volunteers

No

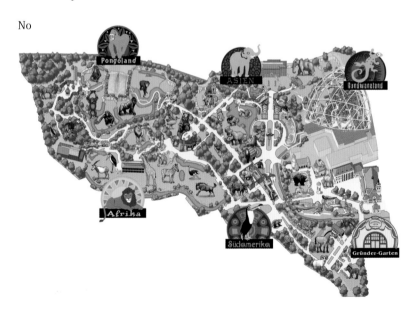

Zoo Leipzig

General Site Description

A historic zoo site, extended several times within the city area. A fine setting with a river running through the site and with good mature tree cover and varied vegetation. The zoo is in the final stages of metamorphosis to "Zoo of the Future" incorporating a mixture of well-renovated historic and impressive new exhibits. Leipzig zoo is of particular scientific research importance through close co-operation with the Max Planck Institute in Pongoland. Gondwanaland, Europe's largest zoo tropical hall, is to open on 01.07.2011.

Indoor Exhibits

Great Apes House (Pongoland), Aquarium, Terrarium, Elephant House, Bird House, Giraffe House, Monkey House

Star Attractions

Pongoland (Chimpanzees, Gorillas, Orang Utans and Bonobos), African Savannah (including Giraffe House), Lions, Meerkats, Spotted Hyena, Elephants, Sloth Bears, Tigers, Fur Seal, Asiatic Bird Volière, Pelicans, Manchurian Crane, Gondwanaland (from 01.07.2011)

Time required

whole zoo: 6 - 8 hours   star attractions: 3 - 4 hours

Contact

	Name	Jardim Zoologico de Lisboa/ Lisbon Zoo
	Address	Praça Marechal Humberto Delgado, Sete-Rios Lisbon, P
	Phone	+351 (0) 217 232 900
	Fax	+351 (0) 217 232 901
	Email	info@zoolisboa.pt
	Website	www.zoo.pt

Opening Hours

Open every day of the year
Summer Late March to Late September   10.00 to 20.00
Winter Late September to Late March   10.00 to 18.00

Entrance Prices 2011

	EUR
Adult	17.00
Child 3-11	12.50
Child under 3	Free
Annual Card – Adult	83.00
Annual Card – Child	60.00
Annual Card – Family	60.00 each family member
Concessions: Over 65s	

Transport Access

Car	2ª Circular Road to Estrada da Luz then signposted to Zoo
Car Park	Yes, at Zoo, Some Free of Charge
Bus	16, 31, 54, 70, 701, 725, 746, 755, 768 and 96 aeroshuttle
Metro	Linha Azul (Blue Line) to Station Jardim Zoologico
Nearest Station	Linha de Sul (South Line) Sete-Rios to Station Jardim Zoologico

Ownership of Zoo   Private Non Profit   Private Institution, non-profit, municipal support

Area of Zoo   24 Ha

Date of Foundation   1884

Visitor Numbers   Circa 730,000

Animal Inventory at 31.12.2009

	Number	Species
Mammals	611	120
Birds	644	129
Reptiles	359	51
Amphibians	15	5
Fish	7	1

Facilities	Catering (zoo owned): Restaurant, Café, Kiosks, Picnic Place - Animax catering facilities at zoo attractive water feature outlook just outside zoo entrance Retail (zoo owned): Zoo shop, Zoo Train, Cable Car Children's Zoo: Yes, Children's Farm Children's Playground: Yes
Dogs	Allowed on leads: No Kennel Facilities: No
Feeding by Visitors	Strictly prohibited
Shows, etc	Yes, Free Flying Bird Show, Dolphins and Sea Lions, Snakes and Lizards Presentation, Tiger Information Exhibit and Great Apes Information Exhibit
Education	Zoo keeper talks: Yes Zoo School/Education Centre: Yes Biodiversity Centre: No Zoo Guidebook: Yes, EUR 25.90 Signage on Exhibits: Portuguese and English Star Rating: ***
Friends of the Zoo	Yes, Amigos do Zoo Membership at 31.12.2009 - Circa 1,800 and circa 180 corporate members
Volunteers	Yes, Circa 100
General Site Description	Lisbon is a fine, historic, attractive, city centre zoological garden with varied colourful vegetation both temperate and sub-tropical. The zoo has a fine animal collection, excellent signage and a delightful vibrant atmosphere. Some substandard enclosures are being systematically addressed. There are few indoor houses open to the public but here you will find good animal and conservation information, imaginative flair and enthusiastic animal presentations. There are several moated islands, good water features and good visibility of the animals in most enclosures.

Indoor Exhibits Temple of the Apes, Dolphinarium, Reptile House

Star Attractions Chimpanzees, Red Pandas, Okapis, Dolphins, Meerkats, Colobus Monkeys, Tigers Porcupines, Free Flying Bird Display

Time required whole zoo: 6 - 8 hours
star attractions: 3 - 4 hours

Contact

Name	Zoo Ljubljana
Address	Vecna Pot 70,
	1000 Ljubljana, SLO
Phone	+386 (0) 1 2442 188
Fax	+386 (0) 1 2442 185
Email	info@zoo.si
Website	www.zoo.si

Opening Hours

Open every day of the year

April to September	09.00 to 19.00
October and March	09.00 to 18.00
November to February	09.00 to 17.00

Entrance Prices 2011

	EUR
Adult	7.00
Child Under 2	Free
Child Pre school 2-6	4.00
School Children	5.00
Students and Seniors	6.00
Dogs	1.50
Annual Card – Adult	35.00
Annual Card – Preschool	20.00
Annual Card – School Children	25.00
Annual Card – Students and Seniors	30.00
Annual Card – Dogs	7.50
Concessions: Students, Seniors, Disabled Visitors and their Carers	

Transport Access

Car	Ljubljana Bypass Exit 16 Brno then signposted to zoo
	The zoo is on the west side of Ljubljana
Car Park	Yes, at Zoo, Free of Charge
Bus	23 from City Centre 5 times daily
Nearest Station	Ljubljana Central Station

Ownership of Zoo   Municipal   100% Ljubljana City Council

Area of Zoo   20 Ha

Date of Foundation   1949

Visitor Numbers   Circa 275,000

Animal Inventory at 31.12.2009

	Number	Species
Mammals	157	34
Birds	109	31
Reptiles	34	17
Amphibians	2	2
Fish	0	0

Facilities

Catering (sub-contract): Cafeteria
Retail (zoo owned): Zoo shop
Children's Zoo: Yes, including a farmyard　　Children's Playground: Yes

Dogs

Allowed on leads: Yes　　Kennel Facilities: No

Feeding by Visitors

In general strictly prohibited. However, a coupon can be purchased and for the Activity of Keeper Supervised feeding.

Shows, etc

No

Education

Zoo keeper talks: Yes, Zoo Adventure every weekend and daily in July and August. Animal encounter and information opportunities for example tarantula or snake handling
Zoo School/Education Centre: Yes
Biodiversity Centre: No
Zoo Guidebook: No
Signage on Exhibits: Slovene　　Star Rating: *

Friends of the Zoo

No

Volunteers

Yes, Circa 18

General Site Description	An excellent location, 2 km from the city centre, in the protected green area adjacent to the large recreational municipal Tivoli park gives Ljubljana zoo advantage and potential. The site, partly on a hillside, has good natural features including a varied landscape and natural forest. There is fine natural indigenous vegetation but there are no botanical displays here in the zoo. The zoo's disadvantage is that it lacks water features. The few animal houses are in need of replacement or renovation: this is clearly recognised in the zoo's 5 year master plan and will be addressed in stages.
Indoor Exhibits	Elephant House, Chimpanzee House, Giraffe House, Vivarium
Star Attractions	Ruffed Lemurs, Red Panda, Wallaby/Kangaroo, Ibex, Chamois, Lechwe/Ostrich, Mountain Goats
Time required	whole zoo: 4 hours star attractions: 1 hour

ZSL London

Contact

	Name	ZSL London Zoo
	Address	Regent's Park, London NW1 4RY, UK
	Phone	+44(0) 207 722 3333
	Fax	+44(0) 207 586 5743
	Email	info@zsl.org
	Website	www.zsl.org

Opening Hours

Open every day of the year except Christmas Day

April to October	10.00 to 17.30
November to March	10.00 to 16.00

Entrance Prices 2011

Daily Ticket Prices Include a 10% Voluntary Conservation Donation	
Mid, Peak and Winter Prices apply – Mid prices given here	
	GBP
Adult	19.00
Child 3-15	15.50
Child under 3	Free
Annual Card ZSL Member Adult	69.00
Annual Card ZSL Member Child	45.00
Concessions: 60+, students, disabled visitors and their carers and online tickets Family Day tickets available online in advance only	

Transport Access

Navi	Sat Nav NW1 4RY
Car	Regent's Park Outer Circle
Car Park	Yes, at Zoo GBP 12.50, Gloucester Slips Car Park on Regent's Park Outer Circle
Bus	274, C2
Cycle	Cycle racks opposite main entrance, TfL Barclays Cycle Hire Scheme Docking Stations opposite main entrance and at Gloucester Slips Car Park.
Nearest UndergroundStations	Regent's Park, Baker Street, Camden Town, or Chalk Farm
Nearest Mainline Stations	Euston, Kentish Town
By Waterbus on Regent's Canal	London Waterbus Company from Camden Lock or Little Venice to Zoo

Ownership of Zoo

Charitable Society, 100% Zoological Society of London (ZSL)

ZSL London

Area of Zoo	15 Ha / 36 Acres

Date of Foundation	1828

Visitor Numbers	Circa 1,050,000

Animal Inventory at 31.12.2009

	Number	Species
Mammals	315	73
Birds	603	118
Reptiles	259	70
Amphibians	285	28
Fish	4711	220

Facilities

Catering (zoo owned):
Restaurant, Café, Kiosks, Picnic Place - Oasis Restaurant and Oasis Coffee Bar
Retail (zoo owned): Zoo shop - enlarged for 2011
Children's Zoo: Yes, New Children's Zoo opened 2009, a major new attraction
Children's Playground: Yes

Dogs

Allowed on leads: No   Kennel Facilities: No

Feeding by Visitors

Strictly prohibited

Shows, etc

Yes, Animals in Action. Feeds, demonstrations and encounters -
see daily programme

Education

Zoo keeper talks: Yes
Zoo School/Education Centre: Yes
Biodiversity Centre: Yes, BUGS
Zoo Guidebook: Yes, GBP 4.00
Signage on Exhibits: English   Star Rating: **

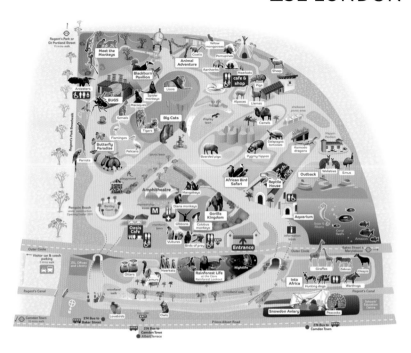

Friends of the Zoo

No, but members ZSL
Membership at 31.12.2009 - Circa 45,000

Volunteers

Yes, Circa 300

General Site Description

This famous historic city zoo is situated on a flat site within the classical oasis of Regent's Park and the Regent's Canal and Outer Circle Road running through the site. London Zoo has several architecturally interesting historic listed buildings: the Blackburn Bird Pavilion has recently been well restored. There are several mature trees and bird enclosures make excellent use of water. Recent years have seen some imaginative new developments and planting such as Rainforest Lookout. The levels of educational and conservation information are high throughout the zoo and BUGS is both exemplary and fascinating. 2011 will see the new Penguin Beach exhibit for Humboldt and Macaroni Penguins.

Indoor Exhibits

BUGS, Reptile House, Komodo Dragons House, Blackburn Bird Pavilion, Okapi House, Tapir House, Gorilla House, Clore Rainforest Lookout, Giraffe House, Casson Building, Aquarium

Star Attractions

BUGS, Komodo Dragons, Lions, Gorillas, Galapagos Tortoises, Otters, Pelicans, Children's Zoo, Birds of Prey, Birds of Africa Walk Through, Blackburn Bird Pavilion, Clore Rainforest Lookout, Squirrel Monkeys Walk Through

Time required

whole zoo: 5 - 7 hours   star attractions: 3 hours

Contact

	Name	Zoo - Aquarium de Madrid
	Address	Casa de Campo, s/n - 28011, Madrid, E
	Phone	+34(0)91 512 3770
	Fax	+34(0)91 711 8163
	Email	comzoo@zoomadrid.com
	Website	www.zoomadrid.com

Opening Hours

Open every day of the year
Madrid Zoo has variable opening times: check the website for the specific date of visit. In general the zoo is open as follows:

Summer	always 10.30 to 19.00 and later on holidays and at weekends
Winter	always 11.00 to 18.00 and later on holidays and at weekends

Entrance Prices 2011

	EUR
Adult	18.80
Child 3-7	15.25
Child under 3	Free
Family Card Each Adult pays	11.10
Family Card Each Child pays	7.60
Concessions: 65+, Advance internet tickets and Corporate Card Holders (Parques Reunidos Attractions)	

Transport Access

Car	Route National V Exit 5A
Car Park	Yes, at Zoo, No charge
Bus	Linea 33
Nearest Station	Metro – Lineas 5 and 10 to Station Casa de Campo

Ownership of Zoo

Private Company	100% Parques Reunidos
Municipal Concession	Site owned by City Council

Area of Zoo   22 Ha

Date of Foundation   1774

Visitor Numbers   Circa 1,050,000

Animal Inventory at 31.12.2009

	Number	Species
Mammals	525	99
Birds	1195	117
Reptiles	350	93
Amphibians	0	0
Fish	5860	680

Facilities

Catering (zoo owned):
Restaurant, Cafeteria, Kiosks, Picnic Place - La Terraza (Plaza Central),
Restaurant Bagaray
Retail (zoo owned): Zoo shop
Children´s Zoo: Yes, La Granja (Children's Farm)
Children´s Playground: Yes

Dogs

Allowed on leads: No   Kennel Facilities: No

Feeding by Visitors

Strictly prohibited

Shows, etc

Yes, Dolphins, Birds of Prey, Sea Lions, Parrots

Education

Zoo keeper talks: Yes, see daily programme
Zoo School/Education Centre: Yes
Biodiversity Centre: No
Zoo Guidebook: Yes, EUR 4.90
Signage on Exhibits: Spanish   Star Rating: **

Friends of the Zoo   No

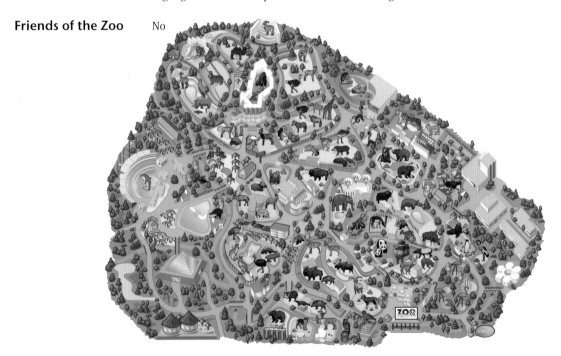

ZOO MADRID

Volunteers   Yes, Circa 70

General Site   Situated within an 100 Ha municipally owned park, Madrid zoo is located on
Description   an attractive sloping site with good vegetation and a small stream running
                        through it. There is a very open feel to the zoo with many moated enclosures
                        affording visitors excellent visibility. An improvement programme is underway
                        to update many of the older enclosures. Madrid is one of only two European
                        zoos currently to exhibit both Giant Pandas and Koalas and successfully to
                        breed the former.
                        At certain times the Lemur Walk Though and the Wallaby Walk Through
                        exhibits are open to visitors.
                        There is an additional charge of EUR 3.00 per visitor per Walk Through.

Indoor Exhibits   Dolphinarium, Aquarium, Gorilla House, Koalas, Vivarium

Star Attractions   Dolphins, Koalas, Turtles, Giant Pandas, Gorillas, Wallabies Walk Through,
                        Bird Lake (Flamingos, Pelicans, Ibis, Crested Crane)

Time required   whole zoo: 6 - 8 hours   star attractions: 2 - 3 hours

ZOOLOGISCHER GARTEN
MAGDEBURG

ZOO MAGDEBURG

Contact

	Name	Zoologischer Garten Magdeburg
	Address	Zoo Allee 1, 39124 Magdeburg, D
	Phone	+49(0) 391 280 900
	Fax	+49(0) 391 280 905 100
	Email	info@zoo-magdeburg.de
	Website	www.zoo-magdeburg.de

Opening Hours

Open every day of the year

Summer	09.00 to 19.00
Winter	09.00 to dusk

Summer and Winter according to change of clocks

Entrance Prices 2011

	EUR
Adult	8.00
Child 4-15	4.00
Child under 4	Free
Dogs	2.00
Annual Card – Adult	30.00
Annual Card - Child	15.00
Annual Card – Family 1 Parent and children	50.00
Annual Card – Family 2 Parents and children	78.00
Concessions: students, pensioners, disabled visitors and their carers, armed services personnel	

Transport Access

Car	A2 Exit MD Centrum to B71 Signposted to Zoo
Car Park	Yes, at Zoo. No charge until end 2011
Tram	10 to Stop Zoo
Nearest Station	Magdeburg Hbf

Ownership of Zoo

Municipal Company   Zoologischer Garten Magdeburg gGmbH
90% City of Magdeburg
10% District of Barleben

Area of Zoo

20 Ha

Date of Foundation

1950

Visitor Numbers

Circa 330,000

Animal Inventory at 31.12.2009

	Number	Species
Mammals	277	71
Birds	385	65
Reptiles	71	21
Amphibians	60	10
Fish	0	0

Facilities

Catering (sub-contract):
Restaurant, Cafeteria, Kiosks, Picnic Place - Bio Zoo-Bistro, Serengeti Camp
Retail (zoo owned): Zoo shop
Children's Zoo: Yes   Children's Playground: Yes

Dogs

Allowed on leads: Yes   Kennel Facilities: No

Feeding by Visitors

Strictly Prohibited, except for Goats in Children's Zoo

Shows, etc

Programme of Exhibitions in Zoowelle

Education

Zoo keeper talks: Yes - see daily programme
Zoo School/Education Centre: Yes
Biodiversity Centre: No
Zoo Guidebook: No
Signage on Exhibits: German   Star Rating: **

Friends of the Zoo

Yes, Förderverein Zoofreunde Magdeburg e. V.
Membership at 31.12.2010, Circa 440

Volunteers

No

ZOO MAGDEBURG

General Site Description

Visitors enter Magdeburg Zoo through the impressive and well-designed Zoowelle building and then walk through parkland with well managed and catalogued trees before arriving in the main zoological gardens. A stream, a tributary of the Elbe river, runs through the zoo and is transformed to become a major feature. The spacious outdoor enclosures are designed to allow visitors to be close to the animals. The recently opened Tapir and Rhino Houses have tropical vegetation and use cambark extensively for a pleasing naturalistic atmosphere: these buildings are setting the style for future developments in the zoo.

Indoor Exhibits

Zoowelle, Apes House, Giraffe House, Rhino House, Elephant House; Tapir House

Star Attractions

Tapir House (coatis, tapirs, capybaras), Lynx, Snow Leopards, Dwarf Mongooses, Flamingos, Black Rhinos, Reeves' Muntjac, Pelicans, Giant Anteaters, Tamarins, Blue Magpies, Meerkats, Mona Monkeys, Eagle Owls

Time required

whole zoo: 4 - 5 hours   star attractions: 2 hours

Marwell Wildlife

Contact	Name Marwell Wildlife Zoological Park
	Address Thompsons Lane, Colden
	Common, Winchester,
	Hampshire, SO21 1JH, UK
	Phone +44(0)1962 777 407
	Fax +44(0)1962 777 511
	Email marwell@marwell.org.uk
	Website www.marwell.org.uk

Opening Hours

Open every day except Christmas Day and Boxing Day

Peak Days (School Summer holidays, Easter, May/June half term)
10.00 to 18.00

Standard Days (April to October Except School Holidays)
10.00 to 17.00

Off Peak Days (January to March and November and December Except half term and Easter holidays)   10.00 to 16.00

Entrance Prices 2011

Daily Ticket Prices Include a 10% Voluntary Conservation Donation	
Standard Day prices are given: Peak Days add 12% Off Peak Days deduct 12%	
	GBP
Adult	16.00
Child 3-16	12.00
Child under 3	Free
Carers of Disabled Visitors	Free
Family Day Ticket - 2 Adults and 2 Children	50.00
Annual Card - Adult	52.50
Annual Card - Child	33.50
Concessions: Students, 60+, Disabled Visitors	
Annual Card Holders are entitled to free entry at reciprocal zoos	

Transport Access	Navi	Sat Nav SO21 1J H
	Car	M3 Junction 11 or M27 Junctions 10 W or 5 E
		Marwell is just off the B2177 between Bishops Waltham and Colden Common. Follow large brown tourist signs to Zoo
	Car Park	Yes, at Zoo, Free of charge
	Bus	Community Bus Service from Eastleigh Park and Ride
	Nearest Station	Eastleigh Station - 5 miles from Zoo
		Southampton Airport Park - 7 miles from zoo
		Winchester Station - 8 miles from Zoo

Ownership of Zoo	Registered Charity	100% Marwell Wildlife

Area of Zoo	50 Ha / 120 acres

Animal Inventory at 31.12.2008

	Number	Species
Mammals	874	109
Birds	410	48
Reptiles	151	33
Amphibians	47	9
Fish	154	14

Date of Foundation 1972

Visitor Numbers Circa 505,000

Facilities
Catering (zoo owned):
Restaurant, Cafeteria, Kiosks, Picnic Areas - Café Graze views across the African Valley, Squirrel Snacks, African BBQ and Bushtucker Bites and Café in the Shop Retail (zoo owned): Zoo shop - The Ark shop, Marwell Express Zoo train GBP 2.00 per person
Children's Zoo: Yes   Children's Playground: Yes, several

Dogs
Allowed on leads: No   Kennel Facilities: No

Feeding by Visitors Strictly prohibited, unless under special supervision

Shows, etc Yes

Education
Zoo keeper talks: Yes, 7 daily – see website or information in zoo for daily programme. Keeper talks or animal encounters from 11.00 to 16.00 daily. Children's Story Telling for over 3s every hour from 11.00 to 15.00
Zoo School/Education Centre: Yes
Biodiversity Centre: No
Zoo Guidebook: Yes, GBP 3.00
Signage on Exhibits: English   Star Rating: **

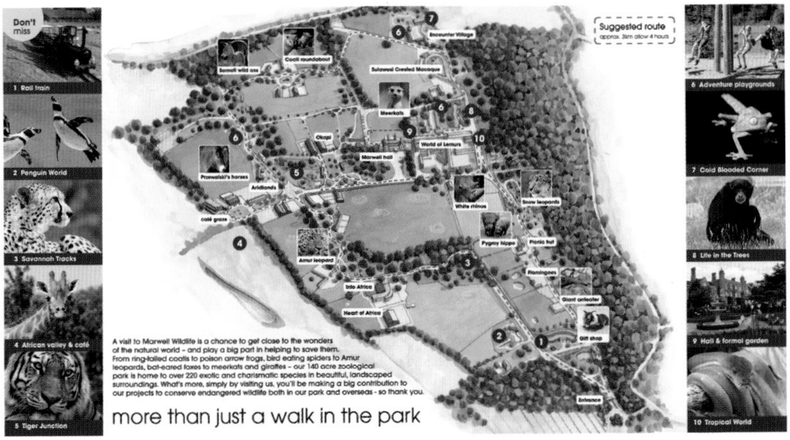

more than just a walk in the park

MARWELL ZOO

Friends of the Zoo	Yes, small membership Also, Annual Card Membership Holders at 31.12.2009 - Circa 18,000
Volunteers	Yes, Circa 120
General Site Description	A large mainly open site ideally suited to Savannah hoofstock. There is limited tree cover and water features are sparse The large new Café Graze gives an excellent view of the large and impressive African Savannah which was opened in 2009. The "Encounter" Village brings together several delightful exhibits and a lovely Wallaby walk through area. In this section the animals are individually named. The world of Lemurs is an exhibit that delights visitors.
Indoor Exhibits	Giraffe House, Tropical World, Okapi House, Tiger House, Rhino House, Lemur House, Aridlands House, Hippo and Tapir House
Star Attractions	Leopard, Snow Leopard, Red Panda, Fossa, Tiger, Giraffe, Macaque, Small Clawed Otter, Ocelot, African Savannah, Zebra, Bennet's Wallaby Walk Through, Lemurs, Bat-Eared Fox
Time required	whole zoo: 5 - 6 hours star attractions: 2 - 3 hours

ZOO MULHOUSE

Contact

Name	Parc Zoologique et Botanique de Mulhouse/Zoo Mulhouse
Address	51 Rue du Jardin Zoologique, 68100 Mulhouse, F
Phone	+33(0) 3 69 77 65 65
Fax	+33(0) 3 69 77 65 80
Email	zoomulhouse@mulhouse-alsace.fr
Website	www.zoo-mulhouse.com

Opening Hours

Open every day of the year

April and September	09.00 to 18.00
May to August	09.00 to 19.00
October, November and March	09.00 to 17.00
December to February	10.00 to 16.00

Entrance Prices 2011

	EUR
Adult	12.00
Child 6-16	6.50
Child Under 6	Free
Annual Card - Adult	60.00
Annual Card - Child 6 -16	26.00
Annual Family Card 2 Adults and 2 Children	52.00
Concessions: reduced winter rates apply to all residents of region Alsace, students, over 65s	

Transport Access

Car	A36 Exit Mulhouse Centre and signposted
Car Park	Yes, at Zoo, Free of Charge
Bus	30 Zoo Stop
Tram	Ligne 1 Stop Gare then Bus 30
Nearest Station	Mulhouse

Ownership of Zoo   Municipal/Regional, 100% Mulhouse and 32 Towns

Area of Zoo   25 Ha

Date of Foundation   1868

Visitor Numbers   Circa 350,000

Animal Inventory at 31.12.2009

	Number	Species
Mammals	305	69
Birds	540	84
Reptiles	100	7
Amphibians	0	0
Fish	0	0

Facilities

Catering (sub-contract):
Restaurant, Kiosks, Picnic Place - Restaurant (Auberge Alsacienne)
Retail (zoo owned): Zoo shop
Children's Zoo: Yes   Children's Playground: Yes

Dogs

Allowed on leads: No   Kennel Facilities: No

Feeding by Visitors

Strictly prohibited

Shows, etc

No

Education

Zoo keeper talks: Yes, several opportunities – see daily programme in zoo
Zoo School/Education Centre: Yes
Biodiversity Centre: No
Zoo Guidebook: No
Signage on Exhibits: French and German   Star Rating: *

ZOO MULHOUSE

Friends of the Zoo   Yes, La Société des Amis du Zoo de Mulhouse - Circa 200

Volunteers   No

General Site Description   This is a fine, varied site combining zoological and botanical gardens with an unused wooded area. The zoo borders the "Tannenwald Waldeck" forest and has a good collection of unusual trees. The site is sloping and attractive but lacks water features. The zoo specialises in Lemurs.

Indoor Exhibits   Monkey House, South American Monkey House

Star Attractions   Ring Tailed Lemurs, Black Vulture, Red Ruffed lemurs, Chile Flamingos, Leopards, Lake Birds Walk Through, Madagascar Boas

Time required   whole zoo: 3 - 4 hours   star attractions: 1 hour

TIERPARK HELLABRUNN

Der Zoo der Stadt München

Contact

Name	Tierpark Hellabrunn/Munich Zoo
Address	Tierparkstr. 30,
	D-81543 München, D
Phone	+49(0) 89 62 508-0
Fax	+49(0) 89 62 508 32
Email	office@tierpark-hellabrunn.de
Website	www.tierpark-hellabrunn.de

Opening Hours

Open every day of the year
April to September   09.00 to 18.00
October to March   09.00 to 17.00

Entrance Prices 2011

	EUR
Adult	11.00
Child 4-14	4.50
Child under 4	Free
Large Family Card for 2 Adults & children at the same postal address	25.00
Small Family Card for 1 Adult & children at the same postal address	14.00
Annual Card Adult	49.00
Annual Card Child	25.00
Annual Card Students and Pensioners	42.00
Annual Card Larger Family	98.00
Annual Card Small Family	49.00
Concessions: students, pensioners, disabled, armed forces personnel, München Card Holders and Kombi Tickets for Zoo and Deutsches Museum	

Transport Access

Car	A 8 -> Innerer Ring -> Thalkirchen
Car Park	P1 Tierparkstr. P2 Siebenbrunner Str. Both EUR 3.50 per day
Park and Ride	Several U Bahn and S Bahn stations offer park and ride
	Listed at www.muenchener.de/umweltzone
Bus	Linie 52 from Marienplatz to Tierpark
U-Bahn	U3 to Station Thalkirchen (Tierpark)
Nearest Station	Munich Hbf

Ownership of Zoo

Municipal AG
93% City of Munich - Münchener Tierpark Hellabrunn AG
7% Private Individuals

Area of Zoo 36 Ha

Date of Foundation 1911

Visitor Numbers Circa 1,500,000

Animal Inventory at 31.12.2009

	Number	Species
Mammals	1035	99
Birds	1028	92
Reptiles	361	55
Amphibians	91	8
Fish	7100	267

Facilities Catering (sub-contract):
Restaurant, Pizzeria, Kiosks, Picnic Place - Tierpark Restaurant
Retail (zoo owned): Zoo shop
Children's Zoo: Yes, New Guinea Pig area of special note, Camel Rides
Children's Playground: Yes

Dogs Allowed on leads: Yes - on a short lead only and not in animal houses.
Kennel Facilities: No

Feeding by Visitors Strictly prohibited – except certain species from food dispensers in the zoo.

Shows, etc Yes, from April to October, Birds of Prey Show, Elephant Show, Dove Show, Sea Lion Parade

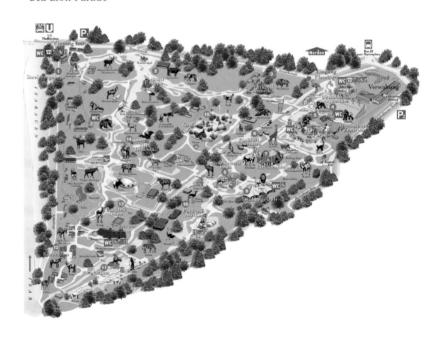

Education

Zoo keeper talks: No
Zoo School/Education Centre: Yes
Biodiversity Centre: Yes, Artenschutz Centrum open 10.00 to 17.00 in Summer and 10.00 to 16.00 in Winter
Zoo Guidebook: Yes, EUR 3.00
Signage on Exhibits: German   Star Rating: **

Friends of the Zoo

Yes, Tierparkfreunde Hellabrunn e. V.   Membership at 31.12.2009 - Circa 7000

Volunteers

Yes, Circa 50

General Site Description

Hellabrunn has a wonderful site, a spacious city parkland with plenty of mature trees and the added advantage of the tributaries of the adjacent river Isar running through the zoo. Characterful older animal houses such as the elephant house combine with excellent modern buildings such as those for apes and monkeys with their excellent vegetation. Free flying bird displays fill the sky twice daily and when the zoo is quiet the squirrel monkeys' tree canopy allows the visitor to get close to them. The Polar Bear exhibit has a well designed Tundra area Hellabrunn was the first zoo to be founded as a geo zoo: this is an on-going development principle.

Indoor Exhibits

Villa Dracula Nocturnal House, Dschungelzelt (big cats), Rhino/Tapir House, Aquarium, Monkey House, Jungle House, Orang Utan Paradise, Elephant House, Giant Tortoise House

Star Attractions

Polar Bears, Squirrel Monkeys, Bird Volière, Giant Tortoises, Orang Utans, Snow Leopards, African Savannah, Ring Tailed Lemurs, Chimpanzees, Red Pandas, Gorillas, Banded Mongooses, Wolverines, Elk, Asian Elephants, Penguins, Takin, Green Iguanas, Teju Lizards, Parakeets, Ibex

Time required

whole zoo: 8 - 10 hours   star attractions: 3 hours

**Allwetterzoo
Münster**

ALLWETTERZOO MÜNSTER

Contact	Name	Allwetterzoo Münster
	Address	Sentruperstr. 315
		48161 Münster, D
	Phone	+49(0)251/8904-0
	Fax	+49(0)251/8904-130
	Email	info@allwetterzoo.de
	Website	www.allwetterzoo.de

Opening Hours

Open every day of the year

March and October	09.00 to 17.00
April to September	09.00 to 18.00
November to February	09.00 to 16.00

Entrance Prices 2011

	EUR
Adult	14.00
Child 3-17	7.00
Child under 3	Free
Dog	Free
Annual Card - Adult	70.00
Annual Card - Child	35.00
Annual Card – Family 2 Adults and their children	145.00
Concessions: Carers of Disabled Visitors	
Annual Card holders qualify for NRW discount	

Transport Access

Car	A1/A43 Kreuz Münster, Richtung Innenstadt
Car Park	Yes, at Zoo EUR 2.00
Bus	14
Nearest Station	Münster Hbf

Ownership of Zoo

Municipal Company, Westfälischer Zoologischer Garten Münster gGmbH
Non Profit, Zoo-Verein 51%, City of Münster 49%

Area of Zoo

30 Ha

Date of Foundation

1875, on present site
since 1974

Visitor Numbers

Circa 1,000,000

Animal Inventory at 31.12.2009

	Number	Species
Mammals	541	61
Birds	502	72
Reptiles	91	23
Amphibians	37	8
Fish	1068	80

Facilities

Catering (sub-contract):
Restaurant, Cafeteria, Kiosks
Retail (sub-contract): Zoo shop
Children's Zoo: Yes   Children's Playground: Yes

Dogs

Allowed on leads: Yes   Kennel Facilities: No

Feeding by Visitors

In general, Strictly prohibited,
Supervised feeding: Elephants, Loris, Penguins and in Children's Zoo

Shows, etc

Dolphins: Daily – seasonal variation in times see website,
Westfalisches Pferdemuseum / Horse Museum, Penguin March

Education

Zoo keeper talks: Yes
Zoo School/Education Centre: Yes
Biodiversity Centre: Yes, Biocity
Zoo Guidebook: Yes, EUR 4.50
Signage on Exhibits: German, English   Star Rating: **

Friends of the Zoo

Yes, Zoo-Verein Münster e. V., Membership at 31.12.2009 – Circa 8,000

Volunteers

No

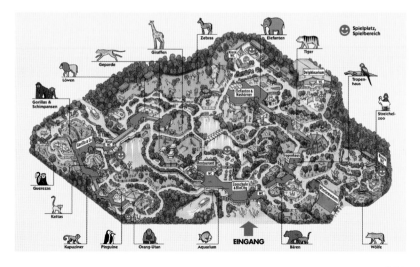

ALLWETTERZOO MÜNSTER

General Site Description

The Allwetterzoo is a delightful zoological garden, located near the Aasee lake on the south west side of the city of Münster. The site is a pleasing mixture of gardens, lakes and mature trees. Cambark is widely used both in animal enclosures and on visitor walkways. The African Panorama, opened in 2010, with its small river and lake, rocks, trees and fine slopes is well designed, moated and ideal for visitor viewing of the 8 species inhabiting the area.
The Colobus walk through with more than 10 free roaming monkeys is unique amongst the surveyed zoos and a wonderful visitor experience.

Indoor Exhibits

Elephant and Rhino House, Apes House, Aquarium, Bears House, Monkey House, Tropical House/ Reptile House, Dolphinarium, Carnivore House, Orang Utan House, Giraffe House

Star Attractions

African Panorama - (Zebra, Antelope, Ostriches), Ruffed Lemurs, Gundis, Colobus Walk- Through, Brown Capuchins, Elephant Feeding, Ring Tailed Lemur Walk- Through, Coatis, Lori Feeding, Dolphins, European Wolves, Penguin March, Gorillas and Mangabeys, Sun Bears, Orang-Utans and Small Clawed Otters, Weaver Birds

Time required

whole zoo: 6 - 8 hours   star attractions: 3 - 4 hours

Tiergarten
Nürnberg

Contact

Name	Tiergarten Nuremberg
Address	Am Tiergarten 30,
	90480 Nürnberg, D
Phone	+49(0) 911 5454 - 6
Fax	+49(0) 911 5454 - 802
Email	tiergarten@stadt.nuernberg.de
Website	www.tiergarten.nuernberg.de

Opening Hours

Open every day of the year
Summer   08.00 to 19.30
Winter   09.00 to 17.00

Entrance Prices 2011

	EUR	EUR
	Zoo	Dolphinarium
Adult	9.00	4.50
Child 4-13	4.50	2.00
Child under 4	Free	Free
Family Card - Adults & their children up to 17	21.00	10.50
Annual Cards	Zoo Only	Zoo + Dolphinarium
Annual Card Main Card Holder Adult	60.00	80.00
Annual Card Additional Adult	45.00	55.00
Annual Card Child	27.00	35.00
From August 2011 there will be Combi Tickets for the Zoo and the Dolphinarium		
Concessions: Students, Pensioners, Disabled Visitors, Armed Services Personnel, Unemployed, Visitors on the last Monday of each month except holidays		

Transport Access

Car	A3 Exit Nürnberg-Mögeldorf or
	A9 Exit Nürnberg Fischbach
Car Park	Yes, at Zoo, Free of Charge
Bus	Linie 65
Tram	Linie 5 from Nuremberg Hbf
Nearest Station	Nuremberg Hbf

Ownership of Zoo

Municipal
100% City of Nuremberg

Area of Zoo

70 Ha

Date of Foundation

1912

Visitor Numbers

Circa 1,080,000

Animal Inventory at 31.12.2009

	Number	Species
Mammals	644	79
Birds	436	51
Reptiles	69	18
Amphibians	69	5
Fish	527	57

Facilities

Catering (sub-contract):
Restaurant, Cafeteria, Kiosks, Picnic Places, Café Restaurant Waldschänke
Bistro at Dolphinarium, New Restaurant in Laguna from August 2011
Retail (sub-contract): Zoo shop
Children's Zoo: Yes   Children's Playground: Yes

Dogs

Allowed on leads: No   Kennel Facilities: No

Feeding by Visitors

Strictly prohibited except in the petting zoo using food from zoo dispensers only

Shows, etc

Dolphinarium, Sea Lions

Education

Zoo keeper talks: Yes, several opportunities in conjunction with feeding –
see daily programme in Zoo
Zoo School/Education Centre: Yes
Biodiversity Centre: Yes, Naturkundehaus
Zoo Guidebook: Yes, EUR 3.00
Signage on Exhibits: German   Star Rating: **

Friends of the Zoo

Yes, Verein der Tiergartenfreunde Nürnberg e. V.
Membership at 31.12.2009 - Circa 2,000

Volunteers

No

General Site Description

Nuremberg Zoo, birthplace of Flocke, the famous polar bear cub born in December 2007, is set in the Reichswald, an attractive, extensive parkland. The zoo has a substantial number of beautiful mature deciduous trees, particularly oak, beech, hornbeam and linden. A wide variety of terrains within the zoo includes shrubberies, woodland areas and marshy patches. One of the joys of Nuremberg Zoo is, therefore, the opportunity this lovely varied terrain gives for many species to have enclosures with the most natural and suitable of habitats. Part of the site is steep with substantial natural sandstone rock features: these too are well used in enclosures for appropriate species and the visitor pathways ways and the perspectives on enclosures are excellent.

The historic Lion and Tiger House has been beautifully restored. A magnificent Dolphin and Manatee Laguna is due to open in August 2011; it will include other species and a Butterfly House.

Indoor Exhibits

Dolphinarium, Giraffe House, Reptile House, Naturkundehaus, Rhino House, Tapir House, Lion/ Tiger House, Monkey House

Star Attractions

Yellow Throated Martens, Dwarf Mongoose, Squirrel Monkeys, Otters, Lions, Spanish Wolves, Bird Lake, Red Panda, Tigers, Walk Through Aviary, Sea Lions, Penguins, Dolphins, Manatees, Baboons, Takins, Ibex Rock

Time required   whole zoo: 7 - 8 hours   star attractions: 3 hours

ODENSE ZOO

Contact
Name	Odense ZooAddress
	Sdr. Boulevard 306
	5000 Odense C, DK
Phone	+45 (0) 66 11 13 60
Fax	+45(0) 65 90 82 28
Email	odensezoo@odensezoo.dk
Website	www.odensezoo.dk

Opening Hours

Open every day of the year*

November to March	10.00 to 16.00
April, September, October	10.00 to 17.00
May, June	10.00 to 18.00
July, August	10.00 to 19.00

*Weekends and Holidays open longer

Entrance Prices 2011

	DKK
Adult	160.00
Child 3-11	85.00
Child under 3	Free
Annual Card - Adult	340.00 or Lux Version 440.00
Annual Card - Child 3-11	180.00 or Lux Version 280.00
Concessions: 65+, students, disabled visitors and their carers	
Annual card also gives free entry to 3 other Danish Zoos	

Transport Access
Car	E20 Exit 52 then signposted
Car Park	Yes, at Zoo
Bus	11,12,31
Nearest Station	Odense Central Station

Ownership of Zoo Municipal Non–profit company

Area of Zoo 8.5 Ha

Date of Foundation 1930

Visitor Numbers Circa 450,000

**Animal Inventory
at 31.12.2009**

	Number	Species
Mammals	479	45
Birds	370	56
Reptiles	117	19
Amphibians	17	2
Fish	975	28

Facilities

Catering (zoo owned):
Restaurant, Café, Kiosks, Picnic Place: Restaurant Kathmandu, Café Darwin, in July Barbeque evenings on Thursdays and zoo open until 22.00
Retail (zoo owned): Zoo shop, Zoo train weekends and school holidays DKK 10.00
Children's Zoo: Yes   Children's Playground: Yes

Dogs

Allowed on leads: No   Kennel Facilities: No

Feeding by Visitors

Strictly prohibited

Shows, etc

Sea Lions, Tiger Training Presentation, Lion Training Presentation

Education

Zoo keeper talks: Yes, daily programme of up to 9 feeding and training events.
Between 11.00 and 15.00 – see daily programme.
Zoo School/Education Centre: Yes
Biodiversity Centre: No
Zoo Guidebook: Yes
Signage on Exhibits: Danish, some English and German   Star Rating: *

Friends of the Zoo   Yes - Membership at 31.12.2009 Circa 1,500

Volunteers   No

General Site Description   Odense Zoo has a river running through the zoo, a large lake area and good water features. The site is relatively flat and has some deciduous tree cover. The zoo's limited range of mammal species is to be expanded in the near future with the acquisition of additional adjacent land from the adjoining municipal owner.

The impressive Oceanium with its manatees and antarctic penguins forms the most important part of a new South American area. A new Savannah exhibit, called Kiwara, is due to open in June 2011.

For a small zoo, there are a significant number of star attractions. The magic of Hans Christian Andersen lives on here in the zoo .

Indoor Exhibits   Chimps House, Africa House, Tropical House, Giraffe House, South America House, Penguin House, Giant Tortoise House

Star Attractions   Chimpanzees, Dwarf Mongooses, Tamarins, Amur Tigers, Manatees, Bird Walk Through, Aldabra Tortoises, Flamingos, Pelicans, Kiwara Complex – includes largest aviary in Europe with free flying pelicans and flamingos

Time required   whole zoo: 4 - 6 hours   star attractions: 2 - 3 hours

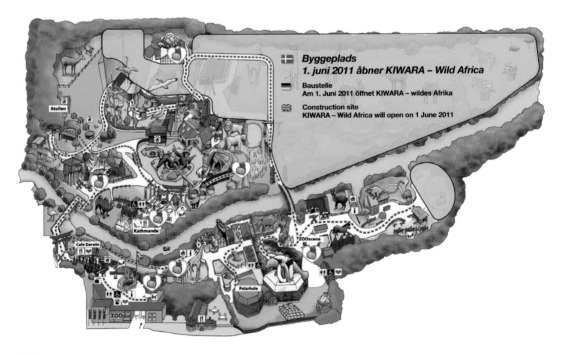

ZOO OSNABRÜCK

Contact

	Name	Zoo Osnabrück
	Address	Klaus-Strick-Weg 12, 49082 Osnabrück, D
	Phone	+49 (0)541 951 050
	Fax	+49 (0)541 951 0522
	Email	zoo@zoo-osnabrueck.de
	Website	www.zoo-osnabrueck.de

Opening Hours

Open every day of the year	
Summer - when clocks change	08.00 to 18.30
Winter to when clocks change	09.00 to 17.00
Christmas Eve and New Year's Eve	09.00 to 14.00
Christmas Holiday Days and New Year's Day	09.00 to 17.00

Entrance Prices 2011

	EUR
Adult	13.50
Child 3-14	8.50
Annual Card – Single Person	45.00
Annual Card – Family	89.00
Concessions: students, disabled visitors and their carers, armed services personnel and unemployed.	

Transport Access

Car	A30 Exit 18 then signposted to Zoo
Car Park	Yes, at Zoo, Free of Charge
Bus	Linie 21 to Kreishaus/Zoo
Nearest Station	Osnabrück Hbf

Ownership of Zoo

Charitable Society
Zoogesellschaft Osnabrück e. V.
100% Private Shareholders including Sponsoring Companies

Area of Zoo 25 Ha

Date of Foundation 1936

Visitor Numbers Circa 850,000

Animal Inventory at 31.12.2009

	Number	Species
Mammals	468	72
Birds	417	77
Reptiles	175	38
Amphibians	14	3
Fish	1120	78

Facilities

Catering (sub-contract):
Restaurant, Café, Kiosks, Picnic Place - Restaurant in Makatanda Village, Zoo Gaststätte with sun terrace, Samburu Restaurant overlooking giraffes, Tigerhütte Restaurant
Retail (sub-contract): Zoo shop
Children's Zoo: Yes - Two children's Zoos
Children's Playground: Yes, Makatanda is a wonderfully designed playground; it is based on an authentic African tree house village with painted spirits. Climbing opportunities are combined with imaginative play possibilities. Also, Kinderland and Giraffe Spielplatz.

Dogs

Allowed on leads: Yes, but not in all houses.   Kennel Facilities: No

Feeding by Visitors

Strictly prohibited except when on a zoo guided tour.

Shows, etc

Climate Change, Untererdischer/ Subterranean Zoo with interactive terminals

Education

Zoo keeper talks: Yes
Zoo School/Education Centre: Yes
Biodiversity Centre: No
Zoo Guidebook: No, but hand held electronic guide available at no charge.
Signage on Exhibits: German   Star Rating: **

Friends of the Zoo

Yes, Zoogesellschaft Osnabrück e. V.
Membership at 31.12.2009, Circa 1,000

Zoo Osnabrück

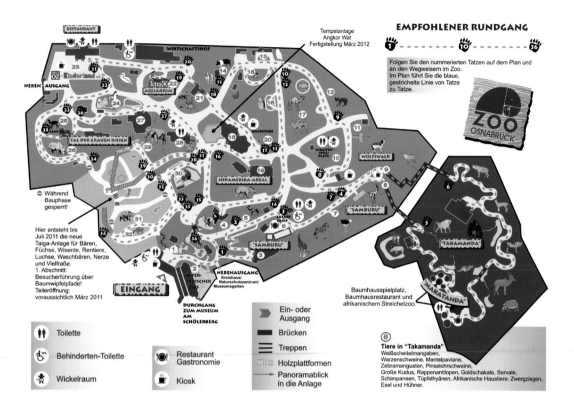

EMPFOHLENER RUNDGANG

Folgen Sie den nummerierten Tatzen auf dem Plan und an den Wegweisern im Zoo. Im Plan führt Sie die blaue, gestrichelte Linie von Tatze zu Tatze.

Tempelanlage Angkor Wat Fertigstellung März 2012

Während Bauphase gesperrt!

Hier entsteht bis Juli 2011 die neue Taiga-Anlage für Bären, Füchse, Wisente, Rentiere, Luchse, Waschbären, Nerze und Vielfraße.
1. Abschnitt: Besucherführung über Baumwipfelpfade!
Teileröffnung: voraussichtlich März 2011

Baumhausspielplatz, Baumhausrestaurant und afrikanischem Streichelzoo

Tiere in "Takamanda"
Weißscheitelmangaben, Warzenschweine, Mantelpaviane, Zebramangusten, Pinselohrschweine, Große Kudus, Rappenantilopen, Goldschakale, Servale, Schimpansen, Tüpfelhyänen, Afrikanische Haustiere: Zwergziegen, Esel und Hühner.

Toilette

Behinderten-Toilette

Wickelraum

Restaurant Gastronomie

Kiosk

Ein- oder Ausgang

Brücken

Treppen

Holzplattformen

Panoramablick in die Anlage

Volunteers	No
General Site Description	A fine, varied and partially hilly site with excellent tree cover and natural vegetation. Recent major extension to accommodate the African themed Takamanda development includes a fine elevated walkway offering interesting perspectives from tree top level. Locally made customised themed wooden litter bins are an interesting aspect of this well managed, clean zoo site. This zoo has expanded and developed well recently. The new Taiga with an improved bears' exhibit opens in 2011.
Indoor Exhibits	Chimpanzee House, Unterirdischer (subterranean) Zoo, Spider Monkeys, Elephant House, Orang Utan House, South America House, Monkey House, Tiger House, Tetra Aquarium, Giraffe House
Star Attractions	Takamanda exhibit - Chimpanzees, Spotted Hyena, Serval, Jackal and Mangabey, Samburu Savannah exhibit - Giraffes and Zebras, Coati, Spider Monkeys, Ibis and Stork Volière, Dhole, Small Clawed Otter, Unterirdischer (subterranean) Zoo, Eurasian Wolf, Marmoset/Tamarin, Weaver Birds
Time required	whole zoo: 6 - 8 hours star attractions: 2 - 3 hours

Environmental Park

PAIGNTON ZOO

Contact	Name	Paignton Zoo Environmental Park
	Address	Totnes Road, Paignton, Devon TQ4 7EU, UK
	Phone	+44(0)1803 697 500 0844 474 2222
	Fax	+44(0)1803 523 457
	Email	info@paigntonzoo.org.uk
	Website	www.paigntonzoo.org.uk

Opening Hours

Open every day except Christmas Day

Spring and Summer	10.00 to 17.00
Winter	10.00 to 16.30

Entrance Prices 2011

Daily Ticket Prices Include a 10% Voluntary Conservation Donation	
	GBP
Adult	13.10
Child 3-15	9.25
Child under 3 and Carers of Disabled Visitors	Free
Family Day Ticket 2 Adults and 2 Children	41.25
Annual Card - Adult	45.00
Annual Card - Child	30.00
Annual Card - Joint 2 Adults	80.00
Annual Card - Family	125.00
Concessions: Students, 60+ and disabled visitors	
Annual Card Holders are entitled to free entry at reciprocal zoos	

Transport Access	Navi	Sat Nav TQ4 7EU
	Car	Paignton Zoo is located on A3022 Totnes Road 1 mile from Paignton
	Car Park	Yes, free Parking at Paignton Zoo
	Bus	First Western National Bus 66 from Brixham to Torquay stops at the Zoo
	Nearest Station	Paignton Station 1 mile
	Bicycle	Secure Bicycle Racks at Zoo

Ownership of Zoo Registered Charity   100% The Whitley Wildlife Conservation Trust

Area of Zoo 34 Ha / 83 acres

Date of Foundation 1923

Visitor Numbers Circa 530,000

Animal Inventory at 31.12.2009

	Number	Species
Mammals	442	68
Birds	964	151
Reptiles	262	51
Amphibians	120	21
Fish	23	4

Facilities

Catering (zoo owned):
Restaurant, Café, Kiosks, Picnic Place - Island Restaurant, Snack Shack
Retail (zoo owned): Living World Gift Shop
Children's Zoo: Yes   Children's Playground: Yes

Dogs

Allowed on leads: No   Kennel Facilities: No

Feeding by Visitors

Strictly prohibited

Shows, etc

Yes, Feathered Feats Bird Shows - in Summer

Education

Zoo keeper talks: Yes, 7 opportunities 10.45 to 15.15 - see daily programme in zoo
Zoo School/Education Centre: Yes, includes a Discovery Centre
Biodiversity Centre: No
Zoo Guidebook: Yes, GBP 2.50
Signage on Exhibits: English   Star Rating: **

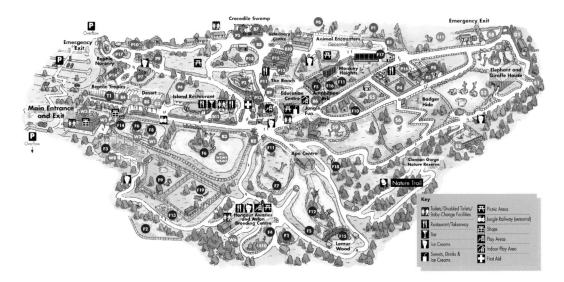

Friends of the Zoo   No but Annual Membership Scheme
Membership at 31.12.2009 – Circa 13,000

Volunteers   Yes, Circa 115

General Site Description   This fine zoological site, adjacent to the South Devon Coast, is bounded by a nature reserve. It is sloping in many parts, has good paths and has good tree cover with a wide variety of mature deciduous trees. The botanical gardens are a great feature exhibiting indigenous, spectacular, endangered, medicinal and culinary plants.
The zoo is organised in 6 Zones: Savannah, Forest, Wetland, Tropical Forest, Desert and "Primley" which is the historic name of the oldest part of the zoo. Paignton is a delightful zoo to visit with its zoological and botanical exhibits its awareness of the interdependence of animal and plant species and the need to create a natural habitat for the animals.

Indoor Exhibits   Monkey Heights, Apes Centre, Desert House, Crocodile Swamp, Rhino House, Elephant and Giraffe House, Reptile Tropics House

Star Attractions   Monkey Heights, Marmosets, Ruffed Lemurs, Cassowary, Red Panda, Maned Wolf, Gibbons, Pelicans, Red River Hog, Grey Kangaroo, Giant Tortoise

Time required   whole zoo: 6 - 8 hours   star attractions: 2 - 3 hours

Contact

	Name	Pairi Daiza
		(formerly Parc Paradisio)
	Address	Domaine de Cambron
		7940 Brugelette, B
	Phone	+32(0) 68 250 850
	Fax	+32(0) 68 455 405
	Email	info@pairidaiza.eu
	Website	www.pairidaiza.eu

Opening Hours

Open Early April to Early November

April, May, June	10.00 to 18.00
July and August	10.00 to 19.00
September and October	10.00 to 18.00

Opening dates vary by a few days each year – check website for exact dates

Entrance Prices 2011

	EUR
Adult	22.00
Child 3-11	17.00
Child under 3	Free
Annual Card - Adult	45.00
Annual Card - Child	35.00
Concessions: 60+ and disabled visitors	

Transport Access

Car	Sat Nav Le Domaine 1 à 7940 Brugelette
Car Park	Yes, at Zoo purchase token for EUR 4.00
Nearest Station	Cambron-Casteau, 10 minutes' walk

Ownership of Zoo

Private Company
100% Parc Paradisio SA Majority Shareholder – Eric Domb

Area of Zoo   55 Ha

Date of Foundation   1994

Visitor Numbers   Circa 900,000

Animal Inventory at 31.12.2009

	Number	Species
Mammals	310	40
Birds	2800	320
Reptiles	1600	100
Amphibians	50	10
Fish	950	150

Facilities

Catering (zoo owned):
Restaurant, Café, Kiosks and Picnic Place: Restaurant Karibuni, Café Orangerie, Brasserie Mersus, L'Oasis, L'Orangerie
Retail (zoo owned): Zoo shop, Miniature Railway
Children's Zoo: Yes, Children's farm   Children's Playground: Yes

Dogs

Allowed on leads: No   Kennel Facilities: No

Feeding by Visitors

Generally not permitted but some controlled feeding opportunities.

Shows, etc

Yes, Birds of Prey

Education

Zoo keeper talks: No
Zoo School/Education Centre: No
Biodiversity Centre: No
Zoo Guidebook: Yes
Signage on Exhibits: French and Flemish   Star Rating: *

Friends of the Zoo

No

Volunteers

No

General Site Description

This is a fascinating zoo with several dimensions. Set in a former 13th century monastery with characterful protected buildings and interesting ruins, Pairi Daiza has fine gardens and a huge lake which has been imaginatively used. Originally opened as a Bird Park as Parc Paradisio, Pairi Daiza has the largest bird collection of all the 80 zoos in the survey. The walk-through aviaries are a true delight.

A huge lake provides an ideal setting for marine mammals, such as hippos. Mature weeping willows near the lake are a special feature.

The zoo gives the visitor a fascinating cultural experience: both the extensive Chinese Garden and the Indonesian archipelago themed "Ganesha" allow the visitor to experience ethnic cultures, buildings, artefacts and plants and to see indigenous species in their appropriate settings.

The zoo is currently planning to extend its mammal collection and to add indoor facilities with a view to all year round opening.

Indoor Exhibits

Oasis Tropical House, Nautilus, Mersus Emergo

Star Attractions

Squirrel Monkeys, American Bison, African Fish Eagles, Birds of Prey Walk-Through, Ring Tailed Lemurs, Capybara/Rhea, Shoebill Storks, Bird Volière, Ruffed Lemurs, Pelicans, Sarus Cranes, Budgerigars, Rat Kangaroos, Flamingos, Parrots

Time required

whole zoo: 6 - 8 hours   star attractions: 3 - 4 hours

PARIS MÉNAGERIE

Contact

Name	Ménagerie du Jardin des Plantes/ Paris Ménagerie
Address	57 rue Cuvier, 75005 Paris, F
Phone	+33(0) 1 40 79 37 94
Fax	+33(0) 1 40 79 37 93
Email	valhuber@mnhn.fr
Website	www.mnhn.fr

Opening Hours

Open every day of the year

Summer	09.00 to 18.00
Winter	09.00 to 17.00

Entrance Prices 2011

	EUR
Adult	8.00
Child / Young Person 4-25	6.00
Child Under 4	Free
Concessions: students	

Transport Access

Car	Signposted Jardin des Plantes/ MNHN
Car Park	No Parking at Zoo
Bus	24, 57, 61, 63, 67, 89, 91
Métro and RER	Jussieu or Austerlitz and RER-C
Nearest Station	SNCF Austerlitz or Gare de Lyon

Ownership of Zoo

National
100% Government   Museum National d'Histoire Naturelle (MNHN)

Area of Zoo

5.5 Ha

Date of Foundation

1794

Visitor Numbers

Circa 720,000

Animal Inventory at 31.12.2009

	Number	Species
Mammals	221	48
Birds	357	81
Reptiles	206	53
Amphibians	126	8
Fish	0	0

Facilities

Catering (sub-contract):
Snack Bar and Picnic area
Retail: No
Children´s Zoo: Yes   Children´s Playground: No

Dogs

Allowed on leads: No   Kennel Facilities: No

Feeding by Visitors

Strictly prohibited

Shows, etc

No

Education

Zoo keeper talks: Yes, Orang Utans, Red Pandas and Aldabra Tortoises
Zoo School/Education Centre: Yes
Biodiversity Centre: No
Zoo Guidebook: Yes, EUR 6.00
Signage on Exhibits: French   Star Rating: **

PARIS MÉNAGERIE

Friends of the Zoo

Yes, Société d' Encouragement pour la Conservation des Animaux Sauvages - SECAS - Circa 1500 members

Volunteers

No

General Site Description

This famous historic city zoo, contained on a very restricted site, has lost its previous large mammal collection and today exhibits smaller and rare species. The several historic buildings have been maintained but there has been little investment in new facilities. There is a pleasant feel to the site which has good vegetation. The zoo temporarily houses some of the animals from its sister zoo, Parc Zoologique de Paris at Bois de Vincennes which is closed for renovation until 2014.

Indoor Exhibits

Monkey House, Reptile House, African Aviary, Wild Cat House, Vivarium

Star Attractions

Red Pandas, Vicunas, Bush Dogs, Flamingos, Maras, Cassowarys, Pudus, Gaboon viper, Macaws, Anoas, Takins, Gaurs

Time required

whole zoo: 3 - 4 hours   star attractions: 1 hour

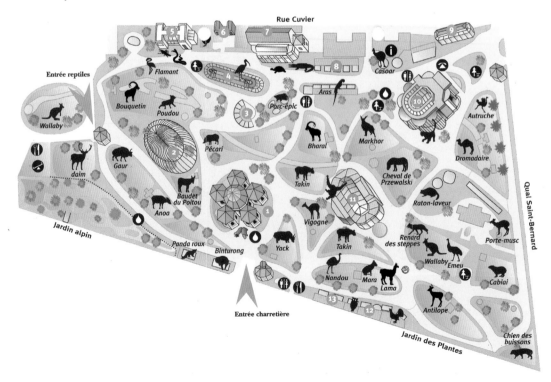

DIERENPARK PLANCKENDAEL

Contact

Name	Dierenpark Planckendael
Address	Leuvensesteenweg 582
	2812 Muizen- Mechelen, B
Phone	+32(0) 1541 4921
Fax	+32(0) 1542 2935
Email	info@planckendael.be
Website	www.planckendael.be

Opening Hours

Open every day of the year	
May, June and September	10.00 to 18.00
July and August	10.00 to 19.00
October, March and April	10.00 to 17.30
November to February	10.00 to 16.45

Entrance Prices 2011

	EUR
Adult	21.00
Child 3-17	17.00
Child under 3	Free
Annual Card - Adult	93.00
Annual Card 2 Adults and children under 18	164.00
Concessions: 60+, disabled visitors and their carers, Antwerp Combi Ticket	

Transport Access

Car	E19 Exit 11 Zemst then Signposted to Zoo
Car Park	Yes, at Zoo EUR 15.00
Bus	284, 285 from Mechelen Station
Tram	Ligne 1 Stop Gare then Bus 30
Nearest Station	Muizen and Mechelen
Boat	From Mechelen Station (high season only)

Ownership of Zoo

Private Foundation Non Profit
100% KMDA, Royal Zoological Society of Antwerp with financial support from
Antwerp Council and Flanders Regional Government

Area of Zoo   40 Ha

Date of Foundation   1956

Visitor Numbers   Circa 850,000

DIERENPARK PLANCKENDAEL

Animal Inventory at 31.12.2009

	Number	Species
Mammals	321	62
Birds	667	110
Reptiles	54	10
Amphibians	8	3
Fish	25	3
Excluded from the birds: circa 400 White Storks		

Facilities

Catering (zoo owned):
Restaurant, Café, Kiosks - De Ooievaar, Toepaja, Restaurant Wapiti
Retail (zoo owned): Zoo shop
Children's Zoo: Yes, Children's Farm
Children's Playground: Yes, 5 different playgrounds including trampoline park

Dogs

Allowed on leads: No   Kennel Facilities: No

Feeding by Visitors

Strictly prohibited

Shows, etc

No

Education

Zoo keeper talks: No
Zoo School/Education Centre: No
Biodiversity Centre: No
Zoo Guidebook: No
Signage on Exhibits: Flemish, French and English   Star Rating: *

Friends of the Zoo

No, but Members' of KMDA Scheme
200,000 members Antwerp and Planckendael combined

Volunteers

Yes, 1

General Site Description

Under common ownership with Antwerp Zoo, Planckendael is being developed for species requiring much space. Recent new enclosures are for giraffes and cheetahs and will be followed by a 3 Ha elephant house and enclosure. The zoo park is situated on a flat Manor House site with many mature trees and excellent water features. A major environmental project in the zoo is the recycling and purification of water through plants and reed beds.

Indoor Exhibits

Giraffe House, Bee House, Bonobo House, Asian Green House, Koala House

Star Attractions

Bonobos, African Savannah, White Handed Gibbons, Koalas, Cheetahs, Bush Dogs, Small Clawed Otters, Spotted Hyenas, Golden Headed Lion Tamarins and Marmosets

Time required

whole zoo: 5 - 7 hours   star attractions: 2 - 3 hours

ZOOLOGICKÁ
A BOTANICKÁ
ZAHRADA
MĚSTA PLZNĚ

Contact

Name	Plzen Zoological and Botanical Gardens
Address	Pod Vinicemi 9, 30116 Plzen, CZ
Phone	+420(0) 378 038 325
Fax	+420(0) 378 038 302
Email	zoo@plzen.eu
Website	www.zooplzen.cz

Opening Hours

Open every day of the year
April to October   08.00 to 19.00
November to March   09.00 to 18.00

Entrance Prices 2011

	CZK	CZK
	Summer	Winter
Adult	75.00	50.00
Child 4-15	45.00	30.00
Child under 4	Free	Free
Annual Card – Adult	300.00	
Annual Card – Child 4-15	200.00	
Annual Card – Family 2 Adults and 3 Children	600.00	
Concessions: Students, Over 65s, Disabled Visitors		

Transport Access

Car	From Plzen Town Centre via Rooseveltova Ul.
Car Park	Yes, at Zoo
Bus	41
Tram	1, 4
Nearest Station	Plzen Main Station

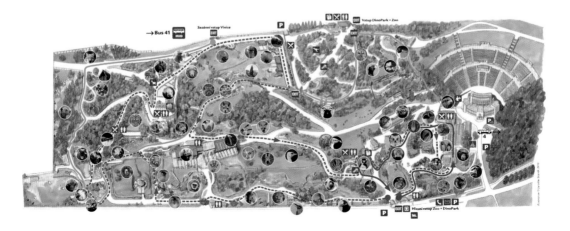

ZOO PLZEN

Ownership of Zoo Municipal   100% Plzen City Council

Area of Zoo 21 Ha

Date of Foundation 1926 relocated to present site in 1963

Visitor Numbers Circa 460,000

Animal Inventory at 31.12.2009

	Number	Species
Mammals	1514	241
Birds	1845	505
Reptiles	1325	248
Amphibians	472	59
Fish	692	90

Facilities Catering (sub-contract):
Restaurant, Cafeteria, Kiosks - Restaurant Kiboko, Restaurant at Lemur,
Siberian Log House
Retail (sub-contract): Zoo shop
Children's Zoo: Yes, in fine weather Camel Rides
Children's Playground: Yes

Dogs Allowed on leads: No   Kennel Facilities: No

Feeding by Visitors Strictly prohibited

Shows, etc Birds of Prey Show in Amphitheatre, Luftnerka Farmhouse, Dino Park

Education Zoo keeper talks: Yes, 3 Opportunities in Winter at feeding times
5 Opportunities in Summer at feeding times - see daily programme in zoo
Zoo School/Education Centre: Yes
Biodiversity Centre: No
Zoo Guidebook: Yes, CZK 75.00
Signage on Exhibits: Czech   Star Rating: *

Friends of the Zoo Yes, circa 30 members

Volunteers No

General Site Description

The only combination of Zoological and Botanical Gardens in the Czech Republic is in Plzen. Situated close to the river Mze in the south and bordered by high rocks in the north, the zoo is being organised as a Geo zoo with major new developments opened in 2010. The majority of the species here cannot be seen elsewhere in the Czech Republic. There is a fine Japanese garden, Showa-en, and a Greenhouse for Succulents.

Indoor Exhibits

Giraffe House, Madagascar House, Mysterious World of African Night, Rhino House, Tropical Pavilion, Lion House, Pygmy Hippo House, African Animals House, Apes House

Star Attractions

African Savannah Tortoises South America Pampas, Pygmy Hippos, Red Titi, Lion Tailed Macaque, Brown Bears, Dwarf Mongooses, Snow Leopards

Time required

whole zoo: 6 - 7 hours   star attractions: 1 - 2 hours

PRAGUE ZOO

Contact

Name	Zoological Garden of the City of Prague
Address	U Trojskéno Zámku 3/120, Troja 171 00 Prague 7, CZ
Phone	+420(0) 296 112 230
Fax	+420(0) 233 540 287
Email	pr@zoopraha.cz
Website	www.zoopraha.cz

Opening Hours

Open every day of the year

April, May, September, October	09.00 to 18.00
June to August	09.00.to 19.00
March	09.00 to 17.00
November to February	09.00 to 16.00

Entrance Prices 2011

	CZK
Adult	150.00
Child 3-15	100.00
Child under 3	Free
Family Day Ticket 2 Adults and 2 Children	450.00
Dog on Lead	20.00
Annual Card - Family	1,200.00
Annual Card – Adult	500.00
Annual Card – Child 3-15	300.00
Annual Card – Dog on Lead	100.00
Concessions: Over 65s, Special Needs Visitors, Students	
Combi Ticket Available for Zoo/Botanical Gardens/Castle	

Transport Access

Car	Follow signposts to Zoo/Troja
Car Park	Yes, at Zoo CZK 100.00
Bus	112
Tram	14,17 to Trojská and then Bus 112
Metro Station	Nadrazi Holesovice and then Bus 112
Boat	To Troja on Vlatava in Summer

Ownership of Zoo

Municipal
100% Prague City Council

Area of Zoo

60 Ha

Date of Foundation

1931

Visitor Numbers

Circa 1,300,000

Animal Inventory at 31.12.2009

	Number	Species
Mammals	1200	169
Birds	1428	270
Reptiles	851	120
Amphibians	52	10
Fish	1009	52

Facilities

Catering (sub-contract): 2 Restaurants, Café, Kiosks, Picnic Facilities
Retail (sub-contract): Zoo shop, Cable Car CZK 20.00
Children's Zoo: Yes   Children's Playground: Yes, several

Dogs

Allowed on leads: Yes   Kennel Facilities: No

Feeding by Visitors

Strictly prohibited, except in Children's Zoo

Shows, etc

Yes, Exhibitions in the Education Centre

Education

Zoo keeper talks: Yes, in fine weather 16 - 21 opportunities - see daily programme in zoo
Zoo School/Education Centre: Yes
Biodiversity Centre: No
Zoo Guidebook: Yes, CZK 159.00
Signage on Exhibits: Czech with summary English, German and Russian
Star Rating: **

Friends of the Zoo

Yes, Zoo Fan Club - Circa 500 members

Volunteers

No

General Site Description

On an attractive rocky slope, imaginatively used for many exhibits and providing natural habitats for many species and rising high above the Vltava river, the lower half of this fine zoo suffered badly from the flooding in 2002 which

submerged half the zoo. Many animals suffered and some were lost; but the rescue work was amazing and Slávek, the hippo born in the zoo, survived. Major investment followed and Prague Zoo is now a real delight.

The Indonesia Jungle house is a fine development with very good entrance Indonesia information exhibition. Good water availability in the zoo has enabled the development of many moated islands for the monkeys. The Lemur Walk Through is a real delight: several duck species share this beautiful enclosure with the different Lemur species. There is a spacious feel to the zoo which has lovely vegetation, several Walk Through exhibits and good perspectives on enclosures. Prague Zoo has the finest animal collection in former Eastern Europe.

Indoor Exhibits

Indonesia Jungle, Chambal Gharial House, Bird House Sichuan, Giraffe House, Gorilla House, Elephant/Hippopotamus House, Big Cats and Terrarium, Africa House, Penguin House, Giant Tortoise House

Star Attractions

Orang Utans, Pigtail Macaques, Ring Tailed Lemurs Walk Through, Cuban and Blue Iguanas, Lar Gibbons, Barbary Macaques, Water Birds Walk Through, Red Pandas, Gharials, Small Clawed Otters, Binturongs, Birds of Prey Aviary, Fur seals, Canadian Otters, Giraffes, Pelicans, Gorillas

Time required

whole zoo: 8 - 10 hours   star attractions: 3 hours

OUWEHANDS DIERENPARK

Contact

Name	Ouwehands Dierenpark /	
	Ouwehands Zoo Rhenen	
Address	Grebbeweg 111,	
	3911 AV Rhenen, NL	
Phone	+31 (0) 317 650 200	
Fax	+31 (0) 317 613 727	
Email	info@ouwehand.nl	
Website	www.ouwehand.nl	

Opening Hours

Open every day of the year

Summer	09.00 to 18.00
Winter	10.00 to 17.00

Check website for opening hours which can vary from day to day

Entrance Prices 2011

	EUR
Adult	19.00
Child 3-9	16.00
Child Under 3	Free
Annual Card - Adult	48.50
Annual Card - Child	48.50
Annual Card – 2 Adults and Children	194.00
Concessions: over 65s, Disabled Visitors	
Annual card includes magazine and reduced price entry to other Dutch NVD zoos.	

OUWEHANDS DIERENPARK

Transport Access

Car	A12 Exit Veenendaal or A15 Exit Ochten
Car Park	Yes, at Zoo EUR 5.00 per day
Bus	45, 50, 87
Tram	Ligne 1 Stop Gare then Bus 30
Nearest Station	Rhenen Station 800 m to Zoo

Ownership of Zoo Private Company – Non Profit 100% Van Ouwehands Dierenpark B.V.

Area of Zoo 22 Ha

Date of Foundation 1932

Visitor Numbers Circa 910,000

Animal Inventory at 31.12.2009

	Number	Species
Mammals	345	44
Birds	466	77
Reptiles	95	15
Amphibians	16	5
Fish	0	0

Facilities

Catering (zoo owned):
Restaurants, Café, Kiosks - Jungle Restaurant, Ravot Apia Restaurant, Café Passaro
Retail (zoo owned): Zoo shop
Children's Zoo: Yes
Children's Playground: Yes, including Ravot Aapia, Europe's largest indoor jungle playground covering 0.4 Ha.
It includes zoo themed playground equipment and play opportunities as well as some animal exhibits.

Dogs

Allowed on leads: Yes
Kennel Facilities: No

Feeding by Visitors Strictly prohibited

Shows, etc Yes, Sea Lions

Education

Zoo keeper talks: Yes, in Summer
3 opportunities per day – see daily programme
Zoo School/Education Centre: Yes
Biodiversity Centre: No
Zoo Guidebook: Yes, EUR 3.50
Signage on Exhibits: Dutch
Star Rating: **

OUWEHANDS DIERENPARK

Friends of the Zoo   No

Volunteers   Yes, circa 45

General Site Description

This interesting zoo is on a flat but well wooded site with mature deciduous trees. Ouwehands is certainly different with its huge indoor zoo playground and its 2 Ha bear forest supported by Alertis, the foundation for mistreated bears and nature conservation. Visitors have the opportunity to see the bears and wolves at close quarters in natural surrounding from a raised walkway across the enclosure and to get close to many other animals including polar bears, one of the zoos specialities.

Indoor Exhibits

Elephant House, Umkhosi – African Mammals, Giraffe House, Urucu – South American Jungle, Orang Utan House, Aquarium, Passaro – Tropical Birds

Star Attractions

Harbour Seals, Small Clawed Otters, Penguins, Polar Bears, Warthogs, Hornbills White Handed Gibbons, Zebras, Volière – Tropical Birds, The Bear Forest – Alertis Brown Bears and Wolves, Saddleback Storks, African Black Eagles, Peacocks, Pheasants

Time required   whole zoo: 4 - 6 hours   star attractions: 2 - 3 hours

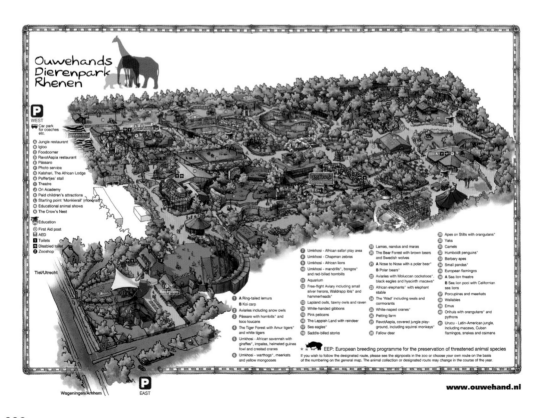

RIGA ZOO

RĪGAS
NACIONĀLAIS ZOOLOĢISKAIS DĀRZS

Contact

Name	Riga National Zoological Garden
Address	Meza Prospekts 1, Riga LV 1014
Phone	+371 (0) 6751 84 09
Fax	+371 (0) 6754 00 11
Email	info@rigazoo.lv
Website	www.rigazoo.lv

Opening Hours

Open every day of the year
Mid April to Mid October   10.00 to 19.00
Mid October to Mid April   10.00 to 17.00

Entrance Prices 2011

	LS
Adult	4.00
Child 4-18	3.00
Child under 4	Free
Family Day Ticket - 2 Adults and Children	12.00
Annual Card - Adult	40.00
Annual Card - Family	60.00
Annual Card - 1 Adult and 1 Child	50.00
Concessions: Students, Over 62s, Disabled Visitors and their Carers	

Transport Access

Car	Zoo is located in Mežaparks
Car Park	Yes, at Zoo 2 Ls per visit
Bus	48 from Plavnieki or Sarkandaugava
Tram	11 from City Centre

Ownership of Zoo	Municipal 100% Riga City Council

Area of Zoo — 22 Ha

Date of Foundation — 1912, originally German Speaking Society

Visitor Numbers — Circa 375,000

Animal Inventory at 31.12.2010

	Number	Species
Mammals	490	88
Birds	377	74
Reptiles	241	61
Amphibians	1265	54
Fish	634	63

Facilities
Catering (sub-contract):
Cafés, Kiosks and Picnic Places
Retail (zoo owned): Zoo shop
Children's Zoo: Yes   Children's Playground: Yes

Dogs
Allowed on leads: No   Kennel Facilities: No

Feeding by Visitors
Strictly prohibited

Shows, etc
Grey Seal Show, Winter Night Visiting – see Calendar

Education
Zoo keeper talks: Yes, 8 opportunities – see daily programme in zoo
Zoo School/Education Centre: Yes
Biodiversity Centre: No
Zoo Guidebook: No
Signage on Exhibits: Latvian and Russian   Star Rating: **

Friends of the Zoo
No

Volunteers
Yes, Circa 10

General Site Description
A varied, fairly flat zoological garden in the large Mežaspark, bordering the attractive Baltic coastal waters in the north east of the city. Nevertheless the site lacks natural water features but has reasonable natural tree cover. Some space and enclosures are available for expansion. Many buildings need modernisation or renovation but in 2008 the zoo invested in an excellent new giraffe house and there is a programme of further improvements.

RIGA ZOO

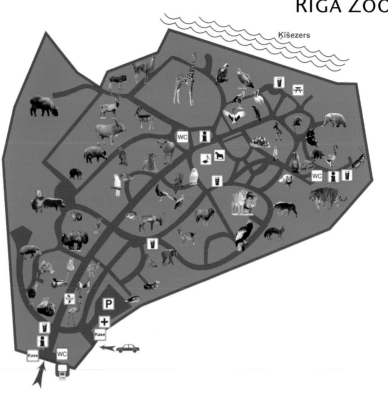

Kīšezers

Indoor Exhibits	Giraffe House, Nocturnal House, Aquarium, Hippo House, Tropical House
Star Attractions	Giraffes, Marmosets, Water Dragons, Coatis, Forest Reindeer, Frogs, Goeldi's Monkeys, Markhors, Toads, African Savannah
Time required	whole zoo: 4 - 6 hours star attractions: 1 - 2 hours

Contact

	Name	Bioparco di Roma
	Address	Viale Giardino Zoologico 20
		00197 Rome, I
	Phone	+39 06 360 82 11
	Fax	+39 06 320 73 89
	Email	info@bioparco.it
	Website	www.bioparco.it

Opening Hours

Open every day of the year except Christmas Day

Summer: April to October	09.30 to 18.00
Summer Weekends and Public Holidays	09.30 to 19.00
Winter: October to March	09.30 to 17.00
December to February	10.00 to 16.00

Summer and Winter follow Change of Clocks

Entrance Prices 2011

	EUR
Adult	12.50
Child Under 1 metre high	Free
Children up to 12 years	10.50
Annual Card – Adult	100.00
Annual Card – 1 Adult and 1 Child	120.00
Annual Card – 2 Adults and 1 Child	150.00
Annual Card – 2 Adults and 2 Children	175.00
Concessions: Students, Seniors 60+, Disabled Visitors and their Carers, Armed Services Personnel	

Transport Access

Car	Exit Salaria Centro – Parioli'del GRA
Car Park	Public Parking near zoo at Villa Borghese EUR 18.00 per day
Bus	3, 52, 53, 217, 360, 910 and 926
Tram	No 19 to Bioparco
Metro Station	Red line to Flaminio and Spagna

Ownership of Zoo

Municipal
100% City of Rome

Area of Zoo

18 Ha

Date of Foundation

1911

Visitor Numbers

Circa 540,000

Animal Inventory at 31.12.2009

	Number	Species
Mammals	319	45
Birds	380	65
Reptiles	316	64
Amphibians	98	12
Fish	0	0

Facilities

Catering (sub-contract):
Restaurant Mascagni, Cafè del Parco and Cafè del Ninfeo
Retail (zoo owned): Zoo shop – Bioparco Shop, Zoo train, EUR 1.00 per person
Children's Zoo: Yes, includes five breeds of Italian donkey, small farm with Italian domestic farm animals
Children's Playground: Yes, several playgrounds and meeting rooms

Dogs

Allowed on leads: No   Kennel Facilities: No

Feeding by Visitors

Strictly prohibited

Shows, etc

No

Education

Zoo keeper talks: Yes, 8 opportunities at weekends and on public holidays – see programme in zoo
Zoo School/Education Centre: No
Biodiversity Centre: No but "BIODIVERSITALIA" for Italian indigenous species
Zoo Guidebook: Yes, EUR 8.00
Signage on Exhibits: Italian and English   Star Rating: **

Friends of the Zoo

No

BIOPARCO DI ROMA

Volunteers

No

General Site Description

Part of the famous Villa Borghese Park area, the zoo has unfortunately been reduced in size in recent years. This is a true city zoo combining zoological and botanical aspects. There are over 1000 trees, some of which are very rare and very old. Semi tropical vegetation including much bamboo gives a lush feel. Peacocks are ubiquitous!

Indoor Exhibits

Reptile House, Biodiversitalia House

Star Attractions

Bird Volière, Wolves, Spoonbills, Brown bears, Bird Lakes, Chimpanzees, Sacred Ibis

Time required

whole zoo: 5 - 6 hours
star attractions: 2 hours

Contact	Name	Zoologischer Garten Rostock GmbH
	Address	Rennbahnalle 21, 18059 Rostock, D
	Phone	+49(0)381 20 820
	Fax	+49(0)381 493 4400
	Email	office@zoo-rostock.de
	Website	www.zoo-rostock.de

Opening Hours

Open every day of the year

April to October	09.00 to 19.00
November to March	09.00 to 17.00
24/12 and 31/12	09.00 to 14.00

Entrance Prices 2011

	EUR
Adult	11.50
Child 3-16	6.00
Child under 3	Free
Dog	6.00
Family Card 1 Adult and up to 3 children	21.00
Family Card 2 Adults and up to 3 children	31.00
Annual Card – Adult	35.00
Annual Card – Child 3-16	16.00
Annual Card – Family 2 Adults, 3+ children	102.00
Annual Card – Dog	16.00
Concessions: students, apprentices and handicapped visitors	

Transport Access

Car	A19 Exit Rostock East then B105
	A20 Exit Rostock West then B103
	B105 from East or West
Car Park	Yes, at Zoo
Bus	28
Tram	3, 6
Nearest Station	Rostock Hbf

Ownership of Zoo

Municipal Company, Zoologischer Garten Rostock gGmbH
99.56% City of Rostock, 0.44% Rostocker Zooförderverein e. V.

Area of Zoo

42 Ha

Date of Foundation

1899

Visitor Numbers

Circa 555,000

ZOO ROSTOCK

Animal Inventory at 31.12.2009

	Number	Species
Mammals	329	64
Birds	455	82
Reptiles	51	15
Amphibians	28	6
Fish	386	51

Facilities

Catering (zoo owned and sub-contract):
Restaurant, Cafeteria, Kiosks, Picnic Place: Restaurant Elefantenlodge,
Café Käfer, Café Toralk
Retail (zoo owned): 2 Zoo shops
Children's Zoo: Yes
Children's Playground: Yes, particularly interesting. Specifically related to
bionics, environment and zoo animals

Dogs

Allowed on leads: Yes   Kennel Facilities: Yes, no charge

Feeding by Visitors

Strictly prohibited

Shows, etc

Edutainment (Darwin Box), The Green Egg

Education

Zoo keeper talks: Yes
Zoo School/Education Centre: Yes
Biodiversity Centre: Yes – Bionics Centre
Zoo Guidebook: Yes
Signage on Exhibits: German   Star Rating: **

Friends of the Zoo

Yes, Rostocker Zooförderverein e. V.
Membership at 31.12.2009 – Circa 150

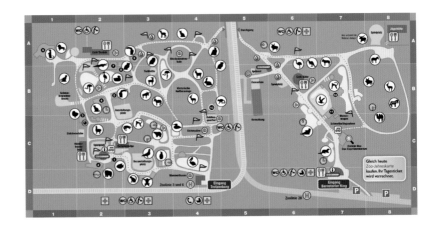

ZOO ROSTOCK

Volunteers

Yes, Circa 10

General Site Description

Rostock Zoo is situated in an extensive zoological park with excellent mature tree cover and varied vegetation. This includes renowned displays of dahlias and rhododendrons.

The site is generally level with imaginatively used, attractive landscape and some fine water features. The zoo is being extended through the construction of the future DARWINEUM project which will transform the Zoo's apes and monkey exhibits as well as enabling the addition of new species.

Indoor Exhibits

Elephant House, Rain Forest Pavilion, Bird and Reptile House, Lion House, South America House, Crocodile Hall, Monkey House, Aquarium
Under construction for 2012 - DARWINEUM

Star Attractions

Jaguar, Otters and Racoons, Patas Monkeys, Meerkats, Arctic Foxes, Bactrian Camels, Capuchin Monkeys, Pelicans, Tamarins,
Walk Through Volière – coastal sea birds, Fur Seals and Sea Lions, Falcons, Antelope Savannah, Muntjac and Cranes

Time required   whole zoo: 8 hours   star attractions: 2 - 3 hours

Diergaarde
BLIJDORP
rotterdam zoo

DIERGAARDE BLIJDORP

Contact

Name	Diergaarde Blijdorp/ Rotterdam Zoo
Address	Blijdorplaan 8, 3041 JG Rotterdam, NL
Phone	+31(0) 10 443 1431
Fax	+31(0) 10 467 7811
Email	info@rotterdamzoo.nl
Website	www.rotterdamzoo.nl

Opening Hours

Open every day of the year
Summer   09.00 to 18.00
Winter   09.00 to 17.00

Entrance Prices 2011

	EUR
Adult	19.50
Child 3-9	16.50
Child under 3	Free
Annual Card - Adult	71.00
Annual Card - Child	50.00
Annual Card 2 Adults and children	179.00
Concessions: 64+ and disabled visitors	

Transport Access

Car	A20 Exit 13 Blijdorp Signposted
Car Park	Yes, at Zoo EUR 7.00 per day
Buses	32, 33 to Main Entrance; 44, 49 to Riviera Hall Entrance
Trams	3 to Riviera Hall Entrance
Nearest Station	Rotterdam Central 12 minute walk

Ownership of Zoo

Private Foundation Non Profit
100% Royal Rotterdam Zoological Society with financial support from
Rotterdam City Council

Area of Zoo   28 Ha

Date of Foundation   1857

Visitor Numbers   Circa 1,600,000

**Animal Inventory
at 31.12.2009**

	Number	Species
Mammals	1235	84
Birds	1287	148
Reptiles	595	88
Amphibians	151	14
Fish	6828	257

Facilities

Catering (zoo owned):
Restaurants, Café, Kiosks, Picnic Place:
Restaurant Terraszaal, Restaurant de Lepelaar, Caribbean Café
Retail (zoo owned): Zoo shop, Zoo train
Children's Zoo: Yes   Children's Playground: Yes

Dogs

Allowed on leads: No   Kennel Facilities: No

Feeding by Visitors

Strictly prohibited

Shows, etc

Yes, Birds Species Show from May to October

Education

Zoo keeper talks: Yes, at least six opportunities daily – see programme in zoo
Zoo School/Education Centre: Yes
Biodiversity Centre: No
Zoo Guidebook: Yes, EUR 3.50
Signage on Exhibits: Dutch and English   Star Rating: **

Friends of the Zoo

Yes, Friends of Rotterdam Zoo - Circa 6,500 members
Zakenkring (Business Circle) 160 members

Volunteers

Yes, circa 400

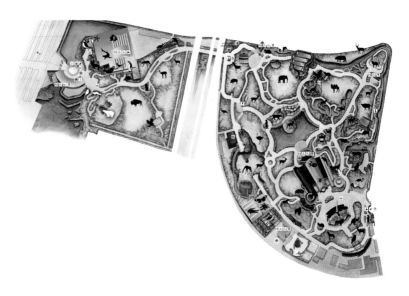

DIERGAARDE BLIJDORP

General Site Description

The Royal Rotterdam Zoological and Botanical Gardens are situated on a flat site with fine vegetation including seven varieties of bamboos and a Chinese garden. This old established city centre zoo is being transformed. Impressive new buildings have been opened in the past ten years and outdoor enclosures have been redeveloped to resemble natural habitats more closely. The zoo is being reorganised as a geo zoo.

The extremely impressive Oceanium "water world" exhibits are situated in the new area, separated from the historic zoo by the railway line which straddles the enlarged zoo: visitors will be surprised to see storks happily nesting on the railway posts.

Indoor Exhibits

Oceanium, Elephant House, Lion House, Crocodile House, Riviera Hall, Giraffe House, Tiger House, Komodo Dragon House, Tropical House, Apes House, Okapi House, Polar Bear Exhibit

Star Attractions

Oceanium, Amur Leopards, Nile Crocodiles, Bird Walk Through (Lake), Elephants, Pallas Cat, Caimans, Bird Walk Through (Ibis), Giraffes, Fishing Cat, Komodo Dragons, Birds of Prey Walk Through, Polar Bears, Colobus, Red River Hogs, Manchurian Cranes, Sea Lions, White Handed Gibbons, Bactrian Camel, Puffins/ Guillemots, King Penguins

Time required

whole zoo: 6 - 8 hours   star attractions: 3 - 4 hours

Contact

Name	Sóstó Zoo
Address	Nyíregyházi Állatpark Nonprofit Kft. 4431 Sóstófürdo, Sóstói út, H
Phone	+36 20 297 68 62
	+36 20 297 89 38
Fax	+36 42 402 031
Email	info@sostozoo.hu
	office@sostozoo.hu
Website	www.sostozoo.hu

Opening Hours

Open every day of the year

Summer: April to October   09.00 to 19.00

Winter: November to March   09.00 to 16.00

Entrance Prices 2011

	HUF
Adult	2,200
Child 3-17	100
Family Ticket - 2 Adults and 1 child	5,800
Family Ticket - 2 Adults and 2 children	7,200
Family Ticket - 2 Adults and 3 children	8,400
Concessions: Students, Pensioners	

Transport Access

Car	M3 Exit Nyiregyhaza Centrum then signposted
Car Park	Yes, at Zoo no charge
Bus	No 8 from Nyiregyhaza Station to Zoo
Nearest Station	Nyiregyhaza

Ownership of Zoo   Municipal
100% Nyiregyhaza
City Council

Area of Zoo   40 Ha

Date of Foundation   1996

Visitor Numbers   Circa 500,000

Animal Inventory at 31.12.2009

	Number	Species
Mammals	531	98
Birds	524	96
Reptiles and Amphibians	275	33
Fish and Molluscs	1361	112

Facilities

Catering (zoo owned hotel and sub-contract catering):
Hotel, Restaurant, Café, Kiosks, Picnic Place: The Jungle Hotel,
Bamboo Restaurant in the Green Pyramid
Retail (sub-contract): Zoo shop
Children´s Zoo: Yes   Children´s Playground: Yes

Dogs

Allowed on leads: No   Kennel Facilities: Yes

Feeding by Visitors

Strictly prohibited

Shows, etc

Yes, Sea Lions, Birds of Prey, Macaws

Education

Zoo keeper talks: Yes
Zoo School/Education Centre: Yes
Biodiversity Centre: No
Zoo Guidebook: Yes, HUF 200
Signage on Exhibits: Hungarian   Star Rating: *
Summary Information Boards and new signage also in English ,German,
Slovakian and Ukranian

Friends of the Zoo

Yes,
Membership at 31.12.2009 – Circa 60

Volunteers

Yes, Circa 20

SóStó Zoo

General Site Description

Situated within the 700 Ha Sóstó oak forest in the east of Hungary, the zoo occupies a relatively flat site with both large open and wooded areas. Botanical gardens were commenced in 2004 and are being systematically extended. This is a relatively new zoo with an impressive animal collection. Sóstó zoo opened milestone developments, the impressive Green Pyramid with viewing of the Indonesian rainforest from four levels and the Tarzan Trail and African Savannah in 2010. Visitors are able to get close to large animals in natural surroundings.

Indoor Exhibits

The Green Pyramid - Indonesia House and Oceanarium, South America House, Elephant House, Tropical House

Star Attractions

The Green Pyramid – Orang Utans, Komodo Dragons, Gibbons, Sharks and Sting Rays, African Savannah – Giraffes, Zebras, Antelopes and Pelicans, Elephants, Sea Lions, Parrots, Gorillas, Loris, Oceanarium

Time required

whole zoo: 6 - 8 hours
star attractions: 2 - 3 hours

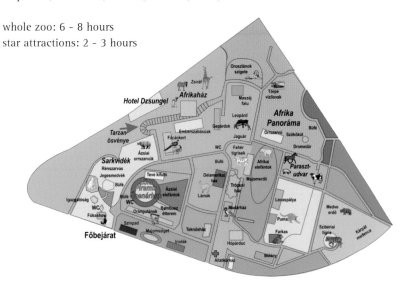

Contact

Name	Wilhelma - Zoologisch-Botanischer Garten Stuttgart
Address	Wilhelma 13, 70376 Stuttgart, D
Phone	+49(0) 711 540 20
Fax	+49(0) 711 540 2222
Email	info@wilhelma.de
Website	www.wilhelma.de

Opening Hours

Open every day of the year

May to August	08.15 to 18.00
April and September	08.15 to 17.30
March and October	08.15 to 17.00
November to February	08.15 to 16.00

These times are for ticket purchase: the zoo stays open until dusk or 20.00

Entrance Prices 2011

	Summer Mar to Oct	Winter Nov to Feb
	EUR	EUR
Adult	12.00	8.00
Child 6-17	6.00	4.00
Child Under 6	Free	Free
Family Ticket - 1 Parent and children	18.00	12.00
Family Ticket - 2 Parents and their children	30.00	20.00
Annual Card - Adult	52.00	
Annual Card – Child 6 -17	36.00	
Annual Card - Family 1 Parent and children	67.00	
Annual Card – Family 2 Parents and their children	99.00	
Concessions: Students, Disabled Visitors and their Carers, Armed Services Personnel. In Summer visitors entering the zoo after 16.00 pay Winter price.		

Transport Access

Car	A81 or A8 Exit Centrum and then signposted Wilhelma
Car Park	Yes, Parkhaus at Zoo Charge EUR 1.00 per hour/ EUR 5.00 per day
Bus	52, 55, 56 to Rosensteinbrücke
S Bahn	1, 2, 3 to Bahnhof Bad Canstatt and 4, 5, 6 to Nordbahnhof
Stadt Bahn	U14 Stop Wilhelma
Nearest station	Stuttgart Hbf then Stadt Bahn U14

Ownership of Zoo

Regional   100% Land Baden-Württemberg

Area of Zoo   30 Ha

Date of Foundation   1837 Gardens   1949 Zoo

Visitor Numbers   Circa 2,400,000

Animal Inventory at 31.12.2009

	Number	Species
Mammals	655	114
Birds	1023	199
Reptiles	370	87
Amphibians	318	32
Fish	4923	503

Facilities

Catering (sub-contract):
Restaurant, Cafeteria, Kiosks, Picnic Place: Wilhelma Restaurant,
Restaurant am Schaubauernhof, Bistro Belvedere
Retail (sub-contract): Zoo shop - new in 2010
Children's Zoo: Yes, pony rides in Summer
Children's Playground: Yes, new adventure playgrounds 2011

Dogs

Allowed on leads: No
Kennel Facilities: Yes

Feeding by Visitors   Strictly prohibited

Shows, etc   Yes, Damaszenerhalle Exhibition Hall

Education

Zoo keeper talks: Yes, opportunities daily – see daily programme
Zoo School/Education Centre: Yes, New Centre opens 2011
Biodiversity Centre: No
Zoo Guidebook: Yes, EUR 3.50
Signage on Exhibits: German
Star Rating: *

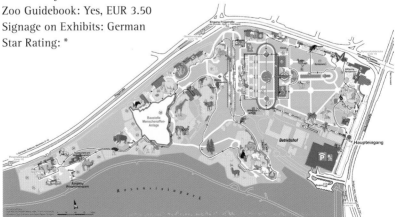

Friends of the Zoo Yes, Verein der Freunde und Förderer der Wilhelma e. V.
Membership at 31.12.2009 – Circa 24,000

Volunteers Yes, circa 50

General Site Description

These famous zoological and botanical gardens are on the site of the Moorish style Palace of the Swabian King Wilhelm 1 of Württemberg and benefit from the wonderful, well maintained 19th Century Palm Houses of the former royal park and gardens. The formal gardens include a Belvedere and Terracotta Terraces: these are immaculately maintained and make this zoo a botanical and a photographer's delight.

A rather less fortunate inheritance has been some 1960s concrete structures which are now systematically being replaced with state-of-the-art animal enclosures. The sloping and wooded areas provide fine outdoor enclosures for many species as do many beautiful water features on the lower area. Wilhelma combines a renowned botanical centre of excellence with an extremely comprehensive animal collection. Many other zoos in this survey benefit from Wilhelma's expertise obtaining tropical vegetation from them. Wilhelma is, understandably, Baden-Württemberg's most visited paid attraction.

Indoor Exhibits

Amazonia House, Hippo and Tapir House, Aquarium, Carnivores House, Giraffe and Okapi House, Terrarium and Crocodile Hall, Apes House, Monkey House, Butterfly House and Insektarium, Elephant and Rhino House, Palm House with Tropical Birds, Tropical House

Star Attractions

Amazonia Haus, Okapis, Bush Dogs, Curassows, Crocodile Hall, Spectacled Bears, Fennec Foxes, Congo Peafowl, Bird Volière Walk Through, Tamarins and Marmosets, Goeldi's Monkeys, Storks, Palm House, White Faced Sakis, Caimans, Water Dragons

Time required whole zoo: 6 - 8 hours star attractions: 2 - 3 hours

TALLINN ZOO

Contact
Name	Tallinn Zoo
Address	North Gate is on Paldiski Mnt 145, West Gate is on Ehitajate tee 150, 13522 Tallinn, EST
Phone	+372 (0) 694 33 00
Fax	+373 (0) 657 89 90
Email	zoo@tallinnzoo.ee
Website	www.tallinnzoo.ee

Opening Hours

Open every day of the year
May to August	09.00 to 19.00
September, October, March, April	09.30 to 17.00
November to February	09.30 to 15.00

Visitors can remain another 2 hours after stated times

Entrance Prices 2011

	Summer 01/05 to 30/09	Winter 01/10 to 30/04
	EUR	EUR
Adult	5.80	3.20
Child 3-17	2.90	2.00
Child under 3	Free	Free
Family Day Ticket 2 Adults and Children	11.20	6.00
Annual Card – Adult	35.00	
Annual Card – Family	63.60	
Concessions: Over 70s, Special Needs Visitors, Students		

Transport Access
Car	Paldiski Mnt Road on West side of Tallin signposted to zoo
Car Park	Yes, 2 Car Parks at Zoo Free of Charge at North Gate and Charged at West Gate
Bus	22 and Trolleybus 6 from City Centre to Zoo
Nearest Station	Baltic Railway Station Bus 21 and Trolleybus 7 to Zoo

Ownership of Zoo

Municipal
100% Tallinn City Council

Area of Zoo

89 Ha

Date of Foundation

1939 but on present site since 1983

Visitor Numbers

circa 330,000

Animal Inventory at 31.12.2009

	Number	Species
Mammals	984	95
Birds	601	120
Reptiles	145	47
Amphibians	148	17
Fish	2575	133

Facilities

Catering (zoo owned):
Cafés, Kiosks, Picnic Place
Retail: No
Children's Zoo: Yes   Children's Playground: Yes

Dogs

Allowed on leads: No   Kennel Facilities: No

Feeding by Visitors

In general, Strictly prohibited but visitors are permitted to feed fish, waterfowl and domestic goats with food bought from zoo dispensers.

Shows, etc

No

Education

Zoo keeper talks: No
Zoo School/Education Centre: Yes
Biodiversity Centre: No
Zoo Guidebook: No
Signage on Exhibits:
Estonian and Russian
Star Rating: **

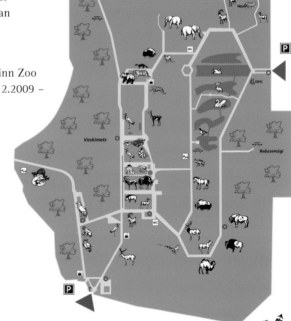

Friends of the Zoo

Yes, Friends of Tallinn Zoo
Membership at 31.12.2009 –
Circa 360

Volunteers

No

General Site Description

The zoo is situated on the outskirts of the city on a large flat partly wooded site. There is a good lakeland area which is home to many bird species.

Outdoor enclosures are generally large but most indoor facilities are in need of enlargement, renovation and improvement.

This is an unusually large and interesting collection with a special emphasis on mountain goats and sheep, eagles and cranes from temperate and northern areas. It is planned that Tallinn will in the future be organised as a GEO-Zoo.

Indoor Exhibits   Elephant House, Tropical House

Star Attractions   Elephants, Lions, Mountain Sheep, Snow Leopards, Tortoises, Cranes, Amur Leopards, Mountain Goats, Striped Hyena, Waterfowl ponds and lakes

Time required   whole zoo: 6 - 8 hours   star attractions: 1 - 2 hours

Contact

Name	Twycross Zoo
Address	Burton Road, Atherstone, Warwickshire CV9 3PX, UK
Phone	+44 0844 474 1777
Fax	+44 0844 474 1888
Email	info@twycrosszoo.org
Website	www.twycrosszoo.org

Opening Hours

Open every day except Christmas Day
Summer: Late March to Late October   10.00 to 17.30
Winter: Late October to Late March   10.00 to 16.00
Summer BST and Winter GMT - follow dates for clock change

Entrance Prices 2011

	GBP
Adult	13.00
Child 3-16	9.00
Child under 3 and Carers of Disabled Visitors	Free
Family Day Ticket 2 Adults and 2 Children	40.00
Family Day ticket 1 Adult and 2 Children	28.00
Annual Silver Card – Adult	46.80
Annual Silver Card – Child	32.40
Annual Silver Card – Family 2 Adults and 2 Children	140.00
Annual Gold Cards add circa 10%	
Concessions: Students, 60+ and Disabled/ Special Needs Visitors Annual Gold Card Holders are entitled to free entry at reciprocal zoos	
Daily Ticket Prices Include a 10% Voluntary Conservation Donation	

Transport Access

Car	A5 or M42 onto A444 and follow brown tourist attraction signs
Car Park	Yes, at zoo and free of charge
Bus	Buses from Nuneaton and Ashby de la Zouch
Nearest Station	Nuneaton
Bicycle	Bicycle Racks at Zoo

Ownership of Zoo   Registered Charity   100% East Midlands Zoological Society

Area of Zoo   18 Ha/ 43 acres

Date of Foundation   1963

Visitor Numbers   Circa 550,000

**Animal Inventory
at 31.12.2009**

	Number	Species
Mammals	536	78
Birds	371	86
Reptiles	63	19
Amphibians	8	3
Fish	73	5

Facilities

Catering (zoo owned):
Restaurant, Café, Kiosks, Picnic Place: Himalaya Restaurant, Café Tibet,
Gorilla Outpost, Anty's Kitchen, The Dome Café
Retail (zoo owned): 2 Zoo shops Bazaar and Gallery
Children's Zoo: Yes   Children's Playground: Yes

Dogs

Allowed on leads: No. Dogs must not be left in cars in the car park.
Kennel Facilities: No

Feeding by Visitors

Strictly prohibited

Shows, etc

Yes

Education

Zoo keeper talks: Yes
Zoo School/Education Centre: Yes
Biodiversity Centre: No
Zoo Guidebook: Yes, GBP 2.99
Signage on Exhibits: English   Star Rating: *

Friends of the Zoo

No, but 1,000 annual card holders / members of Twycross Zoo Association

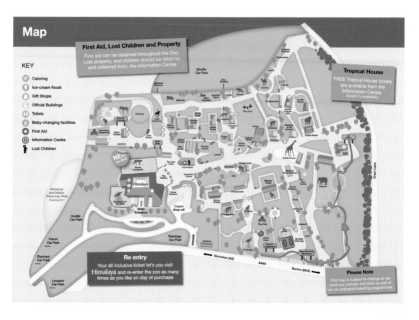

Volunteers	Yes, circa 10

General Site Description

Twycross Zoo is on a relatively flat open site. However, recent spectacular innovations have done much to make the site more interesting. These include a recent natural garden and spectacular wild flower bank behind Himalaya, excellent use of the reed beds in the vicinity of the Bornean Longhouse and enlarged elephant paddocks where the viewing area has been naturally landscaped in a most imaginative and appropriate way providing interesting perspectives on the enclosure.

Twycross was historically developed by Molly Banham and Nathalie Evans who focused on collecting all species of primates. The story of the zoo's origin is in their book Molly's Zoo. Twycross Zoo has a unique and comprehensive collection of Apes and Monkeys and is appropriately marketed as The World Primate Centre.

Indoor Exhibits

Himalaya, Tropical House, 2 Chimps' Houses, Elephant House, Borneo Long-house, Orang Utan House, Giraffe House, 2 Gorilla Houses, Bonobo House. Various small monkey houses have a walk through corridor.

Star Attractions

Elephants / Ude Walwe, 2 Bird Volières, Pelicans, Borneo Longhouse, Marmosets, Meerkats, Snow Leopards, Bat eared fox, Extent of Primate Collection

Time required   whole zoo: 6 hours   star attractions: 2 hours

Bioparc
VALENCIA

BIOPARC VALENCIA

Contact

	Name	Bioparc Valencia
	Address	Avenida Pio Baroja 3
		46015 Valencia, E
	Phone	+34(0) 902 250 340
	Fax	+34(0) 902 875 350
	Email	info@bioparcvalencia.es
	Website	www.bioparcvalencia.es

Opening Hours

Open every day of the year

April to June	10.00 to 20.00
July and August	10.00 to 21.00
September to Mid October	10.00 to 19.00
Mid October to March	10.00 to 18.00

Entrance Prices 2011

	EUR
Adult	21.50
Child 4-12	16.00
Child under 4	Free
Annual Card - Adult	51.00
Annual Card - Child	39.00
Concessions: Students, Large Families, 64+ and Disabled Visitors	

Transport Access

Car	A7/N340 or A3 (from Madrid) or N234
Car Park	Yes, at Zoo EUR 5.00 per day
Buses	95 from Valencia North or Bus Station
Metro	Lines 3 and 5 to stop Nou d'Octubre
Nearest Station	Valencia North

Ownership of Zoo

Private Company   100% Rain Forest S.L.

Area of Zoo

16 Ha

Date of Foundation

2008

Visitor Numbers

Circa 575,000

Animal Inventory at 31.12.2009

	Number	Species
Mammals	326	55
Birds	263	48
Reptiles	28	12
Amphibians	0	0
Fish	2626	36

Facilities

Catering (zoo owned):
Restaurants, Café, Kiosks, Picnic Place - Restaurante Samburu, Parrilla Ndoki
Retail (zoo owned): 2 Zoo shops
Children's Zoo: No   Children's Playground: Yes

Dogs

Allowed on leads: No   Kennel Facilities: No

Feeding by Visitors

Strictly prohibited

Shows, etc

Yes, educational presentations on Predators and Prey of African Savannah – Birds of Prey and Jackals

Education

Zoo keeper talks: Yes, Various opportunities –see programme in zoo
Zoo School/Education Centre: Yes
Biodiversity Centre: Yes, Biodiversity Hall
Zoo Guidebook: No
Signage on Exhibits: Spanish, Valencian and English   Star Rating: **

Friends of the Zoo

No

Volunteers

Yes

General Site Description

Bioparc Valencia is the newest zoo in the survey and is still being developed. The Zoo has been designed as an "immersion experience" for visitors. The philosophy is to display animals in natural surroundings appropriate to their wild habitats. Social animals that live together in groups are exhibited as well as groups of different species that coexist in the same habitat. Hidden barriers give a sense of continuity between the space occupied by the animals and that occupied by the visitors.
At present, only African species are exhibited in four separate zones – Savannah, Equatorial Africa, Madagascar and Kitum Cave. The site has been transformed from a flat unattractive area into a splendid and spectacular one: it incorporates excellent vegetation, attractive landscaping, huge rock and hill features, several waterfalls and lakes. It is very clean throughout and environmentally conscious.

BIOPARC VALENCIA

Indoor Exhibits
Gorillas, Chimpanzees, Reptiles, Termite Hill, Kitum Cave - Hippos, Crocodiles and Turtles

Star Attractions
African Elephants, Zebras, Dromedaries, Giraffes, Hippos, Red Buffaloes, White Rhinos, Pygmy Hippos, Banded Mongooses, Angolan Lions, Lemurs Walk Through, Rock Hyrax/Klipspringer, Gorillas/Mangabeys/Guenons, Red River Hogs, Walk Through Volière, Nile Crocodiles, Aardvarks, Thomson's Gazelles, Drills/Talapoins, Red-Flanker Duiker

Time required
whole zoo: 4 - 6 hours   star attractions: 2 - 3 hours

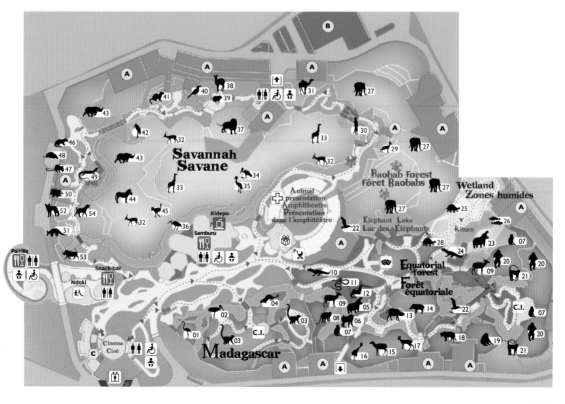

TIERGARTEN
SCHÖNBRUNN
Arten schützen & erhalten
www.zoovienna.at

Contact

Name	Tiergarten Schönbrunn / Vienna Zoo
Address	Maxingstr. 13b 1130 Vienna, A
Phone	+43(0) 1 877 9294-0
Fax	+43(0) 1 877 9641
Email	info@zoovienna.at
Website	www.zoovienna.at

Opening Hours

Open every day of the year	
April to September	09.00 to 18.30
October and March	09.00 to 17.30
November, December, January	09.00 to 16.30
February	09.00 to 17.00

Entrance Prices 2011

	EUR
Adult	14.00
Child / Young Person 6-19	6.00
Children under 6	Free
Annual Card – Adult	35.00
Annual Card – Child / Young person 6-19	18.00
Family Ticket book 4x Adult and 6x Child Young Persons	60.00
Concessions: Disabled Visitors and their Carers	
Various Combination Passes Available with Palm House, Wüstenhaus and Schönbrunn Palace	

Transport Access

Car	Park and Ride U6 Hütteldorf and U6 Siebenhirten
Car Park	In Elisabeth Allee
Bus	15A, 51A, 56B and 156B
Tram	10, 58, 60
Nearest Station	U4 Hietzing

Ownership of Zoo

National Government Company
100% Schönbrunner - Tiergarten Gesellschaft mbH

Area of Zoo   17 Ha

Date of Foundation   1752

Visitor Numbers   Circa 2,500,000

Animal Inventory at 31.12.2009

	Number	Species
Mammals	651	94
Birds	1186	116
Reptiles	326	59
Amphibians	453	34
Fish	2412	186

Facilities

Catering (Zoo owned):
Restaurant, Cafeteria, Kiosks, Picnic Place - Gasthaus Tirolergarten, Kaiser
Pavilion, Café Atelier Nonja in ORANG.erie, Café Hietzing, Jumbo Buffet
Retail (sub-contract): Zoo shop, Panorama Diesel Train Adult EUR 2.00 Child
EUR 1.00
Children's Zoo: Yes, plus Tyroler Farm   Children's Playground: Yes, several

Dogs

Allowed on leads: No   Kennel Facilities: No

Feeding by Visitors

Strictly prohibited

Shows, etc

Yes

Education

Zoo keeper talks: 18 different opportunities – see programme in zoo
Zoo School/Education Centre: Yes, major new facility in ORANG.erie
Biodiversity Centre: No
Zoo Guidebook: Yes, EUR 3.00
Signage on Exhibits: German, English   Star Rating: ***

VIENNA ZOO

Friends of the Zoo	Yes, Verein der Freunde des Tiergarten Schönbrunn Membership at 31.12.2009 – Circa 10,000
Volunteers	Yes - circa 50
General Site Description	Situated in the south eastern of the former Habsburg Summer Residence, Tiergarten Schönbrunn has the magnificent combination of high quality animal houses and exhibits combined with a wonderful setting of gardens, woods and parkland on a partially hilly site. Houses restored from the eighteenth century Habsburg period, on part of the UNESCO protected Schönbrunn palace site, give a unique feel to this world class zoological garden. Closing time in the zoo is announced, just as it has been for the last 240 years, by the Kaiserglöckerl bell; it is still rung by hand and was formerly used to announce the arrival of the Emperor and the Archdukes. Centuries of history blend with a thoroughly up to date zoo to make a visit here an unforgettable experience. There are so many superb exhibits that it is difficult to select spectacular highlights: however, possibly the Giant Panda Exhibit and the Rainforest House are exemplary. It is not surprising that Vienna Zoo is number 1 on my ranking list. Vienna Zoo has a continuous improvement programme: the renovated Monkey House is expected to be ready in 2011.
Indoor Exhibits	Regenwald Haus, Rhino House, Vivarium, Monkey House, ORANG.erie, Hippo House, Terrarium, Australia House, Elephant House, Giant Panda House, Crocodile House, Insect House, South America House, Koala House, Bird House, Tyrolean House, Giraffe House, Lion House, Wuestenhaus – additional entrance fee
Star Attractions	Giant Pandas, Penguins, Regenwald House, Bee Eaters, Avocets, Orang Utans, Ring Tailed Lemurs, Red Pandas, Rhinoceros Iguanas, Koalas, White Handed Gibbons, Parma Wallabies, Anacondas, African Elephants, Spectacled Bears, Giant Tortoises, Manchurian Crane and Serow, Rhinos, Coatis, Nile Crocodiles, Collared Peccary, South America Park – Giant Anteaters, Tapirs, Vicunas, Capybaras, Rheas and Seriemas
Time required	whole zoo: 6 - 8 hours star attractions: 4 - 5 hours

ZOO WARSAW

Contact

Name	Warsaw Zoological Gardens
Address	Ul. Ratuszowa 1/3
	03-461 Warsaw, PL
Phone	+48(0) 22 619 4041
Fax	+48(0) 22 619 5898
Email	zoo@zoo.waw.pl
Website	www.zoo.waw.pl

Opening Hours

Summer	09.00 until 19.00
Winter	09.00 until dusk

Entrance Prices 2011

	PLN
Adult	16.00
Child 3-12	11.00
Child under 3	Free
Family Day Ticket 2 Adults and 3 Children	55.00
Annual Card - 2 Persons	100.00
Concessions: 60+, disabled visitors and their carers	

Transport Access

Car Park	Yes, at Zoo
Bus	101, 127, 135, 160, 162, 170, 174, 190, 509, 527
Tram	4, 13, 23, 26, 46
Nearest Station	Warsaw Central Bus 444 to Zoo May to September

Ownership of Zoo   Municipal   100% City of Warsaw

Area of Zoo   40 Ha

Date of Foundation   1928

Visitor Numbers   Circa 720,000

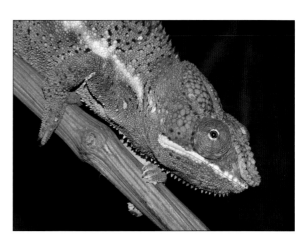

**Animal Inventory
at 31.12.2010**

	Number	Species
Mammals	434	67
Birds	1016	194
Reptiles	239	72
Amphibians	385	24
Fish	715	71

Facilities

Catering (sub-contract):
Restaurant, Café, Kiosks and Picnic Place - Belwederek Restaurant,
Zeppelin Café, Gibon
Retail (sub-contract): Zoo shop
Children's Zoo: Yes, the Fantasy Zoo is an imaginative story based concept
allowing children to feed and have contact with the animals.
Children's Playground: Yes

Dogs

Allowed on leads: No   Kennel Facilities: No

Feeding by Visitors

Strictly prohibited

Shows, etc

Yes, Feathers and Eggs in Birdhouse, Elephant's Sculptures

Education

Zoo keeper talks: Yes, 4 opportunities in Summer only
Zoo School/Education Centre: Yes
Biodiversity Centre: No
Zoo Guidebook: Yes, PLN 10.00 A particularly good English version
Signage on Exhibits: Polish   Star Rating: **

Friends of the Zoo	Yes, Friends of Warsaw Zoo Circa 150 members Panda Foundation – fundraising organisation
Volunteers	Yes, Circa 50
General Site Description	A splendid zoological garden which has been much improved since 1995 with many valuable mature trees and fine outdoor enclosures. This is a real oasis within the city with well-tended lawns and varied colourful flowerbeds. The newly opened Apes' House (2008) and Hippo House (2009) do credit to the zoo following on from the Elephant House (2003) with its splendid tropical vegetation and two level viewing which includes a forest view of the elephants from the upper level.
Indoor Exhibits	Apes House, Giraffe House, Bird House, Invertebrate House, Hippo House, Rhino House, Reptile House, Elephant House, Monkey House, Aquarium
Star Attractions	Chimpanzees, Hippos, Mountain Goats, Gorillas, Przewalski's Horses, Marabou Storks, Red Pandas, Llamas, White Storks, Squirrel Monkeys, Rock Hyrax, Elephants
Time required	whole zoo: 6 - 8 hours star attractions: 3 - 4 hours

ZSL WHIPSNADE

Contact

Name	ZSL Whipsnade Zoo
Address	Dunstable, Bedfordshire
	LU6 2LF, UK
Phone	+44(0) 1582 872 171
Fax	+44(0) 1582 872 649
Website	www.zsl.org

Opening Hours

Open every day except Christmas Day

April to October	10.00 to 17.00
November to March	10.00 to 16.00

Entrance Prices 2011

Daily Ticket Prices Include a 10% Voluntary Conservation Donation	
Prices vary according to the time of year: the price range is given here	
	GBP
Adult	17.00 to 19.50
Child 3-15	14.00 to 15.00
Child under 3	Free
Annual Card ZSL Member - Adult	69.00
Annual Card ZSL Member - Child	45.00
Concessions: Students, 60+, Disabled Visitors and advance online ticket purchase	

Transport Access

Car	M1 Junction 9 from South Junction 12 from North and follow elephant signpost
Car Park	Yes GBP 4.00, Car Entry to Zoo GPB 16.00
Bus	X31 from Luton Station
Nearest Station	Luton Station

Ownership of Zoo

Charitable Society   100% Zoological Society of London (ZSL)

Area of Zoo

260 Ha / 600 Acres

Date of Foundation

1931

Visitor Numbers

Circa 475,000

Animal Inventory at 31.12.2009

	Number	Species
Mammals	1847	79
Birds	339	66
Reptiles	108	30
Amphibians	25	3
Fish	721	19

ZSL WHIPSNADE

Facilities
Catering (zoo owned):
Restaurant, Cafeteria, Kiosks, Picnic Areas - Wild Bite Café/Restaurant
Retail (zoo owned): Zoo shop, Jumbo Express (train ride)
Children's Zoo: Yes   Children's Playground: Yes

Dogs
Allowed on leads: No   Kennel Facilities: No

Feeding by Visitors
Strictly prohibited

Shows, etc
Yes, Bird Arena with Birds of the World, Sea Lion Splash, Discovery Centre, Elephant Walk and Display

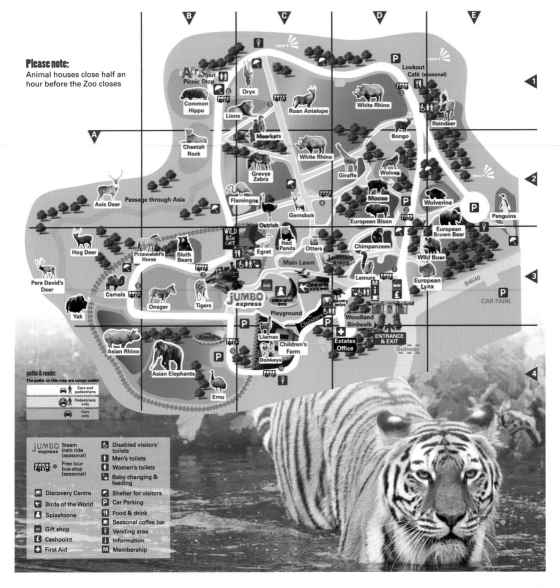

Please note:
Animal houses close half an hour before the Zoo closes

paths & roads:
The paths on this map are colour coded:
- Cars and pedestrians
- Pedestrians only
- Cars only

jUMBO express — Steam train ride (seasonal)
— Free tour bus-stop (seasonal)
- Discovery Centre
- Birds of the World
- Splashzone
- Gift shop
- Cashpoint
- First Aid

- Disabled visitors' toilets
- Men's toilets
- Women's toilets
- Baby changing & feeding
- Shelter for visitors
- Car Parking
- Food & drink
- Seasonal coffee bar
- Vending area
- Information
- Membership

ZSL WHIPSNADE

Education

Zoo keeper talks: Yes
Zoo School/Education Centre: Yes
Biodiversity Centre: No
Zoo Guidebook: Yes, GBP 4.00
Signage on Exhibits: English   Star Rating: **

Friends of the Zoo

No, but members of ZSL   Membership at 31.12.2009 - Circa 45,000

Volunteers

Yes

General Site Description

The largest zoo in the survey, this extensive open site on the edge of the Chiltern Hills with spectacular views over Dunstable Downs has large outdoor enclosures well suited to herds of hoofstock. The zoo has many imaginative outdoor exhibits; most recently the fine addition of formerly indigenous British large mammal species now extinct in the wild. The area has relatively little tree cover and there is a scarcity of water. It provides an excellent area for children to be energetic: there is the opportunity to travel around the site on the miniature Steam Railway and for an additional charge cars can be taken into the zoo and the circular route with frequent parking bays followed.

Indoor Exhibits

Elephant House, Discovery Centre, Chimpanzees House, Rhino House, Giraffe House, Hippo House

Star Attractions

Cheetah Rock, Lions, Brown Bears, Elephants, Tigers, Indian Rhinos, Chimpanzees, Lynx, Ring Tailed Lemur Walk Through

Time required

whole zoo: 8 hours
star attractions: 2 - 3 hours

Contact

Name	Zoo Wroclaw sp.z o.o.
Address	Ul. Wróblewskiego 1 – 5
	51-618 Wroclaw, PL
Phone	+48 71 348 30-24, -25, or -26
Fax	+48 71 348 37 68
Email	lutra@zoo.wroc.pl
Website	www.zoo.wroclaw.pl

Opening Hours

Open every day of the year

April to September	09.00 to 18.00
November to February	09.00 to 16.00
March and October	09.00 to 17.00

Entrance Prices 2011

	PLN
Adult	25.00
School Aged Child 7-18	20.00
Child 3-7	15.00
Child under 3 and Adults over 75	Free
Family Ticket	70.00
Annual Card - Adult	120.00
Annual Card - Child and All Concessions	70.00
Concessions: 75+, Disabled Visitors and All Visitors on Thursdays.	

Transport Access

Car	A4/E40 then Road No 455 and signposted to Zoo
Car Park	Vis a vis by Centennial Hall (Hala Stulecia)
Bus	Line E 145, 146 to Stop Hala Stulecia
Tram	1, 2, 4, 10 and 19
Nearest Station	Wroclaw Glowny

Ownership of Zoo

Limited Liability Company
Zoo Wroclaw LLC
100% City of Wroclaw

Area of Zoo

33 Ha

Date of Foundation

1865 (Breslau)

Visitor Numbers

Circa 650,000

Animal Inventory at 31.12.2009

	Number	Species
Mammals	551	105
Birds	624	149
Reptiles	806	161
Amphibians	652	47
Fish	2069	168

Facilities

Catering (sub-contract):
Restaurant, Cafeteria, Kiosks, Picnic Place - Zoo Restaurant Przystanek,
Restaurant Letney, Koala Grill
Retail (sub-contract): Zoo shop
Children´s Zoo: Yes   Children´s Playground: Yes

Dogs

Allowed on leads: No   Kennel Facilities: No

Feeding by Visitors

Strictly prohibited, except in Children's Zoo and at Baboon Exhibit using food only from Zoo dispensers

Shows, etc

Yes, Fur Seals, Elephant Training

Education

Zoo keeper talks: Yes, various opportunities in Summer - see programme in zoo
Zoo School/Education Centre: Yes
Biodiversity Centre: No
Zoo Guidebook: Yes, PLN 10.00
Signage on Exhibits: Polish   Star Rating: *

Zoo Wroclaw

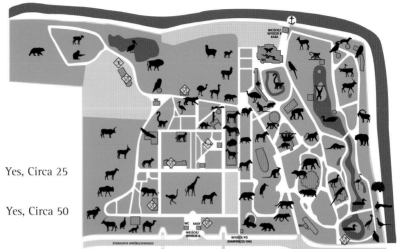

Friends of the Zoo   Yes, Circa 25

Volunteers   Yes, Circa 50

General Site Description

This zoo, the oldest in Poland, occupies a flat site on the eastern edge of the city of Wroclaw. There is a programme of improvement for some relatively poor old buildings and many of the improved exhibits are very good. An excellent extensive wooded area has been allocated to an interesting brown bear exhibit. Wroclaw Zoo, the first in Poland to have its own company, is embarking on the ambitious, major project Africarum, a tropical hall, which will be the first purpose-built ,large-scale, multi-species exhibit indoor facility in Poland. Africarum, life giving waters of Africa, will have a complex of enclosures representative of various ecosystems from the Red Sea to Namibia and the Congo Basin.

Indoor Exhibits

Pachyderm House, Madagascar House, Terrarium and Butterfly House, Apes House, Monkey House, Bird House, Sahara Animals House, Primates House

Star Attractions

Gibbons, Brown Bears, Fur Seals, Ring tailed Lemurs, Black and White Ruffed Lemurs, Sea Eagles, Madagascar House, Terrarium

Time required   whole zoo: 6 - 8 hours   star attractions: 2 hours

ZOO WUPPERTAL

Contact

	Name	Zoo Wuppertal
	Address	Hubertusallee 30
		42117 Wuppertal, D
	Phone	+49(0) 202 563 3600
	Fax	+49(0) 202 741 888
	Email	kontakt@zoo-wuppertal.de
	Website	www.zoo-wuppertal.de

Opening Hours

Open every day of the year except 25/12
Summer: April to October   08.30 to 18.00
Winter: November to March   08.30 to 17.00
Summertime CEST/ MESZ and Wintertime CET/MEZ as per change of clocks

Entrance Prices 2011

	EUR
Adult	10.00
Child 4-16	5.00
Child Under 4	Free
Family – 1 Adult and up to 3 children	18.00
Family – 2 Adults and up to 3 children	27.00
Annual Card - Adult	40.00
Annual Card - Child	20.00
Annual Card – Family 2 Adults and 2 Children	105.00
Concessions: students, Combi Ticket VRR	
Annual Card holders qualify for NRW discount	

Transport Access

Car	A46 or L74 or B224 Exit Kreuz Sonnborn and signposted to zoo/stadion
Car Park	Car Park Zoo/Stadion Free of Charge
Schwebebahn	Stop Zoo/ Stadion
S Bahn	8 or 9 to Wuppertal Zoologischer Garten
Nearest Station	Wuppertal Zoologischer Garten

Ownership of Zoo

Municipal
100% City of Wuppertal

Area of Zoo

24 Ha

Date of Foundation

1881

Visitor Numbers

Circa 630,000

Animal Inventory at 31.12.2009

	Number	Species
Mammals	410	67
Birds	1050	166
Reptiles	133	33
Amphibians	18	4
Fish	1033	109

Facilities

Catering (sub-contract):
Restaurant, Cafeteria, Kiosks, Picnic Place - Restaurant Zoogaststätte,
Waldschänke in Summer only
Retail (Zoo–Verein Wuppertal e. V.): Zoo shop: Zoo Truhe
Children's Zoo: No   Children's Playground: Yes

Dogs

Allowed on leads: No   Kennel Facilities: No

Feeding by Visitors

Strictly prohibited

Shows, etc

Yes, Sea Lion Feeding and Commentary

Education

Zoo keeper talks: Yes, Elephants
Zoo School/Education Centre: Yes
Biodiversity Centre: No
Zoo Guidebook: Yes, EUR 3.00
Signage on Exhibits: German   Star Rating: **

Friends of the Zoo

Yes, Zoo - Verein Wuppertal e. V.
Membership at 31.12.2010 – Circa 1,200

Volunteers

Yes, Circa 30

ZOO WUPPERTAL

**General Site
Description**

A delightful zoological garden situated in a hilly park landscape with rare, mature trees and good footpaths, Wuppertal Zoo provides a city oasis in the western part of the city. A variety of habitats have been created with several recent major investments such as the very spacious enclosure for the lions and the well - designed enclosures for the tigers. A wonderful new Penguin House (2009) accommodates King and Gentoo Penguins. Visitors have a spectacular view of these charismatic birds swimming and diving overhead from a 15 m long acrylic glass tunnel. This superb exhibit fully justifies the Zoo's Penguin logo. Amongst new developments, the Okapi enclosures are being improved.

Indoor Exhibits

Elephant House, Lion House, Aquarium/Terrarium, Tapir House, Penguin House, Small Cat House, Apes House, Monkey House, Bird House

Star Attractions

Penguins – 4 species, Lions, Amur Tigers, Wattled Cranes, Orang Utans, Gorillas, Elephants, White Handed Gibbons, Baird's Tapirs, Kodiak Bears, Drills, South American Pampas

Time required

whole zoo: 5 - 7 hours   star attractions: 2 - 3 hours

ZÁMEK LEŠNÁ

ZOO ZLIN

Contact

Name	ZOO a zámek Zlin - Lešná/Zoo Zlin
Address	Lukovská 112, 76314 Zlin 12, CZ
Phone	+420(0) 577 914 180
Fax	+420(0) 577 914 053
Email	office@zoozlin.eu
Website	www.zoozlin.eu

Opening Hours

Open every day of the year

April to September	08.30 to 18.00
October	08.30 to 17.00
December to March	08.30 to 16.00

Entrance Prices 2011

	CZK
Adult	120.00
Child 3-15	80.00
Child under 3	Free
Family Day Ticket - 2 Adults and up to 3 Children	360.00
Annual Card - Adult	600.00
Annual Card - Family 2 Adults and up to 3 Children	1300.00
Concessions: Students , Seniors	

Transport Access

Car	4 Kms from Zlin Centre Direction Holesov
Car Park	Yes, at Zoo CZK 60.00 or 80.00
Bus	34 and 36 to Namesti Prace
Nearest Station	Zlin Station

Ownership of Zoo Municipal 100% City of Zlin

Area of Zoo 52 Ha

Date of Foundation 1948

Visitor Numbers Circa 525,000

Animal Inventory at 31.12.2009

	Number	Species
Mammals	229	46
Birds	737	133
Reptiles	111	18
Amphibians	9	2
Fish	71	11

Zoo Zlin

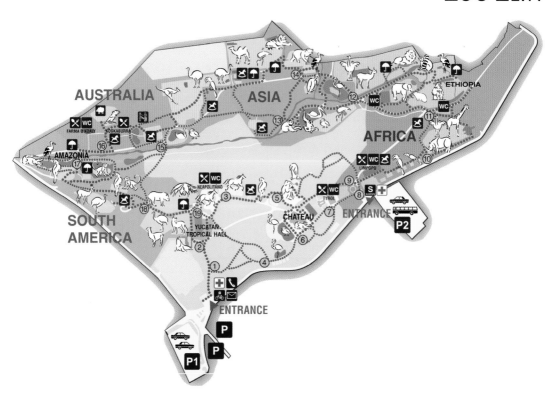

Facilities

Catering (zoo owned):
Restaurant, Café, Kiosks, Picnic Facilities - Restaurant Tyrol, Restaurant Limpopo, Restaurant Neapolitano, Restaurant Koala, Café Bar Kookaburra
Retail (zoo owned): 2 Zoo shops
Children´s Zoo: Yes   Children´s Playground: Yes

Dogs

Allowed on leads: No   Kennel Facilities: No

Zoo Zlin

Feeding by Visitors	Strictly prohibited except for flamingos, rheas and fish with food from one of 6 dispensers in zoo.
Shows, etc	Birds of Prey – in July and August
Education	Zoo keeper talks: Yes – see programme in Zoo Zoo School/Education Centre: Yes Biodiversity Centre: Yes, Centre Caudata Zoo Guidebook: Yes, CZK 10.00 Signage on Exhibits: Czech Star Rating: **
Friends of the Zoo	No
Volunteers	No
General Site Description	Zlin Zoo has a wonderful ambiance; it is set in the English-style gardens of the Art Nouveau Chateau Lešná built in the 19th C on the site of a former Moravian Castle. The Zoo benefits from the chateau's fine gardens with over 1000 mature trees and shrub species and exotic plants and is truly both a zoological and a botanical garden. The site slopes down to a small river and there are several large lakes and wooded areas. Several new exhibits have been built here recently but the site has capacity for further development.
Indoor Exhibits	Yucatan Tropical House, Elephant House, Vivarium, Gorilla House, Monkey House, Giraffe House
Star Attractions	Yucatan Tropical House, Banded Mongooses, Sarus Cranes, Ring Tailed Lemurs Walk Through, Squirrel Monkeys, Macaws, Wallaby and Emu Walk Through, Sea Lions, Flamingos, Addax/Lechwe/Ostrich Exhibit, Alligators, Bird Lakes, Ethiopia 1 – Gelada Baboons, Vultures Walk Through, Caracaras
Time required	whole zoo: 6 - 8 hours star attractions: 2 - 3 hours

Contact

Name	Zoo Zürich
Address	Zürichbergstraße 221, 8044 Zürich, CH
Phone	+41 (0) 44 254 2500
Fax	+41 (0) 44 254 2510
Email	zoo@zoo.ch
Website	www.zoo.ch

Opening Hours

Open every day of the year

March to October	09.00 to 18.00
November to February	09.00 to 17.00

Entrance Prices 2011

	CHF
Adult	22.00
Child Under 6	Free
School Children Child 6-16	11.00
Young Persons 16-25	16.00
Family Day Ticket 2 Adults and their Children	60.00
Annual Card – Adult	120.00
Annual Card – Family 2 Adults and their Children	180.00
Annual Card – School Children 6-16	60.00
Annual Card – Young persons and Students 16-25	80.00
Concessions: Seniors, Disabled Visitors and their Carers	

Transport Access

Car	A1 Exit 65 Direction Dübendorf and Signed from City Centre
Car Park	Yes, At zoo CHF 0.50 per hour also Park and Ride
Bus	751 and 39
Tram	6 from Bahnhofstraße,
Nearest Station	Zurich Hbf then Tram 6 direction Zoo

Ownership of Zoo

Zoo Zürich AG
Non-Profit Public Company
Non-Profit Stock Company
75% 5500 Private shareholders,
12.5% City of Zürich,
12.5% Canton of Zürich

Area of Zoo

27 Ha

Date of Foundation

1929

Visitor Numbers

Circa 1,800.000

Animal Inventory
at 31.12.2009

	Number	Species
Mammals	464	65
Birds	808	113
Reptiles	380	39
Amphibians	401	20
Fish	23	79

Facilities

Catering (zoo owned):
Restaurant, Café, Kiosks, Picnic Place - Siesta Restaurant, Outpost Restaurant, Altes Klösterli Restaurant, Masoala Restaurant
Retail (zoo owned): 2 Zoo shops - Südamerica Shop and Masoala Shop
Children's Zoo: Zoolino Nature Workshop   Children's Playground: Yes

Dogs

Allowed on leads: No   Kennel Facilities: Yes

Feeding by Visitors

Strictly prohibited - except in children's zoo using food from zoo dispensers

Shows, etc

Darwin – Evolution Exhibition, Masaola Information Centre, Shopping to Preserve the Rainforest Exhibition, Info Centre African Mountains, Bat Protection Centre

Education

Zoo keeper talks: 10 per day from 10.30 to 16.00 - see daily programme

Zoo School/Education Centre: Yes
Biodiversity Centre: Yes, Masoala House
Zoo Guidebook: Yes, CHF 19,80
Signage on Exhibits: German, French, Italian, English   Star Rating: ***

Friends of the Zoo

Tiergarten-Gesellschaft Zürich (TGZ)
Membership at 31.12.2009 - Circa 35,000

Volunteers

Yes, Circa 300

General Site Description

Situated at the top of a hill overlooking Zürich, this site is undulating, varied and well organised. Excellent vegetation, including plentiful bamboo, gives a luxuriant feel to this interesting zoological garden which has a high standard of enclosures and signage.

Zürich Zoo displays its animals in environments similar to their natural habitats: different habitats are colour coded and displayed on enclosure signage.

The Masaola Madagascan Rainforest House, representative of the largest unbroken forest area on the island, genuinely reflects Masaola's rainforest. It is both a delight to experience and a wonderful conservation and education exhibit.

The South America House will be completed in 2011 and Zürich Zoo is being extended through the construction of the new Elephant Park.

Indoor Exhibits

Masaola Rainforest House, Giant Tortoise House, Lion House, Elephant House, Apes House, Antelope House, Exotarium – Aquarium/Terrarium, Infopavilion, Africa House

Star Attractions

Masaola Rainforest House, Spectacled Bears, Gelada Baboons, Asian Lions, Coatis, Mongolian Wolves, Amur Tigers, Fish Otters, Swamp Wallabies and Emus, Snow Leopards, Red Pandas, Galapagos Tortoises, Volière – Ibis and Spoonbills, Waterway Bird Walk Through, Pileated Gibbons

Time required

whole zoo: 6 - 8 hours   star attractions: 3 - 4 hours

CHAPTER 18

Conclusion

This is the first time I have written a book. It has been hard work but immensely enjoyable to spend three years immersed in the tremendously wide range of activities of the leading zoological gardens of Europe. I have learned a great deal about these organisations and been unfailingly impressed by their scope of activity and the dedication, inspiration and commitment of people who work in and for them. I hope this book assists zoos to promote a greater awareness of their multi- facetted roles.

This is an unashamedly pro-zoo book but it is not uncritical. It is intended to help zoos by collating information not easily available elsewhere, by benchmarking and so providing assistance in their negotiations for the substantial investment funds urgently required to enable them both to improve sub-standard exhibits and provide new attractions for their visitors.

Equally, it is intended to encourage zoo visitors, to increase their knowledge, to visit other zoos, to recommend zoo visiting to their family and friends, and to spread and support the increasingly important and urgent conservation message. The exciting new attractions in build and in planning should encourage increasing visitor numbers, on which the zoos depend.

Finally, thank you for buying and reading this book: by doing so you are helping conservation as all profits are being donated to Stiftung Artenschutz, the German in-situ conservation charity, supported by more than 20 of the zoos in my survey. This donation will support a specific project for Gibbons in Vietnam, one of the most threatened primate species in this conservation hotspot region of south-east Asia.

Anthony Sheridan
01. 03 20111

Stiftung Artenschutz and my project for gibbon conservation

Stiftung Artenschutz, whose office is at Allwetterzoo Münster, is an in-situ conservation co-operative organisation, supported by about 40 European zoos, dedicated to modest specific conservation projects primarily in tropical countries. It works with low overheads and includes representatives from leading conservation and zoo organisations, including WWF, VDZ and Conservation International.

Gibbon Conservation Project. All profits from this book will go directly to Stiftung Artenschutz for a new project "Conservation of Yellow-cheeked Crested Gibbons (Nomascus gabriellae) in Nam Nung Nature Reserve in Nông Province, Vietnam. This is situated in the highland centre of Vietnam and the Nature Reserve has an area of nearly 11,000 Ha. The first phase of the project, due to commence in mid-2011, will assess the current status and distribution of, identify threats to, identify priority areas for conservation of, give recommendations for long-term conservation of and train local protected area staff for these gibbons.

CHAPTER 19

Acknowledgements

Many people have helped me over the past three years with my project, leading up to this book. I thank everybody concerned for their help, support and encouragement. In connection with this book, I am particularly indebted to the following for their help. The views expressed in this book are my own, not all of which are necessarily agreed by those named below.

Dr. Clemens Becker, Deputy Director, Zoo Karlsruhe

Dr. Bernhard Blaszkiewitz, Director, Berlin Zoo and Tierpark Berlin

Dipl.-Kfm. Andreas Busemann, Director, Zoo Osnabrück

Dr. Peter Dollinger, Director VDZ and past Director WAZA

Dr. Iain Douglas-Hamilton, Save the Elephants

Mr. John Edwards, Council Member, ZSL

Mr. Lyndon Estes, EAWLS

Mrs. Fiona Fisken, Editor, International Zoo Yearbook, ZSL

Mr. Daniel Gehring, Director, El Remanso Lodge, Costa Rica

Dr. Stephan Hering-Hagenbeck, Executive Director, Tierpark Hagenbeck Hamburg

Dr. Alex van Hooff, Director, Burgers' Zoo Arnhem

Dr. Jörg Junhold, Director, Zoo Leipzig

Mrs. Ulrike Kölsch, blue! advancing european projects

Mr. Dino Martins, EAWLS

Dr. Mike Norton-Griffiths, Council Member, EAWLS

Hon. Professor Dr. Helmut Pechlaner, past Director, Tiergarten Schönbrunn

Professor Gordon McGregor Reid, past Director, Chester Zoo

Mr. Herman Reichenbach, Gruner + Jahr AG

Mr. Alan Roocroft, Elephant Consultant

Dr. Kees Rookmaaker, Rhino Resource Center

Mr. Tim Rowlands, Curator, Chester Zoo

Dr. Alex Rübel, Director, Zoo Zürich

Mr. Harry Schram, past Director, EAZA

Dr. Dagmar Schratter, Director, Tiergarten Schönbrunn

Dr. Harald Schwammer, Deputy Director, Tiergarten Schönbrunn

Dr. Miranda Stevenson, Director, BIAZA

Mr. Erik Van Vliet, Dierenpark Amersfoort

Dr. Paul Vogt, past Director, Zoo Krefeld

Photo Credits

If no name is given, all copyrights with the according zoo

Front Cover - Yang Yang (mother) with Fu Long (son) (Vienna; Jane Sheridan)
Inside Front Cover - map from www.stepmap.de
Inside Back Cover - Fu Hu (Vienna; Jane Sheridan)
Chapter 1 - p.6 (Hamburg), Chapter 2 - p.8 (La Palmyre), p.9 (Dresden; Jane Sheridan), p.12 (Nuremberg; Jane Sheridan), Chapter 3 - p.15 (Arnhem; Photo: Burgers' Zoo), Chapter 4 - p.17 (Lisbon; Jane Sheridan), p.18 (Basel; Jane Sheridan), p.20 (Basel; Jane Sheridan), p.21 (Hamburg; Götz Berlik), Chapter 5 - p.24 (Lisbon; Jane Sheridan), p.27 (Bussolengo; Jane Sheridan), p.28 top (Cologne; Jane Sheridan), bottom (Vienna), Chapter 6 - p.29 (Beauval; Jane Sheridan), p.32 (Warsaw), p.36 (Dresden), p.38 (Hamburg; Lutz Schnier), Chapter 7 - p.39, 41 & 51 (Kenya; Rachel Sheridan), p.40 & 46 (El Remanso Lodge, Costa Rica; Daniel Gehring), Chapter 8 - p.53 (Basel; Jane Sheridan), p.55 (Dresden; Jane Sheridan), p.57 (Copenhagen; Jane Sheridan), p.58 (Twycross; Jane Sheridan), Chapter 9 - p.59 (Gelsenkirchen), p.60 (Osnabrück), p.63 (Chester), p.65 (Münster; Peter Grewer), p.66 (La Fléche), Chapter 10 - p.67, 69 & 71 (Vienna; Jane Sheridan), p.73, 75 & 76 (Leipzig), p.78 (Arnhem; Photos: Burgers' Zoo), p.80 (Colchester), p.82 (Colchester; Jane Sheridan), Chapter 11 - p.90 (Bussolengo), Chapter 12 - p.92 (Duisburg; Photo: Zoo Duisburg, Kuster/www.zoo-foto.de), Chapter 13 - p.98 (Vienna), p.108 top (Odense), bottom (Rhenen), Chapter 14 - p.111 (Berlin; Jane Sheridan), p.112 (Münster; Tilmann Roßmöller), p.115 (Emmen), p.117 (Zurich), p.119 (Odense), p.120 (Dortmund; Karl-Rainer Ledvina), p.122 (Wuppertal; Barbara Scheer), p.124 (Warsaw), Chapter 15 - p.130 top (Beauval; Jane Sheridan), bottom (Beauval; Gérard Lacz), Chapter 16 - p.136 (Wien; Tiergarten Schönbrunn/Norbert Potensky), Chapter 17 - 139 (Dublin), p.140 (Cologne; Rolf Schlosser), Chapter 18 - p.382 left (Stiftung Artenschutz; Jörg Adler), right (Stiftung Artenschutz; Sven P. Peter), p.387 (Anthony D. Sheridan; Jane Sheridan)

Zoo Profiles:
Amsterdam: entrance (Jonne Niesing), other photos (Roonald van Weeren), Arnhem: all photos (Burgers' Zoo), Basel: all photos (Torben Weber), Beauval: Zoo Parc de Beauval, Berlin Tierpark: all photos (Klaus Rudloff), Berlin Zoo: photos of entrance & bison house (Klaus Rudloff), photos of polar bear & hippo (Peter Griesbach), Bojnice: photo of bongo (Zuzana Mihalovova), other photos (Peter Luptak), Budapest: photo of rhinos (Bagosi Zoltan), Cologne: all photos (Ralf Schlosser), Doué-la-Fontaine: all photos (Bioparc: P. Chabot), Duisburg: all photos (Foto: Zoo Duisburg, Kuster/www.zoo-foto.de), Frankfurt: entrance (Jürgen Kircher), porcupine and tiger (Anna Schmitz), gorilla (Jens Hoffmann), Heidelberg: all photos (Heidrun Knigge & Rose von Selasinsky), Helsinki: all photos (Markku Bussman), Karlsruhe: all photos (Archiv Zoo Karlsruhe), Kronberg: all photos (Archiv Opel-Zoo), La Palmyre: elephants (D. Narbeburu), all other photos (F. Perroux/Zoo de La Palmyre), Madrid: pandas (Jeroen Jacobs), all other photos (Zoo Madrid), Mulhouse: all photos (Zoo Mulhouse), Münster: entrance (Allwetterzoo), guereza (Daniel Morsey), penguins (Peter Grewer), sun bears (Christoph Matzke), Osnabrück: subterranean zoo (Stephan Schulte), Paignton: entrance (Paignton Zoo), other photos (Ray Wiltshire), Rome: all photos (Massimiliano Di Giovanni, Bioparco's Photo), Rostock: all photos (Joachim Kloock, Zoo), Tallinn: mountain goats (Maaja Kitsing), all other photos (Inari Leiman), Vienna: panda and ORANG.erie (Tiergarten Schönbrunn/Norbert Potensky), entrance and pavillon (Daniel Zupanc), Wuppertal: restaurant (Birgit Klee), all other photos (Diedrich Kranz)

CHAPTER 20

Abbreviations

AIZA	Asociación Ibérica de Zoos y Acuarios (Spanish & Portuguese Zoos + Aquaria)
ANPZ	Association Nationale de Parcs et Jardins Zoologiques Privés
BIAZA	British and Irish Association of Zoos and Aquariums
CBSG	Conservation Breeding Specialist Group
CEAF	Central European Association of Zoo Friends
CEO	Chief Executive Officer
CITES	Convention on International Trade in Endangered Species
DAZA	Danish Association of Zoos and Aquaria
DEFRA	Department for Environment, Food and Rural Affairs (UK Government)
DTG	Deutsche Tierpark Gesellschaft e. V.
DWV	Deutscher Wildgehegeverband e. V.
EAWLS	East African Wildlife Society
EAZA	European Association of Zoos and Aquaria
EEA	European Economic Area
EEP	European Endangered Species Programme
ESB	European Regional Studbook
EU	European Union
FHZ	Federation of Hungarian Zoos
IFAW	International Fund for Animal Welfare
IRF	International Rhino Foundation
ISIS	International Species Information System
IUCN	International Union for the Conservation of Nature
KWS	Kenya Wildlife Service (Kenya Government)
MPI	Max-Planck-Institute
NGO	Non-Governmental Organisation
NP	National Park
NR	National Reserve
NRW	Nordrhein-Westfalen (North Rhine Westphalia)
NVD	Nederlandse Vereniging van Dierentuinen (Dutch Zoos Association)
NWDA	North West Regional Development Authority
OZO	Österreichische Zoo Organisation (Austrian Zoos Association)
PZS-SZG	Polish Zoological Society + Directors of Polish Zoological Gardens + Aquariums
SAZA	Swedish Association of Zoos and Aquaria
SDF	Svenska Djurparksföreningen
SNDPZ	Syndicat National des Directeurs de Parcs Zoologiques Français
TAG	Taxon Advisory Group
UCSZ	Union of Czech and Slovakian Zoos
UIZA	Unione Italiana degli Zoo ed Acquari (Italian Association of Zoos and Aquaria)
UK	United Kingdom of Great Britain and Northern Ireland
VDZ	Verband Deutscher Zoodirektoren e. V.
WAZA	World Association of Zoos and Aquaria
WKZPF	Wolfgang Köhler Zentrum für Primatenforschung
WWF	World Wildlife Fund for Nature
ZIMS	Zoological Information Management System
ZSL	Zoological Society of London

Zoo-Verein Wuppertal e.V.

Der Verein und seine Ziele

Der Zoo-Verein Wuppertal e.V. wurde als eingetragener Förderverein des Zoologischen Gartens Wuppertal am 27. Oktober 1955 gegründet. Er hat über 1.000 Mitglieder und ist seit 2001 Mitglied in der Gemeinschaft Deutscher Zooförderer GDZ.

Der Zoo-Verein bemüht sich um die Erhaltung und Erweiterung des Wuppertaler Zoos, seiner Einrichtungen und seiner Anlagen. Daneben fördert er Forschungsprogramme und unterstützt Naturschutzprojekte vor Ort zur Erhaltung bedrohter Tierarten.

Zahlreiche Gebäude und Anlagen im Wuppertaler Zoo sind mit Hilfe des Zoo-Verein Wuppertal e.V. bereits entstanden, z. B.:

Gibbonhaus (1966 & 1981)

Freiflughalle (1993)

Brillenpinguinanlage (2006)

1962	Ponystall (heute Zebustall)
1966	Gibbonhaus
1971	Pinguinanlage (inzwischen durch die neue Pinguinanlage ersetzt)
1981	Erweiterung Gibbonhaus, Hirschhaus, Biberanlage
1985	Erweiterung Affenhaus (Außenanlage für Lemuren), Zooschule
1993	Freiflughalle für tropische Vögel
2003	Orang Utan-Freianlage
2006	Brillenpinguinanlage
2007	Übergangsanlage für Königspinguine
2009	Neue Pinguinanlage für Königs- und Eselspinguine

Mit der Hilfe des Zoo-Vereins sind bislang Gebäude und Anlagen im Wert von über 7 Mio. € im Zoo entstanden. Diese Mittel stammen aus Mitgliedsbeiträgen, Spenden, Erbschaften, Nachlässen, Stiftungen und von Sponsoren.

Zooschule (1985)

Orang Utan-Freianlage (2003)

Neue Pinguinanlage (2009)

Und in Zukunft?

Der Zoo-Verein hat noch viele Ideen, wie er den Zoo zum Wohle seiner Bewohner und Besucher weiter fördern kann. Dazu benötigt er Ihre Unterstützung. Helfen Sie mit Ihrer Spende und werden Sie Mitglied im Zoo-Verein Wuppertal e.V.!

Was bietet der Verein?

- Zooführungen unter fachkundiger Leitung
- Vorträge, Film- und Diavorführungen
- Tagesausflüge in Nachbarzoos
- Mehrtägige Reisen zu Zoos im In- und Ausland
- Kostenlose Zusendung des Vereinsmagazins „Pinguinal" zweimal pro Jahr

Wie wird man Mitglied?

Den Infoprospekt mit Beitrittsformular gibt es in der Zoo-Truhe am Zooeingang.
Der Mitgliedsbeitrag beträgt:
20 € / Jahr für Einzelpersonen
25 € / Jahr für Eheleute
40 € / Jahr für Firmen

A good example of Friends of the Zoo activities.

Anthony D. Sheridan, B.Sc (Econ), FZS

Anthony Sheridan is a life long wildlife enthusiast, a member of the East African Wildlife Society since 1965 and a Fellow of the Zoological Society of London since 1976. Since retiring from working in the electronics industry in 2007, he has spent the past 3 years visiting, analysing and getting to know 80 leading European zoological gardens in 21 countries. He speaks German and some French.

A graduate of the LSE (London School of Economics) in economics, politics and statistics, he spent his early post-university years in politics and education, serving as Chairman of Hertfordshire County Council Education Committee and being a county councillor and governor of many schools, colleges and universities.

His business career commenced in his father's electronics company, including establishing a manufacturing plant in India, before setting up his own manufacturing and sales company in the same industry employing up to 250 in UK and other European countries; he continues to be a non-executive Director in a medium size Germany company near Dresden. He has travelled widely throughout Europe during his business career.

He has been a member of the European Movement in London since its inception, and has been an European enthusiast since leaving university. Anthony is a Freeman of the City of London.